CCDA Self-Study
CCDA Exam Certification Guide
Second Edition

A. Anthony Bruno, CCIE No. 2738
Jacqueline Kim

Cisco Press

Cisco Press
800 East 96th Street
Indianapolis, IN 46240 USA

CCDA Exam Certification Guide, Second Edition

A. Anthony Bruno, CCIE No. 2738
Jacqueline Kim

Copyright © 2004 Cisco Systems, Inc.

Published by:
Cisco Press
800 East 96th Street
Indianapolis, IN 46240 USA

Printed in the United States of America 5 6 7 8 9 0

Fifth Printing December 2005

Library of Congress Cataloging-in-Publication Number: 2002115118

ISBN: 1-58720-076-7

Warning and Disclaimer

This book is designed to provide information about the CCDA exam. Every effort has been made to make this book as complete and as accurate as possible, but no warranty or fitness is implied.

The information is provided on an "as is" basis. The authors, Cisco Press, and Cisco Systems, Inc., shall have neither liability nor responsibility to any person or entity with respect to any loss or damages arising from the information contained in this book or from the use of the discs or programs that might accompany it.

The opinions expressed in this book belong to the author and are not necessarily those of Cisco Systems, Inc.

Feedback Information

At Cisco Press, our goal is to create in-depth technical books of the highest quality and value. Each book is crafted with care and precision, undergoing rigorous development that involves the unique expertise of members from the professional technical community.

Readers' feedback is a natural continuation of this process. If you have any comments regarding how we could improve the quality of this book, or otherwise alter it to better suit your needs, you can contact us through e-mail at feedback@ciscopress.com. Please make sure to include the book title and ISBN in your message.

We greatly appreciate your assistance.

Trademark Acknowledgments

All terms mentioned in this book that are known to be trademarks or service marks have been appropriately capitalized. Cisco Press or Cisco Systems, Inc., cannot attest to the accuracy of this information. Use of a term in this book should not be regarded as affecting the validity of any trademark or service mark.

Corporate and Government Sales

Cisco Press offers excellent discounts on this book when ordered in quantity for bulk purchases or special sales.
For more information, please contact:
U.S. Corporate and Government Sales 1-800-382-3419 corpsales@pearsontechgroup.com

For sales outside of the U.S., please contact:
International Sales 1-317-581-3793 international@pearsontechgroup.com

Publisher: John Wait

Editor-in-Chief: John Kane

Executive Editor: Brett Bartow

Cisco Representative: Anthony Wolfenden

Cisco Press Program Manager: Sonia Torres Chavez

**Manager, Marketing Communications,
Cisco Systems:** Scott Miller

Cisco Marketing Program Manager: Edie Quiroz

Production Manager: Patrick Kanouse

Acquisitions Editor: Michelle Grandin

Development Editor: Deb Doorley

Project Editor: San Dee Phillips

Copy Editor: Kris Simmons

Technical Editors: Dave Nichols
Donnie Williams
Ken Zuhr

Team Coordinator: Tammi Barnett

Book Designer: Gina Rexrode

Cover Designer: Louisa Adair

Composition: Octal Publishing, Inc.

Indexer: Brad Herriman

CISCO SYSTEMS

Corporate Headquarters
Cisco Systems, Inc.
170 West Tasman Drive
San Jose, CA 95134-1706
USA
www.cisco.com
Tel: 408 526-4000
800 553-NETS (6387)
Fax: 408 526-4100

European Headquarters
Cisco Systems International BV
Haarlerbergpark
Haarlerbergweg 13-19
1101 CH Amsterdam
The Netherlands
www-europe.cisco.com
Tel: 31 0 20 357 1000
Fax: 31 0 20 357 1100

Americas Headquarters
Cisco Systems, Inc.
170 West Tasman Drive
San Jose, CA 95134-1706
USA
www.cisco.com
Tel: 408 526-7660
Fax: 408 527-0883

Asia Pacific Headquarters
Cisco Systems, Inc.
Capital Tower
168 Robinson Road
#22-01 to #29-01
Singapore 068912
www.cisco.com
Tel: +65 6317 7777
Fax: +65 6317 7799

Cisco Systems has more than 200 offices in the following countries and regions. Addresses, phone numbers, and fax numbers are listed on the
Cisco.com Web site at www.cisco.com/go/offices.

Argentina • Australia • Austria • Belgium • Brazil • Bulgaria • Canada • Chile • China PRC • Colombia • Costa Rica • Croatia • Czech Republic
Denmark • Dubai, UAE • Finland • France • Germany • Greece • Hong Kong SAR • Hungary • India • Indonesia • Ireland • Israel • Italy
Japan • Korea • Luxembourg • Malaysia • Mexico • The Netherlands • New Zealand • Norway • Peru • Philippines • Poland • Portugal
Puerto Rico • Romania • Russia • Saudi Arabia • Scotland • Singapore • Slovakia • Slovenia • South Africa • Spain • Sweden
Switzerland • Taiwan • Thailand • Turkey • Ukraine • United Kingdom • United States • Venezuela • Vietnam • Zimbabwe

About the Authors

A. Anthony Bruno, CCIE No. 2738, is a principal consultant with International Network Services (INS) with more than 12 years experience in the internetworking field. His other network certifications include CIPTSS, CCDP, MCSE, CNX in Ethernet, and CWNA. He has consulted for many enterprise and service-provider customers in the design, implementation, and optimization of large-scale, multiprotocol networks. Anthony has worked on the design and implementation of large network mergers, Voice over IP (VoIP), virtual private networks (VPNs), wireless LANs, and multi-homed Internet access. Prior to INS, Anthony was a U.S. Air Force Captain working in network operations and management. He completed his M.S. in electrical engineering at the University of Missouri-Rolla in 1994 and his B.S. in electrical engineering at the University of Puerto Rico-Mayaguez in 1990. Anthony is also a part-time instructor for the University of Phoenix-Online, teaching networking courses.

Anthony is the author of the *Cisco Press CCIE Routing and Switching Exam Certification Guide*, co-author of the *CCDA Exam Certification Guide*, First Edition, and a contributor and the lead technical reviewer for *Cisco CCIE Fundamentals: Network Design and Case Studies*, Second Edition. Anthony contributed a chapter to a Syngress publication titled "Designing Wireless Networks." He also performed technical reviews of the *Cisco Press CID Exam Certification Guide* and *Internetworking Troubleshooting Handbook*.

Jacqueline Kim is the vice president of consulting services at IPLogic, LLC in New York. She has 10 years of experience in the networking industry ranging from engineering to management consulting. Jacqueline consults for Fortune 500 executives to develop technology strategies and manages the solution planning and delivery process. Her passions lie in supporting the development of other networking professionals through training, presenting seminars and workgroups, and engaging in organizational development projects. She has held advisory roles with Cisco and Novell and has earned numerous certifications with Cisco.

About the Contributing Authors

Gert De Laet, CCIE No. 2657, is a CCIE in routing and switching and also a CCIE in security. Gert has more than 10 years of experience in internetworking and works in Brussels, Belgium, for the worldwide CCIE team as product manager for CCIE security at Cisco Systems. Gert holds an engineering degree in electronics. He wrote Chapter 1 of this book.

Anthony Sequeira holds many Cisco certifications, including CCDP and CCNP. He is a certified Cisco Systems instructor currently teaching Cisco Internetworking for KnowledgeNet. Anthony lives in Massachusetts with his wife and new daughter, and—when not studying Cisco networking—he studies general aviation. Anthony wrote Chapters 5, 6, and 7 for this book.

About the Technical Reviewers

Dave Nichols, throughout more than 20 years of systems implementation, support, and training, has maintained a love of technology as well as a healthy skepticism. He joined Cisco Systems in 1999, moving down the protocol stack from the application layer to Layers 2 and 3. A degree in mathematics and a love of radio and politics have led Dave through proprietary and nonproprietary systems, client/server technologies, and database management to IP telephony. As a member of the Cisco Internet Learning Solutions Group, Dave reviews training materials for clarity and accuracy. Dave resides in New England. In addition to his other duties, he is the network administrator for a small in-home network, keeping the kids' IM running.

Donnie Williams is a senior network systems consultant for International Network Services and possesses more than 10 years of experience in the data communications industry. He has provided design, implementation, troubleshooting, and optimization expertise in both enterprise LAN/WAN and service-provider networks. Donnie currently holds several professional or expert-level certifications, such as Microsoft MCSE; Foundry FCNE; Cisco CCNP, CCDP, CIPTSS, CIPTDS, and CIPTOS; Lucent LCTE; and Planet3 CWNA.

Ken Zuhr is an educational specialist in the Internet Learning Solutions Group with Cisco Systems. A certified Cisco Systems instructor, he has been with Cisco for more than 7 years working with routing, WAN switching, voice, and call center products. His more than 25 years working with technology include experience with applications, database systems, operating systems, and networking. He is a member of the Computer Society and the Communications Society of the IEEE. Ken lives in Gilroy, California. His interests include family activities, church choir, and toddling through the California countryside in his Miata with the top down.

Dedication

This book is dedicated to my loving wife, Ivonne, and to our daughters, Joanne Nichole and Dianne Christine. Your support during the development of this book is greatly appreciated. Thank you, Ivonne and kids!

Also, I dedicate this book to my parents, Augustus Anthony Bruno, Sr., and Iris Belia Bruno. Thanks for your guidance and teaching during my "growing up" years. Dad: Thanks for the Commodore VIC20 computer. Finally, I would like to dedicate this book to my sister, Anjanette.

—Anthony Bruno

To my loving and supporting family. Mom, Dad, and Jeanette: I love you very much.

—Jacqueline Kim

Acknowledgments

This book would not have been possible without the efforts of many dedicated people. First, thanks to Michelle Grandin, acquisitions editor, for her dedication and guidance during the development of this book. A special thanks to Deb Doorley, development editor, whose guidance and expertise helped me become a better writer. Deb's special attention to detail significantly improved this book. Thanks to Andrew Cupp for his guidance. Thanks to San Dee Phillips, project editor, for taking care of the final, significant details. Thanks to Brett Bartow, executive editor, for his vision. And special thanks to John Kane, Editor-in-Chief; thanks for getting me started with Cisco Press in 1999. Thanks to all other Cisco Press team members who worked behind the scenes to make this a better book. A special thanks to the technical reviewers: Dave Nichols, Donnie Williams, and Ken Zuhr. Their technical advice and careful attention to detail made this book accurate. Very special thanks to Anthony Sequeira and Gert De Laet for arriving at the last minute to contribute some of the chapters of this book. Finally, I would like to thank my management for their understanding during the development of this book.

—Anthony Bruno

I would like to thank Michelle Grandin, my editor, for her support and strength. Thanks to Deb Doorley, without whom the book could not be possible. Most of all, thanks to John Kane for the opportunities that made my dream a reality. Next, I would like to thank Ken Yanneck, Mike Connally, Ernie Small, and Mark Graber at IPLogic. Thank you, gentlemen, for giving me more than a workplace and being more than just coworkers. Although it wouldn't be possible to thank each member of the IPLogic team individually, your support and knowledge has helped me to complete this project. To Bob Burdick: You were the first friend I made in Albany, and now I can't imagine my life without you. You have taught me a great deal about friendship in the short time I have known you; I couldn't have asked for a better teacher.

—Jacqueline Kim

Contents at a Glance

Contents

Icons Used in This Book

 Router

 Bridge

 Hub

 DSU/CSU

 Catalyst Switch

 Multilayer Switch

 Modem

 ATM Switch

 ISDN/Frame Relay Switch

 Communication Server

 Gateway

 Access Server

PC

PC with Software

 Sun Workstation

 Macintosh

 Terminal

Cisco Works Workstation

 Web Server

File Server

 Laptop

Printer

 IBM Mainframe

Front End Processor

 Cluster Controller

———————— Line: Ethernet

 Line: Serial

- - - - - - - Line: Switched Serial

Token Ring

FDDI

 Network Cloud

Command Syntax Conventions

The conventions used to present command syntax in this book are the same conventions used in the IOS Command Reference. The Command Reference describes these conventions as follows:

- Vertical bars (|) separate alternative, mutually exclusive elements.

- Square brackets [ ] indicate optional elements.

- Braces { } indicate a required choice.

- Braces within brackets [{ }] indicate a required choice within an optional element.

- **Boldface** indicates commands and keywords that are entered literally as shown. In actual configuration examples and output (not general command syntax), boldface indicates commands that are manually input by the user (such as a **show** command).

- *Italics* indicate arguments for which you supply actual values.

Foreword

CCDA Exam Certification Guide, Second Edition, is a complete study tool for the CCDA exam, allowing you to assess your knowledge, identify areas to concentrate your study, and master key concepts to help you succeed on the exams and in your daily job. The book is filled with features that help you design routed and switched network infrastructures involving LAN, WAN, and dial access services. This book was developed in cooperation with the Cisco Internet Learning Solutions Group. Cisco Press books are the only self-study books authorized by Cisco for CCDA exam preparation.

Cisco and Cisco Press present this material in text-based format to provide another learning vehicle for our customers and the broader user community in general. Although a publication does not duplicate the instructor-led or e-learning environment, we acknowledge that not everyone responds in the same way to the same delivery mechanism. It is our intent that presenting this material through a Cisco Press publication will enhance the transfer of knowledge to a broad audience of networking professionals.

Cisco Press will present study guides on existing and future exams through these Exam Certification Guides to help achieve Cisco Internet Learning Solutions Group's principle objectives: to educate the Cisco community of networking professionals and to enable that community to build and maintain reliable, scalable networks. The Cisco Career Certifications and classes that support these certifications are directed at meeting these objectives through a disciplined approach to progressive learning. In order to succeed on the Cisco Career Certifications exams, as well as in your daily job as a Cisco certified professional, we recommend a blended learning solution that combines instructor-led, e-learning, and self-study training with hands-on experience. Cisco Systems has created an authorized Cisco Learning Partner program to provide you with the most highly qualified instruction and invaluable hands-on experience in lab and simulation environments. To learn more about Cisco Learning Partner programs available in your area, please go to www.cisco.com/go/training.

The books Cisco Press creates in partnership with Cisco Systems meet the same standards for content quality demanded of our courses and certifications. It is our intent that you find this and subsequent Cisco Press certification and training publications of value as you build your networking knowledge base.

Thomas M. Kelly
Vice-President, Internet Learning Solutions Group
Cisco Systems, Inc.
August 2003

Introduction

So you have worked on Cisco devices for a while, designing networks for your customers, and now you want to get certified? There are several good reasons to do so. The Cisco certification program permits network analysts and engineers to demonstrate their competence in different areas of networking and at different levels. The prestige and respect that come with a Cisco certification will definitely help you in your career. Your clients, peers, and superiors will recognize you as an expert in networking.

The Cisco Certified Design Associate (CCDA) is the entry-level certification, which represents knowledge of the foundation of the design of Cisco internetwork infrastructure.

The routing and switching path has various levels of certification. CCDA is the entry-level certification in the Network Design track. The next step, Cisco Certified Design Professional (CCDP), requires you to demonstrate advanced knowledge of network design. The Cisco Certified Internetwork Expert (CCIE) requires an expert level of knowledge on internetworking.

The test to obtain CCDA certification is called Designing for Cisco Internetwork Solutions (DESGN) Exam #640-861. It is a computer-based test that has between 70 and 80 questions and a 75-minute time limit. Because all exam information is managed by Cisco Systems and is therefore subject to change, candidates should continually monitor the Cisco Systems site for course and exam updates at www.cisco.com/go/training.

You can take the exam at Sylvan Prometric or VUE testing centers. You can register with Prometric at http://www.2test.com. You can register with VUE at http://www.vue.com. The cost of the exam is US$125. The CCDA certification is valid for three years.

The CCDA exam measures your ability to design networks that meet certain requirements for performance, security, capacity, and scalability. The exam focuses on small- to medium-sized networks. The candidate should have at least one year of experience in the design of small- to medium-sized networks using Cisco products. A CCDA candidate should understand internetworking technologies, including the Enterprise Composite Network Model, routing, switching, WAN technologies, LAN protocols, voice networks, and network management.

Cisco suggests working through the course Designing for Cisco Internetwork Solutions (DESGN) before you take the CCDA exam. For more information on the various levels of certification, career tracks, and Cisco exams, go to the Cisco Learning and Events page at www.cisco.com/go/training.

About This Book

CCDA Exam Certification Guide, Second Edition, is intended to help you prepare for the design portion of the CCDA exam, recognize and improve your areas of weakness, and increase your chances of passing the test. The book is designed to provide you with mastery of the CCDA design objectives. It is recommended that you take the DESGN course or acquire an equivalent amount of on-the-job training before solidifying your CCDA knowledge with this book.

Because the scope of this book is helping you master the CCDA exam design objectives, the authors assume that you have a certain level of internetworking knowledge. If you lack experience with internetworking technologies, it is strongly recommended that you review the *Internetworking Technologies Handbook*, Second Edition, from Cisco Press.

At the beginning of each chapter, you will find a "Do I Know This Already?" quiz to help you assess the degree to which you need to review the subject matter covered in that chapter. You can then read the entire chapter thoroughly or skip directly to only those sections that you need to review further. In addition, at the end of each chapter is a "Q&A" review quiz. Use it after you read the chapter to determine your knowledge of the topics.

Objective of This Book

The objective of this book is to help you fully understand, remember, and recall details of the design topics covered on the CCDA exam. The CCDA exam will be a stepping stone for most people as they progress through the other Cisco certifications; passing the exam because of a thorough understanding and recall of the topics will be incredibly valuable at the next steps.

This book prepares you to *pass the CCDA exam* by doing the following:

- Helping you discover which design topics you have not mastered

- Providing explanations and information to fill in your knowledge gaps

- Supplying exercises and case studies that enhance your ability to recall and deduce the answers to test questions

- Providing a practice exam and exercises on the CD-ROM that help you assess your overall progress and preparation level for the CCDA exam

Who Should Read This Book?

This book is intended to tremendously increase your chances of passing the CCDA exam. This book is intended for an audience who has taken the course Designing for Cisco Internetwork Solutions or has an equivalent level of on-the-job experience. Although others might benefit from using this book, the book is written assuming that you want to pass the exam.

Why should you want to pass CCDA? For many reasons: to get a raise; to show your manager you are working hard to increase your skills; to fulfill a manager's requirement (before he will spend money on another course); to enhance your résumé; because you work in a presales job at a reseller and want to eventually become CCDP certified; or to prove you know the topic, if you learned through on-the-job experience rather than from the prerequisite classes.

Have You Mastered All the Exam Objectives?

The exam tests you on a wide variety of topics; most people will not remember all the topics on the exam. Because some study is required, this book focuses on helping you obtain the maximum benefit from the time you spend preparing for the design portion of the exam. You can access many other sources for the information covered on the exam; for example, you can read the Cisco documentation CD-ROM. This book, however, provides a proven format of effective, late-stage preparation for the exam.

You should begin your exam preparation by spending ample time reviewing the exam objectives listed in the section "CCDA Exam Objectives," later in this introduction. Because exam objectives change from time to time, check out the Cisco website for any future changes to the list of objectives.

How This Book Is Organized

This book contains the following parts:

Part I: General Network Design (Chapters 1–3)

Part II: LAN and WAN Design (Chapters 4–8)

Part III: The Internet Protocol and Routing Protocols (Chapters 9–14)

Part IV: Security, Convergence, and Network Management (Chapters 15–19)

Part V: Comprehensive Scenarios (Chapter 20)

Part VI: Appendixes

The book begins with a chapter that generally defines the design topics that are covered by the CCDA exam. Before you begin studying for any exam, it is important that you know the topics that might be covered. With the CCDA exam, knowing what is on the exam is seemingly straightforward; Cisco publishes a list of CCDA objectives. The objectives, however, are certainly open to interpretation.

Chapters 1 through 19 cover the Cisco CCDA exam design objectives and provide detailed information on each objective. Each chapter begins with a quiz so that you can quickly determine your current level of readiness. Each chapter ends with a review summary and Q&A quiz.

Chapter 20, "Comprehensive Scenarios," provides scenario-based questions for further comprehensive study. Some of the questions in the CCDA test might be based on a scenario design.

Appendix A, "Answers to Chapter 'Do I Know This Already?' Quizzes and Q&A Sections," provides the answers to the various chapter quizzes.

Appendix B, "The OSI Reference Model and Numeric Conversion," reviews the Open Systems Interconnection (OSI) reference model, which provides a better understanding of internetworking. The appendix also reviews the techniques to convert between decimal, binary, and hexadecimal numbers. Although there might not be a specific question on the exam about converting a binary number to decimal, it is necessary to know how to convert these numbers in order to do problems in the test.

Appendix C, "References and Recommended Readings," provides a list of references used in this book and recommended reading. The books, URLs, and RFCs listed include additional information on the covered subjects.

The book also includes a glossary of the most important CCDA terms and acronyms.

Finally, in the back of the book you will find an invaluable CD-ROM. It contains exercise questions on study cards and flash cards that provide answer explanations and links to the appropriate section in an electronic version of the book. The CD-ROM also enables you to take a timed practice CCDA exam that is similar in format to the actual CCDA exam you will be taking. The practice exam is complete with both general knowledge and case-study questions. The practice exam has a database of more than 200 questions, so you can test yourself more than once.

Features of This Book

This book features the following:

- **"Do I Know This Already?" Quizzes**—Each chapter begins with a quiz that helps you determine the amount of time you need to spend studying that chapter. If you follow the directions at the beginning of the chapter, the "Do I Know This Already?" quiz directs you to study all or particular parts of the chapter.

- **Foundation Topics**—These are the core sections of each chapter. They explain the protocols, concepts, and configuration for the topics in that chapter. If you need to learn about the topics in a chapter, read the "Foundation Topics" section.

- **Foundation Summaries**—Near the end of each chapter, a summary collects the most important information from the chapter summarized in lists, tables, and figures. The "Foundation Summary" section is designed to help you review the key concepts in the chapter if you scored well on the "Do I Know This Already?" quiz. This section is an excellent tool for last-minute review.

- **Q&A**—Each chapter ends with a "Q&A" section that forces you to exercise your recall of the facts and processes described inside that chapter. The questions are generally harder than the actual exam. These questions are a great way to increase the accuracy of your recollection of the facts.

- **Case Studies**—Chapter 20 is a complete chapter of case studies that you should read and work on after you feel you have mastered all the objectives presented in the book. The CCDA exam will most likely include some questions based on a design case study.

- **Test Questions**—Using the test engine on the CD-ROM, you can take simulated exams. You can also choose to be presented with several questions on an objective that you need more work on. This testing tool provides you with practice to make you more comfortable when you actually take the CCDA exam.

CCDA Exam Objectives

Cisco lists the objectives for CCDA exam on its website at http://www.cisco.com/warp/public/10/wwtraining/certprog/testing/current_exams/640-861.html. The list provides key information about what the test covers. Table I-1 lists the CCDA exam design objectives and the corresponding parts in this book that cover those objectives. Each part begins with a list of the objectives covered. Use these references as a road map to find the exact materials you need to study to master the CCDA exam design objectives. Note, however, that because all exam information is managed by Cisco Systems and is therefore subject to change, candidates should continually monitor the Cisco Systems site for course and exam updates at www.cisco.com/go/training.

Table I-1 *CCDA Design Objectives and the Parts Where They Are Covered*

Objective	Description	Part
Analysis		
1	Gather and evaluate information regarding an organization's existing social requirements.	I
2	Gather and evaluate information regarding a network owner's current data network and future needs.	I
3	Gather and evaluate information regarding a network owner's current voice network and future needs.	I, IV
4	Identify possible opportunities for network improvement.	I, V
5	Validate gathered information.	I
6	Document relevant findings.	I

Table I-1 *CCDA Design Objectives and the Parts Where They Are Covered (Continued)*

Objective	Description	Part
Modeling		
7	Given a network design or set of requirements, evaluate a solution that meets IP addressing needs.	III, V
8	Given a network design or a set of requirements, evaluate a solution that meets routing-protocol needs.	III
9	Given a network design or a set of requirements, evaluate a solution that meets network-management needs.	IV
10	Given a network design or a set of requirements, evaluate a solution to incorporate equipment and technology within a campus design.	I, II
11	Given a network design or a set of requirements, evaluate a solution to incorporate equipment and technology within an Enterprise Edge design.	I, II, V
12	Design solutions to meet network-owner needs applying the Enterprise Composite Network Model.	I, V
13	Evaluate solutions addressing the issues of delivering voice traffic over a data network.	IV, V
14	Evaluate solutions for compliance with SAFE.	IV
Planning		
15	Develop an implementation plan.	I
16	Develop a prototype-testing plan.	I
17	Develop a verification plan.	I

Table I-2 shows which objectives are covered in each part.

Table I-2 *Part-by-part List of CCDA Design Objectives*

Part	Objective
I	1, 2, 3, 4, 5, 6, 10, 11, 12 15, 16, 17
II	10, 11
III	7, 8
IV	3, 9, 13, 14
V	4, 7, 11, 12, 13

If your knowledge of a particular chapter's subject matter is strong, you might want to proceed directly to that chapter's exercises to assess your true level of preparedness. If you have difficulty with those exercises, make sure to read over that chapter's "Foundation Topics." Also, be sure to test yourself by using the CD-ROM's test engine. Finally, if you are lacking in certain internetworking-technologies knowledge, be sure to review the reference materials provided in the appendixes. No matter your background, you should begin with Chapter 1.

Test Preparation, Test-Taking Tips, and Using This Book

This section contains recommendations that you can choose to follow to increase your probability of passing the CCDA written exam.

The following are some additional suggestions for using this book and preparing for the exam:

- Familiarize yourself with the exam objectives in Table I-1 and thoroughly read the chapters on topics that you are not familiar with. Use the assessment tools provided in this book to identify areas where you need additional study. The assessment tools include the "Do I Know This Already?" quizzes, the "Q&A" questions, and the sample exam questions on the CD-ROM.

- Take all quizzes in this book and review the answers and the answer explanations. It is not enough to know the correct answer, but you need to also understand why it is correct and why the others are incorrect. Retake the chapter quizzes until you pass with 100 percent.

- Take the CD-ROM test in this book and review the answers. Use your results to identify areas where you need additional preparation.

- Review other documents, RFCs, and the Cisco website for additional information. If this book references an outside source, it's a good idea to spend some time looking at it.

- Review the chapter questions and CD-ROM questions the day before your scheduled test. Review each chapter's "Foundation Summary" when you are making your final preparations.

- On the test date, arrive at least 20 minutes before your test time. This plan will give time to register and glance through your notes before the test without feeling rushed or anxious.

- If you are not sure which is the answer to a question, attempt to eliminate incorrect answers.

- You might need to spend more time on some questions than others. Remember, you have an average of 1 minute to answer each question.

PART I: General Network Design

This part covers the following CCDA exam objectives (to view the CCDA exam outline, visit http://www.cisco.com/go/training):

- Gather and evaluate information regarding an organization's existing social requirements.
- Gather and evaluate information regarding a network owner's current data network and future needs.
- Gather and evaluate information regarding a network owner's current voice network and future needs.
- Identify possible opportunities for network improvement.
- Validate gathered information.
- Document relevant findings.
- Given a network design or a set of requirements, evaluate a solution to incorporate equipment and technology within a campus design.
- Given a network design or a set of requirements, evaluate a solution to incorporate equipment and technology within an Enterprise Edge design.
- Design solutions to meet network-owner needs applying the Enterprise Composite Network Model.
- Develop an implementation plan.
- Develop a prototype-testing plan.
- Develop a verification plan.

Exam Topics in This Chapter

- Organizational Network Policies and Procedures

- Top-Down Design Practices

- Requirements and Constraints

- Return on Investment (ROI)

- Design Activities, Tools, and Techniques

CHAPTER 1

Design Principles

This chapter describes the importance of an organization's network policies through an introduction of the global network business model and covers other significant design principles, such as top-down design, requirements and constraints, and network design tools.

More specifically, this chapter discusses design principles, examining the requirements and constraints of a network both from a business and a technical perspective after explaining the global network business model and the top-down design concepts.

This chapter explores design tools through some of the activities, techniques, and tools used in today's network-design process, for auditing networks and analyzing and simulating network traffic.

"Do I Know This Already?" Quiz

The purpose of the "Do I Know This Already?" quiz is to help you decide whether you need to read the entire chapter. If you already intend to read the entire chapter, you do not necessarily need to answer these questions now.

The 10-question quiz, derived from the major sections in the "Foundation Topics" portion of the chapter, helps you determine how to spend your limited study time.

Table 1-1 outlines the major topics discussed in this chapter and the "Do I Know This Already?" quiz questions that correspond to those topics.

Table 1-1   *"Do I Know This Already?" Foundation Topics Section-to-Question Mapping*

Foundation Topics Section	Questions Covered in This Section
Organizational Network Policies and Procedures	1, 2, 3
Top-Down Design Practices	4, 5
Requirements and Constraints	6, 7, 8, 9
Design Activities, Tools, and Techniques	10

> **CAUTION** The goal of self-assessment is to gauge your mastery of the topics in this chapter. If you do not know the answer to a question or you are only partially sure of the answer, you should mark this question wrong for purposes of the self-assessment. Giving yourself credit for an answer you correctly guess skews your self-assessment results and might provide you with a false sense of security.

1. What is a global network business?

    a. A model that explains requirements and constraints when opening corporate information to all key constituencies

    b. A model that leverages the network for competitive advantage by allowing direct access to necessary corporate information by all key constituencies

    c. A model that explains the necessary design tools required for opening corporate information to all key constituencies

    d. A model that explains the economical constraints when opening corporate information to all key constituencies

    e. A model that explains the political constraints when opening corporate information to all key constituencies

2. Global network businesses are built on what three principles?

    a. Customer focus, decentralization, and core versus context

    b. Customer focus, decentralization, and core versus edge

    c. Customer focus, centralization, and core versus context

    d. Customer focus, continuous standardization, and core versus context

    e. Customer focus, continuous standardization, and core versus edge

3. What is the promise of the global network business model?

    a. Increased productivity with a slightly higher cost

    b. Increased productivity and reduced cost

    c. Improvement of core versus context but lower productivity

    d. Improvement of core versus context with a slightly higher cost

    e. Creates a lot of overhead in your organization

4. What is critical for the top-down design concept?

    a. Engagement of the top executives during the design process

    b. Engagement of the top executives once the design process is finalized

    c. Engagement of the employees working on the top floors in the building during the design process

    d. Engagement of the HR representatives during the design process

    e. Engagement of the marketing representatives during the design process

5. Departments using Internet capabilities can be categorized and grouped at which of the following levels? (The answer is stated in relative terms.)

    a. Lagging, leading, emerging

    b. Lagging, market parity, leading

    c. Lagging, market parity, leading, emerging

    d. Lagging, market parity, leading, high

6. The network-design process is limited by a number of external constraints. What are origins of these constraints?

    a. Technological, political, social, and economical

    b. Technological, worldwide standards, social, and managerial

    c. Technological, cost, social, and economical

    d. Managerial, political, social, and economical

7. What are technical constraints when designing a network infrastructure?

    a. Manpower

    b. Partnership agreements

    c. Cost

    d. Processor speed, buffer capacity

8. What are political constraints when designing a network infrastructure?

    a. Manpower

    b. Partnership agreements

    c. Cost

    d. Processor speed, buffer capacity

9. What are economical constraints when designing a network infrastructure?

    a. Manpower

    b. Partnership agreement

    c. Cost

    d. Processor speed, buffer capacity

10. Define some of the activities, tools, and techniques used in today's network-design process. (Choose three.)

    a. Analyzing network traffic

    b. Network auditing

    c. Filtering incoming network traffic

    d. Simulation of network traffic

    e. Network traffic hacking

The answers to the "Do I Know This Already?" quiz appear in Appendix A, "Answers to Chapter 'Do I Know This Already?' Quizzes and Q&A Sections." The suggested choices for your next step are as follows:

- **8 or less overall score**—Read the entire chapter. It includes the "Foundation Topics," "Foundation Summary," and "Q&A" sections.

- **9-10 overall score**—If you want more review on these topics, skip to the "Foundation Summary" section and then go to the "Q&A" section. Otherwise, move to the next chapter.

Foundation Topics

This chapter describes the design principles and the importance of organizational network policies and procedures. It includes a discussion of top-down design practices; the requirements and constraints involved with such; and the design activities, tools, and techniques, including auditing existing networks.

Fundamentally, you break the network-design process into manageable blocks so that the network functions within the performance and scale limits of applications, protocols, and network services.

The network infrastructure itself is an important component in the design process because it transports the application and network-management traffic. The designed network infrastructure must meet at least three high-level goals:

- It should provide timely and reliable transport.
- It should be adaptable to satisfy ever-changing application demands.
- The cost of future growth to meet the needs of business or information expansion should be appropriate to the extent of the required changes.

Building a network infrastructure requires a lot of planning, designing, modeling, and, most importantly, information-gathering. Network designers have many technologies to consider. The functionality of the selected technology and networking equipment is important because it might need to conform to standards to provide interoperability and it must be able to perform the tasks required by the network architecture.

The network architecture, an intermediate network design, provides a "blueprint" for the detailed design activities required to realize a functioning network infrastructure.

When designing networks, it is important to look at available resources you have to implement the new network architecture but also be sensitive to the quantity and quality of the resources available to operate and manage the network.

Organizational Network Policies and Procedures

Organizations, and their leadership teams, realize how networks can deliver operational efficiencies for current activities. The network can seamlessly link organizations to their direct customers, clients, business partners, suppliers, and employees, allowing them to share information and conduct business worldwide. To effectively operate globally, organizations must use their networks, and the Internet, as fully integrated components of all activities. The benefits of becoming a global network organization include improved productivity and greater economic efficiency. These benefits can be substantial. Cisco itself offers a prime example for other organizations seeking to leverage the power of their networks for business advantage. In the early 1990s, Cisco was a young technology company experiencing high growth and global expansion. Orders were escalating. The operations and support groups were stretched to their limits. As its business grew, Cisco had to find a way to minimize the required growth of staff and business systems yet still maintain, or improve, high levels of quality and customer satisfaction. For today's uncertain environment, this model has been altered toward the networked virtual organization model.

What Is a Global Network Business?

A global network business can be best described as a model that provides access to all relevant corporate data and information for users required to fulfill their day-to-day activities. These users, from key constituencies, use all available network resources, both private and public, to gain access to all information in a timely fashion. The main advantage of the model being more responsive and efficient instead of a model that protects information independent and isolated from the users of that information.

In general, a global network business spans all geographies, encouraging close relationships with customers, clients, partners, prospects, suppliers, and employees.

How the Global Network Business Evolved

In this context, it is important to know the organization's core competencies and start developing trusted business advisors and technology partnerships with companies that have the experience and share a similar long-term vision. Operating as a global network organization often leads to continuing changes in the use of the Internet that require coordination across multiple organizations. This effort is eased by shared goals and objectives. An increasingly common realization of the global networked business is the network virtual organization, in which cooperating organizations are connected by a common network infrastructure.

The models presented presume three underlying principles. They are customer or client focus, continuous standardization, and core versus context.

Customer Focus

Customer focus helps all participants in the activities that define the global network business or network virtual organization to look and move in the same direction. The improved responsiveness to changing requirements and increased satisfaction with provided goods and services that result from customer focus should provide an economic justification for the network investments.

Continuous Standardization

Continuous standardization works to use the network in ways that reduce the costs of providing goods and services through decreased service times and reduced redundancy. Standardizing the format allows increased direct data sharing, whereas standardizing internetworking technologies smoothes the flow of data through the combined organizations by increasing the transparency of the underlying network.

Core Versus Context

Logically joining organizations allows each participant to focus on core activities, investing in the materials, tools, and technologies that allow effective transformation of physical and intellectual materials to goods and services in ways that improve the organization's economic efficiency. The context in which each organization operates is provided by the interconnected mesh of cooperating suppliers and partners, each investing in its core activities.

Network Design and the Global Network Business

Ultimately, the model used by an organization provides an environment for the execution of a plan. It is the model, the plan, and the execution that together provide the economic returns which justify the networking investment. The network design must be sensitive to all. The model is a starting point, subject to constant re-examination. No fixed model is appropriate for every organization all the time. The benefits derived from a model can be reduced, or enhanced, by unexpected external issues and events. In some organizations, information is the product, amplifying investments in information technology. Other organizations measure success in terms of revenue growth or cost containment. Capital investment can be seen as a foundation or an anchor that restricts mobility. Sensitivity to the view of an organization's executives is critical in providing a satisfactory network design.

Top-Down Design Practices

For organizations to ensure long-term success, it is important to understand the contribution of networking, and more particularly internetworking, to the activities of the organization. Increased overall financial and operational performance is enabled, and sustained, by the investment in internetworking.

It is critical to identify and measure an organization's internetworking and Internet capabilities. This process should become an organization-wide pursuit directed by the highest executives. For many organizations, this process might require transforming the organization and the processes of the organization. The rest of this discussion addresses some strategies and tactics that you can employ to facilitate success. These design practices must originate from the very top of the organization with details based on the current situation, including the current network.

Requirements for Top-Down Design Practices

One of the basic requirements for a successful implementation and strategic use of internetworks and the Internet is the engagement of the top executives, particularly the company's CEO, during the design phase. Strategic use of the Internet to extend the organization's reach outward to customers, clients, vendors, and partners cannot become a core part of an organization's business philosophy until all the top executives assume an active leadership role in the process. Top executive support speeds the development of an organization's Internet capabilities; when the CEO recognizes that the efficiencies enabled by the Internet are key to future growth and survival, cultural transitions and adoption rates are bound to happen faster.

It is good practice to perform a periodic executive review and to restate or revise an organization's goals. Given the effort required to gather input from the various constituencies, and the value of executive time, annually is a reasonable frequency for this effort. For instance, the leadership team of Cisco selected "Leadership in Internet capabilities in all functions" as one of its top three goals. Every group throughout the company identified areas in which the Internet could impact its business area, defined how it can become one of the best in those areas, and regularly reported progress on those plans. In other words, its Internet strategy was integrated with its business strategy, and it had to have measurable and reportable results. Getting executive support not only aids in the allocation of necessary resources, but it also sends the right message throughout the company. At the end of the day, the entire company needs to be involved in promoting network-enabled business initiatives.

Evaluation of Top-Down Design Practices

One of the steps is evaluating every activity in the organization. Look at how the organization is using the Internet and networking capabilities to transform the way business is done. In practice, have the IT team, perhaps assisted by outside consultants, visit with senior executives to discuss the Internet and networking strategy. In some organizations, this review will validate and reinforce existing practice. In other situations, the evaluation group might realize that although they already use the network for several functions, the company has no cohesive strategy for using its Internet and networking capabilities to better benefit the organization.

Find a reference or benchmark company or organization outside of your own that is "best in class" for every function in the organization, whether it is customer care, e-commerce, e-learning, supply-chain management, web foundation, or workforce optimization. Complete the following objectives during the design process, and keep them in the back of your mind during the course of the evaluation:

■ Recommendations for the best solutions delivering the greatest competitive edge for your organization

■ Prioritization for the deployment of those solutions to generate the maximum value and return on investment

■ Identification and alignment of the resources required to put your networking plan in action

Also during this phase, the organization needs to find out how good (or bad) the different internal units are effectively using the Internet and networking capabilities of the organization. The efforts of the units in using these technologies as compared to other organizations can be categorized in one of four ways: lagging others, at market parity or average, leading others, or emerging. This evaluation should be validated by conversations with external peers performing equivalent functions when possible.

Deployment and Team Building for Top-Down Design Practices

When implementing new procedures and policies, you need to understand that organizations must embrace a new style and new set of rules all the way from the top to the bottom of the organization.

In general, the majority of projects that fail to deliver the expected benefits do so because of cultural, organizational, and leadership gaps between the IT teams and the organization's functional units. A leadership team that can bridge this gap will create a far more integrated and focused enterprise, increasing the probability of a desirable cycle of IT and business success.

For any projects, and more particularly for Internet and networking projects involving multiple departments within an organization, it is important to get participation from a broad base of people, from the technical experts to department managers and end users. These virtual teams must band together quickly and execute on tight schedules, requiring strong leadership and a sense of the common goals.

Creating the right team culture is not an easy task for most organizations, especially for organizations where the corporate history has been one of command and control. The necessary changes are not trivial, but the rewards that are a direct result of these changes will be exceptional.

The Final Word on Top-Down Design Practices

It definitely depends on the size of the organization, but consider creating a core team in charge to streamline the new processes. It will be its task to continually work with the departmental teams to develop new strategies based on best-practices experience throughout the organization and coordinate quarterly meetings with the senior leadership team.

Most organizations tend to compromise this important step, and after they have reaped the benefits, they don't identify or follow through on the next steps. This point is where the review process can help.

Set aside a good amount of time for every leader to determine the areas of redundancy and overlap. All members of the senior management team should participate in these review sessions. The review meetings provide good information for everyone regarding redundancies and overlooked opportunities. One of the key things to remember: Creating added value is changing your processes as you implement the new strategies. These changes are part of an ongoing process, providing a better leverage of the investments and also providing better coordination for the organization as a whole.

Requirements and Constraints

As described in the introduction, network design is an exercise in meeting new and old requirements while also working with certain constraints. These constraints can be technological, social, political, or economic.

Technological Constraints

The impact of the technological developments used to implement the latest global network business models and network virtual organizations in conjunction with the changing needs of consumers and society in general is obvious. All these developments are the reason Internet traffic doubles annually. CPU processing speed takes approximately 18 months to double. The difference in doubling periods and the inability of most organizations to augment capital equipment budgets to support these growth rates mean that CPU resources are a design constraint that you must address through network design and device configuration. Typically, the computation (processing) limitations that apply to network design are associated with processing routing-table calculations, encrypting and decrypting secured packets, accounting, implementing incoming and outgoing access lists, or just forwarding packets.

Device memory size also plays a significant role during the design phase, more or less for the same reasons.

Other resource considerations that can affect a network design include configurable buffer capacity, device port density, interface bandwidth, and backplane capacity constraints. In all cases, greater capacity increases the cost of the implementation. Another technological constraint involves ensuring that appropriate ventilation, air-conditioning, and other environmental requirements are met in the operations and laboratory facilities used to house the equipment.

Social Constraints

Manpower or labor in general is a clear concern in any network design. The more often a task must be executed (for instance, the amount of effort and skill required to connect a new user to the network or expand the capacity of the network infrastructure), the more the design should focus on making that particular task simple and efficient to manage. Including network-management services in the design can mitigate some of the labor concerns through the automation of monitoring and reporting functions. This automation should reduce the quantity of highly skilled employees required for the ongoing operation of the network.

Political Constraints

Political concerns could include the compulsory use of standards and installed applications that are difficult to understand, implement, and use.

Some organizations might have a single vendor pre-arranged partnership agreement, whereas other team members desire a multivendor type of environment.

Economic Constraints

Economic constraints play a major role for all network designers. Doing "more with less" is a common requirement, partially enabled by advances in semiconductor technology. Even when the restatement "achieving the best possible service at the lowest possible cost" is acceptable, there are design consequences. Common areas of design compromise for minimizing network acquisition and operations costs include WAN bandwidth, quality-of-service (QoS) guarantees, availability, security, and manageability. Ultimately, the network designer satisfies selected requirements to maximize the benefits from the network-built subject constraints of both cost and time. Other requirements with a lower priority, or less visibility, get deferred to later implementation phases or canceled.

Return on Investment (ROI)

A strategic part of the network design process is a tracking mechanism to measure the profit for a specific investment. A company's management team uses this simple tool as a financial metric to make business investment decisions and to measure the company's performance over time.

Return on Investment (ROI) is often calculated and defined in percentage terms and results in the return a customer can expect from the investment made. ROI is calculated by dividing the profit (return) by the total investment cost. Sometimes, the ROI is also specified as a ratio or break-even number. The latter has a time ratio in the calculation and results in the exact timeframe until the investment is returned.

Most customers in today's business environment try to understand or ask for a value justification; this is where the ROI calculation plays a significant role.

Design Activities, Tools, and Techniques

During the network-design process, there might be tools available to facilitate some of the activities. Some of the activities supported by tools include network auditing, traffic analysis, and network simulation. The choice of tools is very much determined by the value of the network investment and the consequences of network failure. This section discusses some of the tools and techniques used in today's network-design process for auditing networks and analyzing and simulating network traffic.

Having tools available to support every stage of the design process reduces risk (for instance, new equipment in the network), increases understanding (how certain components work in your environment), and improves responsiveness to design opportunities (getting technical analysis and business cases quickly).

Auditing an Existing Network

Network audit tools will help you generate specific reports on certain parts of your network and analyze how these segments of the network are performing. The network audit process should provide detailed recommendations to address the challenges, opportunities, and problems identified in the audit. The audit will also help the network-engineering team proactively identify and resolve potential network troubles before major problems are encountered.

Following is a list of reports that are often generated as part of a network audit:

- Performance reports
- Configuration reports
- Software reports
- Hardware reports

In general, a network audit will identify specific opportunities to improve the network utilization, availability, and stability, resulting in a reduced operation cost and a maximum return on the investment in the network infrastructure.

Analyzing Network Traffic

Network traffic analysis collects and analyzes data, which allows the network designer to balance the network load, troubleshoot and resolve network problems, optimize network performance, and, last but not least, plan future network growth. Traffic analysis is often performed as part of a network audit to generate performance reports.

The analysis tools help engineers and network designers better understand traffic patterns in the network. There are many analysis-tool suites on the market. Some provide only basic calculations. Others give extensive detail, including a complex analysis of traffic patterns, capacity availability, delay, and operational stability. Some tools allow the designer to re-run the analysis as the design is developed. Traffic analysis conducted during deployment allows timely adjustment of the design based on issues encountered at various locations or times.

Simulating Network Traffic

Network simulation has at least two distinct realizations. The first models the network using software to emulate the traffic sources and sinks, network devices, and the links that connect them. By varying model parameters, the designer can approximate the impact of more or less traffic demand or network resources. Although simulation software is expensive, for a large network it is far less expensive than building a flawed design. The second kind of simulation uses special hardware and software to generate traffic for injection into a live network for subsequent traffic analysis.

This testing activity is useful for validating and adequately testing QoS, latency, adaptive protocols, multicasting, and so on.

Traffic generation is also appropriate to estimate how the existing network will respond as you add new applications and services. Dynamic bandwidth utilization and latency are relatively difficult to estimate as compared to simple traffic delivery. Loss is relatively obvious. You can use adaptive protocols and applications with traffic generators to validate the expected behaviors.

A final use of traffic generation is testing multicast delivery. A large, complex test environment requires tools to ensure reasonable test coverage.

Foundation Summary

The "Foundation Summary" section of each chapter lists the most important facts from the chapter. Although this section does not list every fact from the chapter that will be on your CCDA exam, a well-prepared CCDA candidate should at a minimum know all the details in each "Foundation Summary" before going to take the exam.

Organizations, and their respective leadership teams, are beginning to realize how their networks can deliver process efficiencies that impact revenue, cost, and schedule.

Therefore, these organizations increasingly focus on network-design principles, including the recommended steps of internetworking design and organizational network policies and procedures. Organizations implementing a global network business model using top-down design concepts must make sure that they consider and manage all the requirements and constraints.

You can use a set of activities, techniques, and tools in today's network-design process.

Global Network Business Model

In general, a global network business spans all geographies, encouraging close relationships with customers, clients, partners, prospects, suppliers, and employees.

Top-Down Design

When implementing new procedures and policies, it is important that organizations embrace a new style and new set of rules for leadership and management all the way down from the top to the bottom of the organization.

Requirements and Constraints

Network design is an exercise in meeting new and old requirements while also working with certain constraints. These constraints can be technological, social, political, or economic.

Network-Design Tools

During the network-design process, you have a set of tools to facilitate some of the work. Some of the tools and techniques used in today's network-design process are network audits, network traffic analysis, and network simulation.

Q&A

As mentioned in the introduction, you have two choices for review questions. The questions that follow give you a bigger challenge than the exam itself by using an open-ended question format. By reviewing now with this more difficult question format, you can exercise your memory better and prove your conceptual and factual knowledge of this chapter. The answers to these questions appear in Appendix A.

For more practice with exam-like question formats, use the exam engine on the CD-ROM.

1. What is a global network business?

2. On what principles are global network businesses built?

3. What does the global network business model achieve?

4. What is critical for the top-down design concept?

5. Which levels can you define on how departments are leveraging Internet capabilities?

6. What are the four general categories of constraints encountered by a network designer?

7. What are technological constraints when designing a network infrastructure?

8. What are social constraints when designing a network infrastructure?

9. What are political constraints when designing a network infrastructure?

10. Define some of the activities supported by the tools used in today's network-design process.

This chapter covers the following subjects:

- Design Methodology

- Planning

- Design

- Implement, Operate, and Optimize

- Network Documentation

- Network Prototype

CHAPTER 2

Network Design Methodology

Design methodology is a critical process to network directors, administrators, consultants, and architects. Many organizations have grown their in-house expertise to include network designers because of the frequency of network changes. The growing role of the network as a business enabler has forced rapid and dynamic changes for both the network and the IT organization. This chapter delivers a comprehensive, yet simple, design methodology based on the extensive experience of Cisco.

"Do I Know This Already?" Quiz

The purpose of the "Do I Know This Already?" quiz is to help you decide if you need to read the entire chapter. If you already intend to read the entire chapter, you do not necessarily need to answer these questions now.

The 10-question quiz, derived from the major sections in the "Foundation Topics" portion of the chapter, helps you determine how to spend your limited study time.

Table 2-1 outlines the major topics discussed in this chapter and the "Do I Know This Already?" quiz questions that correspond to those topics.

Table 2-1   *"Do I Know This Already?" Foundation Topics Section-to-Question Mapping*

Foundation Topics Section	Questions Covered in This Section
Design Methodology	1, 2, 7
Planning	3
Network Documentation	4, 5, 8
Network Prototype	6, 9, 10

> **CAUTION** The goal of self assessment is to gauge your mastery of the topics in this chapter. If you do not know the answer to a question or you are only partially sure of the answer, you should mark this question wrong for purposes of the self assessment. Giving yourself credit for an answer you correctly guess skews your self-assessment results and might provide you with a false sense of security.

1. What does the acronym PDIOO stand for?

    a. Purpose, design, install, operation, optimization

    b. Plan, design, install, operation, optimization

    c. Plan, design, implement, operate, optimize

    d. Purpose, design, implement, operate, optimize

    e. Plan, designate, install, operate, optimization

2. Which of the following statements represents a likely starting point for planning network changes?

    a. Protocol assessment

    b. Determining the application requirements

    c. Determining the design requirements

    d. Determining the business needs

    e. Network assessment

3. True or False? A top-down network design process indicates that the network designer starts identifying the technology to use before defining the abstract concepts.

4. Which part of the network documentation would the chief financial officer (CFO) who is approving the project typically read?

    a. Design requirements

    b. Customer requirements

    c. Network topology diagram

    d. Executive summary

    e. Summary

5. In which part of the document, provided by the network designer, would the proposed network diagram appear?

   a. Executive summary

   b. Design requirements

   c. Design solution

   d. Summary

   e. Financial summary

6. Which of the following are steps to prototyping the network?

   a. Develop a test plan.

   b. Define success criteria.

   c. Purchase and prepare devices.

   d. Understand alternative proposals.

   e. Document the results.

7. Developing a network design based on layers such as core and distribution is an example of which type of design methodology?

   a. Flat design

   b. PDIOO

   c. Top-down

   d. Hierarchical structured design

8. In which section of the network document does Cisco recommend a discussion of performance, scalability, capacity, security, and traffic needs?

   a. Design requirements

   b. Design solution

   c. Executive summary

   d. Design summary

   e. Appendix

9. During which stage of the prototyping process is the prototype tested prior to being reviewed by the customer?

   a. Step 1: Review requirements.

   b. Step 4: Develop a test plan.

   c. Step 5: Purchase and prepare equipment.

   d. Step 6: Practice.

   e. Step 7: Conduct final tests and demonstrations.

10. During which stage of the prototyping process would you determine possible problem areas that might affect your design?

   a. Step 1: Review requirements.

   b. Step 2: Determine prototype extend.

   c. Step 3: Understand alternative proposals.

   d. Step 4: Develop a test plan.

   e. Step 5: Purchase and prepare equipment.

The answers to the "Do I Know This Already?" quiz appear in Appendix A, "Answers to Chapter Quizzes and Q&A Sections." The suggested choices for your next step are as follows:

■ **8 or less overall score**—Read the entire chapter. This includes the "Foundation Topics," "Foundation Summary," and "Q&A" sections.

■ **9-10 overall score**—If you want more review on these topics, skip to the "Foundation Summary" section and then go to the Q&A section. Otherwise, move to the next chapter.

Foundation Topics

In this section, you learn a design methodology that helps the network designer define the network's technical and business requirements and work through all phases of the technology lifecycle of planning, design, implementation, operation, and optimization (PDIOO). With the importance of organizational network policies and procedure, as discussed in Chapter 1, "Design Principles," this chapter discusses documenting the gathered information and relevant findings.

Design Methodology

As network expectations have changed, so have design principles. Enterprises no longer rely on a single vendor, technology, or protocol. The design strategy has changed dramatically to include security and scalability as primary criteria. Security is having a large impact on network design. Placing access servers and WAN routers is more complex and deliberate.

Large, flat, bridged networks with thousands of users have almost disappeared. Networks are subnetted to manageable sizes to limit broadcast domains and manage functional workgroups. Advances in microprocessor technology have allowed the development of multilayer switches that can perform routing and other high-level network functions at speeds formerly only attainable with large switched networks.

Redesigned networks transport only IP packets; instead of bridging or routing non-IP packets, networks encapsulate these protocols into IP before the router transmits them. In a LAN, a common design technique is to place all local-area transport (LAT) or Systems Network Architecture (SNA) devices on one VLAN so bridged traffic is not required.

There is greater redundancy in network designs; since September 11, business continuity has become a priority. New levels of redundancy are required, and disaster recovery is no longer optional. Redundancy is taking many forms, including separate power sources, multiple WAN carriers, alternate cable routes, and redundant hardware. Network connectivity and services are critical components of enterprise operations. The cost of downtime is increasing at a phenomenal rate.

Enterprises are no longer locked into using a single vendor, technology, or protocol; many technologies have standardized, but it is still not a trivial factor to design a network. Assessing the design criteria enables you to understand the network and what it was meant to do. Network designs must easily adapt to implement the next generation of technology. Many network designers are planning for IP telephony; these network-design plans are not for new networks but are improvements on existing ones. Properly planning networks based on sound architecture makes necessary network redesigns easier.

PDIOO Stages of the Network

Design is just one component of a network lifecycle. Planning, design, implementation, operation, and optimization (PDIOO) are the different stages of the network lifecycle. Each stage builds on its predecessor, developing a sound network that maintains its effectiveness through changing business needs. You can apply the PDIOO methodology to all technologies. During this PDIOO process, you define key deliverables and associated actions, with a direct correlation to the added value and benefit for the client's network. For example, understanding business goals, usage characteristics, and network requirements helps you avoid unnecessary upgrades and network redesigns, reducing time for introducing new services in the network. Discussions in this chapter revolve around these five main stages.

Planning

The role of the network is undergoing constant change due to the changing demands on business and changes in network products and technologies. Changes to the network, whether small or large, reflect the PDIOO lifecycle. As an example, imagine a typical small network consisting of 200 users in the healthcare market. This company plans to double its revenue by adding five remote offices. Now, its original network becomes a hub site to these remote offices. It would be unmanageable, and potentially costly, to have Internet access at each of these remote offices, so the hub site is the central point of Internet access.

This change to the network begins with planning. At this stage, it is important to define the following:

- Business requirements and strategy
- Project-success criteria
- Network architecture

The following is a list of architectural inquiries you must answer to define the strategy:

- Determine performance requirements for the network. How will the network ensure performance as the network scales?
- Determine availability requirements. How much network redundancy is required? What are the critical components of the network?
- How will network management be deployed throughout the network? What components need out-of-band management? How will the IT resources manage multiple network-down situations?
- What is the state of the current network?

This list is just a sample of the types of questions you can encounter during the network-planning stage. The responses to these questions are not products or configurations: They are strategies.

Planning is a stage where you can test the logic of your future design and determine whether there are any flaws. Planning helps you avoid replicating a logical mistake in a network design that you would use as a template across five locations.

Design Assessment

When planning for changes to an existing network, it is critical to understand the state of the existing network. This type of assessment provides a starting point. It also provides you with an understanding of how the network and the user community operate together. Not taking the user community into account can become a major problem during the implementation.

Therefore, it is critical to identify and measure your Internet and networking capabilities, which should become a company-wide process. This approach is a top-down approach to network design. Top-down means that you begin with abstract concepts and application requirements first before identifying technologies to use. The abstract concepts are the business requirements, the network architecture, and then the network design. The process is often iterative because the design changes as you uncover more information about the needs of the network. Note that the results of each stage of the PDIOO network lifecycle affect the network design.

Design

After completing the planning stage, you have enough information to develop a network design. If a network is already in place, use this phase to review and validate it. At this stage, you choose products, protocols, and features based on criteria defined in the planning stage. You develop network diagrams to illustrate what changes will occur in the network to achieve the desired results. The more detailed the network diagram and plan, the better you can anticipate the challenges during the implementation.

NOTE In addition to the PDIOO lifecycle, Cisco recommends an architecture for building complex networks using structured design practices. This functional model provides central management and a site backbone, or core, which offers transport services to hierarchies of distribution and access modules that support user connectivity, servers, and WAN connectivity to other sites, organizations, and individuals. This model is also the basis of the Security Architecture for Enterprise (SAFE) blueprint, which evolved from the Cisco Architecture for Voice, Video, and Integrated Data (AVVID).

Following a structured design enables you to predict traffic behavior, routing paths, and capacity requirements. It is recommended that the structured network design begins with the outermost layers, such as the access and the applications, and then move inward to distribution and core.

Implement, Operate, and Optimize

The implementation stage provides detailed customized deliverables to help avoid risks, meet expectations, and so on. The operate and optimization phase, also known as the operational-support phase, is designed to protect your network investment and help your staff prevent problems, maximize system utility, and accelerate problem resolution. The following sections describe the steps in more detail.

Implementation

A sound implementation plan ensures smooth deployment, even when issues arise. Communicating the implementation plan to all stakeholders provides you with an opportunity to assess the viability of the plan. It is better to find mistakes on the drawing board than during the implementation. Good processes such as change control can effectively handle issues that occur during the deployment. In addition, change control provides flexibility because it is impossible to plan for every contingency, especially if the implementation has a long duration.

Operability and Support Maintenance

Eventually, you have to support and ensure the operability of what you build. Network-management strategy is equally important as the network design, and you must address it in the planning and design stage. There is no doubt that networks are getting larger and more complex, but so are the support requirements for the network. You can resolve issues with resource constraints and increased support hours, in part, with a well-planned network-management solution. Remember, after the excitement and newness of the network installation has worn off, you are still left with a network that you have to manage.

Assigning Ownership of Network Management

All organizations, unless they completely outsource all aspects of the network, have some level of ownership of network management. With the growing demands on network managers, they must make an assessment. Is it realistic and cost-effective to develop network-management staff and tools in-house to meet the service expectations? How long can the current support provided by the existing network-management solution remain viable? What changes must you make to ensure its viability? What is your network-management solution's total cost of ownership? You must explore this topic in the process of deciding who owns the network-management solution in-house.

Outsourcing Network Management with MSPs

Network management has traditionally been the responsibility of the network managers, engineers, and operators. If an organization outsourced management, engineering, and operations, it also outsourced network management. But recent years have seen the rise of managed service providers (MSPs), companies that monitor the network but do not take ownership of the configuration and troubleshooting of the network.

Typical MSPs offer basic fault management, monitoring the up/down status of key network devices as determined by the customer. When a device goes down, the MSP pages or calls a designated customer contact who is responsible for resolution. It is also common for MSPs to offer performance-management capabilities, monitoring bandwidth usage on WAN links. The MSP usually monitors the network over an encrypted Internet session.

MSPs solve a common problem with implementing a network-management system—how to pay for the software, systems, and services necessary for a network-management system, which, depending on the size and needs of the organization, can vary from $10,000 to more than $1,000,000. With an MSP, the organization pays a monthly fee based on the number of monitored devices.

MSPs offer the advantage of providing monitoring services 24-by-7, often exceeding the customer requirements, at a reduced implementation price. Monthly payments to the MSP can eventually exceed the cost of building an owned management system.

MSPs might not be able to provide all the services that the customer requires. For example, the MSP might not be able to provide reports according to the customer's standards. Remember, you are using the MSP services for your purposes, but they might not be an exact match to your needs.

Optimization

The last step in the PDIOO process is the optimization of the network. A sound design still requires optimization and "tweaking" to gain its full potential. The optimization of the network can be as simple as hardening servers against security threats or adding quality of service (QoS) to the network for latency-sensitive traffic. Optimization can even lead to a redesign of the network, so the cycle would begin again.

Network Documentation

After completing a design, the next step is to document it so that you can properly communicate your solution. The documentation can be in the form of a response to a Request for Proposal (RFP) or a design document, also referred to as a proposal. The following are the minimum recommended sections of the design document, all of which are described in detail in the sections that follow:

■   Executive summary

■   Design requirements

■   Design solution

■   Summary and appendixes

Executive Summary

The first section is an executive summary, which is typically one page in length. The executive summary describes the network requirements and how the proposed design meets those requirements. The audience for the executive summary is the decision makers for the project. The following is a list of suggested topics:

■   State the goals of the project and how it relates to the business needs.

■   Describe how your solution addresses these business needs. Outline the network-design strategy.

■   Describe the implementation concerns such as integration issues, training, support, and transition issues.

■   Outline the benefits of the solution.

It is important that you write the executive summary clearly and concisely. Remember that the audience needs to understand the project based on this one- or two-page description.

Design Requirements

This section describes the results of investigating the organization's business and technical needs. Some of the methods for understanding the design requirements can include characterizing the existing network and the logical network requirements, such as performance, scalability, capacity, security, and traffic needs. It is helpful in this section to organize the design requirements to be easily understandable. Remember to refer back to the business needs as appropriate.

Design Solution

Present the recommended solution in this section based on the priority of the organization. This section should include a network diagram of the proposed solution. The network diagram should contain addressing and naming conventions. Also included are listings of the hardware and software recommendations for the LAN and WAN and the recommended protocols for routing and application. Finally, with any implementation, you should write a section addressing how the network will be managed after it is installed.

Figure 2-1 uses logical symbols, not pictures of specific products. The architecture development process commonly uses this type of diagram.

Figure 2-1 *Logical Diagram for a Simple Network*

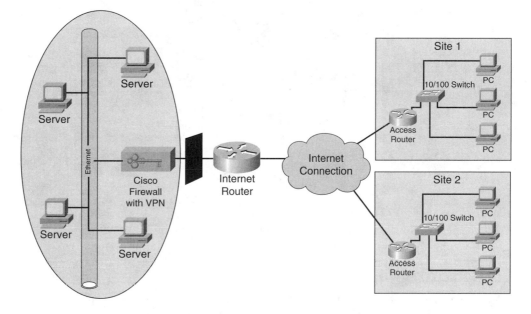

Summary and Appendixes

Use this section to summarize your solution and relate specific design details to the project requirements and goals. Use appendixes to provide supplemental information to better illustrate the proposed solution. The appendixes can include the following:

- Contact information of project consultants and Cisco representatives
- A project plan
- Details of addressing and naming schemes that you developed for the project
- Results of prototype test results and any performance measurements you performed on the current network
- Workflow diagrams

Figure 2-2 is an example of a workflow diagram for an implementation.

Figure 2-2 *Sample Workflow Diagram for Implementation*

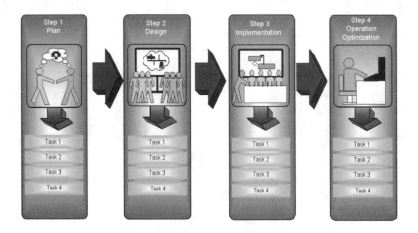

You can use Figure 2-2 to illustrate a complex project plan in phases or milestones. This illustration helps the customers visualize the project with which you are familiar.

Network Prototype

A complex network design can be a financial drain and a resource drain on an organization. It is necessary to demonstrate that the design meets the project requirements. A network prototype can provide this "trial run" at a minimal cost but with the capability to demonstrate almost all the functionality of the network, resulting in a prototype.

A prototype is a complex and full trial run of the network design used to prove that the design works. A prototype is usually a large-scale, fully functional form of a new design that you can use to prove a large implementation. It is necessary to decide whether the need to prove the design justifies the cost of setting up a prototype, and Table 2-2 summarizes the criteria for choosing the prototype.

Table 2-2 *Criteria for Prototype*

Criteria	Prototype
Size of the network design	Used on a subset of a large network design that can span both LANs and WANs
Demonstration of functionality	Used to prove complex functionality, such as connectivity; applications, such as email; and routing
Cost	Costlier because it requires more equipment and resources
Customer requirement	Used when a proof of full functionality of the design is necessary

Creating a Prototype

After you determine the testing needs, you must perform the appropriate steps for creating a prototype. Table 2-3 lists the steps for creating a prototype.

Table 2-3   *Steps for Creating a Prototype*

Steps	Description
Step 1: Review the requirements.	Determine the major goals. Outline the proof required to demonstrate that your design works. Determine possible problem areas that might affect your design.
Step 2: Determine the extent of the prototype.	Determine how much of the design must be built into a prototype to be effective. Identify the tools you can use to simplify the prototype.
Step 3: Understand alternative proposals.	Work with others to identify the products and designs in alternative proposals. If information is not available, speculate on what competing proposals might use. Research information on alternative products by referencing websites, industry articles, and evaluations.
Step 4: Develop a test plan.	Draw a network diagram. List tools for the test. List the plan scheduling, resources, and milestones. Prepare the demonstrations. Determine how each test will prove that the design meets the requirements. Determine how each test will show that the alternative products provide an inferior solution.

Table 2-3   *Steps for Creating a Prototype (Continued)*

Steps	Description
Step 5: Purchase and prepare equipment.	You must acquire and prepare some or all of the following equipment: Network-simulation tools Protocol analyzers Industry tests Network hardware and software Routers Switches Network-management tools End-system hardware and software Application servers File servers
Step 6: Practice.	Practice your demonstration to include the necessary elements from the previous step.
Step 7: Conduct final tests and demonstrations.	Test your configuration using the following tools: Cisco IOS Software commands Protocol analyzers Simulation tools

The sections that follow describe in detail all the steps outlined in Table 2-3.

Step 1: Reviewing the Requirements

Having a clear goal for building your prototype is essential. In fact, you should create the prototype design using the same approach you used to determine requirements for the original design.

Begin by doing the following:

- List the major goals.

- Identify the requirements for performance, security, capacity, and scalability.

- Consider other requirements such as return-on-investment (ROI) issues, management of the new network, equipment reuse, and the cost of implementing the prototype test.

- Determine what specific advantages you can illustrate with the prototype.

Plan the ideas you illustrate to ensure that the prototype is complete and that it serves as a useful vehicle to demonstrate these points.

Just as it is important to list the good ideas, you also want to be ready for any problems or issues that might negatively affect the success of the project. Take the time to list the cons to the prototype so that you are ready to address them as well.

Step 2: Determining the Extent of the Prototype

Creating the right-size prototype is critical. You must determine how much of the design you should include in the prototype to meet the test expectations. The scope of your prototype is a factor that you must determine before work can begin. The cost and the purpose of the prototype often determine the size of the demonstration. For example, if one of the primary concerns is time, you might focus your effort on a specific problem. If it is necessary to roll out the design in multiple locations, it might be possible to implement a full prototype in one of the organization's many locations.

> **TIP**   Remember that the network goals are the deciding factor in determining how much of the network design you should implement to prove its value.

When proving the effectiveness of your design, you can use tools and investigative services to simplify the development of the prototype by simulating some of the equipment and their effect on the network.

These simulations generally remove the need to purchase, install, and configure actual equipment to make the task of creating the prototype less costly.

> **TIP**   You can use a network analyzer to simulate traffic. It also works as a tool to prove the effectiveness of the network design. The Network General's Sniffer is one of several network analyzers.

Competing products sometimes endure third-party industry tests. You can use these tests and their results to prove your design without building a test yourself. An example of one of these tests is the Strategic Networks Consulting, Inc. (SNCI) switch test, available from the SNCI website. It performed this test on Cisco's Catalyst 5000 switches and Cabletron's MMAC-Plus switches. Go to the SNCI website at http://www.zdnet.com/zdtag/snci/ to review the test and other similar comparisons.

Step 3: Understanding Alternative Proposals

For a large design that requires a prototype, there are probably several competing design alternatives. It is important to plan this particular prototype to highlight the advantages that your design can offer above the competition. Working with the account manager and sales team can help you find the alternative proposals. Taking the time to gather as much information on other proposals is always a good way to double-check your own design and to make sure that you did not miss a point.

If it is not possible to get information on the alternatives, make some assumptions on what might be proposed to meet the project requirements by referencing websites or product descriptions. You can make a comparison list of features based on the requirements or draw up a list of pros and cons about the alternatives. Then, use this information to build your strategy.

Step 4: Developing a Test Plan

After you prepare to create the prototype, the next step is to create the test plan to use on the prototype. The best tool available to a designer is a topology map of the prototype test network. You can use this one diagram to view the entire network, and it can be the single most important document of a prototype. On this diagram, you can include major configuration parameters, such as network speeds, topology information, WAN line speeds, and descriptions of specific network devices, such as firewalls.

A topology map of the test environment proves invaluable. The prototype topology map can include a list of simulation tools, Cisco hardware and software, and non-Cisco hardware and software you need for the prototype. Some of the non-Cisco hardware you might want to use includes cables, modems, null modems, WAN connections, Internet access, workstations, servers, design-simulation tools, telephone-equipment simulators, and so on.

When compiling a list of the resources you need, it is important also to list and plan the tests that you will perform on the prototype network. The test plan should reflect the goals you decided upon when you created the design for the prototype: Remember that you designed these goals to meet the project needs.

Demonstration

Performing a demonstration might be complicated and might require the involvement of multiple people to ensure its success. If you require help from coworkers or collaboration from others, remember to request the help with ample time to coordinate your resources. To make sure that everyone understands what to do for the test, be sure to develop and review a script.

Table 2-4 shows a table included in a script that maps out the roles and responsibilities of the people involved in the presentation. If you clearly define this type of information, people are better prepared to contribute to the success of the presentation.

Table 2-4 *Creating a Script*

Role	Contributions to the Project and Script
Design consultant	Review the design and define the goals. Provide the network diagram. Review the benefits of the design.
Project manager	Develop a schedule. Map milestones. Develop an implementation plan. Provide contact information.
Account manager	Handle customer contact. Compile competitive information.
Network engineers	Create detailed implementation plans. Draw up testing overviews.

Test the script ahead of time at a lab. Preparation only reinforces the testing, which in turn shows that your team is coordinated and professional and also might point out any unforeseen problems that you must resolve before you present the final product

Finally, the test should highlight the strengths of the design and point out how the alternatives might not prove as useful. Remember to review the test to avoid issues that might arise later during the demonstration.

Step 5: Purchasing and Preparing Equipment

Remember that it is important to prepare for the prototype demonstration well in advance so that you can purchase and configure the equipment with ample time. Because equipment purchases can be delayed or other unforeseen problems can arise, you should gather and configure the equipment as soon as you compile a list. This list would include the following:

- Network-simulation tools
- Network hardware and software
- End-system hardware and software

Remember to prepare an inventory sheet to help you track the products as they arrive. It's also important to stage some of the equipment with basic testing. *Staging* is a method of setting up the equipment for basic configuration and testing the hardware. It is also a good time to develop an inventory to help you sort your equipment.

Step 6: Practicing

Performing the demonstration is a complex task. It is important to practice with the members of your team to coordinate your presentation; it is especially important if you are going to demonstrate the equipment. You want to make sure that your demonstration does not have any surprises that would adversely affect your success. Make sure that you give yourself ample time to practice several times.

Step 7: Conducting Final Tests and Demonstrations

During the final step, you must present the prototype design for usability testing. Some common basic tools that can make demonstrations more effective are

- Protocol analyzers
- Simulation tools
- Cisco IOS commands

An insightful design methodology helps the network designer define the network's technical and business requirements and work through all phases of the technology lifecycle of PDIOO. Documenting the gathered information is critical, and a complex network design might require demonstrating that the design meets the project requirements using a network prototype.

Foundation Summary

The "Foundation Summary" section of each chapter lists the most important facts from the chapter. Although this section does not list every fact from the chapter that will be on your CCDA exam, a well-prepared CCDA candidate should, at a minimum, know all the details in each "Foundation Summary" before taking the exam.

PDIOO

The network lifecycle is a simple process of planning, designing, implementing, operating, and optimizing. Whether you face a simple design change or a new network, the five steps are applicable. If you begin with proper planning, you can ensure a smoother implementation.

Each stage of the lifecycle, although described in one word, represents a complex grouping of tasks. Those tasks change depending on the project at hand. However, creating clear and realistic objectives for each stage is the key to developing subsequent tasks. Treat each stage as if it were its own project, with the same level of concentration and completeness.

Network Documentation

After completing a network design, you must present it in a manner that is concise and accurate. Cisco recommends that the network documentation have the following five components:

- Executive summary
- Design requirements
- Design solution
- Summary
- Appendix

The documentation is the "gift wrapping" on your project, but remember that it leaves an impression and you should not take it lightly.

Steps for Prototyping

Table 2-5 lists the steps involved in a prototype. This type of process is great for challenging and complex projects. It enables you to test a design, identify potential issues, and gain the confidence of the customer.

Table 2-5 *Steps in Prototype Process*

Steps	Description
Step 1: Review the requirements.	Determine the major goals.
	Outline the proof required to demonstrate that your design works.
	Determine possible problem areas that might affect your design.
Step 2: Determine the extent of the prototype.	Determine how much of the design must be built into a prototype to be effective.
	Identify the tools you can use to simplify the prototype.
Step 3: Understand alternative proposals.	Work with others to identify the products and designs in alternative proposals.
	If information is not available, speculate on what competing proposals might use.
	Research information on alternative products by referencing websites, industry articles, and evaluations.
Step 4: Develop a test plan.	Draw a network diagram.
	List tools for the test.
	List the plan scheduling, resources, and milestones.
	Prepare the demonstrations.
	Determine how each test will prove that the design meets the requirements.
	Determine how each test will show that the alternative products provide an inferior solution.

Table 2-5 *Steps in Prototype Process (Continued)*

Steps	Description
Step 5: Purchase and prepare equipment.	You must acquire and prepare some or all of the following equipment:
	Network-simulation tools
	Protocol analyzers
	Industry tests
	Network hardware and software
	Routers
	Switches
	Network-management tools
	End-system hardware and software
	Application servers
	File servers
Step 6: Practice.	Practice your demonstration to include the necessary elements from the previous step.
Step 7: Conduct final tests and demonstrations.	Test your configuration using the following tools:
	Cisco IOS Software commands
	Protocol analyzers
	Simulation tools

Q&A

As mentioned in the introduction, you have two choices for review questions. Some of the questions that follow give you a bigger challenge than the exam itself by using an open-ended question format. By reviewing now with this more difficult question format, you can exercise your memory better and prove your conceptual and factual knowledge of this chapter. The answers to these questions appear in Appendix A.

For more practice with exam-like question formats, use the exam engine on the CD-ROM.

1. What is the name of the design process that begins with understanding business processes and objectives before creating a network design?

2. What is the second process in the Cisco network lifecycle?

3. What is the name of the stage where you perform moves, adds, and changes on the new network?

4. After a network is in place, and you need to incorporate new application such as video, what stage of the PDIOO process would this need represent?

5. Where would the customer find a description of the network strategy used to address the business issues identified during the design process?

6. A network diagram that uses general icons to represent network functions such as routing and firewalling is called what type of diagram?

7. Which step of the network prototype-testing process follows after the develop-and-test-plan step?

8. During which stage of the prototyping process would you order and stage the equipment?

9. How many steps are involved in developing a prototype based on Cisco's recommendations?

10. What is the first process in the Cisco network lifecycle?

11. During which stage of the network prototype-testing phase do you need the proof to demonstrate that your design works?

12. Which tool available to network designers is often described as "one diagram to view the entire network?"

13. For what purposes do you use a network analyzer during the network-design process?

14. Which part of the network document contains the proposed network diagram?

15. What is the importance of a design assessment during the planning phase for making changes to an existing network?

16. Which part of the network document do you use to summarize the solution and relate specific design details to the project requirements and goals?

This chapter covers the following subjects:

- Hierarchical Network Models

- Enterprise Composite Network Model

- Network Availability

CHAPTER 3

Network Structure Models

This chapter reviews the hierarchical network model and introduces the Enterprise Composite Network model. It addresses the use of device, media, and route redundancy to improve network availability.

"Do I Know This Already?" Quiz

The purpose of the "Do I Know This Already?" quiz is to help you decide whether you need to read the entire chapter. If you already intend to read the entire chapter, you do not necessarily need to answer these questions now.

The eight-question quiz, derived from the major sections in the "Foundation Topics" portion of the chapter, helps you determine how to spend your limited study time. Table 3-1 outlines the major topics discussed in this chapter and the "Do I Know This Already?" quiz questions that correspond to those topics.

Table 3-1 *"Do I Know This Already?" Foundation Topics Section-to-Question Mapping*

Foundation Topics Section	Questions Covered in This Section
Hierarchical Network Models	1, 3
Enterprise Composite Network Model	2, 5, 6, 7
Network Availability	4, 8

CAUTION The goal of self assessment is to gauge your mastery of the topics in this chapter. If you do not know the answer to a question or you are only partially sure of the answer, you should mark this question wrong for purposes of the self assessment. Giving yourself credit for an answer you correctly guess skews your self-assessment results and might provide you with a false sense of security.

1. In the hierarchical network model, which layer is responsible for fast transport?

    a. Network

    b. Core

    c. Distribution

    d. Access

2. Which Enterprise Composite Network model component interfaces with the service provider (SP)?

    a. Campus infrastructure

    b. Access layer

    c. Enterprise Edge

    d. Edge distribution

3. In the hierarchical network model, at which layer does security filtering, address aggregation, and media translations occur?

    a. Network

    b. Core

    c. Distribution

    d. Access

4. Which is a method for workstation-to-router redundancy in the access layer?

    a. AppleTalk Address Resolution Protocol (AARP)

    b. Hot Standby Redundancy Protocol (HSRP)

    c. Routing Information Protocol (RIP)

    Answer options:

    a. Answers b and c

    b. Answers a, b, and c

5. The network-management module has tie-ins to which components?

    a. Campus infrastructure

    b. Server farm

    c. Enterprise Edge

    d. SP Edge

Answer options:

   a. Answers a and b

   b. Answers a, b, and c

   c. Answers a, b, c, and d

6. Which is an SP Edge module in the Enterprise Composite Network model?

   a. Public Switched Telephone Network (PSTN) service

   b. Edge distribution

   c. Server farm

   d. Core layer

7. In which module would you place a Cisco Call Manager (CM)?

   a. Campus core

   b. E-commerce

   c. Server farm

   d. Edge distribution farm

8. High availability, port security, and rate limiting are functions of which hierarchical layer?

   a. Network

   b. Core

   c. Distribution

   d. Access

The answers to the "Do I Know This Already?" quiz appear in Appendix A, "Answers to Chapter 'Do I Know This Already?' Quizzes and Q&A Sections." The suggested choices for your next step are as follows:

- **6 or less overall score**—Read the entire chapter. It includes the "Foundation Topics," "Foundation Summary," and "Q&A" sections.

- **7–8 overall score**—If you want more review on these topics, skip to the "Foundation Summary" section and then go to the "Q&A" section. Otherwise, move to the next chapter.

Foundation Topics

With the complexities of network design, the CCDA needs to understand network models used to simplify the design process. The hierarchical network model was one of the first Cisco models that divided the network into core, distribution, and access layers.

The Enterprise Composite Network model is a model that provides a functional modular approach to network design. In addition to a hierarchy, modules organize server farms, network management, and the Enterprise Edge. Chapters that follow focus on the technologies and solutions in each of these modules.

Hierarchical Network Models

Hierarchical models enable you to design internetworks that use specialization of function combined with an hierarchical organization. Such a design simplifies the tasks required to build a network that meets current requirements and can grow to meet future requirements. Hierarchical models use layers to simplify the tasks for internetworking. Each layer can focus on specific functions, allowing you to choose the right systems and features for each layer. Hierarchical models apply to both LAN and WAN design.

Benefits of the Hierarchical Model

The benefits of using hierarchical models for your network design include the following:

- Cost savings
- Ease of understanding
- Modular network growth
- Improved fault isolation

After adopting hierarchical design models, many organizations report cost savings because they are no longer trying to do everything in one routing or switching platform. The modular nature of the model enables appropriate use of bandwidth within each layer of the hierarchy, reducing the provisioning of bandwidth in advance of actual need.

Keeping each design element simple and functionally focused facilitates ease of understanding, which helps control training and staff costs. You can distribute network-monitoring and management-reporting systems to the different layers of modular network architectures, which also helps control management costs.

Hierarchical design facilitates changes. In a network design, modularity lets you create design elements that you can replicate as the network grows. As each element in the network design requires change, the cost and complexity of making the upgrade is contained to a small subset of the overall network. In large, flat network architectures, changes tend to impact a large number of systems. Limited mesh topologies within a layer or component, such as the campus core or backbone connecting central sites, retain value even in the hierarchical design models.

Structuring the network into small, easy-to-understand elements improves fault isolation. Network managers can easily understand the transition points in the network, which helps identify failure points.

Today's fast-converging protocols were designed for hierarchical topologies. To control the impact of routing-protocol processing and bandwidth consumption, you must use modular hierarchical topologies with protocols designed with these controls in mind, such as Open Shortest Path First (OSPF).

Hierarchical network design facilitates route summarization. Route summarization reduces the routing-protocol overhead on links in the network and reduces routing-protocol processing within the routers.

Hierarchical Network Design

As Figure 3-1 illustrates, a traditional hierarchical LAN design has three layers:

■ The core layer provides fast transport between distribution sites within the enterprise campus.

■ The distribution layer provides policy-based connectivity.

■ The access layer provides workgroup and user access to the network.

Each layer provides necessary functionality to the enterprise campus network. You do not need to implement the layers as distinct physical entities. You can implement each layer in one or more devices or as cooperating interface components sharing a common chassis. Smaller networks can "collapse" multiple layers to a single device with only an implied hierarchy. Maintaining an explicit awareness of hierarchy is useful as the network grows.

Figure 3-1 *A Hierarchical Network Design Has Three Layers: Core, Distribution, and Access*

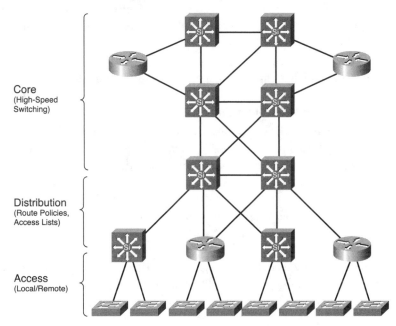

Core Layer

The core layer is the high-speed switching backbone of the network, which is crucial to corporate communications. The core layer should have the following characteristics:

- Fast transport

- High reliability

- Redundancy

- Fault tolerance

- Quick adaptation (adapt to changes quickly)

- Low latency and good manageability

- Avoidance of slow packet manipulation caused by filters or other processes

- Limited and consistent diameter

When a network uses routers, the number of router hops from edge to edge is called the *diameter*. As noted, it is considered good practice to design for a consistent diameter within a hierarchical network. The trip from any end station to another end station across the backbone should have the same number of hops. The distance from any end station to a server on the backbone should also be consistent.

Limiting the diameter of the internetwork provides predictable performance and ease of trouble-shooting. You can add distribution layer routers and client LANs to the hierarchical model without increasing the diameter of the core layer. Use of a block implementation isolates existing end stations from most effects of network growth.

Distribution Layer

The distribution layer of the network is the isolation point between the access and core layers of the network. The distribution layer can have many roles, including implementing the following functions:

- Policy (for example, ensuring that traffic sent from a particular network is forwarded out one interface while all other traffic is forwarded out another interface)
- Security filtering
- Address or area aggregation or summarization
- Departmental or workgroup access
- Broadcast or multicast domain definition
- Routing between virtual LANs (VLANs)
- Media translations (for example, between Ethernet and Token Ring)
- Redistribution between routing domains (for example, between two different routing protocols)
- Demarcation between static and dynamic routing protocols

You can use several Cisco IOS Software features to implement policy at the distribution layer, including the following:

- Filtering by source or destination address
- Filtering on input or output ports
- Hiding internal network numbers by route filtering
- Static routing
- Quality-of-service (QoS) mechanisms (for example, ensuring that all devices along a path can accommodate the requested parameters)

The distribution layer provides aggregation of routes providing route summarization to the core. In the campus LANs, the distribution layer provides routing between VLANs that also apply security and QoS policies.

Access Layer

The access layer provides user access to local segments on the network. The access layer is characterized by switched- and shared-bandwidth LAN segments in a campus environment. Microsegmentation using LAN switches provides high bandwidth to workgroups by reducing collision domains on Ethernet segments and reducing the number of stations capturing the token on Token Ring LANs. Some functions of the access layer include the following:

■ High availability

■ Port security

■ Rate limiting

■ Address Resolution Protocol (ARP) inspection

■ Virtual access lists

■ Trust classification

You implement high-availability models at the access layer. The section "Network Availability" later in this chapter covers availability models. The LAN switch in the access layer can control access to the port and limit the rate at which traffic is sent to and from the port. You can implement access by identifying the MAC address using ARP, trusting the host, and using access lists.

Other chapters of this book cover the other functions in the list.

For small office/home office (SOHO) environments, the entire hierarchy collapses to interfaces on a single device. Remote access to the central corporate network is through traditional WAN technologies such as ISDN, Frame Relay, and leased lines. You can implement features such as dial-on-demand routing (DDR) and static routing to control costs. Remote access can include virtual private network (VPN) technology.

Hierarchical Model Examples

You can implement the hierarchical model by using either routers or switches. Figure 3-2 is an example of a switched hierarchical design. In this design, the core provides high-speed transport and the routing functionality resides in the distribution layer. Figure 3-3 shows examples of a routed hierarchical design. In this design, the core uses multilayer switches to offer line-speed transport with Layer 3 (routing) functionality.

Figure 3-2   *Example of a Switched Hierarchical Design*

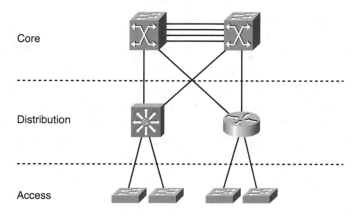

Figure 3-3   *Example of a Routed Hierarchical Design*

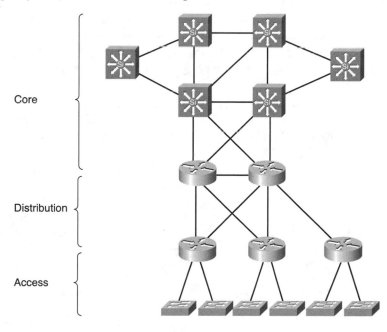

Enterprise Composite Network Model

The Cisco Enterprise Composite Network model facilitates the design of larger, more scalable networks. As networks become more sophisticated, it is necessary to use a more modular approach to design than just WAN and LAN core, distribution, and access layers. The model divides the network into functional components, functional areas containing network modules. It maintains the concept of distribution and access components connecting users, WAN services, and server farms through a high-speed campus backbone. The modular approach in design should be a guide to the network architect. In smaller networks, the layers can collapse into a single layer, even a single device, but the functions remain. The Enterprise Composite Network model divides the network into three major functional components:

- Enterprise Campus
- Enterprise Edge
- SP Edge

Figure 3-4 shows the Enterprise Composite Network model. The Enterprise Campus functional component consists of the campus infrastructure with server farms and network management. An edge-distribution module provides distribution from the campus infrastructure to the Enterprise Edge. The Enterprise Edge consists of the Internet, VPN, and WAN modules that connect the enterprise with the SP's facilities. The SP Edge provides Internet, PSTN, and WAN services.

Figure 3-4   *Enterprise Composite Network Model*

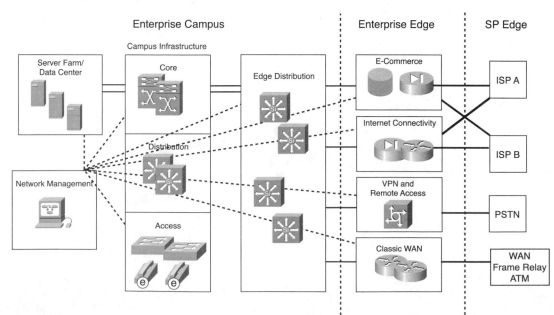

In brief, the enterprise infrastructure consists of core, distribution, and access layers. The network-management servers reside in the campus infrastructure but have tie-ins into all the components in the enterprise network for monitoring and management.

> **TIP** LAN environments also refer to the enterprise infrastructure as the campus backbone, building distribution, and building access layers. The functions are similar to those of the core, distribution, and access layers.

The Enterprise Edge connects to the edge-distribution module of the enterprise campus. In small and medium sites, the edge distribution can collapse into the campus-backbone component. It provides connectivity to outbound services that are further described in later sections. And the server-farms module provides high-availability network service for campus servers.

Enterprise Campus Modules

The Enterprise Campus consists of the following modules:

- Enterprise infrastructure
- Edge distribution
- Server farms
- Network management

Figure 3-5 shows the enterprise-campus model. The campus infrastructure consists of the core, building distribution, and access layers. The server farm or data center provides high-speed access and high availability (redundancy) to the servers. The CM is located in the server farm for IP telephony networks.

An enterprise-campus infrastructure can apply to small, medium, and large locations. In most instances, large campus locations have a three-tier design with a wiring-closet component (building-access layer), a building-distribution layer, and a campus-core layer. Small campus locations likely have a two-tier design with a wiring-closet component (Ethernet access layer) and a backbone core (collapsed core and distribution layers). It is also possible to configure distribution functions in a multilayer building-access device to maintain the focus of the campus backbone on fast transport. Medium-sized campus network designs sometimes use a three-tier implementation or a two-tier implementation, depending on the number of ports, service requirements, manageability, performance, and availability required.

Figure 3-6 shows an example of a campus-wide design. Workgroup switches in the building-access layer provide access to the network. Ports are assigned a VLAN for access. Trunking protocols connect building access, building distribution, and campus backbone switches. Multilayer switches and servers use FastEtherchannel or Gigabit Ethernet media. Chapter 4, "LAN Design," covers LAN designs in more detail.

Figure 3-5 *Enterprise Campus Model*

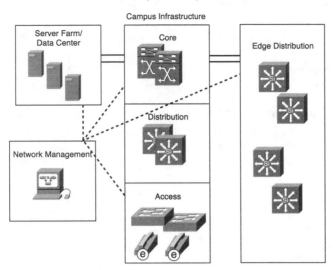

Figure 3-6 *Campus-Wide Design*

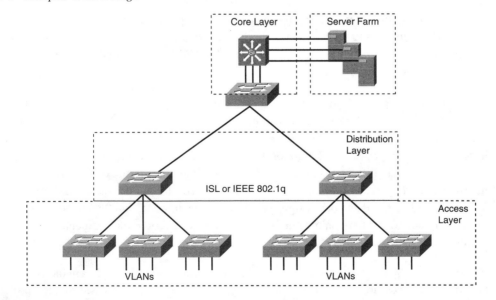

Enterprise Edge Modules

The Enterprise Edge consists of the following modules:

- E-commerce networks and servers
- Internet connectivity
- VPN and remote access
- Classic WAN

E-Commerce Module

The e-commerce module provides highly available networks for business services. It uses the high-availability designs of the server-farm module with the Internet connectivity of the Internet module. Design techniques are the same as those described for these modules.

Internet Module

Several models connect the enterprise to the Internet. The simplest form is to have a single circuit between the enterprise and the SP, as shown in Figure 3-7. The drawback is that you have no redundancy or failover if the circuit fails.

Figure 3-7 *Simple Internet Connection*

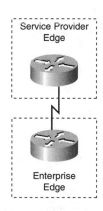

You can use multihoming solutions to provide redundancy or failover for Internet service. Figure 3-8 shows several Internet multihoming options. The four options follow:

- Option 1: Single router, dual links to one Internet service provider (ISP)
- Option 2: Single router, dual links to two ISPs
- Option 3: Dual routers, dual links to one ISP
- Option 4: Dual router, dual links to two ISPs

Option 1 provides link redundancy but does not provide ISP and local router redundancy. Option 2 provides link and ISP redundancy but does not provide redundancy for a local router failure. Option 3 provides link and local router redundancy but does not provide for an ISP failure. Option 4 provides for full redundancy of the local router, links, and the ISPs.

Figure 3-8 *Internet Multihoming Options*

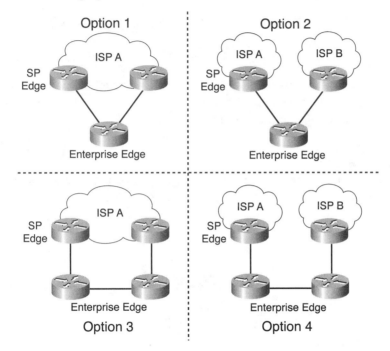

VPN/Remote Access Module

The VPN/remote access module provides remote-access termination services, including authentication for remote users and sites. If you use a remote-access terminal server, this module connects to the PSTN network. Today's networks often prefer VPNs over remote-access terminal servers and dedicated WAN links. VPNs reduce communication expenses by leveraging the infrastructure of SPs. For critical applications, the cost savings might be offset by a reduction of enterprise control and the loss of deterministic service. Remote offices, mobile users, and home offices access the Internet using the local SP with secured IP Security (IPSec) tunnels to the VPN/remote access module via the Internet module.

Figure 3-9 shows an example of a VPN design. Branch offices obtain local Internet access from an ISP. Home users also obtain local Internet access. VPN software creates secured VPN tunnels to the VPN server that is located in the VPN module of the Enterprise Edge.

Figure 3-9 *VPN Architecture*

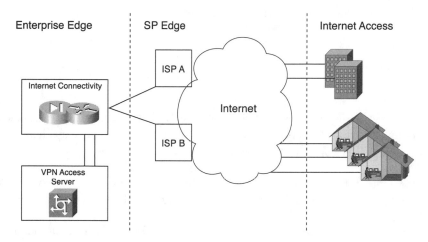

WAN Module

The Enterprise Edge includes access to WANs. WAN technologies include the following:

- Wireless
- PSTN
- Leased lines
- Synchronous Optical Network (SONET) and Synchronous Digital Hierarchy (SDH)
- PPP
- Frame Relay
- ATM
- Cable
- Digital subscriber line (DSL)

Chapters 5 through 8 cover these WAN technologies. Figure 3-10 shows an example of the WAN module connecting with the Frame Relay SP Edge. The Enterprise Edge routers in the WAN module connect to the Frame Relay switches of the SP.

Figure 3-10 *WAN Module*

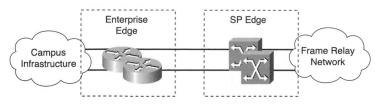

Service Provider (SP) Edge

The SP Edge consists of edge services such as the following:

- Internet services
- PSTN services
- WAN services

Enterprises use SPs to acquire network services. ISPs offer enterprises access to the Internet. ISP have the ability to route the enterprise's networks to their network and to upstream and peer Internet providers. Some SPs can provide Internet services with DSL access.

For voice services, PSTN providers offer access to the global public voice network. WAN SPs offer Frame Relay, ATM, and other WAN services for Enterprise site-to-site connectivity.

The SP Edge is not a test topic. For the test, focus on the Enterprise Campus and Enterprise Edge modules of the Enterprise Composite Network model.

Network Availability

This section covers designs for high-availability network services in the access layer.

When designing a network topology for a customer who has critical systems, services, or network paths, you should determine the likelihood that these components will fail and design redundancy where necessary. Consider incorporating one of the following types of redundancy into your design:

- Workstation-to-router redundancy in the building-access layer
- Server redundancy in the server farm module
- Route redundancy within and between network components
- Media redundancy in the access layer

The sections that follow discuss each type of redundancy.

Workstation-to-Router Redundancy

When a workstation has traffic to send to a station that is not local, the workstation has many possible ways to discover the address of a router on its network segment, including the following:

- ARP
- Explicit configuration
- Router Discovery Protocol (RDP)
- RIP
- HSRP

The sections that follow cover each of these methods.

ARP

Some IP workstations send an ARP frame to find a remote station. A router running proxy ARP can respond with its data link layer address. Cisco routers run proxy ARP by default.

Explicit Configuration

Most IP workstations must be configured with the IP address of a default router, which is sometimes called the default gateway.

In an IP environment, the most common method for a workstation to find a server is via explicit configuration (a default router). If the workstation's default router becomes unavailable, you must reconfigure the workstation with the address of a different router. Some IP stacks enable you to configure multiple default routers, but many other IP implementations only support one default router. HSRP provides a solution for hosts with only one default router.

RDP

RFC 1256 specifies an extension to the Internet Control Message Protocol (ICMP) that allows an IP workstation and router to run RDP to let the workstation learn the address of a router.

RIP

An IP workstation can run RIP to learn about routers. You should use RIP in passive mode rather than active mode. (Active mode means that the station sends RIP frames every 30 seconds.) Usually in these implementations, the workstation is a UNIX system running the **routed** UNIX process.

HSRP

The Cisco HSRP provides a way for IP workstations to keep communicating on the internetwork even if their default router becomes unavailable. HSRP works by creating a phantom router that has its own IP and MAC addresses. The workstations use this phantom router as their default router.

HSRP routers on a LAN communicate among themselves to designate two routers as *active* and *standby*. The active router sends periodic hello messages. The other HSRP routers listen for the hello messages. If the active router fails and the other HSRP routers stop receiving hello messages, the standby router takes over and becomes the active router. Because the new active router assumes both the IP and MAC addresses of the phantom, end nodes see no change at all. They continue to send packets to the phantom router's MAC address, and the new active router delivers those packets.

HSRP also works for proxy ARP. When an active HSRP router receives an ARP request for a node that is not on the local LAN, the router replies with the phantom router's MAC address instead of its own. If the router that originally sent the ARP reply later loses its connection, the new active router can still deliver the traffic.

Figure 3-11 shows a sample implementation of HSRP.

Figure 3-11 *Example of HSRP: The Phantom Router Represents the Real Routers*

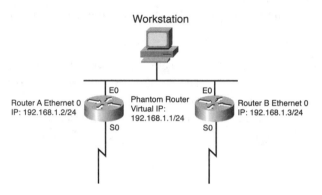

In Figure 3-11, the following sequence occurs:

1. The workstation is configured to use the phantom router (192.168.1.1) as its default router.

2. Upon booting, the routers elect Router A as the HSRP active router. The active router does the work for the HSRP phantom. Router B is the HSRP standby router.

3. When the workstation sends an ARP frame to find its default router, Router A responds with the phantom router's MAC address.

4. If Router A goes offline, Router B takes over as the active router, continuing the delivery of the workstation's packets. The change is transparent to the workstation.

Server Redundancy

Some environments need fully redundant (mirrored) file and application servers. For example, in a brokerage firm where traders must access data to buy and sell stocks, two or more redundant servers can replicate the data. Also, you can deploy CM servers in clusters for redundancy. The servers should be on different networks and power supplies.

Route Redundancy

Designing redundant routes has two purposes: balancing loads and increasing availability.

Load Balancing

Most IP routing protocols can balance loads across parallel links that have equal cost. Use the **maximum-paths** command to change the number of links that the router will balance over for IP; the default is four, and the maximum is six. To support load balancing, keep the bandwidth consistent within a layer of the hierarchical model so that all paths have the same cost. (The Cisco Interior Gateway Routing Protocol (IGRP) and Enhanced IGRP (EIGRP) are exceptions because they can load balance traffic across multiple routes that have different metrics by using a feature called *variance*.)

A hop-based routing protocol does load balancing over unequal bandwidth paths as long as the hop count is equal. After the slower link becomes saturated, packet loss at the saturated link prevents full utilization of the higher capacity links; this scenario is called pinhole congestion. You can avoid *pinhole congestion* by designing and provisioning equal bandwidth links within one layer of the hierarchy or by using a routing protocol that takes bandwidth into account.

IP load balancing in a Cisco router depends on which switching mode the router uses. Process switching load balances on a packet-by-packet basis. Fast, autonomous, silicon, optimum, distributed, and NetFlow switching load balance on a destination-by-destination basis because the processor caches information used to encapsulate the packets based on the destination for these types of switching modes.

Increasing Availability

In addition to facilitating load balancing, redundant routes increase network availability.

You should keep bandwidth consistent within a given design component to facilitate load balancing. Another reason to keep bandwidth consistent within a layer of a hierarchy is that routing protocols converge much faster on multiple equal-cost paths to a destination network.

By using redundant, meshed network designs, you can minimize the effect of link failures. Depending on the convergence time of the routing protocols, a single link failure will not have a catastrophic effect.

You can design redundant network links to provide a full mesh or a well-connected partial mesh. In a full-mesh network, every router has a link to every other router, as shown in Figure 3-12. A full-mesh network provides complete redundancy and also provides good performance because there is just a single-hop delay between any two sites. The number of links in a full mesh is $n(n–1)/2$, where n is the number of routers. Each router is connected to every other router. A well-connected partial-mesh network provides every router with links to at least two other routing devices in the network.

Figure 3-12 *Full-Mesh Network: Every Router Has a Link to Every Other Router in the Network*

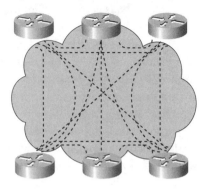

A full-mesh network can be expensive to implement in WANs due to the required number of links. In addition, groups of routers that broadcast routing updates or service advertisements have practical limits to scaling. As the number of routing peers increases, the amount of bandwidth and CPU resources devoted to processing broadcasts increases.

A suggested guideline is to keep broadcast traffic at less than 20 percent of the bandwidth of each link; this amount limits the number of peer routers that can exchange routing tables or service advertisements. When planning redundancy, follow guidelines for simple, hierarchical design. Figure 3-13 illustrates a classic hierarchical and redundant enterprise design that uses a partial-mesh rather than a full-mesh topology. For LAN designs, links between the access and distribution layer can be Fast Ethernet, with links to the core at Gigabit Ethernet speeds.

Figure 3-13 *Partial Mesh Design with Redundancy*

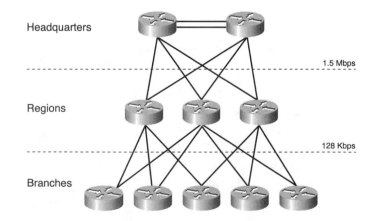

Media Redundancy

In mission-critical applications, it is often necessary to provide redundant media.

In switched networks, switches can have redundant links to each other. This redundancy is good because it minimizes downtime, but it can result in broadcasts continuously circling the network, which is called a *broadcast storm*. Because Cisco switches implement the IEEE 802.1d spanning-tree algorithm, you can avoid this looping in the Spanning Tree Protocol (STP). The spanning-tree algorithm guarantees that only one path is active between two network stations. The algorithm permits redundant paths that are automatically activated when the active path experiences problems.

Because WAN links are often critical pieces of the internetwork, WAN environments often deploy redundant media. As shown in Figure 3-14, you can provision backup links so they become active when a primary link goes down or becomes congested.

Figure 3-14   *Backup Links Can Provide Redundancy*

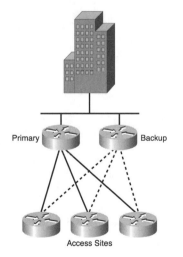

Often, backup links use a different technology. For example, a leased line can be in parallel with a backup dialup line or ISDN circuit. By using *floating static routes*, you can specify that the backup route have a higher administrative distance (used by Cisco routers to select routing information) so that it is not normally used unless the primary route goes down. This design is less available than the partial mesh presented previously. Typically, on-demand backup links reduce WAN charges.

> **NOTE**   When provisioning backup links, learn as much as possible about the physical circuit routing. Different carriers sometimes use the same facilities, meaning that your backup path might be susceptible to the same failures as your primary path. You should do some investigative work to ensure that your backup really is acting as a backup.

You can combine backup links with load balancing and *channel aggregation*. Channel aggregation means that a router can bring up multiple channels (for example, ISDN B channels) as bandwidth requirements increase.

Cisco supports the Multilink Point-to-Point Protocol (MPPP), which is an Internet Engineering Task Force (IETF) standard for ISDN B channel (or asynchronous serial interface) aggregation. MPPP does not specify how a router should accomplish the decision-making process to bring up extra channels. Instead, it seeks to ensure that packets arrive in sequence at the receiving router. Then, the data is encapsulated within PPP and the datagram is given a sequence number. At the receiving router, PPP uses this sequence number to re-create the original data stream. Multiple channels appear as one logical link to upper-layer protocols.

Foundation Summary

The "Foundation Summary" section of each chapter lists the most important facts from the chapter. Although this section does not list every fact from the chapter that will be on your CCDA exam, a well-prepared CCDA candidate should at a minimum know all the details in each "Foundation Summary" before going to take the exam.

The CCDA exam requires that you understand the three layers of a hierarchical network design:

- The core layer and campus-backbone component provide fast transport within sites.
- The distribution layer and building-distribution component provide policy-based connectivity.
- The access layer and building-access component provide workgroup and user access to the network.

The Enterprise Composite Network model divides the network into three major functional components:

- Enterprise Campus (campus infrastructure, edge distribution, server farm, network management)

    The campus infrastructure includes the building-access and building-distribution components and the shared campus-backbone component or campus core. The edge distribution provides connectivity to the Enterprise Edge. High availability is implemented in the server farm, and network management monitors all modules in the Enterprise Campus and Enterprise Edge.

- Enterprise Edge (e-commerce, Internet, VPN/remote access, WAN)

    The e-commerce module provides high availability for business servers and connects to the Internet module. The WAN module provides Frame Relay or other WAN technology. The VPN module provides secure site-to-site remote access over the Internet.

- SP Edge (Internet, PSTN, WAN)

    ISPs offer Internet access to the enterprise. PSTN providers provide voice services. WAN providers in the SP Edge provide Frame Relay and other WAN services by.

Figure 3-15 shows an example of an Enterprise composite Network Model, as described here.

Figure 3-15 *Enterprise Composite Network Model*

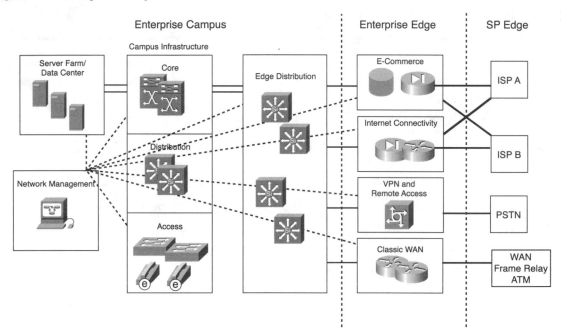

Network availability comes from design capacity, technologies, and device features that implement the following:

- Workstation-to-router redundancy in the building-access module
- Server redundancy in the server-farm module
- Route redundancy within and between network components
- Media redundancy in the access and distribution modules

Q&A

As mentioned in the introduction, you have two choices for review questions. The questions that follow give you a bigger challenge than the exam itself by using various question formats, including some that are in a short-answer format. By reviewing now with more difficult question formats, you can exercise your memory better and prove your conceptual and factual knowledge of this chapter. The answers to these questions appear in Appendix A.

For more practice with exam-like question formats, use the exam engine on the CD-ROM.

1. True or false? The core layer of the hierarchical model does security filtering and media translation.

2. True or false? The access layer provides high availability and port security.

3. You add a CM to the network as part of a Voice over IP (VoIP) solution. In which Enterprise Composite Network model module should you place the CM?

4. True or false? HSRP provides router redundancy.

5. What is the Enterprise Edge module that connects to an ISP?

6. True or false? In the Enterprise Composite Network model, the network-management module does not manage the SP Edge.

7. True or false? You can implement a full-mesh network to increase redundancy and reduce the costs of a WAN.

8. How many links are required for a full mesh of six sites?

9. List and describe four options for multihoming to the SP between the Enterprise Edge and the SP Edge. Which option provides the most redundancy?

10. To what Enterprise Edge module does the SP Edge Internet module connects.

11. What are four benefits of hierarchical network design?

12. In an IP telephony network, in which module or layer are the IP phones and CMs located?

13. Match the redundant model with its description.

i. Workstation-router redundancy

ii. Server redundancy

iii. Route redundancy

iv. Media redundancy

a. Cheap when implemented in the LAN but critical for the WAN

b. Provides load balancing

c. Host has multiple gateways

d. Data is replicated

14. True or false? Small to medium campus networks must always implement three layers of hierarchical design.

15. How many full-mesh links do you need for a network with 10 routers?

Figure 3-16 *Scenario*

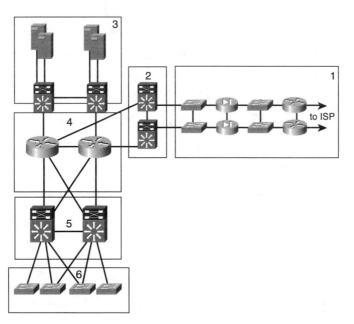

Use Figure 3-16 to answer the following questions:

16. From the diagram in Figure 3-16, which is the enterprise core layer?

17. From the diagram in Figure 3-16, which is the Enterprise Edge?

18. From the diagram in Figure 3-16, which is the enterprise access layer?

19. From the diagram in Figure 3-16, which is the Enterprise Edge distribution?

20. From the diagram in Figure 3-16, which is the enterprise infrastructure distribution layer?

21. From the diagram in Figure 3-16, which is the campus data center?

22. From the diagram in Figure 3-16, which block does not belong to the enterprise campus of the Enterprise Composite Network model?

PART II: LAN and WAN Design

This part covers the following CCDA exam objectives (to view the CCDA exam outline, visit http://www.cisco.com/go/training):

- Given a network design or a set of requirements, evaluate a solution to incorporate equipment and technology within a campus design.

- Given a network design or a set of requirements, evaluate a solution to incorporate equipment and technology within an Enterprise Edge design.

This chapter covers the following subjects:

- LAN Media

- LAN Hardware

- LAN Design Types and Models

CHAPTER 4

LAN Design

This chapter covers the design of local area networks (LANs). It reviews LAN media, components, and design models. The section "LAN Media" reviews the design characteristics of different Ethernet media technologies and wireless LANs.

This chapter covers how you apply hubs, Layer 2 and Layer 3 switches, and routers in the design of LANs. It reviews several design models for large building, campus, and remote LANs.

"Do I Know This Already?" Quiz

The purpose of the "Do I Know This Already?" quiz is to help you decide whether you need to read the entire chapter. If you already intend to read the entire chapter, you do not necessarily need to answer these questions now.

The eight-question quiz, derived from the major sections in the "Foundation Topics" portion of the chapter, helps you determine how to spend your limited study time.

Table 4-1 outlines the major topics discussed in this chapter and the "Do I Know This Already?" quiz questions that correspond to those topics.

Table 4-1 *"Do I Know This Already?" Foundation Topics Section-to-Question Mapping*

Foundation Topics Section	Questions Covered in This Section
LAN Media	2, 4
LAN Hardware	1, 3, 8
LAN Design Types and Models	5, 6, 7

> **CAUTION** The goal of self assessment is to gauge your mastery of the topics in this chapter. If you do not know the answer to a question or you are only partially sure of the answer, you should mark this question wrong for purposes of the self assessment. Giving yourself credit for an answer you correctly guess skews your self-assessment results and might provide you with a false sense of security.

1. What device filters broadcasts?

   a. Layer 2 switch

   b. Hub

   c. Layer 3 switch

   d. Router

   e. Answers a and c

   f. Answers c and d

   g. Answers a, c, and d

2. What is the maximum segment distance for Fast Ethernet over unshielded twisted-pair (UTP)?

   a. 100 feet

   b. 500 feet

   c. 100 meters

   d. 285 feet

3. What device limits the collision domain?

   a. Layer 2 switch

   b. Hub

   c. Layer 3 switch

   d. Router

   e. Answers a and c

   f. Answers c and d

   g. Answers a, c, and d

4. How are wireless LANs identified?

   a. IP network

   b. Service Set Identifier (SSID)

   c. Wired Equivalent Privacy (WEP) key

   d. Internet Group Management Protocol (IGMP)

5. What type of switches are preferred in the campus backbone of an enterprise network?

   a. L2 switches

   b. L3 switches

   c. L3 hubs

   d. hubs

6. What Cisco proprietary protocol can you use in LAN switches to control multicast traffic at the data link layer within a LAN switch?

   a. IGMP

   b. Cisco Group Management Protocol (CGMP)

   c. MAC filters

   d. Cisco Discovery Protocol (CDP)

7. Marking is also known as what?

   a. Classifying

   b. Pinging

   c. Coloring

   d. Tracing

8. Why is switching preferred on shared segments?

   a. Shared segments provide a collision domain for each host.

   b. Switched segments provide a collision domain for each host.

   c. Shared segments provide a broadcast domain for each host.

   d. Switched segments provide a broadcast domain for each host.

The answers to the "Do I Know This Already?" quiz appear in Appendix A, "Answers to Chapter 'Do I Know This Already?' Quizzes and Q&A Sections." The suggested choices for your next step are as follows:

■ **6 or less overall score**—Read the entire chapter. It includes the "Foundation Topics," "Foundation Summary," and "Q&A" sections.

■ **7-8 overall score**—If you want more review on these topics, skip to the "Foundation Summary" section and then go to the "Q&A" section. Otherwise, move to the next chapter.

Foundation Topics

This chapter covers the design of LANs. It reviews LAN media, components, and design models. Figure 4-1 shows the Enterprise Campus section of the Enterprise Composite Network model. Enterprise LANs have a campus backbone and one or more instances of the building-distribution and building-access layers with server farms and an Enterprise Edge to the WAN or Internet.

Figure 4-1 *Enterprise Campus*

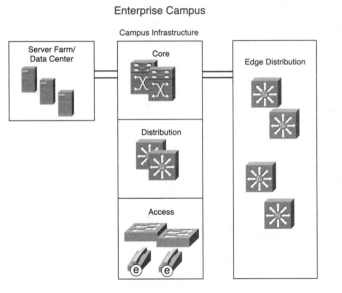

LAN Media

This section identifies some of the constraints that you should consider when provisioning various LAN media types. It covers the physical specifications of Ethernet, Fast Ethernet, and Gigabit Ethernet. It also covers the specifications for Token Ring and Fiber Distributed Data Interface (FDDI).

You must also understand the design constraints of wireless LANs in the campus network. This section covers the specifications for wireless LANs.

Ethernet Design Rules

Ethernet is the underlying basis for the technologies most widely used in LANs. In the 1980s and early 1990s, most networks used 10Mbps Ethernet, defined initially by Digital, Intel, and Xerox (DIX Ethernet Version II) and later by the IEEE 802.3 Working Group. The IEEE 802.3-2002 standard contains physical specifications for Ethernet technologies through 1000Mbps. Table 4-2 describes the specifications. The table also includes some physical (100BASE-T) specifications for Fast Ethernet. Table 4-2 provides scalability information that you can use when provisioning IEEE 802.3 networks.

Table 4-2   *Scalability Constraints for IEEE 802.3*

	10BASE5	**10BASE2**	**10BASE-T**	**100BASE-T**
Physical Topology	Bus	Bus	Star	Star
Maximum Segment Length (Meters)	500	185	100 from hub to station	100 from hub to station
Maximum Number of Attachments per Segment	100	30	2 (hub and station or hub-hub)	2 (hub and station or hub-hub)
Maximum Collision Domain	2500 meters (m) of five segments and four repeaters; only three segments can be populated	2500 m of five segments and four repeaters; only three segments can be populated	2500 m of five segments and four repeaters; only three segments can be populated	See the details in the section "100Mbps Fast Ethernet Design Rules" later in this chapter.

The most significant design rule for Ethernet is that the round-trip propagation delay in one collision domain must not exceed 512 bit times, which is a requirement for collision detection to work correctly. This rule means that the maximum round-trip delay for a 10-Mbps Ethernet network is 51.2 microseconds. The maximum round-trip delay for a 100-Mbps Ethernet network is only 5.12 microseconds because the bit time on a 100-Mbps Ethernet network is 0.01 microseconds as opposed to 0.1 microseconds on a 10-Mbps Ethernet network.

10-Mbps Fiber Ethernet Design Rules

Table 4-3 provides some guidelines for fiber-based 10-Mbps Ethernet media for network designs. The 10BASE-FP standard uses a passive-star topology. The 10BASE-FB standard is for a backbone or repeater-based system. The 10BASE-FL standard provides specifications on fiber links.

Table 4-3   *Scalability Constraints for 10-Mbps Fiber Ethernet (Continued)*

	10BASE-FP	**10BASE-FB**	**10BASE-FL**
Topology	Passive star	Backbone or repeater-fiber system	Link
Maximum Segment Length	500 m	2000 m	1000 or 2000 m
Allows Cascaded Repeaters?	No	Yes	No
Maximum Collision Domain	2500 m	2500 m	2500 m

100-Mbps Fast Ethernet Design Rules

The IEEE introduced the IEEE 802.3u-1995 standard to provide Ethernet speeds of 100Mbps over UTP and fiber cabling. The 100BASE-T standard is similar to 10Mbps Ethernet in that it uses carrier sense multiple access collision detect (CSMA/CD), runs on Category (CAT) 3, 4, and 5 UTP cable, and preserves the frame formats. Connectivity still uses hubs, repeaters, and bridges.

100Mbps Ethernet, or Fast Ethernet, topologies present some distinct constraints on the network design because of their speed. The combined latency due to cable lengths and repeaters must conform to the specifications for the network to work properly. This section discusses these issues and provides sample calculations.

The overriding design rule for 100Mbps Ethernet networks is that the round-trip collision delay must not exceed 512 bit times. However, the bit time on a 100Mbps Ethernet network is 0.01 microseconds, as opposed to 0.1 microseconds on a 10Mbps Ethernet network. Therefore, the maximum round-trip delay for a 100Mbps Ethernet network is 5.12 microseconds, as opposed to the more lenient 51.2 microseconds in a 10Mbps Ethernet network.

The following are specifications for Fast Ethernet, each of which is described in the following sections:

- 100BASE-TX
- 100BASE-T4
- 100BASE-FX

100BASE-TX Fast Ethernet

The 100BASE-TX specification uses CAT 5 UTP wiring. Like 10BASE-T, Fast Ethernet uses only two pairs of the four-pair UTP wiring. If CAT 5 cabling is already in place, upgrading to Fast

Ethernet requires only a hub or switch and network interface card (NIC) upgrades. Because of the low cost, most of today's installations use switches. The specifications are as follows:

- Transmission over CAT 5 UTP or CAT 1 shielded twisted-pair (STP) wire.
- RJ-45 connector (same as in 10BASE-T).
- Punchdown blocks in the wiring closet must be CAT 5 certified.
- 4B5B coding.

100BASE-T4 Fast Ethernet

The 100BASE-T4 specification was developed to support UTP wiring at the CAT 3 level. This specification takes advantage of higher-speed Ethernet without recabling to CAT 5 UTP. This implementation is not widely deployed. The specifications are as follows:

- Transmission over CAT 3, 4, or 5 UTP wiring.
- Three pairs are used for transmission, and the fourth pair is used for collision detection.
- No separate transmit and receive pairs are present, so full-duplex operation is not possible.
- 8B6T coding.

100BASE-FX

The 100BASE-FX specification for fiber is as follows:

- Operates over two strands of multimode or single-mode fiber cabling
- Can transmit over greater distances than copper media
- Uses media interface connector (MIC), Stab & Twist (ST), or Stab & Click (SC) fiber connectors defined for FDDI and 10BASE-FX networks
- 4B5B coding

100BASE-T Repeaters

To make 100-Mbps Ethernet work, distance limitations are much more severe than those required for 10Mbps Ethernet. For repeater networks, there is no five-hub rule; Fast Ethernet is limited to two repeaters. The general rule is that a 100Mbps Ethernet has a maximum diameter of 205 meters (m) with UTP cabling, whereas 10Mbps Ethernet has a maximum diameter of 500 m with 10BASE-T and 2500 m with 10BASE5. Most networks today use switches instead of repeaters, which limits the length of 10BASE-T and 100BASE-TX to 100 m between the switch and host.

The distance limitation imposed depends on the type of repeater.

The IEEE 100BASE-T specification defines two types of repeaters: Class I and Class II. Class I repeaters have a latency (delay) of 0.7 microseconds or less. Only one repeater hop is allowed. Class II repeaters have a latency of 0.46 microseconds or less. One or two repeater hops are allowed.

Table 4-4 shows the maximum size of collision domains, depending on the type of repeater.

Table 4-4   *Maximum Size of Collision Domains for 100BASE-T*

	Copper	Mixed Copper and Multimode Fiber	Multimode Fiber
DTE-DTE (or Switch- Switch)	100 m		412 m (2000 if full duplex)
One Class I Repeater	200 m	260 m	272 m
One Class II Repeater	200 m	308 m	320 m
Two Class II Repeaters	205 m	216 m	228 m

Again, for switched networks, the maximum distance between the switch and the host is 100 m.

Gigabit Ethernet Design Rules

Gigabit Ethernet was first specified by two standards: IEEE 802.3z-1998 and 802.3ab-1999. The IEEE 802.3z standard specifies the operation of Gigabit Ethernet over fiber and coaxial cable and introduces the Gigabit Media Independent Interface (GMII). These standards are superseded by the latest revision of all the 802.3 standards included in IEEE 802.3-2002.

The IEEE 802.3ab standard specified the operation of Gigabit Ethernet over CAT 5 UTP. Gigabit Ethernet still retains the frame formats and frame sizes, and it still uses CSMA/CD. As with Ethernet and Fast Ethernet, full duplex operation is possible. Differences appear in the encoding; Gigabit Ethernet uses 8B10B coding with simple nonreturn to zero (NRZ). Because of the 20 percent overhead, pulses run at 1250 MHz to achieve a 1000 Mbps throughput.

The following section covers the following specifications:

■   1000BASE-LX

■   1000BASE-SX

■   1000BASE-CX

■   1000BASE-T

1000BASE-LX Long Wavelength Gigabit Ethernet

The IEEE 1000BASE-LX uses long wavelength optics over a pair of fiber strands. The specifications are as follows:

- Uses long wave (1300 nanometer [nm])
- Use on multimode or single-mode fiber
- Maximum lengths for multimode fiber are
    — 62.5 micrometer fiber: 440 m
    — 50 micrometer fiber: 550 m
- Maximum length for 9 micron, single-mode fiber is 5 km
- Uses 8B10B encoding with simple NRZ

1000BASE-SX Short Wave Gigabit Ethernet

The IEEE 1000BASE-SX uses short-wavelength optics over a pair of multimode fiber strands. The specifications are as follows:

- Uses short wave (850 nm)
- Use on multimode fiber
- Maximum lengths:
    — 62.5 micrometer: 260 m
    — 50 micrometer: 550 m
- Uses 8B10B encoding with simple NRZ

1000BASE-CX Gigabit Ethernet over Coaxial Cable

The IEEE 1000BASE-CX standard is for short copper runs between servers. The specification is as follows:

- Used on short-run copper
- Runs over a pair of 150 ohm balanced coaxial cable (twinax)
- Maximum length is 25 m
- Mainly for server connections
- Uses 8B10B encoding with simple NRZ

1000BASE-T Gigabit Ethernet over UTP

The IEEE standard for 1000Mbps Ethernet over CAT 5 UTP was IEEE 802.3ab; it was approved in June 1999. It is now included in IEEE 802.3-2002. This standard uses the four pairs in the cable. (100BASE-TX and 10BASE-T Ethernet only use two pairs.) The specifications are as follows:

- CAT 5, four-pair UTP.
- Maximum length is 100 m.
- Encoding defined is a five-level coding scheme.
- 1 byte is sent over the four pairs at 1250 MHz.

Table 4-5 covers Gigabit Ethernet scalability constraints.

Table 4-5 *Gigabit Ethernet Scalability Constraints*

Type	Speed	Maximum Segment Length	Encoding	Media
1000BASE-T	1000 Mbps	100 m	Five-level	CAT 5 UTP
1000BASE-LX (long wave)	1000 Mbps	50 micrometers: 550 m	8B10B	Single/multiple mode fiber
1000BASE-SX (short wave)	1000 Mbps	62.5 micrometers: 260 m 50 micrometers: 500 m	8B10B	Multimode fiber
1000BASE-CX	1000 Mbps	25 m	8B10B	Shielded balanced copper

10 Gigabit Ethernet

IEEE 802.3ae, published in August 2002, specifies a standard for 10Gpbs Ethernet. It is defined only for full-duplex operation over optical media. It allows use of Ethernet frames over distances typically encountered in metropolitan-area networks (MANs) and WANs. Other uses include data centers, corporate backbones, and server farms. More information is available at the 10 Gigabit Alliance website, http://www.10gea.org, and through the IEEE. This is not currently a CCDA test topic.

Fast EtherChannel

The Cisco EtherChannel implementations provide a method to increase the bandwidth between two systems by bundling Fast Ethernet or Gigabit Ethernet links. When bundling Fast Ethernet links, use the term Fast EtherChannel. EtherChannel port bundles allow you to group multiple ports into a single logical transmission path between the switch and a router, host, or another switch. EtherChannels provide increased bandwidth, load sharing, and redundancy. If a link fails in the bundle, the other links take on the traffic load. You can configure EtherChannel bundles as trunk links.

Depending on your hardware, you can form an EtherChannel with up to eight compatibly configured ports on the switch. The participating ports must have the same speed and duplex mode and belong to the same VLAN.

Token Ring Design Rules

Token Ring was developed by IBM in the 1970s. In the 1980s, Token Ring and Ethernet competed as the preferred media for LANs. The IEEE developed the IEEE 802.5 specification based on the IBM Token Ring specifications. The 802.5 working group is now an inactive working group of the IEEE. The most recent specification is IEEE 802.5-1998. More information appears at http://www.8025.org.

Table 4-6 lists some media characteristics for designing Token Ring segments.

Table 4-6 *Scalability Constraints for Token Ring*

	IBM Token Ring	IEEE 802.5
Physical Topology	Star	Not specified
Maximum Segment Length	Depends on type of cable, number of media attachment units (MAUs), and so on	Depends on type of cable, number of MAUs, and so on
Maximum Number of Attachments per Segment	260 for STP, 72 for UTP	250
Maximum Network Diameter	Depends on type of cable, number of MAUs, and so on	Depends on type of cable, number of MAUs, and so on

FDDI Design Rules

FDDI is a 100-Mbps token-passing, dual-ring LAN media that uses fiber-optic cable. FDDI was a high-speed campus-backbone technology before Fast Ethernet and Gigabit Ethernet became available. FDDI uses a dual-counter rotating-ring architecture with a primary and secondary ring. In normal operation, the primary ring is active and the secondary ring is idle. If a failure occurs, the secondary ring provides redundancy.

FDDI media access does not appear in new enterprise networks because Fast and Gigabit Ethernet have replaced it as a preferred Layer 2 LAN and MAN technology. The FDDI specification does not actually specify the maximum segment length or network diameter. It specifies the amount of allowed power loss, which works out to the approximate distances shown in Table 4-7.

Table 4-7 *Scalability Constraints for FDDI*

	Multimode Fiber	Single-Mode Fiber	UTP
Topology	Dual ring, tree of concentrators, and others	Dual ring, tree of concentrators, and others	Star
Maximum Segment Length	2 km between stations	60 km between stations	100 m from hub to station
Maximum Number of Attachments per Segment	1000 (500 dual-attached stations)	1000 (500 dual-attached stations)	2 (hub and station or hub-hub)
Maximum Network Diameter	200 km	200 km	200 km

Wireless LANs

Wireless LANs (WLANs) provide the capability of accessing internetworking resources without having to be "wired" to the network. WLANs applications include inside-building access, LAN extension, outside building-to-building communications, public access, and small office/home office (SOHO) communications.

The first standard for wireless LANs is IEEE 802.11, approved by the IEEE in 1997. The current specification is IEEE 802.11-1999. IEEE 802.11 implemented wireless LANs at speeds of 1 Mbps and 2 Mbps using Direct Sequence Spread Spectrum (DSSS) and Frequency Hopping Spread Spectrum (FHSS) on the physical layer of the Open System Interconnection (OSI) model. DSSS divides data into separate sections; each section travels over different frequencies at the same time. FHSS uses a frequency-hopping sequence to send data in bursts. With FHSS, some data transmits at Frequency 1, and then the system hops to Frequency 2 to send more data, and so on, returning to transmit more data at Frequency 1.

Current implementations use the IEEE 802.11b standard. The IEEE 802.11b standard is referred as "high-rate." It provides speeds of 11, 5.5, 2, and 1 Mbps. An interoperability certification for IEEE 802.11b WLANs is Wireless Fidelity (Wi-Fi). The Wireless Ethernet Compatibility Alliance (WECA) governs the Wi-Fi certification. IEEE 802.11b uses DSSS and is backward compatible with 802.11 systems that use DSSS. The modulation techniques used by IEEE 802.11b follow:

- Complimentary Code Keying (CCK), at 5.5 and 11 Mbps
- Differential Quadrature Phase Shift Keying (DQPSK), at 2 Mbps
- Differential Binary Phase Shift Keying (DBPSK), at 1 Mbps

A description of each modulation technique is well beyond the level of this discussion.

Service Set Identifier (SSID)

WLANs use an SSID to identify the "network name" of the WLAN. The SSID can be 2 to 32 characters in length. All devices in the WLAN must have the same configured SSID to communicate.

WLAN Access Method

The IEEE 802.11 Mandatory Access Control (MAC) layer implements carrier sense multiple access collision avoidance (CSMA/CA) as an access method. With CSMA/CA, each WLAN station listens to see whether there is a station transmitting. If there is no activity, the station then transmits. If there is activity, the station uses a random countdown timer. When the timer expires, the station transmits.

WLAN Modes

WLAN architecture has three modes of operation. The first mode is the Basic Service Set (BSS). In BSS mode, all stations communicate with the access point (AP). The AP provides communication between clients and connects the WLAN network with the wired LAN. As shown in Figure 4-2, in BSS mode clients do not communicate directly with each other; all communication happens through the AP. BSS is also referred as Infrastructure mode.

Figure 4-2   *BSS (Infrastructure) Mode*

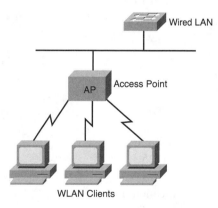

The second mode is the Independent Basic Service Set (IBSS). As shown in Figure 4-3, IBSS mode stations communicate directly with each other without using an AP. IBSS is also known as ad hoc mode.

Figure 4-3   *IBSS (Ad-Hoc) Mode*

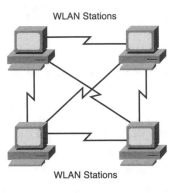

The third mode is the Extended Service Set (ESS). As shown in Figure 4-4, ESS is a set of BSS where APs have connectivity in the wired LAN, providing a distribution system for roaming capabilities.

Figure 4-4   *Wireless ESS Mode*

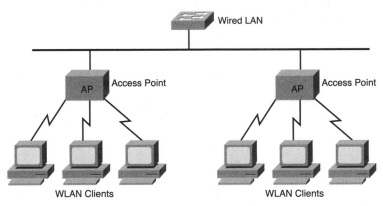

Frequencies Used by Wireless LANs

The IEEE 802.11b standard uses the 2.4 GHz band of the Industrial, Scientific, and Medical (ISM) frequencies. The Federal Communication Commission (FCC) authorizes ISM frequencies for unlicensed use in the United States. The three ISM frequency bands follow:

■   902 to 928 MHz

■   2.4000 to 2.5000 GHz

■   5.725 to 5.875 GHz

IEEE 802.11, 802.11b, and 802.11g standards all use the 2.4 ISM band for unlicensed frequency use.

The IEEE 802.11a standard uses the 5 GHz bands of the Unlicensed National Information Infra-structure (UNII) frequencies. These frequency bands were allocated in addition to the ISM bands for unlicensed used in the U.S. The three UNII bands are

- 5.15 to 5.25 GHz (lower band)
- 5.25 to 5.35 GHz (middle band)
- 5.75 to 5.85 GHz (upper band)

WLAN Security

WLANs provides an effective solution for the hard-to-reach locations and enable mobility to a level that was previously unattainable. WLANs without any encryption present a security risk because publicly available software can snoop the SSIDs. The productivity improvements with WLANs are just beginning, however. The WEP security protocol, used in the IEEE 802.11b standard, is considered faulty and vulnerable to numerous attacks. The 802.11b protocol is the most commonly deployed wireless protocol, and although it has the ability for 64-bit and 128-bit encryption, readily available software can crack the encryption scheme.

Unauthorized Access

A problem that confronts WLANs comes from the fact that wireless signals are not easily controlled or contained. WEP works at the data link layer, sharing the same key for all nodes that communicate. The 802.11 standard was deployed because it allowed bandwidth speed up to 11 Mbps and it is based on DSSS technology. DSSS also enables APs to identify WLAN cards via their MAC addresses. Because traditional physical boundaries do not apply to wireless networks, attackers can gain access using wireless from outside the physical security perimeter. Attackers achieve unauthorized access if the wireless network does not have a mechanism to compare a MAC address on a wireless card to a database that contains a directory with access rights. An individual can roam within an area, and each AP that comes in contact with that card must also rely on a directory. Statically allowing access via a MAC address is also insecure because MAC addresses can be spoofed. Securing the payload and ensuring proper authentication are the two focus areas for the Secure blueprint for Enterprise Networks(SAFE) WLAN design developed by Cisco.

Some APs can implement MAC address and protocol filtering to enhance security or limit the protocols used over the WLAN. Again, attackers can hack MAC address filtering. A user can listen for transmissions, gather a list of MAC addresses, and then use one of those MAC addresses to connect to the AP.

SAFE WLAN Design Approach

The SAFE WLAN design approach makes two assumptions, which this chapter presents. The assumptions are that all WLAN devices are connected to a unique IP subnet and that most services available to the wired network are also available to the wireless nodes. Using these two assumptions, the SAFE WLAN designs offer two basic security approaches:

- The use of the Lightweight Extensible Authentication Protocol (LEAP) to secure authentication
- The use of virtual private networks (VPNs) with IP Security (IPSec) to secure traffic from the WLAN to the wired network

Considering WLAN as an alternative access methodology, remember that the services these WLAN users access are often the same accessed by the wired users. WLAN opens a new world of access for the hacker, and you should consider the risks prior to deployment.

To enhance security, you can implement WLANs with IPSec VPN software, use the IEEE 802.1X-2001 port-based access control protocol, and use dynamic WEP keys.

IEEE 802.1X Port-Based Authentication

IEEE 802.1X-2001 is a port-based authentication standard for LANs. It authenticates a user before allowing services. You can use it on Ethernet, Fast Ethernet, and WLAN networks.

With IEEE 802.1X, client workstations run client software to request access to services. Clients use the Extensible Authentication Protocol (EAP) to communicate with the LAN switch. The LAN switch verifies client information with the authentication server and relays the response to the client. LAN switches use a Remote Authentication Dial-In User Service (RADIUS) client to communicate with the server. The RADIUS authentication server validates the identity of the client and authorizes the client. The server uses RADIUS with EAP extensions to make the authorization.

Dynamic WEP Keys and LEAP

Cisco also offers dynamic per-user, per-session WEP keys to provide additional security over statically configured WEP keys, which are not unique per user. For centralized user-based authentication, Cisco developed LEAP. LEAP uses mutual authentication between the client and the network server and uses IEEE 802.1X for 802.11 authentication messaging. LEAP uses a RADIUS server to manage user information.

LEAP is a combination of 802.1X and the EAP. It combines the capability to authenticate to various servers such as RADIUS and forces the WLAN user to log in to an access point that compares the login information to RADIUS.

Because the WLAN access depends on receiving an address, using Dynamic Host Configuration Protocol (DHCP), and the authentication of the user, using RADIUS, the WLAN needs constant access to these back-end servers. In addition, LEAP does not support one-time passwords (OTP), so you must use good password-security practices. The password issue and maintenance practice is a basic component of corporate security policy.

In the same way you place Domain Name System (DNS) servers accessible via the Internet on a demilitarized zone (DMZ) segment, you should apply a similar strategy to the RADIUS and DHCP servers accessible to the WLAN. These servers should be secondary servers that are on a different segment from their primary counterparts. Such placement ensures that any attacks launched on these servers are contained within that segment.

You should control access to the servers. Consider the WLAN an unsecured segment and apply appropriate segmentation and Layer 3 filtering. Such a step ensures that WLAN access is controlled and directed to only those areas that need it. For example, you do not want to permit WLAN access to management servers, voice networks, and HR servers.

You must also protect these servers against attack. The criticality of these servers makes them an ideal target for denial-of-service (DoS) attacks. Consider using host-based intrusion-detection systems (IDSs) to protect these devices.

Other IEEE WLAN Standards

The IEEE 802.11a standard provides an increase of throughput from IEEE 802.11b with speeds up to 54 Mbps. IEEE 802.11a uses the 5 GHz bands of the UNII frequencies, and for this reason, it is not backward-compatible with IEEE 802.11b WLANs.

IEEE 802.11g is an emerging standard that has been recently approved by the IEEE working group. It provides faster WLAN speeds in the ISM 2.4 GHz band, up to 54 Mbps. IEEE 802.11g is backward-compatible with 802.11b WLANs, albeit at the 802.11b slower data rate.

IEEE 802.11d provides specifications for WLANs in markets not served by the current 802.11, 802.11b, and 802.11a standards. It also provides enhancements to the security and authentication protocols for WLANs.

The emerging IEEE 802.15 standard provides specifications for Wireless Personal Area Networks (WPANs). The emerging IEEE 802.16 standard provides specifications for fixed broadband wireless access.

LAN Hardware

This section covers the hardware devices and how to apply them to LAN design. You place devices in the LAN depending on their roles and capabilities. LAN devices are categorized based on how they operate in the OSI model. This section covers the following devices:

- Repeaters
- Hubs
- Bridges
- Switches
- Routers
- Layer 3 switches

Repeaters

Repeaters are the basic unit in networks that connect separate segments. Repeaters take incoming frames, regenerate the preamble, amplify the signals, and send the frame out all other interfaces. Repeaters operate in the physical layer of the OSI model. Because repeaters are not aware of packets or frame formats, they do not control broadcasts or collision domains. Repeaters are said to be protocol transparent because they are not aware of upper-layer protocols such as IP, Internetwork Packet Exchange (IPX), and so on.

One basic rule of using Ethernet repeaters is the 5-4-3 Rule. The maximum path between two stations on the network should not be more than five segments with four repeaters between those segments and no more than three populated segments. Repeaters introduce a small amount of latency, or delay, when propagating the frames. A transmitting device must be able to detect a collision with another device within the specified time after the delay introduced by the cable segments and repeaters is factored in. The 512 bit-time specification also governs segment lengths. A more detailed explanation of the specification appears at http://www.cisco.com/univercd/cc/td/doc/cisintwk/ito_doc/ethernet.htm. Figure 4-5 illustrates an example of the 5-4-3 Rule.

Hubs

With the increasing density of LANs in the late 1980s and early 1990s, *hubs* were introduced to concentrate Thinnet and 10BASE-T networks in the wiring closet. Traditional hubs operate on the physical layer of the OSI model and perform the same functions as basic repeaters. The difference is that hubs have more ports than basic repeaters.

Figure 4-5 *Repeater 5-4-3 Rule*

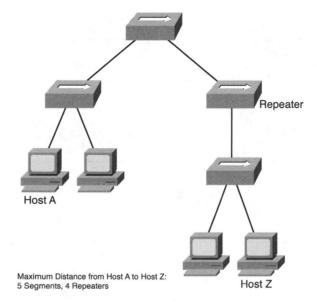

Repeater

Host A

Maximum Distance from Host A to Host Z:
5 Segments, 4 Repeaters

Host Z

Bridges

Bridges connect separate segments of a network. They differ from repeaters in that bridges are intelligent devices that operate in the data link layer of the OSI model. Bridges control the collision domains on the network. Bridges also learn the MAC layer addresses of each node on each segment and on which interface they are located. For any incoming frame, bridges forward the frame only if the destination MAC address is on another port or if the bridge is not aware of its location. The latter is called *flooding*. Bridges filter any incoming frames with destination MAC addresses that are on the same segment from where the frame arrives; they do not forward these frames.

Bridges are store-and-forward devices. They store the entire frame and verify the cyclic redundancy check (CRC) before forwarding. If the bridges detect a CRC error, they discard the frame. Bridges are protocol transparent; they are not aware of the upper-layer protocols such as IP, IPX, and AppleTalk. Bridges are designed to flood all unknown and broadcast traffic.

Bridges implement the *STP* to build a loop-free network topology. Bridges communicate with each other, exchanging information such as priority and bridge interface MAC addresses. They select a root bridge and then implement the STP. Some interfaces are in a blocking state, whereas other bridges have interfaces in forwarding mode. Figure 4-6 shows a network with bridges. With STP, there is no load sharing or dual paths as there is in routing. STP provides recovery of bridge failure by changing blocked interfaces to a forwarding state if a primary link fails. Although DEC and IBM versions are available, the IEEE 802.1d standard is the STP most commonly used.

Figure 4-6 *Spanning Tree Protocol*

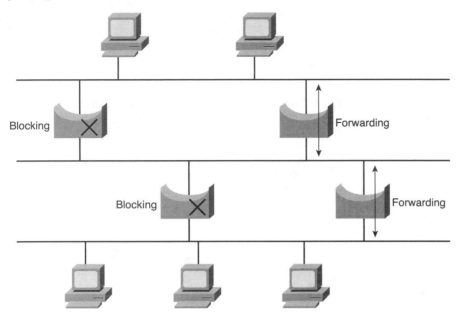

The spanning-tree topology elects a *root bridge* as the root. It places all ports that are not needed to reach the root bridge in blocking mode. The selection of the root bridge is based on the lowest numerical bridge priority. The bridge priority ranges from 0 to 65,535. If all bridges have the same bridge priority, then the bridge with the lowest MAC address becomes the root. The concatenation of the bridge priority and the MAC address is the bridge identification (BID). Physical changes to the network force spanning-tree recalculation.

Switches

Switches use specialized integrated circuits to reduce the latency common to regular bridges. Switches are the evolution of bridges. Some switches have a capability to run in cut-through mode, where the switch does not wait for the entire frame to enter its buffer; instead, it begins to forward the frame as soon as it finishes reading the destination MAC address. Cut-through operation increases the probability that frames with errors are propagated on the network because it forwards the frame before the entire frame is buffered and checked for errors. Because of these problems, most switches today perform store-and-forward operation as bridges do. As shown in Figure 4-7, switches are exactly the same as bridges with respect to collision-domain and broadcast-domain characteristics. Each port on a switch is a separate collision domain. By default, all ports in a switch are in the same broadcast domain. Assignment to different VLANs changes that behavior.

Figure 4-7 *Switches Control Collision Domains*

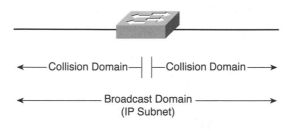

Switches have characteristics similar to bridges; however, they have more ports and they run faster. Switches keep a table of MAC addresses per port, and they implement STP. Switches are data link layer devices. They are transparent to protocols operating at the network layer and above. Each port on a switch is a separate collision domain but part of the same broadcast domain. Switches do not control broadcasts on the network.

The use of LAN switches instead of bridges or hubs is nearly universal. Switches are preferred over shared technology because they provide full bandwidth in each direction when configured in duplex mode. All the devices on a hub share the bandwidth in a single collision domain. Switches can also use VLANs to provide more segmentation. The LAN Design Types and Models section in this chapter discusses VLANs.

Routers

Routers make forwarding decisions based on network layer addresses. In addition to controlling collision domains, routers bound data link layer broadcast domains. Each interface of a router is a separate broadcast domain. Routers do not forward data link layer broadcasts. IP defines network layer broadcast domains with a subnet and mask. Routers are aware of the network protocol, which means they are capable of forwarding packets of routed protocols such as IP, IPX, and AppleTalk. Figure 4-8 shows a router; each interface is a broadcast and a collision domain.

Figure 4-8 *Routers Control Broadcast and Collision Domains*

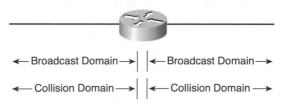

Routers exchange information about destination networks using one of several routing protocols. Routers use routing protocols to build a list of destination networks and to identify the best routes to reach those destinations. The following are routing protocols. The lists are organized by the protocols that can be routed.

For routing TCP/IP, use the following:

■ Enhanced Interior Gateway Routing Protocol (EIGRP)

■ Open Shortest Path First (OSPF)

■ Routing Information Protocol (RIP)

■ Intermediate System-to-Intermediate System (IS-IS)

■ Protocol Independent Multicast (PIM)

For routing Novell, use the following:

■ Novell Routing Information Protocol (Novell RIP)

■ NetWare Link Services Protocol (NLSP)

■ EIGRP

Chapter 11, "Routing Protocol Selection Criteria," discusses routing protocols in further detail.

Routers provide the translation of data link protocols. They are the preferred method of forwarding packets between networks of differing media, such as Ethernet to Token Ring, Ethernet to FDDI, or Ethernet to serial. They also provide methods to filter traffic based on the network layer address, route redundancy, load balancing, hierarchical addressing, and multicast routing.

Layer 3 Switches

LAN switches that are capable of running routing protocols are *Layer 3 switches*. These switches are capable of running routing protocols and communicating with neighboring routers. Layer 3 switches have LAN technology interfaces that perform network layer packet forwarding. Routers must still provide connectivity to WAN circuits. The use of switching technologies at the network layer greatly accelerates packet forwarding between connected LANs, including VLANs. You can use the router capacity you save to implement other features, such as security filtering and intrusion detection.

Layer 3 switches perform the functions of both data link layer switches and network layer routers. Each port is a collision domain. You can group ports into network layer broadcast domains (subnets). As with routers, a routing protocol provides network information to other network layer devices (subnets), and a routing protocol provides network information to other Layer 3 switches and routers.

LAN Design Types and Models

LANs can be classified as large-building LANs, campus LANs, or small and remote LANs. The large-building LAN typically contains a major data center with high-speed access and floor communications closets; the large-building LAN is usually the headquarters in larger companies. Campus LANs provide connectivity between buildings on a campus. Redundancy is usually a requirement in large-building and campus LAN deployments. Small and remote LANs provide connectivity to remote offices with a relatively small number of nodes.

It is important to remember the Cisco Enterprise Composite Network model in network design. First, build a high-speed campus-backbone network to serve the campus or large buildings. Second, build the building-distribution layers, where you can apply policy. Finally, build the building-access layers, where LANs provide access to the network end stations.

Large-Building LANs

Large-building LANs are segmented by floors or departments. The building-access component serves one or more departments or floors. The building-distribution component serves one or more building-access components. Campus and building backbone devices connect the data center, building-distribution components, and the enterprise edge-distribution component. The access layer typically uses Layer 2 switches to contain costs, with more expensive Layer 3 switches in the distribution layer to provide policy enforcement. Current best practice is to also deploy Layer 3 switches in the campus and building backbone. Figure 4-9 depicts a typical large-building design.

Each floor can have more than 200 users. Following a hierarchical model of building access, building distribution, and core, Fast Ethernet nodes can connect to the Layer 2 switches in the communications closet. Fast Ethernet or Gigabit Ethernet uplink ports from closet switches connect back to one or two (for redundancy) distribution switches. Distribution switches can provide connectivity to server farms that provide business applications, DHCP, DNS, intranet, and other services.

> **TIP**   Remember that the access layer should use low-end Layer 2 switches and that the distribution layer should use Layer 2 or Layer 3 switches.

Enterprise Campus LANs

A campus LAN connects two or more buildings within a local geographic area using a high-bandwidth LAN media backbone. Usually the enterprise owns the media (copper or fiber). High-speed switching devices minimize latency. In today's networks, Gigabit Ethernet campus backbones are the standard for new installations. In Figure 4-10, Layer 3 switches with Gigabit Ethernet media connect campus buildings.

Figure 4-9 *Large-Building LAN Design*

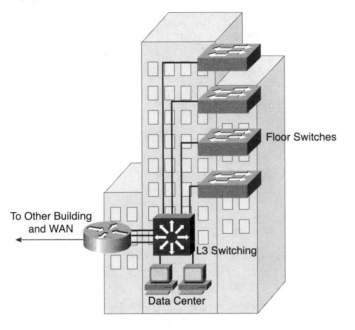

Figure 4-10 *Campus LANs*

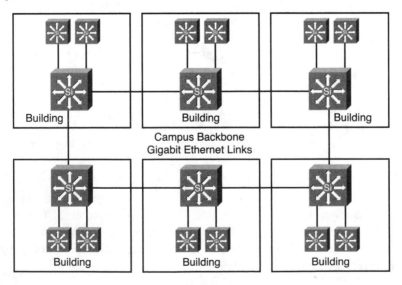

Ensure that you implement a hierarchical composite design on the campus LAN and that you assign network layer addressing to control broadcasts on the networks. Each building should have addressing assigned in such a way as to maximize address summarization. Apply contiguous subnets to buildings at the bit boundary to apply summarization and ease the design. Campus networks can support high-bandwidth applications such as video conferencing. Remember to use Layer 3 switches with high-switching capabilities in the campus-backbone design. In smaller installations, it might be desirable to collapse the building-distribution component into the campus backbone. An increasingly viable alternative is to provide building access and distribution on a single device selected from among the smaller Layer 3 switches now available.

Small and Remote Site LANs

Small and remote sites usually connect to the corporate network via a small router. The LAN service is provided by a small LAN switch. The router filters broadcast to the WAN circuit and forward packets that require services from the corporate network. You can place a server at the small or remote site to provide DHCP and other local applications such as an NT backup domain controller and DNS; if not, you must configure the router to forward DHCP broadcasts and other types of services. As the site grows, you will need the structure provided by the Enterprise Composite Network model. Figure 4-11 shows a typical architecture of a small or remote LAN.

Figure 4-11 *Remote Office LAN*

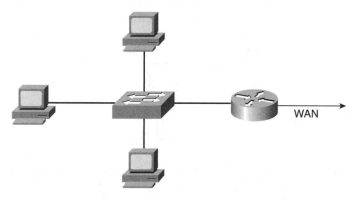

Server-Farm Module

The server-farm or data-center module provides high-speed access to servers for the campus networks. You can attach servers to switches via Fast Ethernet or Gigabit Ethernet. Some campus deployments might need EtherChannel technology to meet traffic requirements. Figure 4-12 shows an example of a server-farm module. Servers are connected via Fast Ethernet or Fast EtherChannel.

The server-farm switches connect via redundant uplink ports to the core switches. The largest deployments might find it useful to hierarchically construct service to the data center using access and distribution network devices.

Figure 4-12 *Server Farm*

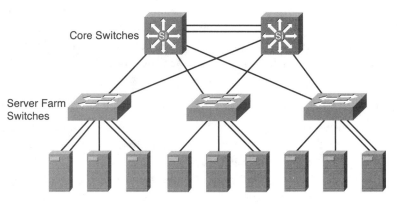

You can use the Server Load Balancing (SLB) feature to provide additional server redundancy. SLB is a Cisco IOS Software feature that provides IP-based server-load balancing. With SLB, a virtual server represents a group of real servers. Clients connect to the virtual IP address, and the SLB load-balancing algorithm selects a real server for the connection. Figure 4-13 shows a diagram of the SLB environment. Client A makes a connection to the virtual IP address, and the SLB algorithm selects Server 1. For Client B, Server 2 is selected. For Client C, Server 3 is selected. The SLB can then select Servers 2 and 1 for Clients D and E.

Quality of Service Considerations

For the access layer of the campus LAN, you can classify and mark frames or packets to apply quality of service (QoS) policies in the distribution or at the Enterprise Edge. Classification is a fundamental building block of QoS and involves recognizing and distinguishing between different traffic steams. For example, you distinguish between web, FTP, and VoIP traffic. Without classification, all traffic would be treated the same.

Marking sets certain bits in a packet or frame that has been classified. Marking is also referred as coloring or tagging. Layer 2 has two methods to mark frames for CoS:

- Inter-Switch Link (ISL)
- IEEE 802.1p/802.1Q

Figure 4-13 *Server Load Balancing*

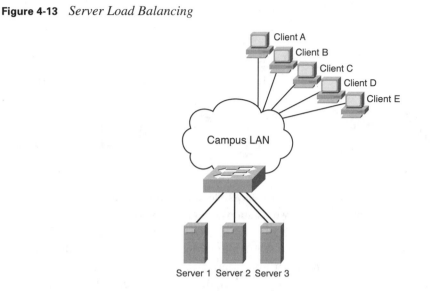

The IEEE 802.1D-1998 standard describes IEEE 802.1p traffic class expediting.

Both methods provide three bits for marking frames. The Cisco ISL is a proprietary trunk-encapsulation method for carrying VLANs over Fast Ethernet or Gigabit Ethernet interfaces. ISL appends tags to each frame to identify the VLAN it belongs to. As shown in Figure 4-14, the tag is a 30-byte header and CRC trailer that are added around the Fast Ethernet frame. This includes a 26-byte header and 4-byte CRC. The header includes a 15-bit VLAN ID that identifies each VLAN. The user field in the header also includes three bits for CoS.

Figure 4-14 *ISL Frame*

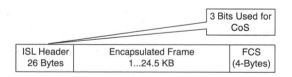

The IEEE 802.1Q standard trunks VLANs over Fast Ethernet and Gigabit Ethernet interfaces, and you can use it in a multivendor environment. IEEE 802.1q uses one instance of STP for each VLAN allowed in the trunk. Like ISL, IEEE 802.1Q uses a tag on each frame with a VLAN identifier. Figure 4-15 shows the IEEE 802.1Q frame. Unlike ISL, 802.1Q uses an internal tag. IEEE 802.1Q also provides support for the IEEE 802.1p priority standard, which is included in the 802.1D-1998 specification. A 3-bit priority field is included in the 802.1Q frame for CoS.

Figure 4-15 *IEEE 802.1Q Frame*

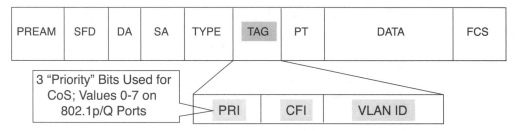

The preferred location to mark traffic is as close as possible to the source. Figure 4-16 shows a segment of a network with IP phones. Most workstations send packets with CoS or IP precedence bits (ToS) set to 0. If the workstation supports IEEE 802.1Q/p, it can mark packets. The IP phone can reclassify traffic from the workstation to 0. VoIP traffic from the phone is sent with a Layer 2 CoS set to 5 or Layer 3 ToS set to 5. The phone also reclassifies data from the PC to a CoS/ToS of 0. With Differentiated Service Code Point (DSCP), VoIP traffic is set to Expedited Forwarding (EF), binary value 101110 (hexadecimal 2E).

As shown in Figure 4-16, switches capabilities vary in the access layer. If the switches in this layer are capable, configure them to accept the markings or remap them. The advanced switches in the distribution layer can mark traffic, accept the CoS/ToS markings, or remap the CoS/ToS values to different markings.

Figure 4-16 *Marking of Frames or Packets*

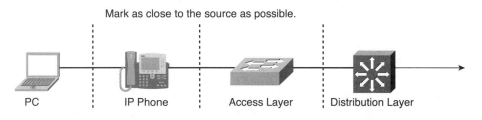

Multicast Traffic Considerations

The protocol between end workstations and the local Layer 3 switch is the IGMP. IGMP is the protocol used in multicast implementations between the end hosts and the local router. RFC 2236 describes IGMP version 2 (IGMPv2). RFC 1112 describes the first version of IGMP. IP hosts use IGMP to report their multicast group memberships to routers. IGMP messages use IP protocol number 2. IGMP messages are limited to the local interface and are not routed.

When campus LANs use multicast media, end hosts that do not participate in multicast groups might get flooded with unwanted traffic. Two solutions are

- CGMP
- IGMP snooping

CGMP

CGMP is a Cisco proprietary protocol implemented to control multicast traffic at Layer 2. Because a Layer 2 switch is not aware of Layer 3 IGMP messages, it cannot restrain multicast packets from being sent to all ports.

As shown in Figure 4-17, with CGMP, the LAN switch can speak with the IGMP router to find out the MAC addresses of the hosts that want to receive the multicast packets. You must also enable the router to speak CGMP with the LAN switches. With CGMP, switches distribute multicast sessions to the switch ports that have group members.

Figure 4-17   *CGMP*

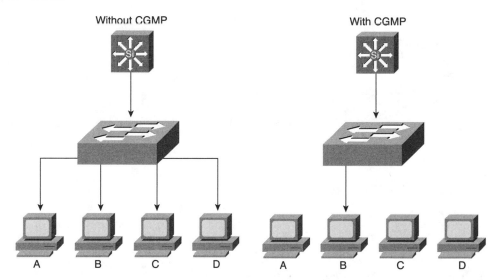

When a CGMP-enabled router receives an IGMP report, it processes the report and then sends a CGMP message to the switch. The switch can then forward the multicast messages to the port with the host receiving multicast traffic. CGMP Fast-Leave processing allows the switch to detect IGMP Version 2 leave messages sent by hosts on any of the supervisor engine module ports. When the IGMPv2 leave message is sent, the switch can then disable multicast for the port.

IGMP Snooping

IGMP snooping is another way for switches to control multicast traffic at Layer 2. They listen to IGMP messages between the hosts and routers. If a host sends an IGMP query message to the router, the switch adds the host to the multicast group and permits that port to receive multicast traffic. The port is removed from multicast traffic if an IGMP leave message is sent from the host to the router. The disadvantage of IGMP snooping is that it must listen to every IGMP control message, which can impact the CPU utilization of the switch.

Foundation Summary

The "Foundation Summary" section of each chapter lists the most important facts from the chapter. Although this section does not list every fact from the chapter that will be on your CCDA exam, a well-prepared CCDA candidate should at a minimum know all the details in each "Foundation Summary" before going to take the exam.

The CCDA exam requires you to be familiar with the following topics that were addressed in this chapter:

- **LAN Media**—Ethernet, Token Ring, and wireless LAN media
- **LAN Hardware**—Components used in LAN networks
- **LAN Design Types and Models**—Building and campus LAN types and LAN design models

The tables that follow provide an overview of the following items that will also assist you in preparing for the CCDA exam:

- Overview and comparison of LAN devices
- Summary of LAN types and their characteristics
- Description of the components of the Enterprise Campus model
- Summary of the modules on the campus infrastructure

Table 4-8 shows a comparison of LAN devices.

Table 4-8 *Device Comparison*

Device	OSI Layer	Protocol Transparent or Aware	Domain Boundary	Understands
Repeaters	Layer 1: Physical	Transparent	Amplify signal	Bits
Hubs	Layer 1: Physical	Transparent	Amplify signal	Bits
Bridges	Layer 2: Data link	Transparent	Collision domain	Frames
Switches	Layer 2: Data link	Transparent	Collision domain	Frames
Routers	Layer 3: Network	Aware	Broadcast domain	Packets
Layer 3 switches	Layer 3: Network	Aware	Broadcast domain	Packets

Table 4-9 provides a summary of LAN types and their characteristics.

Table 4-9 *LAN Types*

LAN Type	Characteristics
Large-building network	Large number of users, data center, floor closet switches, multiple LANs within the building, high-speed backbone switching between distribution devices
Campus network	High-speed backbone switching between multiple buildings in a geographical area
Small or remote LAN	Small number of users, small switches

Table 4-10 provides a description of the components of the Enterprise Campus model.

Table 4-10 *Enterprise Campus Model Components*

Component	Description
Campus infrastructure	Core, building distribution, and building access
Server farm	Connects to the campus backbone; has enterprise servers
Edge distribution	Connects the campus backbone to the Enterprise Edge

Table 4-11 provides a summary of the modules on the campus infrastructure.

Table 4-11 *Campus Infrastructure Modules*

Component	Description
Core or campus backbone	High-end Layer 3 switches
Building distribution	Layer 3 or Layer 2 switches providing redundant distribution to the access layer
Building access	Layer 2 access switches

Q&A

As mentioned in the introduction, you have two choices for review questions. Some of the questions that follow give you a bigger challenge than the exam itself by using a short-answer question format. By reviewing now with more difficult question format, you can exercise your memory better and prove your conceptual and factual knowledge of this chapter. The answers to these questions appear in Appendix A.

For more practice with exam-like question formats, use the exam engine on the CD-ROM.

1. True or false? Layer 2 switches control network broadcasts.

2. What is equivalent to the WLAN network name?

3. What technology can you use to limit multicasts at Layer 2?

4. True or false? Packet marking is also known as coloring.

5. True or false? The IEEE 802.11a wireless technology is backward-compatible with IEEE 802.11b.

6. What does IEEE 802.1x provide?

7. What IOS feature can you use to provide server redundancy?

8. What are two methods to mark frames to provide CoS?

9. Match the LAN media with its original physical specification:

    i. Fast Ethernet   a. IEEE 802.3ab

    ii. Gigabit Ethernet   b. IEEE 802.11b

    iii. WLANs   c. IEEE 802.3u

    iv. Token Ring   d. IEEE 802.5

10. Fill the blank: The _____ interoperability certification exists for IEEE 802.11b WLANs. The certification is governed by _____.

11. Match the WLAN mode with its common description:

    i. BSS   a. Ad-hoc mode

    ii. IBSS   b. Infrastructure mode

    iii. ESS   c. Set of BSS

12. True or false? Layer 3 switches bound Layer 2 collision and broadcast domains.

13. Match the Enterprise Campus component with its description:

    i. Campus infrastructure   a. Consists of backbone, building-distribution, and building-access modules

    ii. Server farm

    iii. Edge distribution   b. Connects the campus backbone to the Enterprise Edge

       c. Provides redundancy access to the servers

14. Match each LAN device type with the description that best describes it:

    i. Hubs   a. Legacy devices that connect 2 data link layer segments

    ii. Bridges

    iii. Switches   b. Network layer devices that forward packets to serial interfaces connected to the WAN

    iv. L3 switches

    v. Routers   c. High-speed devices that forward frames between two or more data link layer segments

       d. High-speed devices that bound data link layer broadcast domains

       e. Devices that amplify the signal between connected segments

15. True or false? IP phones and LAN switches can reassign the CoS bits of a frame.

16. Name two ways to reduce multicast traffic in the access layer.

17. What are two VLAN methods that you can use to carry marking CoS on frames?

18. True or false? You can configure CGMP in mixed Cisco switch and non-Cisco router environments.

19. What security enhancement does the LEAP protocol provide that was missing in WEP?

20. Why does the SAFE WLAN architecture pose a potential support problem for a large client deployment base?

21. What method would you use to manage the issue of LEAP's inability to support OTP?

Figure 4-18   *Enterprise Campus Diagram*

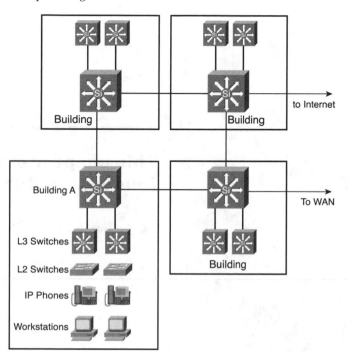

Use Figure 4-18 to answer the following questions:

22.   What media would you recommend for the campus LAN backbone?

23.   The workstations send out frames with the CoS set to 5. What should the IP phones do so that the network gives preference to VoIP traffic over data traffic?

24.   If the Layer 2 switches in Building A do not have the ability to look at CoS and ToS fields, where should these fields be inspected for acceptance or reclassification: in the building L3 switches or in the backbone L3 switches?

25.   Does the network have redundant access to the WAN?

26.   Does the network have redundant access to the Internet?

27.   Does the diagram follow recommended devices for networks designed using the Enterprise Composite Network model?

This chapter covers the following subjects:

- An Introduction to Wide-Area Networking

- Wide-Area Networking Technologies

CHAPTER 5

Wide-Area Networking Technologies

This chapter reviews the basic categories of WAN technologies and describes how these technologies fit within the Enterprise Composite Network model. This chapter also details specific WAN technologies such as Frame Relay, digital subscriber line (DSL), wireless, and many more.

"Do I Know This Already?" Quiz

The purpose of the "Do I Know This Already?" quiz is to help you decide whether you need to read the entire chapter. If you intend to read the entire chapter, you do not necessarily need to answer these questions now.

The 10-question quiz, derived from the major sections in the "Foundation Topics" portion of the chapter, helps you determine how to spend your limited study time.

Table 5-1 outlines the major topics discussed in this chapter and the "Do I Know This Already?" quiz questions that correspond to those topics.

Table 5-1 *"Do I Know This Already?" Foundation Topics Section-to-Question Mapping*

Foundation Topics Section	Questions Covered in This Section
An Introduction to Wide-Area Networking	1, 5, 7, 9
Wide-Area Networking Technologies	2, 3, 4, 8, 10

CAUTION The goal of self assessment is to gauge your mastery of the topics in this chapter. If you do not know the answer to a question or you are only partially sure of the answer, you should mark this question wrong for purposes of the self assessment. Giving yourself credit for an answer you correctly guess skews your self-assessment results and might provide you with a false sense of security.

1. Under what category of WAN technologies does ISDN belong?

   a. Leased lines

   b. Circuit-switched

   c. Packet-switched

   d. Cell-switched

2. Which physical layer WAN technology option transforms PSTN local-loop lines into fast conduits for data, permitting a maximum upstream rate of 2 Mbps and a maximum downstream rate of 8 Mbps?

   a. Frame Relay

   b. ISDN

   c. Cable

   d. Asymmetric DSL (ADSL)

3. Which emerging WAN technology uses DSL coding and digital modulation techniques with Ethernet?

   a. Wireless

   b. Cable

   c. SMDS

   d. Long-Reach Ethernet (LRE)

4. Which WAN data-link technology offers higher throughput at the cost of less robust error detection and control than the earlier X.25 technology?

   a. Frame Relay

   b. ISDN

   c. Dial-up

   d. Switched Multimegabit Data Service (SMDS)

5. Which of the following statements regarding WANs is incorrect?

   a. WANs typically encompass broad geographic areas.

   b. Users of WANs do not typically own all transmission facilities.

   c. In general, WAN technologies function at the middle three layers of the Open System Interconnection (OSI) model.

   d. Switches or concentrators often relay information through the WAN.

6. Given the Enterprise Composite Network model, all WAN connections are terminated in a single functional area. What is the area called?

   a. Enterprise Campus

   b. Service Provider (SP) Edge

   c. Enterprise Edge

   d. Enterprise WAN

7. Under what category of WAN technologies does ATM belong?

   a. Leased lines

   b. Circuit-switched

   c. Packet-switched

   d. Cell-switched

8. You construct a small satellite office in a remote location of Kansas. This location is to host several workstations that require connections to the main office facility. These workstations sporadically need to upload large database transactions. You must keep costs to a minimum if possible. What is the best choice for a WAN service in this case?

   a. Frame Relay

   b. X.25

   c. ATM

   d. ISDN

9. Which of the following is an example of a packet-switched WAN service?

   a. ISDN

   b. ATM

   c. SMDS

   d. Asynchronous

10. Your supervisor is interested in a wireless WAN solution that provides higher bandwidth than point-to-multipoint (p2mp) wireless. Which of the following statements are true?

    a. Service providers cannot install point-to-point (p2p) links from a p2mp hub.

    b. P2p links tend to be slower than p2mp.

    c. P2p wireless connections can provide up to 44 Mbps raw bandwidth.

    d. P2mp wireless connections can provide up to 1.544 Mbps raw bandwidth.

The answers to the "Do I Know This Already?" quiz appear in Appendix A, "Answers to Chapter 'Do I Know This Already?' Quizzes and Q&A Sections." The suggested choices for your next step are as follows:

- **8 or less overall score**—Read the entire chapter. This includes the "Foundation Topics," "Foundation Summary," and "Q&A" sections.

- **9 or 10 overall score**—If you want more review on these topics, skip to the "Foundation Summary" section and then go to the "Q&A" section. Otherwise, move to the next chapter.

Foundation Topics

This chapter introduces the various WAN technologies that a CCDA candidate should understand. In chapters that follow this one, you get more details regarding specific design considerations and WAN backup strategies that a network designer should know.

After an introduction to WANs in general, this chapter details each specific WAN technology and discusses the groups that Cisco uses to categorize these technologies. Several tables assist you in final-exam preparations.

Introduction to Wide-Area Networking

WANs are a constantly evolving and necessary component within internetworks. Increasingly, today's business environments require systems to disseminate greater amounts of information across wider geographical boundaries. Moreover, as the information transmitted across networks increases in complexity and time-sensitivity, WANs need greater bandwidths.

Before the CCDA can begin designing WAN solutions, popular WAN technology options must be understood. These include packet-, cell-, and circuit-switched technologies as well as dedicated leased-line connections. First, define a WAN.

What Is a WAN?

As the name implies, WANs encompass broad geographical areas. Unlike with LANs, private organizations that need the WAN services do not typically own the WAN. In most cases, the costs involved are too high, and sharing WAN resources across multiple organizations lessens the need to support multiple parallel private infrastructures, which reduces right-of-way issues and conflicts. Network providers most often supply connections through their systems and can even provide portions of the hardware required. These network providers charge fees, or tariffs, for use of the WAN. Often set by governmental regulation, these fees can be a fixed periodic amount independent of distance, duration of activity, or metered data volumes, as is typical of small office/home office (SOHO) Internet connectivity. These fees are also typically based on permanent or virtual circuits and some defined relationship for guaranteed access bandwidth, as is common for packet-switched networks. Circuit-switched environments often use time of active connection. Leased-line environments frequently use an amount that considers access bandwidth and distance. As you will learn, it is important to consider all the aspects of these tariffs as you design appropriate WAN solutions.

If the network providers are not actually supplying hardware to the organization, companies are almost certainly relying on network-provider switches or concentrators that relay information as it courses through the WAN. Typically, the organization does not know or care about the actual path data takes as it moves through the provider's LAN. As long as the data reaches its destination (securely) in the timeframe expected, the provider can route the data as needed.

For the most part, WAN technologies operate at the lowest three layers of the OSI model. These layers are the physical, data link, and network layers. Classic examples include X.25, which operates at Layers 2 and 3, and Frame Relay, which operates at Layer 2 only.

Table 5-2 details key typical differences you should know when comparing LAN and WAN technologies.

Table 5-2   *LAN Versus WAN Technologies*

Technology	Area	Ownership	Bandwidth
LAN	Small	Self-owned	High
WAN	Large	Provider-owned	Low

WAN Categories

We often divide WAN technologies into categories that help define their nature. These categories are as follows:

- Leased lines
- Circuit-switched
- Packet-switched
- Cell-switched

Leased Lines

Networking professionals often refer to *leased lines* as point-to-point links. This text uses leased-line terminology because of the frequency with which organizations actually lease these connections from a network or service provider.

Leased lines are typically more reliable (and more expensive) when compared to the other WAN categories because they are completely reserved for transmissions and they are always available. Service providers reserve an entire physical circuit from the network access point to the customer premises. The circuit might be over-dedicated physical media or a channel maintained using frequency modulation (FM) or time-division multiplexing (TDM). Synchronous serial connections are common examples of leased lines. Figure 5-1 shows a typical leased-line WAN connection.

Figure 5-1 *Leased-Line WAN Connection*

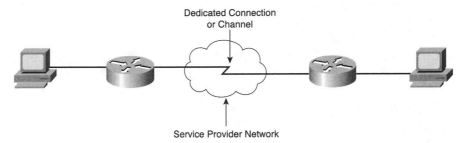

Circuit-Switched Lines

The classic example of a *circuit-switched* communications network is a typical voice telephone call over the PSTN. The call establishes a connection between the two end points and then terminates (or tears down) this connection when communications complete. Realize that with circuit-switched technologies, WAN equipment dedicates a physical path to the communications while they are occurring. No other participants can use the physical medium while communications continue. Classic examples of circuit-switched WAN technologies include ISDN and asynchronous serial connections.

Packet-Switched Lines

Packet-switching technologies typically reduce costs to the organization because the service provider experiences a more efficient use of its equipment. This efficiency is a result of customers sharing the WAN resources in a way that allows the operator of the transport network to interleave traffic from multiple sources to multiple destinations on links within the transport network. With packet switching, network equipment creates "virtual circuits" through the shared WAN provider's network. These virtual circuits transport the data (segmented as packets) through the WAN.

Virtual circuits are typically permanent virtual circuits (PVCs) or switched virtual circuits (SVCs). SVCs tend to have a lower cost for the organization, when available. They are appropriate when users transfer data sporadically over the WAN. With SVCs, network equipment builds connections on demand as needed, and these connections terminate when transmission completes.

PVCs are permanently established connections. Obviously, these circuits are more appropriate for WAN environments where constant data transfers must take place. Although PVCs (which often guarantee bandwidth availability) tend to be more expensive, there is no overhead required with establishing connections, transferring data, and terminating connections, as with SVCs.

Packet-switching WAN technologies include X.25, Frame Relay, and SMDS, such as those shown in Figure 5-2.

Figure 5-2 *Packet-Switching Networks*

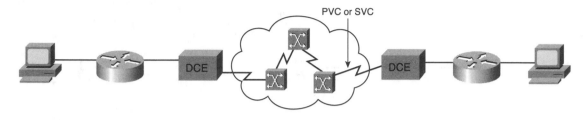

Cell Switching

With *cell-switching* WAN technology, the network divides data into units of a fixed size called cells. The provider can transmit these fixed size cells efficiently over a physical medium. ATM is an example of cell-switching technology.

WANs and the Enterprise Composite Network Model

Cisco built upon the classic hierarchical network model (access, distribution, core) to provide network designers with the Enterprise Composite Network model. The classic hierarchical model always suffered from scalability and manageability weaknesses. Cisco recommends use of the Enterprise Composite Network model to provide the functional components for network design. This model is aligned with the current Cisco "best practice" for building converged networks that provide security and other network services to support the transport of voice, video, and data. Figure 5-3 depicts the Enterprise Composite Network model.

Figure 5-3 *Enterprise Composite Network Model*

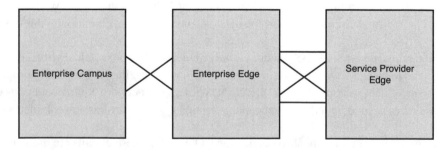

It is interesting to note that this model does not abandon the hierarchical model but rather adopts hierarchy separately within the enterprise campus to meet the specialized needs for user access; for access to application servers; and for access to or from remote users, sites, and external networks.

Initial feedback from network designers regarding the new model has been positive. Network architects can focus on a "divide-and-conquer" approach in which they concentrate on each block of the model and the relationships between them. Designers divide the network into functional areas and focus their efforts more effectively to meet the business needs of their organizations.

Where do WAN technologies fit in the Enterprise Composite Network model? They operate between the Enterprise Edge and the SP Edge using the various technologies in this chapter.

Wide-Area Networking Technologies

Today, there are many technologies available for designing WAN infrastructures. Constant research and development in the area of WAN technologies allows designers to implement increasingly cost-effective WAN designs that take advantage of new mechanisms such as metropolitan Ethernet and virtual private networks (VPNs) using cable and DSL for access. You should acquire a solid comprehension of the technology options available before designing WAN solutions.

Dial-Up

The first of the WAN technologies presented here is one that many readers have used at some point, dial-up. *Dial-up* refers to the use of a modem connected to the PSTN to carry data. Although the available bandwidth is lowest with this technology (the FCC permits download speeds to 53 kbps in the U.S.), it is still a popular remote-access choice for home office and telecommuter environments—because of low costs and almost universal availability. Users can easily achieve dial-up wide-area networking through the acquisition of inexpensive customer premises equipment (CPE) such as the digital modem.

Dial-up WAN services have managed a presence in more than just the home-office environment, in part because of dial-on-demand routing (DDR) capabilities built in to most Cisco devices. DDR enables networking equipment to dynamically dial a connection to a remote WAN destination upon the receipt of "interesting" traffic. Of course, it is up to the Cisco administrator to determine and define these interesting traffic patterns.

Chapter 7, "Backup Options and Sample WAN Designs," details yet another powerful reason why dial-up solutions continue to appear in WAN designs today—WAN backup options.

ISDN

Regional telephone carriers make ISDN a WAN design possibility for many internetwork WAN designs. *ISDN* permits the digitization of access to the telephone network so that existing phone lines are capable of carrying data in a digital form rather than as analog signals.

It is important that network designers understand the devices and reference points in an ISDN WAN. We refer to ISDN terminals that are "ISDN ready" as terminal equipment type 1 (TE1s), whereas non-ISDN terminals are TE2s. To connect a TE2 device to the ISDN network, use a terminal adapter (TA). TE1 and TE2 devices connect to network termination type 1 (NT1) or network termination type 2 (NT2) devices. These devices connect the four-wire subscriber wiring to the two-wire local-loop provider network. In North America, the NT1 is a customer-provided CPE device, whereas in most other parts of the world, this device is part of the carrier's network. NT2s are more complicated devices usually found as components in PBXs. They typically provide Layer 2 and 3 protocol functions and concentration services.

The key reference points within an ISDN network are defined in the ISDN standards produced by the International Telecommunication Union Telecommunication Standardization Sector (ITU-T). The R reference point identifies the area between non-ISDN equipment and the TA. The S reference point identifies the area between user terminals and the NT2. The T reference point identifies the area between the NT1 and NT2 devices. Finally, the U reference point identifies the area between the NT1 devices and line-termination equipment in the carrier network. Obviously, the U reference point is relevant only to ISDN subscribers in North America. Figure 5-4 depicts TE1 and TE2 devices and their respective connections to the ISDN switch with the respective reference points.

Figure 5-4 *ISDN Devices and Reference Points*

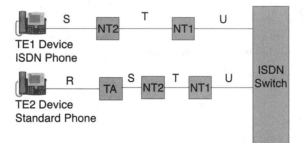

The two types of ISDN services are Basic Rate Interface (BRI) and Primary Rate Interface (PRI).

BRI

ISDN *BRI* offers two bearer (B) channels and a single delta (D) channel. BRI B channels transmit data and operate at 64 Kbps. The BRI D channel handles signaling and operates at 16 Kbps. BRI also provides for framing control and other overhead, thus bringing the total bit rate to 192 Kbps.

PRI

In North America and Japan, *PRI* ISDN over T1 media provides 23 B channels and 1 D channel. Unlike BRI, the D channel in PRI operates at 64 Kbps as well, bringing the total bit rate to 1.544 Mbps. In Europe, Australia, and other parts of the world, PRI is provisioned over E1 media and features 30 B channels and one 64 Kbps D channel for a total bit rate of 2.048 Mbps.

X.25

X.25 is an ITU-T WAN protocol. *Frame Relay* has helped make X.25 mainly a legacy WAN technology, especially in North America. X.25 was designed to operate effectively even over links with relatively high bit-error rates. The packet-switched networks of common carriers have used it. X.25 features high overhead due to built-in error detection and recovery mechanisms. Frame Relay, on the other hand, takes advantage of today's more reliable physical connections and leaves such error recovery to upper layers of the OSI model. The bandwidth saved is available for other uses.

X.25 WAN devices include data terminal equipment (DTE), data circuit-terminating equipment (DCE), and packet-switching exchange (PSE). DTE devices are end systems that communicate across the X.25 network. They might include your actual workstations or other network hosts. DCE devices are communications devices, such as modems and packet switches, that provide the interface between DTE devices and a PSE. DCE devices are generally located in the carrier's facilities. PSEs are switches that compose the bulk of the carrier's network. They transfer data from one DTE device to another through the X.25 PSN.

The packet assembler/disassembler (PAD) is a common device in X.25 networks. X.25 relies upon PADs when an end device cannot implement the full X.25 functionality. The PAD is located between the end device and a DCE device. The PAD performs three primary functions: buffering, packet assembly, and packet disassembly.

X.25 WAN technology maps to the lowest three layers of the OSI reference model. X.25 implementations typically use the following protocols: Packet-Layer Protocol (PLP); Link Access Procedure, Balanced (LAPB); and a variety of physical-layer protocols (such as EIA/TIA-232, EIA/TIA-449, EIA/TIA-530, and G.703).

X.25 supports both SVCs and PVCs. The basic operation of an X.25 virtual circuit begins when the source DTE device specifies the virtual circuit to be used (in the packet headers) and then sends the packets to a locally connected DCE device. The local DCE device examines the packet headers to determine which virtual circuit to use and then sends the packets to the closest switch in the path of that virtual circuit. The switches pass the traffic to the next intermediate node in the path, which can be another switch or the remote DCE device. The remote DCE device examines the packet headers and determines the destination address. This DCE device then sends the packets to the destination DTE device. If communication occurs over an SVC and neither device has additional data to transfer, the virtual circuit terminates.

Although PVCs are more common with Frame Relay, SVCs are more common with X.25 implementations. Also, X.25 requires special addressing. Specifically, X.25 uses X.121 addresses in call setup mode to establish SVCs. The X.121 address field includes the International Data Number (IDN), which consists of two fields: the Data Network Identification Code (DNIC) and the National Terminal Number (NTN). The DNIC is an optional field that identifies the exact PSN in which the destination DTE device is located. X.25 sometimes omits the DNIC in calls within the same PSN. The DNIC has two subfields: country and PSN. The country subfield specifies the country where the destination PSN is located. The PSN field specifies the exact PSN in which the destination DTE device is located. Finally, the NTN identifies the exact DTE device in the PSN for which a packet is destined. This field varies in length.

Frame Relay

Many network designers consider Frame Relay a streamlined version of X.25. This analogy holds true on several different levels. It is certainly appropriate to label the protocol as streamlined because it does not involve the intense error recovery that occurs with X.25. Frame Relay restricts its operations to the lower two layers of the OSI model and allows higher-level protocols to concern themselves with transmission errors.

Frame Relay's designers originally intended the protocol for use across ISDN interfaces. Today, Frame Relay transmissions occur over a variety of other network interfaces as well.

Like X.25, Frame Relay networks rely upon DCE and DTE devices. They also rely upon virtual circuits for the actual transmission of data through the WAN network. These can be SVCs or PVCs, yet Frame Relay PVCs are more common—many carriers do not even provide the option of SVC configurations.

Although X.25 uses X.121 addresses for circuit identification, Frame Relay uses a new concept called data-link connection identifiers (DLCIs). Frame Relay service providers typically assign these values, and they have only local significance. Their values are unique in the LAN but not necessarily in the Frame Relay WAN.

Frame Relay reduces network overhead by implementing simple congestion-notification mechanisms rather than enforcing explicit per-virtual-circuit flow control. Specifically, Frame Relay implements two congestion-notification mechanisms, forward-explicit congestion notifications (FECNs) and backward-explicit congestion notifications (BECNs).

Discard Eligibility

Frame Relay also uses a *Discard Eligibility (DE)* bit to indicate that a frame has a greater probability of loss by discard than other frames. The DE bit is part of the address field in the Frame Relay frame header. DTE devices can set the value of the DE bit of a frame to 1 to indicate that the frame has lower importance than other frames. The DE bit can also be set at the edge of a Frame Relay network to mark packets that are not compliant with the service contract. When the network becomes congested, DCE devices discard frames with the DE bit set before discarding those without. This clever method of congestion management helps to ensure that DCEs do not drop critical data.

Local Management Interface

Another important feature of Frame Relay is *Local Management Interface (LMI)*. LMI is a set of enhancements to the basic Frame Relay specification. Cisco Systems, StrataCom, Northern Telecom, and Digital Equipment Corporation developed the new enhancements in 1990. LMI offers a number of features (called extensions) for managing complex internetworks. These extensions include global addressing, virtual-circuit status messages, and multicasting.

SMDS

SMDS is a high-speed, packet-switched, datagram-based WAN technology used for communication over public data networks (PDNs). SMDS uses fiber- or copper-based media and supports speeds of 1.544 Mbps over Digital Signal Level 1 (DS-1) transmission facilities or 44.736 Mbps over Digital Signal Level 3 (DS-3) transmission facilities. In addition, SMDS data units are large enough to encapsulate entire IEEE 802.3, IEEE 802.5, and Fiber Distributed Data Interface (FDDI) frames.

A typical SMDS network consists of several underlying devices to provide high-speed data service. These devices include CPE, carrier equipment, and the subscriber network interface (SNI). The CPE is terminal equipment typically owned and maintained by the customer. The CPE includes end devices, such as terminals and personal computers, and intermediate nodes, such as routers, modems, and multiplexers. The SMDS carrier, however, sometimes provides intermediate nodes. Carrier equipment generally consists of high-speed WAN switches that must conform to certain network equipment specifications, such as those outlined by Bell Communications Research (Bellcore). These specifications define network operations, the interface between a local-carrier network and a long-distance carrier network, and the interface between two switches inside a single-carrier network.

Notice that the SNI is the interface between the CPE and carrier equipment. This interface is the point at which the customer network ends and the carrier network begins. The function of the SNI is to render the technology and operation of the carrier SMDS network transparent to the customer.

SMDS uses the SMDS Interface Protocol (SIP) for communications between CPE and SMDS carrier equipment. SIP provides connectionless service across the SNI, allowing the CPE to access the SMDS network. SIP derives its origins from the IEEE 802.6 Distributed Queue Dual Bus (DQDB) standard for cell relay across metropolitan-area networks (MANs). DQDB is a perfect basis for SIP because it is an open standard that supports all the SMDS service features.

SMDS protocol data units (PDUs) carry both a source and a destination address. SMDS addresses are 10-digit values resembling conventional telephone numbers. The SMDS addressing implementation offers group addressing and security features. SMDS group addresses allow a single address to refer to multiple CPE stations, which specify the group address in the destination-address field of the PDU. The network makes multiple copies of the PDU and delivers these packets to all members of the group. Group addresses reduce the amount of network resources required for distributing routing information, resolving addresses, and dynamically discovering network resources. SMDS group addressing is analogous to multicasting on LANs.

SMDS implements two security features: source-address validation and address screening. Source-address validation ensures that the PDU source address is legitimate and represents the true SNI from which it originated. Source-address validation prevents address spoofing, in which illegal traffic assumes the source address of a legitimate device. Address screening allows a subscriber to establish a private virtual network that excludes unwanted traffic.

Asynchronous Transfer Mode

Asynchronous Transfer Mode (ATM) is an ITU-T standard for cell relay. ATM was developed to provide converged services for voice, video, and data with better performance characteristics than provided by traditional packet-switched technologies. ATM transmits information in small, fixed-size cells. ATM networks are connection-oriented.

ATM is a cell-switching and multiplexing technology that combines the benefits of circuit switching (guaranteed capacity and constant transmission delay) with those of packet switching (flexibility and efficiency for intermittent traffic). It provides scalable bandwidth from a few megabits per second (Mbps) to many gigabits per second (Gbps).

ATM Cells

ATM cells consist of 53 octets, or bytes. The first 5 bytes contain cell-header information, and the remaining 48 contain the payload (user information). Small, fixed-length cells are well suited to transferring voice and video traffic because such traffic is intolerant of the serialization delay incurred by any large data packet that might precede it in an output queue.

ATM Networks

An *ATM network* consists of a set of ATM switches interconnected by point-to-point ATM links or interfaces. ATM switches support two primary types of interfaces: User-Network Interface (UNI) and Network Node Interface (NNI). A UNI connects an ATM end system (such as hosts and routers) and a private ATM switch or a private ATM switch and the public-carrier ATM network switch node. An NNI connects two network nodes.

ATM networks are connection-oriented, which means that a virtual channel (VC) exists across the ATM network prior to any data transfer. A virtual channel is much like the virtual circuits used by other technologies explored in this chapter.

ATM Connections

The two types of ATM connections are virtual paths and virtual channels. A *virtual path* is a bundle of virtual channels that is identified by a virtual path identifier (VPI) on a particular interface. In a virtual path connection, the traffic is switched through a network node based only on the interface and VPI received. A *virtual channel* is a specific connection through the ATM network. Within any one virtual path, the virtual channel is identified by a virtual channel identifier (VCI). In a virtual channel connection, the traffic is switched through a network node based on the interface and VPI and VCI received. The VPI and VCI values are local to a particular link between two ATM switches or an ATM switch and an end system.

Additional WAN Technologies

In addition to the more widely deployed WAN technologies explored in this section, there are several technologies with increasing visibility for WAN access and transport. Access technologies include DSL, cable, and LRE. Wireless provides WAN connectivity where it is expensive, impractical, or impossible to build a cabled infrastructure.

DSL

DSL technology is a modem technology that uses existing twisted-pair, local-loop telephone lines to transport high-bandwidth data, such as multimedia and video, to service subscribers. The term xDSL covers a number of similar, yet competing, forms of DSL technologies, including ADSL (asymmetric), SDSL (single-line), HDSL (high-data-rate), HDSL-2, G.SHDL (multirate high-data-rate), IDSL (ISDN), and VDSL (very-high-data-rate). xDSL is drawing significant attention from network designers because it delivers high-bandwidth data rates to dispersed locations with relatively small changes to the existing telco infrastructure. Currently, most DSL deployments are ADSL, mainly delivered to residential customers.

ADSL technology provides asymmetric data rates. It allows more bandwidth downstream—from a Network Service Provider's (NSP's) central office to the customer site—than upstream from the subscriber to the central office. This asymmetry, combined with always-on access (which eliminates call setup), makes ADSL ideal for Web surfing, video-on-demand, and remote access, usually using a VPN connection. Users of these applications typically download much more information than they send. ADSL can transmit more than 6 Mbps to a subscriber and as much as 640 Kbps more in both directions. Such rates expand existing access capacity by a factor of 50 or more as compared to analog modem access without new cabling.

ADSL depends on advanced digital-signal processing and algorithms to transmit large amounts of information through twisted-pair telephone lines. To create multiple channels, ADSL modems divide the available bandwidth of a telephone line in one of two ways: frequency-division multiplexing (FDM) or echo cancellation. FDM assigns one band for upstream data and another band for downstream data. TDM divides the downstream path into one or more high-speed channels and one or more low-speed channels. It occurs with the upstream path as well for low-speed channels. Echo cancellation assigns the upstream band to overlap the downstream and separates the two by means of local echo cancellation, a technique well known in V.32 and V.34 modems. With either technique, ADSL splits off a 4 kHz region for basic telephone service at the lower end of the frequency range.

LRE

LRE or Ethernet in the First Mile (EFM) broadband networking technology uses Ethernet technology to deliver 5-15 Mbps performance over existing telephone-grade (Category 1/2/3) wiring. LRE reaches up to 5000 feet and enables simultaneous voice, video, and data applications. This technology actually makes use of DSL coding and digital-modulation techniques with Ethernet framing.

LRE provides a cost-effective, easy-to-deploy technology for service providers and facility operators to use in existing multi-unit buildings (MxU) and enterprise-campus environments with broadband access. MxU buildings include hotels, multidwelling unit (MDU) housing, and multitenant unit (MTU) office buildings.

Cable

Cable is an expanding new technology option for data transport that uses a hybrid of coaxial cable and fiber-optic media over cable distribution systems. Although this WAN technology was at first hampered by a lack of formal standardization, a newly introduced standard, the Data Over Cable Service Interface Specification (DOCSIS) 1.0 has found wide North American acceptance as a method to serve homes and small offices. Remote access to enterprises usually uses a VPN connection. DOCSIS 1.1 is currently in development for the purpose of supporting Voice over IP (VoIP) and advanced security.

The DOCSIS interface specifications enabled the development and deployment of data-over-cable systems on a nonproprietary, multivendor, interoperable basis for transparent bidirectional transfer of IP traffic between the cable system head end and customer locations over an all-coaxial or hybrid-fiber/coax (HFC) cable network. The system consists of a Cable Modem Terminating System (CMTS) at the head end, a coaxial or HFC medium, and a cable modem at the premises of the customer, in conjunction with DOCSIS-defined layers that support interoperability and evolutionary feature capabilities.

From a design perspective, cable is an attractive WAN access technology where cable television is widely deployed.

Wireless

Wireless is an exciting area of telecommunications that uses electromagnetic waves for data transport instead of wire or glass fibers. Current examples of wireless equipment include cellular phones, pagers, global positioning services (GPSs), cordless computer peripherals, satellite television, and wireless LANs.

Currently, many types of wireless technologies exist, containing a large number of subset technologies that range from ATM-based to wireless LAN facilities. Wireless frequencies of the different technologies travel between several hundred feet (wireless LAN) and 25 miles (Multichannel Multipoint Distribution Service [MMDS]).

These different wireless technologies are each unique because of their protocols (ATM or IP), their connection types (p2p or p2mp), and their spectrums (licensed or unlicensed).

Multiprotocol Label Switching

Another exciting WAN technology option is *Multiprotocol Label Switching (MPLS)*, which features a converged network infrastructure that is already replacing some Frame Relay and ATM networks. Due to MPLS, service providers have the ability to provide traditional WAN services and beyond at a fraction of the cost of other WAN technologies. These additional services include traffic engineering, QoS, Layer 2 Tunneling, and virtual private network (VPN) services over IP.

MPLS functions by encapsulating packets as they arrive at the Service Provider Edge network. Packets are "tagged" by this encapsulation to indicate the destination network. Core MPLS routers in the service provider network apply appropriate services based on the label and also forward the packet appropriately based on this special tag information. The MPLS encapsulated information is stripped from the packet upon exciting the service provider network.

MPLS relies upon several equipment types in order to achieve its technology as well as an important protocol. Customer Premise Equipment (CPE) is the network equipment at a customer location, while Edge Label Switch Routers (ELSRs) are located at the ingress point of the service provider network. As its name implies, this equipment is used to assign (remove) labels to packets as they arrive (exit) at the provider. Cisco high-end switches or routers function as the ELSR equipment. Label Switch Routers (LSRs) are located at the core of the MPLS network and are critical for forwarding and traffic engineering functions as they pass MPLS packets at a high rate of speed. The Label Distribution Protocol (LDP) is responsible for distributing label information throughout the network.

MPLS devices use Forwarding Equivalence Classes (FECs) to make forwarding decisions. FECs are responsible for maintaining and communicating the relationship between labels and paths throughout the network.

Because MPLS offers exciting and efficient methods for forwarding many different types of traffic with varying network service needs, MPLS should see more implementations soon.

Foundation Summary

The "Foundation Summary" section of each chapter lists the most important facts from the chapter. Although this section does not list every fact from the chapter that will be on your CCDA exam, a well-prepared CCDA candidate should at a minimum know all the details in each "Foundation Summary" before going to take the exam.

WANs encompass broad geographical areas, and the organizations that use them do not typically own the equipment or media that connects the equipment. Network providers most often supply connections through their systems and might even provide portions of the hardware required. These network providers charge fees, or tariffs, for use of the WAN. It is very important that you consider all aspects of these tariffs as you design appropriate WAN solutions. For the most part, WAN technologies operate at the lowest three layers of the OSI model.

Designers typically divide WAN technologies into four categories: leased lines, circuit-switched, packet-switched, and cell-switched. Leased lines are point-to-point links. Leased lines are typically more reliable (and more expensive) because they are completely reserved for transmissions, and they are always available. An example of a circuit-switched communications network is a typical voice telephone call over the PSTN. The call establishes a connection between the two end points and then terminates this connection when communications complete. Packet-switching technologies typically reduce costs to the organization because they use the service provider's equipment more efficiently, a result of customers sharing the WAN resources. With packet switching, the network creates "virtual circuits" through the shared WAN provider's network. These virtual circuits transport the data (segmented as packets) through the WAN. With cell-switching WAN technology, the network divides data into units of fixed-size chunks called cells. The provider can transmit these fixed-size cells efficiently over a physical medium. ATM is the best example of cell-switching technology.

WAN technologies fit nicely into the Enterprise Composite Network model. They operate between the Enterprise Edge and the SP Edge using the various Layer 2 and Layer 3 technologies in this chapter.

Table 5-3 summarizes the WAN technologies in this chapter.

Table 5-3 *WAN Technology Summary*

Technology	Bandwidth	Time to Connect	Reliability	Availability	Cost
Analog modem dial-up	Low	High	Low	High	Low
ISDN	Low	Medium	Medium	High	Low
X.25	Low	Low	Medium	High	High
Frame Relay	Medium	Low	Medium	High	High
SMDS	High	Low	High	High	High
ATM	High	Low	High	Medium	Medium
DSL	Low/Medium	Low	Medium	Medium	Medium
LRE	Low/Medium	Low	Medium	Low	Medium
Cable	Low/Medium	Low	Low	Medium	Medium
Wireless	Low/Medium	Low	Low	Low	Low

Q&A

As mentioned in the introduction, you have two choices for review questions. Some of the questions that follow give you a bigger challenge than the exam itself by using a short-answer question format. By reviewing now with more difficult question format, you can exercise your memory better and prove your conceptual and factual knowledge of this chapter. The answers to these questions appear in Appendix A.

For more practice with exam-like question formats, use the exam engine on the CD-ROM.

1. For each of the following WAN technologies, indicate whether the appropriate category is leased line, circuit-switched, packet-switched, or cell-switched:

   a. ISDN

   b. Frame Relay

   c. ATM

   d. Synchronous serial

   e. X.25

   f. Dial-up

   g. SMDS

2. In what part of the Enterprise Composite Network model do WAN technologies best fit?

   _____

3. Match the following WAN technologies with their definitions:

   a. Wireless   i. High bandwidth over telephone local-loop copper lines

   b. LRE   ii. Usually over a hybrid of coaxial and fiber optics

   c. DSL   iii. Electromagnetic waves as opposed to wire or glass fiber

   d. Cable   iv. Utilizes coding and digital modulation techniques from DSL

4. You are designing a WAN solution for a customer that is setting up a small satellite office in New York. The customer needs medium- to high-bandwidth access at this location for downloading constant data streams from the headquarters in Los Angeles. The satellite office also needs to upload large amounts of data frequently to headquarters. The client is interested in a mature and time-tested WAN technology. Which WAN technology should you recommend? Why?

5. Describe an ATM cell and explain why cells are well suited for the transmission of voice and video traffic.

6. Describe the ISDN options of BRI and PRI, focusing on available bandwidth for each technology.

7. What is the purpose of FECN and BECN within Frame Relay technology?

8. What is the most common type of virtual circuit used with Frame Relay? With X.25?

9. What is the basic Layer 2 technology behind MPLS encapsulation?

10. What is the purpose of the ELSR in MPLS technology?

This chapter covers the following subjects:

- Analyze, Characterize, Design

- Common Design Factors

- WAN Performance Options

CHAPTER 6

Designing Wide-Area Networking Solutions

Now that you understand the various WAN technologies that a CCDA should know, it is time to examine a process for designing WAN solutions. Chapter 7, "Backup Options and Sample WAN Designs," actually provides sample designs for your examination.

This chapter describes a process a network designer should follow when designing WAN solutions. It also details the most common factors that a network designer should consider when making such design decisions. Finally, this chapter describes various WAN technologies that can dramatically affect the performance of WAN solutions.

"Do I Know This Already?" Quiz

The purpose of the "Do I Know This Already?" quiz is to help you decide whether you need to read the entire chapter. If you intend to read the entire chapter, you do not necessarily need to answer these questions now.

The 10-question quiz, derived from the major sections in the "Foundation Topics" portion of the chapter, helps you determine how to spend your limited study time.

Table 6-1 outlines the major topics discussed in this chapter and the "Do I Know This Already?" quiz questions that correspond to those topics.

Table 6-1 *"Do I Know This Already?" Foundation Topics Section-to-Question Mapping*

Foundation Topics Section	Questions Covered in This Section
Analyze, Characterize, Design	1
Common Design Factors	2, 3
WAN Performance Options	4, 5, 6, 7, 8, 9, 10

> **CAUTION** The goal of self assessment is to gauge your mastery of the topics in this chapter. If you do not know the answer to a question or you are only partially sure of the answer, you should mark this question wrong for purposes of the self assessment. Giving yourself credit for an answer you correctly guess skews your self-assessment results and might provide you with a false sense of security.

1. Which of the following is not a part of the process recommended by Cisco for WAN designs?

    a. Characterize the existing network.

    b. Configure deployed services.

    c. Design the new WAN topology.

    d. Analyze customer requirements.

2. Which of the following WAN access technologies uses copper media, permits downstream bandwidth of up to 8 Mbps downstream, and provides more limited upstream bandwidths?

    a. Long-Reach Ethernet (LRE)

    b. ATM

    c. ISDN

    d. Frame Relay

    e. X.25

    f. Asymmetric Digital Subscriber Line (ADSL)

3. Which of the following terms describes a specific measure of delay often used to describe voice and video networks?

    a. Reliability

    b. Latency

    c. Jitter

    d. Flux

4. Designers should avoid the use of compression in a WAN design if the CPU utilization percentage is at what level or greater?

    a. 45 percentage

    b. 55 percentage

    c. 65 percentage

    d. 75 percentage

    e. 85 percentage

5. Which statement is correct about TCP window size and WAN performance?

    a. Larger window sizes increase the number of acknowledgment packets and thereby increase the performance and reliability of WAN connections.

    b. Smaller window sizes increase the number of acknowledgment packets and thereby increase the performance and reliability of WAN connections.

    c. Larger window sizes decrease the number of acknowledgment packets and can impact the performance of WAN connections.

    d. Smaller window sizes decrease the number of acknowledgment packets and can impact the performance of WAN connections.

6. Which compression algorithm can reduce the size of TCP/IP headers to as few as three bytes?

    a. Van Jacobson

    b. Microsoft Point-to-Point Compression (MPPC)

    c. FRF.9 Frame Relay payload compression

    d. Link Access Procedure, Balanced (LAPB) using Lempel-Ziv Stack (LZS)

7. Which of the following WAN scenarios might be appropriate for queuing solutions?

    a. A WAN connection features consistent congestion problems, and data transfers often suffer.

    b. A WAN connection is rarely congested, and data transfers never suffer.

    c. A WAN connection features occasional periods of congestion, and data transfers have occasionally suffered as a result.

    d. A newly implemented WAN connection has yet to demonstrate sufficient WAN statistics for congestion-level tracking.

8. Which queuing mechanism establishes four interface output queues that designers can use for traffic scheduling?

    a. First-in, first-out (FIFO)

    b. Priority queuing (PQ)

    c. Weighted fair queuing (WFQ)

    d. Custom queuing (CQ)

9. Which queuing mechanism uses 16 queues and ensures each receive some level of attention—improving "fairness?"

   a. FIFO

   b. PQ

   c. WFQ

   d. CQ

10. Which WAN performance option delays excess packets by holding them in buffers and then releasing them at preconfigured rates?

    a. Traffic shaping

    b. Traffic policing

    c. WFQ

    d. CQ

    e. PQ

The answers to the "Do I Know This Already?" quiz appear in Appendix A, "Answers to Chapter 'Do I Know This Already?' Quizzes and Q&A Sections." The suggested choices for your next step are as follows:

■ **8 or less overall score**—Read the entire chapter. This includes the "Foundation Topics," "Foundation Summary," and "Q&A" sections.

■ **9 or 10 overall score**—If you want more review on these topics, skip to the "Foundation Summary" section and then go to the Q&A section. Otherwise, move to the next chapter.

Foundation Topics

A network designer should follow a clear-cut process when designing a completely new network—or the more common occurrence—redesigning an existing network. This section assists you with a network-design challenge and focuses on redesigning an existing network. Perhaps, this redesign is necessary because you must support a new application or network service or because the existing network cannot support current applications or bandwidth requirements. Whatever the reason, the concepts in this section assist you in creating a well-planned, fully functional WAN design.

Analyze, Characterize, Design

Designing the perfect WAN solution for a client involves a careful process. Although there are many possible approaches, Cisco recommends that designers engage in the analysis of requirements, characterization of the existing network, and design of the new WAN topology—at the very least. Although it might sound like a lot of work (and if done properly, it is), keep in mind that some design engagements make it simpler because there is no existing network to begin with!

First, network designers must engage in a careful analysis of the requirements for the network. For an existing network, chances are that business conditions or goals have changed and the network must meet new demands. For example, many organizations are incorporating Voice over IP (VoIP) solutions to save money and consolidate technologies. This major change in a network almost certainly increases and expands the demands placed upon the WAN. A designer should also look as far into the future as possible during this phase, satisfying current requirements and as many upcoming requirements as possible.

The second step in the process is important as well. This step involves a careful analysis of the existing network infrastructure. Not only should a designer carefully document the existing WAN, but he should also focus on the existing WAN's ease of migration to the new design. Can existing network equipment satisfy the new infrastructure requirements? Can the existing infrastructure support new sites? What about the new planned features?

Finally, the network designer must document fully the new proposed network. Obviously, this document should fully describe how the new design meets the technology goals of the organization and how, in turn, the technology of the organization meets the business goals of the organization. Wherever possible, the designer should note the exact service levels possible with the new design.

Common Design Factors

Although network designers should consider many potential design factors before documenting their proposed solutions, Cisco recommends three main categories. Designers should scrutinize the following when designing WAN solutions:

■   Application factors

■   Technical factors

■   Cost factors

Application Factors

Application access is an important factor in modern WAN designs. Almost all network users must access remote applications at some point in their use of the network. This access becomes an even bigger factor as organizations rely more on distributed application platforms. For example, an organization might rely heavily on an SQL Server installation that is located in a data center in a remote region of the business's geography. The most important components in this or any other design example regarding application access are response time, throughput, and reliability.

> **TIP**   Remember that the network designer should prepare detailed design documents while progressing through the new or revised network design. A common design document in this phase would detail the applications running in the environment and key characteristics about them.

Response Time

Response time is a powerful component of application-design criteria. Response time is a simple and often accurate measure of design success or failure. Simply stated, response time is the time between the entry of a command or data at a source system and the target system's execution of the command or the target's response.

Perhaps, response time is such a key measurement because end users of the network are so aware of its value. Nothing in the network warrants more satisfaction-level discussions than slow response times.

Two specific components of response time are *delay* and *jitter*. The ever-increasing amount of voice and video make these measures more critical due to their effect on the quality of the received real-time content. They are typically measured in only one direction, unlike response time. With data traffic, delay contributes directly to response time. In a voice conversation, excessive delay can force a style of communication where one side talks and the other only listens until the roles are explicitly reversed. Jitter is the experienced variation in delay. Digital voice circuits use dejitter buffers to change this random variable delay to a more tolerable fixed delay. Excessive jitter can lead to gaps in the signal stream as traffic is delayed and the dejitter buffer empties or lost conversation if traffic bursts and overflows the dejitter buffer. Streaming video has the same sensitivities and far larger data streams.

Table 6-2 demonstrates that different types of applications feature different levels of tolerance for slow response times.

Table 6-2 *Application Types and Response Times*

	Data File Transfers	Data Interactive	Real-Time Voice	Real-Time Video
Response Time	Lower response times acceptable	Medium response times acceptable	100 ms of delay and low jitter	Minimum possible delay and jitter

The components of delay can be fixed or variable. For a given path through a network, the fixed costs include distance latency, serialization delay, and switching delay. Queuing delays at intermediate devices are the source of delay variation. The dejitter buffers at the edge of the network fix the variable delay. In a connectionless packet network, changes in the path through the network can also change the delay experienced during an exchange. A reasonable estimate for distance latency is 6 ms per 1000 km or 10 ms per 1000 miles. For planning a delay budget, you can expect each switch in the path to add 10 ms to the experienced one-way delay for switching and serialization. Both estimates are intentionally a bit high to allow for the unexpected.

Throughput

Another key factor regarding application considerations is throughput. Of course, *throughput* is the amount of data transferred in a portion of the network during a specific time interval. Again, different applications place different throughput demands on the network. For example, data-file transfer applications force the need for higher throughput even though response-time requirements are lesser. Obviously, network designers and implementers need to schedule the heavy use of throughput-intensive applications for periods of time when the network is not also using response-time–sensitive applications to a high degree.

If an application requires more throughput than a WAN design can deliver, packet loss can result. This packet loss is due to the filling of queues within the devices that attach to the media. Another source of packet loss is the discard of packets damaged in transit by media and signal-path device errors. Damaged packets are typically discarded as discovered. In the telecommunications networking world, this loss is measured as bit-error rate (BER). The BER is the percentage of bits that have errors relative to the total number of bits received. Designers usually express BER as 10 to a negative power. For example, a BER of 10 to the minus 6 indicates 1 bit out of 1,000,000 was transmitted in error. Obviously, high BER measurements for a WAN are a bad sign. One potential solution in such a situation is to slow the transmission rate of data over the WAN, thus reducing the throughput the WAN network can support. Table 6-3 details the throughput requirements for a single instance of typical application categories.

Table 6-3 *Application Types and Throughput*

	Data File Transfers	Data Interactive	Real-Time Voice	Real-Time Video
Throughput	High throughput required	Low throughput	Low throughput	High to medium throughput required

Reliability

Reliability for applications in the network is a measure of how often the application is available when network users attempt to access it. Designers refer to the amount of time an application is unavailable in the network as downtime. Obviously, the less downtime for an application, the better, but some mission-critical applications must offer the highest possible reliability ratings. A common reference to this level of reliability is five 9s. It indicates the application is available 99.999 percent of the time. Designers should consider redundancy in the WAN design when they must support these applications. Redundant WAN designs are a topic of Chapter 7. Designers should also analyze and determine the costs associated with an organization for downtime in an application. Doing so allows an organization to accurately measure the costs that are justifiable for WAN implementations. Table 6-4 details reliability requirements over different application categories. Designers should realize that the table is irrelevant when considering mission-critical applications; they all require the highest availability ratings possible.

Table 6-4 *Application Types and Reliability*

	Data File Transfers	Data Interactive	Real-Time Voice	Real-Time Video
Reliability	Lower requirements	High	Low	Low

What makes designing a WAN to support application traffic such a difficult job for designers is that network users are looking for the best possible response times, yet WAN designers are looking for an effective use of the available bandwidth for a link. Designers want to see the investment in the WAN connectivity pay off for the organization. This payoff means that network users use the WAN link to a high percentage. Obviously, these goals often collide. Too high a link utilization can cause data response times to suffer due to the retransmission of dropped packets and the quality of interactive voice and video to fall dramatically.

Remember, Cisco recommends 50 percent average link utilization as a "sweet spot." This level justifies the purchase of WAN bandwidth while also producing adequate response times for network users. A 50 percent link utilization allows increases in usage during more active times to reach 60 percent, still an acceptable value. Cisco states that 75 percent link utilization typically signals the need for an immediate WAN link upgrade.

Technical Factors

By far, the biggest technical factor when a designer focuses on the WAN is bandwidth. Table 6-5 presents typical bandwidths possible given the use of particular technologies.

Table 6-5   *Typical Bandwidths*

Technology	Media Type	Bandwidth Range
Analog modem dial-up	Copper	48 Kbps
ISDN	Copper	Less than 2 Mbps
X.25	Copper	Less than 2 Mbps
Frame Relay	Copper	Less than 2 Mbps
Switched Multimegabit Data Service (SMDS)	Fiber	Up to 44.736 Mbps
ATM	Fiber	Up to 1 Gbps
DSL	Copper	8 Mbps downstream
LRE	Copper	Up to 15 Mbps
Cable	Coaxial	27 Mbps downstream; 2.5 Mbps upstream
Wireless	Wireless	p2m—up to 22 Mbps downstream; 18 Mbps upstream p2p—up to 44 Mbps

Bandwidth requirements are directly proportional to the amount of data users must transmit on the network. It does vary with the complexity of the data. Electronic images, sound files, and other multimedia-based data files require more bandwidth than the transmission of standard text files, for example.

Obviously, designers face fewer challenges in the LAN design regarding bandwidth. With new advances in Ethernet technologies, including Ethernet switching, data transfers can take place at what Cisco and others call "wire speeds"—meaning the full bandwidth capacity of the Ethernet channels. It can be up to 10 Gbps and even greater! In WAN designs, Table 6-5 places much greater constraints on the bandwidths possible.

Cost Factors

As this chapter and others have already mentioned, costs are a major factor for WAN designers to consider. In fact, a refresher in a college-level accounting class could come in handy. Designers should note fixed costs and recurring variable costs in most WAN designs. Fixed costs include the following:

- **Equipment purchases**—Includes modems, channel service units and data service units (CSU and DSUs), routers and router interfaces, distribution layer switches and modules
- **Circuit-provisioning**—Includes charges for establishing virtual circuits through the provider WAN
- **Network-management tools and platforms**—Includes monitoring and management applications such as CiscoWorks or OpenView

Recurring and often variable costs include the monthly circuit fees from service providers and WAN support and maintenance costs. They might even include any network-management center personnel. As you might guess, these costs tend to vary with the utilization levels of the WAN options.

Remember, from an ownership perspective of the WAN design, the three broad categories are private, leased, and shared.

Privately Owned WAN Designs

If only all WAN designers had unlimited budgets from which to draw. These designers could recommend solutions that incorporate fully private-owned systems and reap immediate performance and security benefits. With privately owned WAN designs, organizations would purchase all the physical layer media (copper, fiber, wireless, coaxial) and the terminal equipment that connects it. Obviously, most organizations find this arrangement cost-prohibitive—most organizations would not possess the expertise and manpower to maintain such a design to begin with.

Leased WAN Designs

Leased WAN arrangements involve dedicated bandwidth leased to the organization by a service provider. The organization leases the terminal equipment involved in the WAN connectivity, or it purchases the equipment for private ownership. Because the organization must pay for the dedicated level of bandwidth (whether this bandwidth is actually used or not), costs tend to be higher with leased connections.

Shared WAN Designs

Shared WAN approaches tend to be the most economical for organizations. Under this arrangement, many companies share the bandwidth that the provider has available. Obviously, organizations must make some sacrifices in the areas of performance and security with this arrangement. It is up to the designer to ensure that these sacrifices do not outweigh the cost savings. As this book detailed in Chapter 5, "Wide-Area Networking Technologies," many technologies such as cell or packet switching can ensure that "private" connections persist through the shared WAN media.

WAN Performance Options

Cisco Systems builds many options for improving the performance of a WAN design right into the WAN equipment. This improvement is possible thanks to the intelligence built into the operating systems that power the network equipment. Any network designer should be familiar with the options for improving WAN link performance included in the operating-system features. Although the feature set varies from operating system to operating system, you must have a thorough understanding of all mechanisms.

Data Compression

The job of *data compression* is to reduce the size of data before transmitting it over the WAN connection. This compression conserves WAN bandwidth at the costs of increased delay and greater terminal equipment costs for software feature sets and optional hardware accelerators. Cisco IOS Software can compress the entire packet before transmission or compress the header or the payload. Cisco IOS Software supports many options for data compression, including the following technologies described here.

FRF.9 Frame Relay Payload Compression

FRF.9 Frame Relay payload compression defines data compression over Frame Relay using the Data Compression Protocol (DCP). The compression operates with both switched virtual circuits (SVCs) and permanent virtual circuits (PVCs). Network equipment negotiates the compression usage at the time the Frame Relay data-link connection identifier (DLCI) initiates. The Frame Relay network transports the compressed payload through the WAN and decompresses the data at its termination point. Thus, FRF.9 is point-to-point or end-to-end technology.

LAPB Payload Compression Using LZS

Designers often refer to this compression as simply Storage Allocation and Coding Program (STAC). In fact, STAC Incorporated developed and marketed this data-compression standard for WAN connections—especially Point-to-Point Protocol (PPP) connections. Many Cisco routers support the method, including most ISDN-capable routers.

HDLC Using LZS

High-Level Data Link Control (HDLC) WAN encapsulations combine with LZS compression technologies.

X.25 Payload Compression of Encapsulated Traffic

Many Cisco routers support payload compression for X.25. Unlike link compression, only the packet's payload (and not its header) receives compression by the equipment.

PPP Using LZS, Predictor

The Predictor compression algorithm tries to predict the next sequence of characters in a data stream by using an index to look up a sequence in the compression dictionary. It then examines the next sequence in the data stream to see whether it matches. If it does, that sequence replaces the looked-up sequence in the dictionary. If there is no match, the algorithm locates the next character sequence in the index, and the process begins again. The index updates itself by hashing a few of the most recent character sequences from the input stream.

Van Jacobson Header Compression for TCP/IP

Van Jacobson TCP/IP header compression reduces the size of the TCP/IP headers to as few as three bytes. It can make a significant improvement on slow serial lines, particularly for interactive traffic. This compression uses the IP-Compression-Protocol configuration option to indicate the ability to receive compressed packets. Each end of the link must separately request this option if bidirectional compression is the desired effect.

MPPC

MPPC is a scheme used to compress PPP packets between Cisco and Microsoft client devices. The companies designed the MPPC algorithm to optimize bandwidth utilization to support multiple simultaneous connections. The MPPC algorithm uses a Lempel-Ziv (LZ) algorithm with a continuous history buffer (dictionary).

Designers often view compression as a "magic pill" that should be immediately prescribed for WAN designs. This belief could not be further from the truth. It is often inappropriate for WAN devices. For example, Cisco recommends that designers avoid compression usage if network-equipment CPU utilization levels are at 65 percent or greater.

Window Size

Another WAN performance factor is TCP window size. The term *window size* refers to the amount of data a device sends on the network before requiring the receipt of an acknowledgment. Acknowledgments occur in reliable protocols to indicate the data actually reached its destination. TCP relies upon these acknowledgments and a window size to ensure the proper end-to-end delivery of data packets.

Designers define window size using frames or bytes depending upon the protocol in question. TCP uses bytes as the window-size measurement.

Window size can have a large impact on WAN performance. For example, if the TCP window size is 8192 bytes, a sending station must stop sending data at this amount if there is no acknowledgment received from the destination. This situation is particularly troubling in WAN environments where there might be long propagation delays due to distance and subsequent long waits for acknowledgment packets. The greater the link bandwidth, the greater the potential problem.

One simple solution to the problem is a simple enlargement of the window size. Designers must approach this solution with caution, however, because sending large amounts of unacknowledged data might result in the retransmission of large amounts of data across the WAN. This retransmission could have more of an adverse effect on bandwidth than the lost time waiting for acknowledgments. Ideal solutions involve network equipment that can adjust window sizes dynamically as WAN line conditions dictate. TCP takes acknowledgment failure as a sign of network congestion and throttles back the data rate.

Queuing Services

Queuing services give network designers a large degree of control in creating a network that meets the demands and requirements of particular applications. Designers do not require queuing services within WAN designs, however, if links are never congested. Moreover, if WAN links consistently demonstrate congestion, queuing is not the answer; an upgrade is more appropriate.

The two types of queues are as follows:

- **Hardware queues**—Use a simple FIFO strategy. Interfaces require this strategy to successfully transmit packets one by one. Designers often refer to the hardware queue as the transmit queue or TxQ.

- **Software queue**—Offers the ability to schedule packets into the hardware queue. Quality of service (QoS) mechanisms can control such scheduling. The CCDA candidate needs to be familiar with three such QoS mechanisms:

    — **Weighted fair queuing (WFQ)**—Addresses a major problem with hardware-based FIFO "scheduling" methods and strict priority methods. The problem is that high-volume senders can "crowd out" low-volume senders. WFQ arranges traffic flows into "conversation sessions" and alternates between such sessions. WFQ biases the queue service to favor smaller traffic flows to ensure that large flows do not monopolize the available bandwidth. WFQ is the default configuration on Cisco interfaces operating at or below 2.048 Mbps. Faster links default to FIFO.

    — **Priority Queuing (PQ)**—Allows designers to give higher priority to certain types of time-sensitive or mission-critical protocols. PQ establishes four interface output queues. The designer assigns each queue a priority and defines traffic types for each queue. PQ then services all traffic in higher-priority queues prior to servicing the lower-priority queues. Obviously, this method ensures that certain traffic types receive absolute priority for forwarding. It risks "starvation" of lower-priority traffic types.

— **Custom Queuing (CQ)**—Establishes up to 16 interface output queues. Here, the designer assigns type, traffic, and size to each of the custom queues. CQ cycles through each queue to send all data, sending the amount from each queue specified by the designer. This approach is a fairer solution in that all traffic types receive some level of service, yet certain traffic types are still prioritized. Custom queuing was developed to address problems with strict priority queuing.

NOTE   Although the CCDA candidate should be well-versed on the queuing technologies in this chapter, there are many other forms of queuing available today, such as low-latency queuing, distributed low-latency queuing, and class-based WFQ.

Traffic Shaping and Policing

Traffic shaping and traffic policing are similar WAN performance options. Both are commonly referred to as committed access rate (CAR). Both inspect traffic and then take action based on traffic characteristics. Traffic shaping delays excess packets by holding them in buffers and then releasing them at preconfigured rates. Traffic policing, on the other hand, typically drops excess traffic or at least modifies them in some way (for example, manipulating IP precedence).

Several methods identify traffic based upon characteristics. For example, policing and shaping can use rate thresholds or header bits (Differentiated Services Control Point [DSCP] or IP precedence) to determine how to affect traffic.

Foundation Summary

The "Foundation Summary" section of each chapter lists the most important facts from the chapter. Although this section does not list every fact from the chapter that will be on your CCDA exam, a well-prepared CCDA candidate should at a minimum know all the details in each "Foundation Summary" before going to take the exam.

Cisco recommends that designers engage in the analysis of customer requirements, the characterization of the existing network, and the design of the new WAN topology as a simple process for designing WAN solutions. Common design factors include application access, technology factors, and cost factors. WAN ownership options include private ownership, leased ownership, or shared ownership.

Designers should also be aware of WAN performance options available with Cisco equipment. These options include compression for bandwidth conservation; TCP window size for increased link utilization; and various congestion management and avoidance mechanisms, including queue service disciplines, traffic shaping, and policing. Compression options include the following:

- FRF.9 Frame Relay payload compression
- LAPB payload compression using LZS
- HDLC using LZS
- X.25 payload compression of encapsulated traffic
- PPP using LZS, Predictor
- Van Jacobson header compression for TCP/IP
- MPPC

Queuing service options include the following:

- FIFO
- WFQ
- PQ
- CQ
- Low-latency queuing
- Class-based WFQ

Congestion management options include the following:

- Traffic shaping
- Traffic policing

Remember, network designs should carefully use these WAN performance options. Queuing, compression, and congestion-management services are all appropriate when network conditions dictate their use. Do not consider these performance options at all when bandwidth or usage levels do not require such services.

Q&A

As mentioned in the introduction, you have two choices for review questions. Some of the questions that follow give you a bigger challenge than the exam itself by using a short-answer question format. By reviewing now with more difficult question format, you can exercise your memory better and prove your conceptual and factual knowledge of this chapter. The answers to these questions appear in Appendix A.

For more practice with exam-like question formats, use the exam engine on the CD-ROM.

1. Describe the Cisco recommended process for designing a WAN solution.

2. Name three common design factors for creating WAN solutions.

3. Describe the options for WAN media and equipment ownership.

4. Match each of the following queuing options with the appropriate definition:

   a. WFQ

   b. PQ

   c. CQ

   i. A queuing method that establishes four interface output queues and allows the designer to assign each queue a priority.

   ii. A queuing methodology that prohibits high-volume senders from "crowding out" low-volume senders.

   iii. A queuing method that establishes up to 16 interface output queues; CQ cycles through each queue to send data.

5. Match each of the following compression technologies with the appropriate definition:

   a. LZS

   b. Predictor

   c. Van Jacobson header compression

   d. MPPC

   e. FRF.9

   i. TCP/IP compression that reduces the size of the TCP/IP headers to as few as three bytes.

   ii. A scheme used to compress PPP packets between Cisco and Microsoft client devices.

   iii. Defines data compression over Frame Relay using the DCP.

   iv. A compression algorithm that tries to guess the next sequence of characters in a data stream by using an index to look up a sequence in the compression dictionary.

   v. Compression standard for WAN connections also known as STAC.

6. Of the ownership options for WAN media and equipment, which option provides companies with the highest level of control and predictability?

7. Match the WAN access technology option with the appropriate available bandwidth value:

a.	Analog modem	i.	Less than 2 Mbps
b.	DSL	ii.	48 Kbps
c.	Cable	iii.	8 Mbps downstream
d.	Frame Relay	iv.	27 Mbps downstream; 2.5 Mbps upstream

This chapter covers the following subjects:

- WAN Backup Design Options

- Sample WAN Designs

CHAPTER 7

Backup Options and Sample WAN Designs

This chapter presents many sample WAN designs covering everything from dedicated, point-to-point connections to shared, switched connections. This chapter also details the various options for redundant WAN designs. Redundancy in the design ensures the network is consistently capable of transferring mission-critical data throughout the entire network.

"Do I Know This Already?" Quiz

The purpose of the "Do I Know This Already?" quiz is to help you decide whether you need to read the entire chapter. If you intend to read the entire chapter, you do not necessarily need to answer these questions now.

The 10-question quiz, derived from the major sections in the "Foundation Topics" portion of the chapter, helps you determine how to spend your limited study time.

Table 7-1 outlines the major topics discussed in this chapter and the "Do I Know This Already?" quiz questions that correspond to those topics.

Table 7-1 *"Do I Know This Already?" Foundation Topics Section-to-Question Mapping*

Foundation Topics Section	Questions Covered in This Section
WAN Backup Design Options	1, 2, 3, 4
Sample WAN Designs	5, 6, 7, 8, 9, 10

CAUTION The goal of self assessment is to gauge your mastery of the topics in this chapter. If you do not know the answer to a question or you are only partially sure of the answer, you should mark this question wrong for purposes of the self assessment. Giving yourself credit for an answer you correctly guess skews your self-assessment results and might provide you with a false sense of security.

1. What Cisco router configuration component does an implementer use to create a floating static route?

   a. Description

   b. Administrative distance

   c. Primary interface

   d. Loopback

2. Which WAN backup methodology fits the following description? A service provider provisions the network with a secondary permanent virtual circuit (PVC); typically, there is no charge for this additional PVC as long as the load on it remains below a defined level.

   a. Dial backup

   b. Backup PVC

   c. Shadow PVC

   d. Internet

3. Which of the following is not a valid option for using the public Internet as a backup WAN medium?

   a. Generic Routing Encapsulation (GRE) tunnels

   b. IP Security (IPSec) tunnels

   c. Shared PVC

   d. IP routing without constraints

4. Which tunneling technology features the authentication of packets and antireplay attack mechanisms?

   a. GRE

   b. IPSec

   c. Shadow PVC

   d. Dial backup

5. Which packet-switched topology provides simplified and centralized management of the WAN topology as well as minimized tariff costs with service providers?

   a. Partial mesh

   b. Full mesh

   c. Point-to-point

   d. Star

6. Which packet-switched topology approach features virtual circuits that connect many but not all the routers in the topology?

   a. Partial mesh

   b. Full mesh

   c. Point-to-point

   d. Star

7. Which packet-switching topology approach features the best possible redundancy and the best possible performance when configured correctly?

   a. Partial mesh

   b. Full mesh

   c. Point-to-point

   d. Star

8. Which packet-switching topology approach typically requires the greatest level of expertise to implement?

   a. Partial mesh

   b. Hub and spoke

   c. Point-to-point

   d. Star

9. Which of the following is not a true disadvantage of the full-mesh topology?

   a. High level of complexity to implement.

   b. Large number of packet replications required.

   c. Central hub router represents a single point of failure in the network.

   d. High costs due to number of virtual circuits.

10. Which of the packet-switched topologies features the easiest implementation and management?

    a. Star

    b. Partial mesh

    c. Full mesh

    d. Point-to-point

The answers to the "Do I Know This Already?" quiz appear in Appendix A, "Answers to Chapter "Do I Know This Already?" Quizzes and Q&A Sections. The suggested choices for your next step are as follows:

- **8 or less overall score**—Read the entire chapter. It includes the "Foundation Topics," "Foundation Summary," and "Q&A" sections.

- **9–10 overall score**—If you want more review on these topics, skip to the "Foundation Summary" section and then go to the "Q&A" section. Otherwise, move to the next chapter.

Foundation Topics

This chapter explores the options for backing up primary WAN connections. This task is critical in ensuring that end users of the network enjoy consistent access to remote network resources. This chapter also examines sample WAN designs and discusses the strengths and weaknesses regarding particular approaches.

WAN Backup Design Options

CCDAs must often design WAN areas in corporate networks that feature high network availability with no single point of failure. In these networks, the failure of a WAN link cannot partition the network, isolating one or more sites. Mission-critical data must reach remote destinations regardless of media or hardware issues.

Dial Backup Routing

Chapter 5, "Wide-Area Networking Technologies," mentioned that dial-up WAN technologies continue to see use today not only for small office/home office (SOHO) WAN connectivity, but also for backup purposes. In fact, this role of backup should ensure that dial-up technologies maintain a place in new network designs for years to come.

Using dial backup, a network designer can ensure connectivity between sites (for example) even in the event of the failure of the main circuit. This main circuit can be a point-to-point leased line or a packet-switched WAN virtual circuit such as Frame Relay.

Network implementers can configure routers to monitor the main circuit. If there is a failure, the backup line initializes and provides WAN connectivity. Implementers can also control when the backup dial-up connection terminates, either immediately upon restoration of the main link or after a period of time has elapsed.

Figure 7-1 details a sample topology that features a dial-up backup to the main Frame Relay WAN connectivity link. The text description that follows also refers to this figure.

Figure 7-1 *Dial Backup Example*

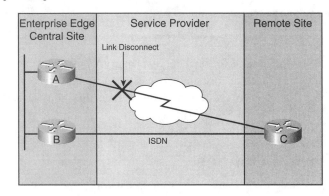

Figure 7-1 is a common example of the use of dial backup. Notice the design uses Frame Relay from Router A in the Enterprise Edge to Router C at a branch-office remote site. The network design relies upon Frame Relay in this example due to the amount of bandwidth required and the costs. If the Frame Relay connection experiences a disconnect, the WAN design still provides connectivity due to an ISDN connection established from Router C to Router B. The following steps provide an example of how this dial backup solution operates:

Step 1   There is a failure of the Frame Relay WAN connection between Routers A and C. The routers use neighbor loss detection to learn of the failure. You should note that often in failures such as this both interfaces might remain in the up state.

Step 2   Router C features an interface configured for backup purposes. This device is notified of the circuit failure by the Frame Relay network or detects loss of connectivity with the transport network.

Step 3   The router selects the configured backup ISDN interface to establish a connection with Router B.

Step 4   The routing protocol specified in the design and configured throughout the management domain or autonomous system recalculates the paths to route traffic in the network.

Step 5   When the provider re-establishes the Frame Relay connection, Router C ends the ISDN connection.

Permanent Secondary WAN Link

Another popular design choice is for the designer to engineer a second and permanent WAN link between sites. This design features more than just the advantage of a redundant backup: It also provides additional bandwidth.

The permanent secondary WAN link design meets the redundancy requirement head on. If the primary WAN link fails, the network uses the secondary permanent link to transmit data. Often, the secondary link is already in use by the network for load sharing. Floating static routes and routing protocols ensure that the link is actually a valid path though the network in the event of a failure.

Another advantage to this redundant design is the increase in bandwidth that can result if the network relies upon the secondary link to carry traffic as well. Load balancing can occur on a per-destination or per-packet basis. If the secondary link is considerably slower, per-packet load balancing is appropriate. If the link is as fast, fast switching can occur with per-destination balancing.

This design methodology is not without its disadvantages, however. The cost of this design is often prohibitive for organizations. This design might also require more robust networking equipment and expertise. For larger networks with many remote offices that the designer must connect with central sites, providing a permanent backup connection for every main link is not financially practical.

Shadow PVC

A WAN backup option that is similar to a permanent secondary WAN link is a shadow PVC. Under the shadow PVC design, a service provider provisions the network with a secondary PVC. It is possible that a service provider will not charge for this additional circuit as long as the load on it remains below a defined level. For example, a plan might specify the shadow PVC at no additional charge if load does not exceed one-fourth of the load on the primary PVC—provided, of course, the primary link is available.

Obviously, much expertise is required when configuring a shadow PVC. The implementer must ensure the load on the secondary virtual circuit is kept to a minimum. You use either floating routes to load only the primary link or some form of policy routing to ensure that only routing-protocol messages and other critical, yet low-volume, traffic routinely uses the shadow circuit.

Internet

Another option for WAN backup is to rely upon the public Internet as a means to transfer data between network locations. Obviously, this arrangement is "best effort," there are no bandwidth guarantees, and security is a significant concern.

Although there are many options for implementing the Internet as a backup option, the CCDA candidate should be aware of three:

■ IP routing without constraints

■ GRE tunnels

■ IPSec tunnels

Some organizations, especially larger ones, work with their service providers to advertise their networks in the Internet. This arrangement enables them to route traffic freely via the Internet. Without payload encryption at the enterprise sites, this method has significant security issues.

Both GRE and IPSec methodologies rely upon tunneling to transmit data over the public Internet. Network-layer tunneling involves one Layer 3 protocol transporting another Layer 3 protocol over the network—usually in a secure fashion.

GRE, a network-layer encapsulation defined by the Internet Engineering Task Force (IETF) RFC 2784, tunnels protocols over IP networks, including the Internet. Specifically, Cisco routers can use GRE to tunnel IP over other IP networks. This setup suits small- to medium-sized Internet backup solutions that do not require the greatest degree of security—or that use protocols incompatible with IPSec.

Figure 7-2 demonstrates a backup GRE tunnel over the Internet. In this example, the primary link is Frame Relay, and a backup GRE tunnel using the Internet ensures connectivity between the central office and the remote site. The Cisco equipment creates the tunnel from a source router (ingress) to the destination router (egress), and the tunnel appears as an actual interface on each router.

Figure 7-2 *Backup GRE Tunnel*

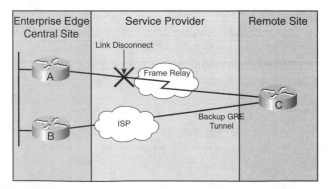

The steps that follow detail the functioning of GRE:

Step 1   The Cisco network designates packets for transmission across the backup GRE tunnel.

Step 2   These packets already contain additional information by way of encapsulation from the transmitting protocol (IP). The ingress router further encapsulates the packets with a new GRE header.

Step 3   The Cisco router places the packets into a tunnel. These packets now feature a destination address of the egress router.

Step 4   The packets arrive at the egress, and this router strips away the GRE encapsulation information.

Step 5   Network equipment forwards the packets, which now contain the original IP headers and destination address information.

IPSec also provides for tunneling IP over IP networks, yet as its name implies, this technology inherently provides security for these transfers. IPSec functions at the network layer and encapsulates and authenticates IP packets between IPSec routers.

The following list details the features and benefits of IPSec as a network solution:

■   IPSec features data confidentiality. Cisco routers encrypt packets prior to their transmission across the network. This feature is obviously a huge benefit given the Internet as a transmission medium.

■   IPSec features data integrity. IPSec receivers can authenticate packets sent from an IPSec sender. This check ensures that the data has not been altered during transmission.

■   IPSec also features data origin authentication. IPSec receivers can authenticate the source of IPSec packets. This check ensures the sending station is legitimately the sending station.

■   IPSec includes antireplay attacks. Cisco routers can detect and reject replay attempts.

■   IPSec features simple deployment for network implementers. Typically, the intermediate systems, such as the backbone Internet service provider (ISP) systems, do not require changes.

■   IPSec is completely transparent to the applications running in the network. They are not and do not need to be aware of the tunneling technology to function.

■   IPSec utilizes Internet Key Exchange (IKE) for the automation of security key management.

■   IPSec interoperates with the public-key infrastructure (PKI).

■   IPSec is compatible with GRE if necessary.

Sample WAN Designs

The remainder of this chapter focuses on sample WAN designs and the technologies used in the implementation of these designs. It also includes new information that these design examples highlight. Because the CCDA examination has candidates examine existing and proposed network designs, this section is extremely important and should not be overlooked.

WAN Technologies for Remote Access

Figure 7-3 shows a network topology in relation to the Enterprise Composite Network Model. This network needs WAN remote-access solutions to accommodate remote users of the network and small offices that do not require constant access.

Figure 7-3   *Remote Access Example*

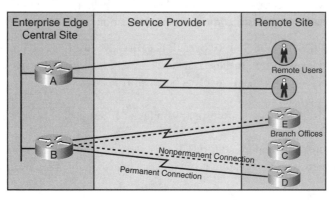

The network designer in this example has gained the following information:

■   The branch-office users should be able to access the central site network seamlessly—as if the users are in that actual network.

■   The remote users need to access the network sporadically to check for e-mail notifications and transfer reports that are typically under 200 KB in size.

■   The branch-office locations require more consistent file transfer access and interactive traffic transfers. Low to medium volume is expected.

■   Two of the branch offices often need to share data directly with each other. This data is mission-critical compared to other traffic sent by the branch offices.

■   The client has indicated no performance specifics for the network.

Given these requirements, a designer might choose permanent connections between the remote offices and the central site using Frame Relay PVCs. Nonpermanent dial-up connections are appropriate for the remote access users.

Packet-Switched Network Designs

Although the design mentioned here certainly meets the requirements put forth by the client, it must still address an important design issue. Specifically, the designer must decide upon the specific Frame Relay topology. Packet-switched networks have three basic designs. (Although Frame Relay is the focus here, note that these designs are also appropriate for other WAN technologies.) These designs are

- Star topology
- Partial-mesh topology
- Full-mesh topology

Star Topology

A star topology specifies a core router that serves as the hub for the WAN connections. Designers often refer to this topology as a hub-and-spoke topology. The core router connects to each of the branch offices; in fact, branch offices can only communicate with each other if they pass their communications through the core (hub) router. The star topology features the advantage of simplified and centralized management of the WAN topology.

Unfortunately, this design topology is not without its problems and disadvantages. These include the following:

- The central hub router represents a single point of failure in the design. If this router fails, WAN communications across all the branch offices are affected.
- Overall performance of the WAN relies upon a single point. This single point is the hub router; all traffic must pass through this potential bottleneck in the design.

Partial-Mesh Topology

The partial-mesh topology approach features virtual circuits that connect many but not all the routers in the topology. This design reduces the number of routers in the topology that require direct connections to each other. It accommodates those sites that do require connectivity directly to each other due to performance or reliability concerns. A partial-mesh design might have several "core" or hub routers that act as collection points for nonmeshed routers to reach each other. Obviously, there are many forms of partially meshed topologies.

The advantages to the partial mesh topology include

- Improved performance
- Improved redundancy
- Fewer virtual circuits than full-mesh designs

The disadvantages of a partial mesh topology include

- Potentially a greater number of virtual circuits than a star topology
- A greater level of expertise

Full-Mesh Topology

In a full-mesh design, each node (router) connects to every other node in the network design. This design features the greatest level of redundancy and performance. Obviously, this approach is nearly impossible in very large networks due to cost concerns.

The advantages of a full-mesh topology include

- Best possible redundancy
- Best possible performance when configured properly

Disadvantages include

- Large costs due to the number of virtual circuits required. There is one for every connection between routers.
- They typically require large numbers of packet and broadcast replications for transmission to all locations in the network.
- Configuring routers in full-mesh environment is quite complex—especially in environments with no multicast support.

Figure 7-4 shows an overview of the WAN design in this example. Notice the use of a partial mesh and both permanent and dial-up options.

Figure 7-4 *Remote Access Design Example*

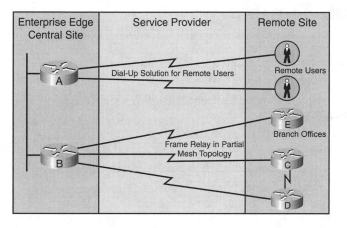

A WAN Connecting Enterprise Sites

Often, the central site might consist of two facilities that are geographically disparate. The designer must connect these two sites using WAN technology to make them appear as one seamless network. Users must be able to access the resources of each site as if they were one site. The sites transmit a high volume of traffic, and each site expects to transfer voice and video traffic to the other site.

Due to the requirements, a designer might recommend the provision of a high-speed point-to-point connection using Synchronous Optical Network (SONET) and Synchronous Digital Hierarchy (SDH). Thanks to the SONET/SDH technology, this organization can enjoy high-speed point-to-point connections of speeds at 155 Mbps or much greater, up to 10 Gbps. The costs of this technology depend almost entirely on the bandwidth required and the distance between the two sites.

Foundation Summary

The "Foundation Summary" section of each chapter lists the most important facts from the chapter. Although this section does not list every fact from the chapter that will be on your CCDA exam, a well-prepared CCDA candidate should at a minimum know all the details in each "Foundation Summary" before going to take the exam.

Remember, the CCDA exam requires that candidates analyze existing or proposed designs and answer detailed questions. This chapter helps prepare candidates for this experience by proposing sample designs and discussing key technologies.

One of the most important areas covered here is the various backup designs that exist for WANs. More networks feature mission-critical data that must be able to reach distant areas of the network. Designing backup WAN solutions helps ensure that the data is successful in reaching their destination.

The CCDA candidate should also be intimately familiar with the design options of a star, partial-mesh, and full-mesh topology. Although Frame Relay networks use them, these topologies are relevant for other WAN technologies as well.

Q&A

As mentioned in the introduction, you have two choices for review questions. Some of the questions that follow give you a bigger challenge than the exam itself by using an open-ended question format. By reviewing now with this more difficult question format, you can exercise your memory better and prove your conceptual and factual knowledge of this chapter. The answers to these questions appear in Appendix A.

For more practice with exam-like question formats, use the exam engine on the CD-ROM.

1. Explain the advantages of IPSec tunneling over GRE tunnels for a backup Internet WAN solution.

2. Match each WAN backup solution with its definition or attribute:

   a. Dial backup

   b. Shadow PVC

   c. Internet

   d. Permanent secondary link

   i. Floating static routes and routing protocols ensure the link is actually a valid path though the network in the event of a failure.

   ii. Options include full IP routing or tunneling solutions.

   iii. The network dynamically engages circuit-switched backups for primary link failures.

   iv. A service provider provisions a backup link.

3. List the advantages of a packet-switched star topology.

4. List the advantages of a packet-switched partial-mesh topology.

5. List the advantages of a packet-switched full-mesh topology.

Refer to Figure 7-5 to answer the questions that follow.

Figure 7-5 *Sample WAN Design*

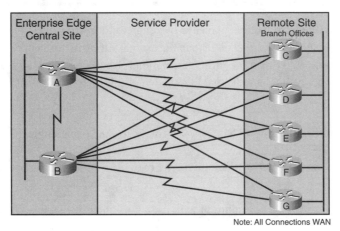

Note: All Connections WAN

6. What is the packet-switched WAN topology used in this enterprise network?

7. What are the disadvantages of this packet-switched topology?

This chapter covers the following subjects:

- DSL Technologies

- VPNs

CHAPTER 8

VPN and DSL WAN Design

This chapter reviews virtual private network (VPN) and digital subscriber line (DSL) technologies for WANs. DSL provides broadband Internet access to business and residential customers at speeds far greater than dial-up with costs less than a leased T1. Enterprise companies are increasingly using DSL coupled with VPN technology to replace their WAN links.

VPNs create private tunnels across the Internet. It uses site-to-site tunnels between offices. The IP Security (IPSec) protocol creates secure tunnels over the Internet.

"Do I Know This Already?" Quiz

The purpose of the "Do I Know This Already?" quiz is to help you decide whether you need to read the entire chapter. If you intend to read the entire chapter, you do not necessarily need to answer these questions now.

The 8-question quiz, derived from the major sections in the "Foundation Topics" portion of the chapter, helps you determine how to spend your limited study time.

Table 8-1 outlines the major topics discussed in this chapter and the "Do I Know This Already?" quiz questions that correspond to those topics.

Table 8-1 *"Do I Know This Already?" Foundation Topics Section-to-Question Mapping*

Foundation Topics Section	Questions Covered in This Section
DSL Technologies	1, 7, 8
VPNs	2, 3, 4, 5, 6

CAUTION The goal of self assessment is to gauge your mastery of the topics in this chapter. If you do not know the answer to a question or you are only partially sure of the answer, you should mark this question wrong for purposes of the self assessment. Giving yourself credit for an answer you correctly guess skews your self-assessment results and might provide you with a false sense of security.

1. What is ADSL?

   a. Asynchronous Digital Subscriber Line

   b. Asymmetric Digital Subscriber Link

   c. Asymmetric Digital Subscriber Line

   d. Asynchronous Digital System Link

2. Which two protocols are used for IP Security?

   a. Generic Routing Encapsulation (GRE) and Internetwork Packet Exchange (IPX)

   b. Authentication Header (AH) and Encapsulating Security Payload (ESP)

   c. Virtual Private Dial-Up Network (VPDN) and GRE

   d. Border Gateway Protocol (BGP) and Enhanced Interior Gateway Routing Protocol (EIGRP)

3. What is the length of the key used with Triple Data Encryption Standard (3DES)?

   a. 56 bits

   b. 64 bits

   c. 128 bits

   d. 168 bits

4. What is MPLS?

   a. Many Protocol Label Switching

   b. Multiprotocol Label Switching

   c. Maximum Path Link Switching

   d. Multipath Label Switching

5. In this ESP mode, only the data is encrypted.

   a. ESP transport mode

   b. ESP tunnel mode

   c. ESP IPSec mode

   d. ESP 3DES mode

6. Which two encryption transforms do both ESP and AH use for authentication?

   a. DES or Hash Message Authentication Code-Message Digest 5 (HMAC-MD5)

   b. HMAC-MD5 or Hash Message Authentication Code-Secure Hash Algorithm-1 (HMAC-SHA-1)

   c. DES or 3DES

   d. 3DES or MD5

7. Which DSL type is marketed as business DSL?

   a. ISDN DSL (IDSL)

   b. ADSL

   c. Symmetric DSL (SDSL)

   d. Very-high-data-rate DSL (VDSL)

8. Which DSL type does residential service use?

   a. IDSL

   b. ADSL

   c. SDSL

   d. VDSL

The answers to the "Do I Know This Already?" quiz appear in Appendix A, "Answers to Chapter 'Do I Know This Already?' Quizzes and Q&A Sections. The suggested choices for your next step are as follows:

- **6 or less overall score**—Read the entire chapter. It includes the "Foundation Topics," "Foundation Summary," and "Q&A" sections.

- **7–8 overall score**—If you want more review on these topics, skip to the "Foundation Summary" section and then go to the "Q&A" section. Otherwise, move to the next chapter.

Foundation Topics

The "Foundation Topics" cover DSL technologies and VPNs. The section "DSL Technologies" covers each of the several DSL technologies and their design characteristics. ADSL is the most popular technology for residential customers. ADSL provides fast download speeds with a slower upload speed. SDSL is the most popular DSL technology for enterprises. SDSL provides the same upload and download speeds.

The section "VPNs" covers the VPN technologies and their design characteristics. GRE is a Cisco tunneling protocol that encapsulates packets into IP headers, creating a virtual point-to-point link between two Cisco routers. Internet tunnels use the IPSec protocol to create secure tunnels over the Internet. IPSec is an internal standard that defines a set of protocols, key management, and algorithms for authentication and encryption.

DSL Technologies

This section reviews the DSL technologies that you can use for access and WANs. When used with VPN technologies, DSL can provide WAN connectivity for remote offices at a lower cost than dedicated services.

DSL increases connectivity options for fixed remote access and extranet offices and users. DSL technology uses existing twisted-pair telephone lines to transport high-bandwidth data, such as multimedia and video, to service subscribers. DSL provides high bandwidth on the existing telephone company infrastructure with dedicated, point-to-point, public network access. With DSL, the user is always connected to the service provider's network. A DSL connection is "always on," providing the specified bandwidth to the user or office. Charges for DSL are typically a fixed monthly fee. In some major markets, private DSL access is available. In this case, permanent virtual circuits (PVCs) extend the enterprise network to the DSL access device.

In North America, DSL is favorably priced based on cost for equivalent bandwidth when compared to dial-up access to a service-provider network by modem or ISDN. It also provides price advantages over leased lines, including full or fractional T1/E1, and packet network services such as Frame Relay. The disadvantages of DSL include spotty availability due to distance and infrastructure quality, lack of guaranteed transport bandwidth through the intermediate public networks, and security issues within the Internet. Where available, cable modems offer comparable service for remote access at a similar cost.

DSL Types

As DSL technology matured, service providers made available different implementations. DSL is an Open System Interconnection (OSI) model physical layer technology. The marketplace has many variations. The two leading schemes are SDSL and ADSL. The forms of DSL include the following:

- ADSL
- SDSL
- IDSL
- High-bit-rate DSL (HDSL)
- VDSL

For Internet DSL providers, the architecture looks like Figure 8-1. DSL modems with Ethernet interfaces at the home office or business location connect to the local-loop connection to the central office. DSL access multiplexers (DSLAMs) aggregate the connections. DSL terminators terminate the virtual circuits and pass the traffic on to the IP networks.

Figure 8-1 *Basic DSL Architecture*

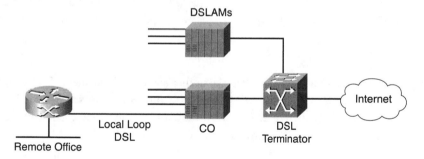

ADSL

ADSL is a DSL technology targeted for residential customers. It is defined by the American National Standards Institute (ANSI) T1.413 standard. It provides asymmetric speed with a downlink speed (from the central office to the customer) faster than the uplink speed. Downstream rates range from 256 kbps to 8 Mbps. Upstream rates range from 16 kbps to 800 kbps. ADSL transmissions work at distances up to 18,000 ft (5488 m) over a single copper twisted pair.

ADSL G.lite is a variant specification that reduces the device requirements of ADSL. It eliminates the requirement for special wiring installation services. ADSL G.lite provides rates up to 1.5 Mbps.

Another variant is Rate Adaptive ADSL (RADSL), which allows the DSL modem to adapt its speed based on the quality and length of the line.

Some examples of services are

- 384 kbps download/128 kbps uplink
- 768 kbps download/ 128 kbps uplink
- 786 kbps download/ 256 kbps uplink
- 1.5 Mbps download/128 kbps uplink
- 1.5 Mbps download/384 kbps uplink
- 6 Mbps download/384 Kbps uplink

HDSL

HDSL provides 2 Mbps of bandwidth but uses two twisted-pair lines (4 wires). The bandwidth rate is symmetrical. The HDSL range is limited to 12,000 ft (3658.5 m). Signal repeaters extend the service beyond the distance. Because it requires two pairs, HDSL is used primarily for digital-loop carrier systems, interexchange points of presence (POPs), and private data networks. A variant, HDSL-2 is a two-wire version that provides the same speeds or double the speed with four wires.

SDSL

SDSL provides equal bandwidth for both the uplink and downlink lines. SDSL is targeted to business customers to replace their more expensive T1 circuits. SDSL uses a single twisted-pair line and has an operating range limited to 22,000 ft. Because of its symmetric capabilities, SDSL is often marketed as business DSL. SDSL provides speeds up to 2.3 Mbps.

Some service examples are

- 144 kbps symmetric
- 192 kbps symmetric
- 384 kbps symmetric
- 768 kbps symmetric
- 1.1 Mbps symmetric
- 1.5 Mbps symmetric

IDSL

IDSL was developed to provide DSL service to locations using existing ISDN facilities by redirecting ISDN traffic to a DSLAM. It maintains all the electrical capabilities of ISDN, allowing for longer local-loop runs that ISDN can support. The customer premises equipment (CPE) is still any ISDN Basic Rate Interface (BRI) bridge/router. The benefit of IDSL is the cost of the service over ISDN. IDSL provides a rate of 144 kbps but uses the D channel in addition to the two B channels. The benefit of IDSL is that it provides a flat rate for the ISDN type service versus the per-call rate of ISDN.

The advantage of IDSL over ISDN is that it can provide the same data capabilities over longer local-loop facilities. Customers can save because IDSL is cheaper than ISDN. For example, a small business with an ISDN service of $0.02 per minute for ISDN B-channel usage might pay as much as $1300 a month. It can pay IDSL service on a flat-rate basis, totaling approximately $150 per month with no per-minute usage charge.

VDSL

VDSL provides asymmetric DSL services at speeds much greater than ADSL. VDSL still uses a single pair to provide up to 52 Mbps downlink speeds and up to 16 Mbps uplink speeds. Only selected areas offer VDSL, and it is limited to 5000 ft from the central office.

Cisco provides Long-Reach Ethernet (LRE) over VDSL that provides Ethernet services over existing Category 1/2/3 twisted-pair wiring at speeds from 5 to 15 Mbps (full duplex) and distances up to 5000 ft.

Table 8-1 summarizes the types of DSL and their specifications and compares to ISDN and T1/E1 service.

Table 8-2 *DSL Specification*

Service	Maximum Distance to Central Office	Max Uplink Speed	Max Downlink Speed	Notes
Full-rate ADSL	18,000 ft (5500 m)	800 kbps	8 Mbps	Asymmetrical.
ADSL G.lite	18,000 ft (5500 m)	384 kbps	1.5 Mbps	No splitter required.
RADSL	18,000 ft (5500 m)	384 kbps	8 Mbps	Rate adapts based on distance and quality.
IDSL	35,000 ft (10,070 m)	144 kbps	144 kbps	DSL over ISDN (BRI).

continues

Table 8-2   *DSL Specification (Continued)*

Service	Maximum Distance to Central Office	Max Uplink Speed	Max Downlink Speed	Notes
SDSL	22,000 ft (6700 m)	2.3 Mbps	2.3 Mbps	Targets T1 replacement. Symmetrical DSL service.
HDSL	12,000 ft (3658 m)	2 Mbps	2 Mbps	Four-wire, similar to T1 service.
HDSL-2	24,000 ft (7333 m)	2 Mbps	2 Mbps	Two-wire version of HDSL or four-wire at 2x rate.
VDSL	5000 ft (1524 m)	16 Mbps	52 Mbps	Few installations.
ISDN (BRI)	18,000 ft (5500 m)	128 kbps	128 kbps	–
T1/E1	24,000 ft (7333 m)	1.5/2.0 Mbps	1.5/2.0 Mbps	–

Because of the high bandwidth capabilities of DSL technology and its reduced cost, it has become a preferred access technology for enterprises to connect remote offices. Even with DSL's spotty presence, it is being used with VPN technologies to connect remote offices to corporate locations. Such setups require VPNs to secure the traffic streams as they traverse the public, untrusted Internet.

VPNs

This section reviews the technologies for VPNs and the design of WANs using VPNs as primary or backup transport.

Enterprise customers should consider the Internet, with the use of VPN technology, as a means to connect corporate locations when bandwidth guarantees are not required to support critical traffic and as an affordable backup for dedicated circuits. VPNs create private tunnels across the Internet. You can create these tunnels from a single host to a VPN concentrator, or you can create site-to-site tunnels between offices. Figure 8-2 shows VPN tunnels between remote sites and the corporate office.

Figure 8-2   *VPN Tunnels*

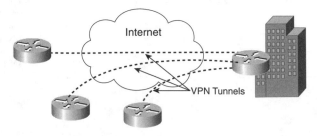

You can use several different technologies to create VPN tunnels:

- GRE
- Point-to-Point Tunneling Protocol (PPTP)
- Microsoft Point-to-Point Encryption (MPPE)
- VPDN
- IPSec
- MPLS

GRE

GRE is a Cisco tunneling protocol that encapsulates entire packets into new IP headers, creating a virtual point-to-point link between two Cisco routers. The new header has the source and destination addresses of the tunnel end points. The virtual link crosses an IP network. GRE is described in RFC 1701; it was created to tunnel IP and other packet types. Encapsulated packets types can be IP packets or non-IP packets, such as Novell IPX or AppleTalk packets.

PPTP

PPTP is described in RFC 2637. It is a network protocol developed by a vendor consortium including Microsoft for transferring data from client PCs to enterprise servers using tunneled PPP through an IP network. PPTP client software is deployed in Windows 95, ME, NT, 2000, and XP. Cisco added support for PPTP to Cisco IOS routers, PIX Firewalls, and VPN concentrators.

MPPE

MPPE is a Microsoft protocol that converts PPP packets into an encrypted form. It is used for creating VPNs over dial-up networks. Most Cisco access platforms support MPPE, which is part of Microsoft's PPTP client VPN solution.

VPDN

VPDN is a Cisco protocol that allows a private dial-in service to span across several remote-access servers (RAS). A VPDN is a network that extends remote access to a private network using a shared infrastructure. VPDNs use Layer 2 tunnel technologies (Layer 2 Forwarding Protocol (L2F), Layer 2 Tunnel Protocol (L2TP), and PPTP) to extend the Layer 2 and higher parts of the network connection from a remote user across an Internet service provider (ISP) network to a private network. VPDNs are a cost-effective method of establishing a long-distance, point-to-point connection between remote-dial users and a private network.

Instead of making connections directly to the network by using Public Switched Telephone Network (PSTN) toll services, access VPDN users need to use only the PSTN to connect to the ISP RAS acting as a local POP. The ISP then forwards the user's PPP session to a tunnel server at the customer network. Forwarding calls through the network as opposed to making a long-distance PSTN call provides dramatic cost savings.

With VPDN, a client dials into a network access server, which forwards the PPP session to a L2F home gateway (HGW) for authentication, as shown in Figure 8-3. The HGW is not collocated with the dialed RAS.

Figure 8-3   *VPDN Tunnel*

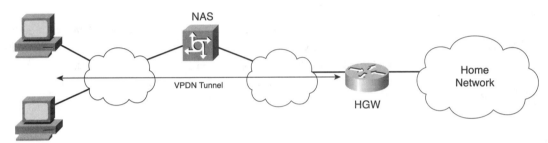

IPSec

IPSec provides a set of security services at the IP layer. The security architecture for IP is defined in RFC 2401. It is an architecture that IPv4 and IPv6 can use. IPSec is a set of protocols, key management, and algorithms for authentication and encryption. Two central protocols for IPSec are

- IP AH
- ESP

IP AH provides data-connection integrity and data-origin authentication for connectionless IP communications. You can use AH alone or with ESP. AH is described in RFC 2402. ESP provides data confidentiality, data-origin authentication, and limited traffic-flow confidentiality. Data confidentiality is just another way to say data encryption. ESP is described in RFC 2406.

IPSec uses the Internet Key Exchange (IKE) protocol for the automatic exchange of keys to form security associations (SA) between two systems. IKE is not used if the SAs are configured manually. IKE eliminates the need to manually specify all of the IPSec SA parameters of both peers and allows encryption keys to change during IPSec sessions. IKE is described in RFC 2409.

Finally, the ESP protocol uses encryption algorithms such as DES and 3DES for bulk encryption and for data confidentiality during IKE key exchange.

IPSec Connection Steps

IPSec operation follows five steps:

- Step 1: Process initiation
- Step 2: IKE Phase 1
- Step 3: IKE Phase 2
- Step 4: Data transfer
- Step 5: Tunnel termination

Process initiation is simply the specification of the type of traffic to be encrypted. You accomplish this step by configuring access lists. IKE Phase 1 authenticates the IPSec peers and sets up a secure channel between the peers to enable IKE exchanges.

After the IKE SA is established, the IKE process negotiates the IPSec SA in IKE Phase 2. When Step 3 is completed, data transfer occurs. The payload of data packets is encrypted using ESP. The tunnel is terminated if the IPSec SA are deleted or their lifetimes expire.

AH

AH provides connectionless integrity (data integrity) for packet headers and data payload and authentication but does not provide confidentiality. Authentication comes from applying a one-way hash function to the packet to create a message digest. As shown in Figure 8-4, the shared keyed hash is applied to both the IP header and packet. The hash creates an authentication header. The receiving IPSec peer applies the same key hash and extracts the transmitted hash from the AH header. If the hashes match, the authentication passes.

Figure 8-4 *Authentication Header Hash*

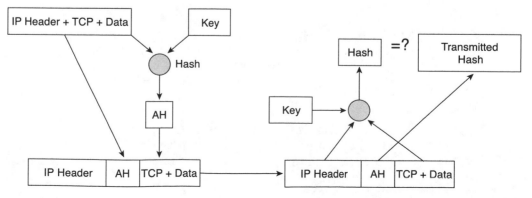

One note with AH is that not all the IP header fields are used to hash the IP header. The fields that change are not part of the hash process. One of these fields is the Time-To-Live (TTL) field, which changes at each router hop.

ESP

ESP provides confidentiality, data-origin authentication, connectionless integrity, an antireplay service (a form of partial sequence integrity), and limited traffic-flow confidentiality as negotiated by the end points when they establish an SA. ESP packet authentication is provided by an optional field. Authentication is performed after encryption is performed. ESP performs encryption by using 56-bit DES and 3DES.

ESP Tunnel or Transport Mode

ESP provides protection of the IP header fields only in tunnel mode. In tunnel mode, the original IP header and payload are encrypted. As shown in Figure 8-5, ESP prepends a new IP header and IPSec header to the encrypted IP header and data. This method provides protection at the IP layer.

Figure 8-5   *ESP Tunnel Mode*

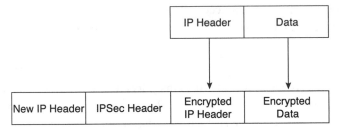

In transport mode, only the IP data is encrypted. As shown in Figure 8-6, ESP inserts an IPSec header between the original IP header and the encrypted data. Only the upper layers are protected in transport mode; it does not protect the IP layer.

Figure 8-6   *ESP Transport Mode*

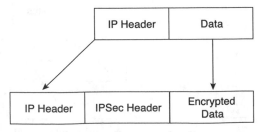

DES and 3DES

DES is an older U.S. Government-approved standard widely used for encryption. DES uses a 56-bit key to scramble and unscramble messages. Exported DES uses a 40-bit bit version. DES breaks data into 64-bit blocks and then processes it with a 56-bit shared secret key.

The latest DES standard uses a 3-by-56 bit key (a 168-bit key called Triple DES), where the input is encrypted three times. 3DES operates like DES in that data is broken into 64-bit blocks. 3DES then processes each block three times, each time with an independent key.

The two IPSec peers must first exchange their shared secret key, which can encrypt and decrypt the message or generate and verify a message authentication code. After the two IPSec peers obtain their shared keys, they can use DES or 3DES for data encryption.

HMACs

Both AH and ESP use HMACs to ensure data integrity and authentication. HMACs use hash functions and private keys to perform message authentication. IPSec specifies the use of HMAC-MD5 and HMAC-SHA-1 for IKE and IPSec.

MD5 is a hash algorithm used to authenticate packet data. MD5 uses a 128-bit key to perform a hash function to produce a 128-bit authentication value of the input data. The message digest serves as a signature of the data. The signature is inserted into the AH or ESP headers. The receiving IPSec peer computes the authentication value of the received packet and compares it to the value stored in the received packet.

SHA-1 is also a hash algorithm used to authenticate packet data. SHA-1 uses a 160-bit secret key to produce a 160-bit authentication value of the input data. As with MD5, the signature is inserted into the AH or ESP headers. The receiving IPSec peer computes the authentication value of the received packet and compares it to the value stored in the received packet.

Diffie-Hellman

Diffie-Hellman is a key-agreement algorithm used by two end devices to agree on a shared secret key. IKE uses Diffie-Hellman for key exchange during IKE Phase 1. These secret keys are then used by encryption algorithms.

Each Diffie-Hellman peer generates a public and private key pair. The public key is calculated from the private key. The private key is kept secret; the public keys are exchanged between the peers. Each peer then computes the same shared secret number by combining the other's public key and its own private key. The shared secret number is converted into a shared secret key. The shared secret key is never exchanged.

WAN Design Using IPSec Tunnels

Enterprise WANs are usually constructed using packet-switched services (Frame Relay, ATM, or MPLS) and private lines encapsulated using PPP and high-level data link control (HDLC). These circuits come at a cost of monthly recurring charges for access and PVCs. Enterprises can reduce their WAN costs by replacing these circuits with site-to-site VPN tunnels over the Internet. Point-to-point IPSec tunnels replace the permanent circuits. Access to the Internet can come from dial-up, cable-modem, or DSL technologies.

Figure 8-7 shows a private WAN that uses Frame Relay circuits. The WAN can use EIGRP as a routing protocol. The service provider makes service guarantees.

Figure 8-7   *Frame Relay WAN*

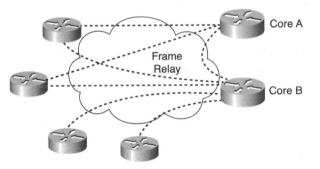

You can replace the Frame Relay WAN with VPN tunnels over the Internet. Figure 8-8 shows the network using VPN. The enterprise might choose to retain a Frame Relay PVC between the core sites with a VPN backup. All the remote sites use redundant tunnels to the core sites. To reduce costs, you can use business SDSL for access to the Internet. EIGRP is still used as a routing protocol between the enterprise routers. The disadvantage of using VPNs for the WAN is that the service guarantees are limited or nonexistent. Traffic depends on the availability of the Internet. You might get service guarantees if a single service provider can provide service to all the sites in the WAN and if it supports IP quality of service (QoS) in its transport network.

MPLS

MPLS is a transport service that can provide VPNs. An advantage of using MPLS for VPN service is the ability to offer service guarantees. Guarantees are not currently possible when using the Internet to transport VPNs.

Figure 8-8 *WAN Using VPN Tunnels*

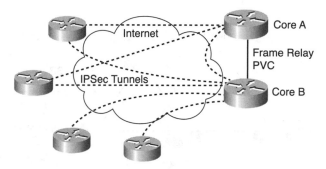

MPLS specifies ways that you can map Layer 3 traffic to connection-oriented Layer 2 transport protocols such as ATM; it adds a label containing specific routing information to each IP packet directing traffic through explicitly defined paths. It allows managers to implement policies to assign labels to various classes of traffic. This arrangement enables the service providers to offer different classes of services (CoSs) to different traffic types or from different customers. The policies could send traffic over a path that is not necessarily the path with the lowest routing metric. With MPLS, service providers can provide VPN services provisioned to give the appropriate priority to premium customers.

MPLS Label

In packet environment, the MPLS label is inserted between the Layer 2 header and the Layer 3 header of a Layer 2 frame. This setup applies for Packet over SONET (POS), Ethernet, Frame Relay, and labels over ATM. In ATM networks with label switching, the label is mapped into the virtual path identifier/virtual channel identifier (VPI/VCI) fields of the ATM header. The MPLS label field is 32 bits in length, with the actual label (tag) being 20 bits.

MPLS adds labels to the packets at the edge of the network and removes them at the other end. The labels are assigned packets based on a grouping. Each group is assigned a service class. The core of the network reads the labels and provides the appropriate services.

MPLS Label Switch Routers

All routers within a MPLS network are Label Switch Routers (LSRs), which forward based on the label and not on routing protocols. If the MPLS network uses ATM, the LSRs are called ATM LSRs. The Edge LSR is responsible for adding the label to the packet. The label is removed before the packet is sent from the MPLS network. Figure 8-9 shows a diagram of these routers.

Figure 8-9 *MPLS LSRs*

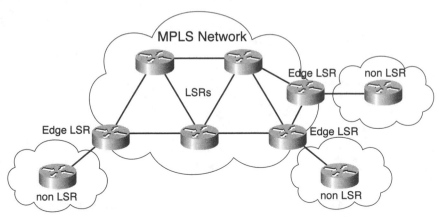

MPLS VPN Router Types

MPLS VPN architectures have four router types:

- **P router**—The service provider's internal core routers. These routers do not have to maintain VPN routes.

- **C router**—The customer's internal routers. They do not connect to the provider. These routers do not maintain VPN routes.

- **CE router**—The edge routers on the customer side that connect to the service provider. These routers do not maintain VPN routes.

- **PE router**—The edge routers on the service-provider side that connect with the customer's CE routers. PE routers maintain VPN routes for the VPNs associated with the connected interfaces.

Figure 8-10 shows a diagram of these routers in a MPLS VPN network.

WAN Design Using MPLS VPNs

One characteristic of MPLS VPNs is that each site in the VPN service is a peer. Because of the peering of all sites, a logical mesh topology is acquired.

Figure 8-11 shows a WAN topology using MPLS VPNs. Each router in the diagram is peered to the others. The service provider contracts CoSs for the enterprise. The provider benefits because it can isolate customers into security groups, provide CoSs, and scale VPN networks.

Figure 8-10 *MPLS VPN Routers*

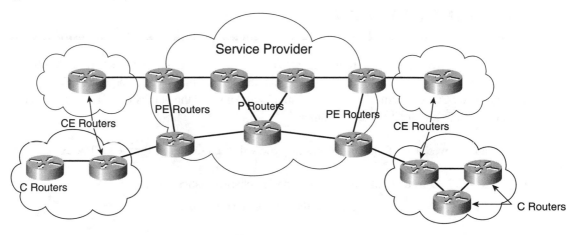

Figure 8-11 *WAN Using MPLS VPN*

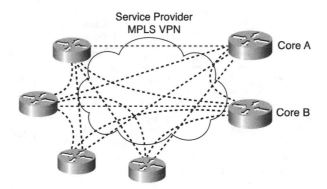

Foundation Summary

The "Foundation Summary" section of each chapter lists the most important facts from the chapter. Although this section does not list every fact from the chapter that will be on your CCDA exam, a well-prepared CCDA candidate should at a minimum know all the details in each "Foundation Summary" before going to take the exam.

This chapter covered the following topics that you will need to master for the CCDA exam:

- **DSL**—The DSL technologies and their design characteristics
- **VPNs**—The VPN technologies and their design characteristics

The tables that follow summarize both the DSL and VPN technologies. Table 8-3 summarizes the different DSL types and specifications.

Table 8-3 *DSL Specifications*

Service	Maximum Distance to Central Office	Max Uplink Speed	Max Downlink Speed	Notes
Full-rate ADSL	18,000 ft (5500 m)	800 kbps	8 Mbps	Asymmetrical.
ADSL G.lite	18,000 ft (5500 m)	384 kbps	1.5 Mbps	No splitter required.
RADSL	18,000 ft (5500 m)	384 kbps	8 Mbps	Rate adapts based on distance and quality.
IDSL	35,000 ft (10,070 m)	144 kbps	144 kbps	Similar to ISDN. DSL over ISDN (BRI).
SDSL	22,000 ft (6700 m)	2.3 Mbps	2.3 Mbps	Targets T1 replacement. Symmetrical DSL service.
HDSL	12,000 ft (3658 m)	2 Mbps	2 Mbps	Often provides T1 service (four-wire). Four-wire, similar to T1 service.
HDSL-2	24,000 ft (7333 m)	2 Mbps	2 Mbps	Two-wire version of HDSL or four-wire at 2x rate.
VDSL	5000 ft (1524 m)	16 Mbps	52 Mbps	Few installations.
ISDN (BRI)	18,000 ft (5500 m)	128 kbps	128 kbps	–
T1/E1	24,000 ft (7333 m)	1.5/2.0 Mbps	1.5/2.0 Mbps	–

Table 8-4 summarizes the different VPN technologies.

Table 8-4 *VPN Technologies*

VPN Technology	Description
GRE	Generic Routing Encapsulation. Cisco tunneling protocol. Encapsulates network-layer packets such as IP, IPX, and AppleTalk.
PPTP	Point-to-Point Tunneling Protocol. Protocol for tunneling PPP from clients used by Microsoft.
MPPE	Microsoft Point-to-Point Encryption. Microsoft protocol that encrypts PPP packets. Used to secure PPTP.
VPDN	Virtual Private Dial-Up Network. Cisco protocol that allows dial-in to span several RASs and forwards the PPP session to an HGW.
IPSec	IP Security. Defines a set of protocols, key management, and algorithms for authentication and encryption. Uses AH and ESP.
AH	Authentication Header. IPSec protocol for connection integrity and data origin. Does not provide data encryption.
ESP	Encapsulating Security Payload. Provides all the features of AH plus data encryption.
IKE	Internet Key Exchange. Eliminates the need to manually configure IPSec SA parameters.
DES	Data Encryption Standard. Uses 56-bit shared key for encryption. Used by ESP.
3DES	Triple DES. Uses 168-bit shared key for encryption. Used by ESP.
HMAC-MD5	Hash Message Authentication Code-Message Digest 5. Uses 128-bit shared key for data authentication. Used by AH or ESP.
HMAC-SHA-1	Hash Message Authentication Code-Secure Hash Algorithm-1. Uses 160-bit shared key for data authentication. Used by AH or ESP.
Diffie-Hellman	Method for generating shared secret keys by using public/private pair keys. DES and MD5 use the secret keys for encryption.
MPLS	Multiprotocol Label Switching. MPLS provides methods to perform traffic engineering, to guarantee bandwidth, and to provision VPNs.

The IPSec connection steps are

Step 1	Process initiation
Step 2	IKE Phase 1
Step 3	IKE Phase 2
Step 4	Data transfer
Step 5	Tunnel termination

Q&A

As mentioned in the introduction, you have two choices for review questions. Some of the questions that follow give you a bigger challenge than the exam itself by using an open-ended format. By reviewing now with this more difficult question format, you can exercise your memory better and prove your conceptual and factual knowledge of this chapter. The answers to these questions appear in Appendix A.

For more practice with exam-like question formats, use the exam engine on the CD-ROM.

1. True or false? ADSL provides greater upload than download speeds.

2. True or false? IPSec uses AH and ESP to provide secure IP communications.

3. True or false? Triple DES (3DES) uses a 192-bit key.

4. True or false? Data is encrypted in both ESP transport and tunnel 9 micron,mode.

5. True or false? ADSL is the preferred DSL technology for enterprise sites.

6. True or false? VDSL provides asymmetric DSL services up to 52 Mbps for the downlink.

7. True or false? GRE supports tunneling IPX and AppleTalk.

8. True or false? MPLS can provide VPNs with different CoS guarantees.

9. Which DSL type do ISDN wired sites use?

    a. IDSL

    b. ADSL

    c. SDSL

    d. VDSL

10. Which protocols do Microsoft operating systems use for secure tunneling during the transfer of data between cooperating systems?

    a. GRE and IPSec

    b. VPDN and MPLS

    c. PPTP and MPPE

    d. GRE and MPLS

11. True or false? AH does not provide data confidentiality.

12. What protocol do you use so that you do not have to manually configure IPSec associations?

13. True or False? VDSL provides symmetric service.

14. Match the DSL types with the descriptions:

i.	ADSL	**a.**	Provides symmetric 144 kbps speed
ii.	IDSL	**b.**	Provides up to 1.544 Mbps symmetrical speeds over four wires
iii.	SDSL	**c.**	Provides asymmetric speeds up to 8 Mbps
iv.	HDSL	**d.**	Provides asymmetric service up to 52 Mbps for the downlink
v.	VDSL	**e.**	Provides symmetric service up to 2.3 Mbps

15. Match the algorithm with the description:

i.	DES	**a.**	Uses 128-bit secret key for authentication
ii.	3DES	**b.**	Uses 168-bit secret key for encryption
iii.	HMAC-MD5	**c.**	Uses 160-bit secret key for authentication
iv.	HMAC-SHA-1	**d.**	Uses 56-bit secret key for data encryption

16. True or false? In MPLS VPN networks, each router is a peer.

17. Which algorithm does IKE Phase 1 use to obtain shared secret keys used by encryption algorithms?

18. True or false? All routers in a MPLS VPN are peers.

19. Match the MPLS VPN router types with the descriptions:

i.	P router	**a.**	Customer internal router
ii.	PE router	**b.**	Provider internal router
iii.	C router	**c.**	Maintains VPN routes
iv.	CE router	**d.**	Customer edge router

20. Match the VPN technology with the description:

i.	GRE	**a.**	Consists of AH and ESP.
ii.	PPTP	**b.**	Provides VPNs with guarantees of service.
iii.	VPDN	**c.**	Cisco tunneling protocol developed to support tunneled remote access.
iv.	IPSec	**d.**	Cisco tunneling protocol. Can tunnel IP, IPX, and AppleTalk.
v.	MPLS	**e.**	Tunneling protocol used by Microsoft operating systems.

PART III: The Internet Protocol and Routing Protocols

This part covers the following CCDA exam objectives (to view the CCDA exam outline, visit http://www.cisco.com/go/training):

- Given a network design or a set of requirements, evaluate a solution that meets IP addressing needs.

- Given a network design or a set of requirements, evaluate a solution that meets routing protocol needs.

This chapter covers the following subjects:

- IPv4 Header

- IPv4 Addressing

- IP Address Subnets

- Address Assignment and Name Resolution

CHAPTER 9

Internet Protocol Version 4

This chapter reviews Internet Protocol Version 4 (IPv4) address structures and IPv4 address types. IPv4 is the version of the protocol that the Internet has used since the initial allocation of IPv4 addresses in 1981. The size of the enterprise indicated the address class that was allocated. This chapter covers the IPv4 header to give you an understanding of IPv4 characteristics. The mid 1990s saw the implementation of classless interdomain routing (CIDR), network address translation (NAT), and private address space to prevent the apparent exhaustion of IPv4 address space. Companies implement variable-length subnet masks (VLSMs) in their networks to provide intelligent address assignment and summarization. The CCDA needs to understand all these concepts to design IPv4 addressing for a network.

"Do I Know This Already?" Quiz

The purpose of the "Do I Know This Already?" quiz is to help you decide whether you need to read the entire chapter. If you intend to read the entire chapter, you do not necessarily need to answer these questions now.

The 10-question quiz, derived from the major sections in the "Foundation Topics" portion of the chapter, helps you determine how to spend your limited study time.

Table 9-1 outlines the major topics discussed in this chapter and the "Do I Know This Already?" quiz questions that correspond to those topics.

Table 9-1 *"Do I Know This Already?" Foundation Topics Section-to-Question Mapping*

Foundation Topics Section	Questions Covered in This Section
IPv4 Header	4
IPv4 Addressing	1, 5, 9
IPv4 Address Subnets	2, 3, 7
Address Assignment and Name Resolution	6, 8, 10

> **CAUTION**   The goal of self assessment is to gauge your mastery of the topics in this chapter. If you do not know the answer to a question or you are only partially sure of the answer, you should mark this question wrong for purposes of the self assessment. Giving yourself credit for an answer you correctly guess skews your self-assessment results and might provide you with a false sense of security.

1. Which of the following addresses is an IPv4 private address?

   a. 198.176.1.1

   b. 172.16.1.1

   c. 191.168.1.1

   d. 224.130.1.1

2. How many IP addresses are available for hosts in the subnet 198.10.100.64/27?

   a. 14

   b. 30

   c. 62

   d. 126

3. What subnet mask should you use in loopback addresses?

   a. 255.255.255.252

   b. 255.255.255.254

   c. 255.255.255.0

   d. 255.255.255.255

4. In what IPv4 field are the precedence bits located?

   a. IP destination address

   b. IP protocol field

   c. Type-of-service field

   d. IP options field

5. What type of address is 225.10.1.1?

    a. Unicast

    b. Multicast

    c. Broadcast

    d. Anycast

6. What protocol maps IPv4 addresses to MAC addresses?

    a. Domain Name System (DNS)

    b. Address Resolution Protocol (ARP)

    c. Neighbor discovery (ND)

    d. Static

7. What is a recommended subnet mask to use in point-to-point WAN links?

    a. 255.255.255.0

    b. 255.255.255.255

    c. 255.255.255.224

    d. 255.255.255.252

8. What is DHCP?

    a. Dynamic Host Control Protocol

    b. Dedicated Host Configuration Protocol

    c. Dynamic Host Configuration Protocol

    d. Predecessor to BOOTP

9. What is the purpose of NAT?

    a. To translate source addresses to destination addresses

    b. To translate between private and public addresses

    c. To translate destination addresses to source addresses

    d. To translate class of service (CoS) to quality of service (QoS)

10. Which protocol maps fully qualified domain names (FQDNs) to IP addresses?

   a. ARP

   b. ND

   c. DNS

   d. WINS

The answers to the "Do I Know This Already?" quiz appear in Appendix A, "Answers to Chapter 'Do I Know This Already?' Quizzes and Q&A Sections. The suggested choices for your next step are as follows:

■ **8 or less overall score**—Read the entire chapter. It includes the "Foundation Topics," "Foundation Summary," and "Q&A" sections.

■ **9–10 overall score**—If you want more review on these topics, skip to the "Foundation Summary" section and then go to the "Q&A" section. Otherwise, move to the next chapter.

Foundation Topics

This chapter reviews IPv4 headers, address classes, and assignment methods.

IP is the network-layer protocol in TCP/IP. IP contains logical addressing and information for routing packets throughout the internetwork. IP is described in RFC 791, which was prepared for the Defense Advanced Research Projects Agency (DARPA) in September 1981.

IP provides for the transmission of blocks of data, called datagrams or packets, from a source to a destination. The sources and destinations are identified by 32-bit IP addresses. The source and destination devices are workstations, servers, printers, and routers. The CCDA candidate must understand IPv4 logical address classes and assignment. The IPv4 protocol also provides for the fragmentation and reassembly of large packets for transport over networks with small maximum transmission units (MTUs). The CCDA candidate must have a good understanding of this packet fragmentation and reassembly.

IPv4 Header

The best way to understand IPv4 is to know the IPv4 header and all its fields. Segments from TCP or the User Datagram Protocol (UDP) are passed on to IP for processing. The IP header is appended to the TCP or UDP segment. The TCP or UDP segment then becomes the IP data. The IPv4 header is 20 bytes in length when it uses no optional fields. The IP header includes the addresses of the sending host and destination host. It also includes the upper-layer protocol, a field for prioritization, and a field for fragmentation. Figure 9-1 shows the IP header format.

Figure 9-1 *IP Header*

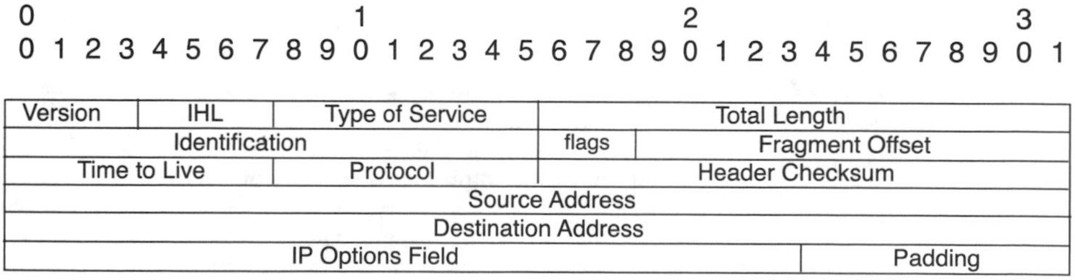

Version	IHL	Type of Service		flags		Total Length	
Identification				flags		Fragment Offset	
Time to Live		Protocol				Header Checksum	
Source Address							
Destination Address							
IP Options Field						Padding	

The following is a description of each field in the IP header:

- **Version**—This field is 4 bits long. It indicates the format, based on the version number, of the IP header. Version 4 is the current version; therefore, this field is set to 0100 for IPv4 packets. This field is set to 0110 in IPv6 networks.

- **IHL**—Internet header length. This field in 4 bits long. It indicates the length of the header in 32-bit words (4 bytes) so that the beginning of the data can be found. The minimum value for a valid header (five 32-bit words) is 5 (0101).

- **ToS**—Type of service. This field is 8 bits in length. The Type of Service field includes 3 bits for IP precedence.

- **Total length**—This field is 16 bits in length. It represents the length of the datagram or packet in bytes, including the header and data. The maximum length of an IP packet can be $2^{16} - 1 = 65,535$ bytes. Routers use this field to determine whether fragmentation is necessary by comparing the total length with the outgoing MTU.

- **Identification**—This field is 16 bits in length. It identifies fragments for reassembly.

- **Flags**—This field is 3 bits in length. It indicates whether the packet can be fragmented and whether more fragments follow. Bit 0 is reserved and set to 0. Bit 1 indicates May Fragment (0) or Do Not Fragment (1). Bit 2 indicates Last Fragment (0) or More Fragments (1) to follow.

- **Fragment offset**—This field is 13 bits in length. It indicates (in bytes) where in the packet this fragment belongs. The fragment has an offset of zero.

- **Time to live**—This field is 8 bits in length. This field indicates the maximum time the packet is to remain on the network. Each router decrements this field by 1 for loop avoidance. If this field is 0, the packet must be discarded. This scheme permits routers to discard undeliverable packets.

- **Protocol**—This field is 8 bits in length. It indicates the upper-layer protocol. The Internet Assigned Number Authority (IANA) is responsible for assigning IP protocol values. Table 9-2 shows some key protocol numbers.

Table 9-2 *IP Protocol Numbers*

Protocol Number	Protocol
1	Internet Control Message Protocol (ICMP)
2	Internet Group Management Protocol (IGMP)
6	TCP
9	Any interior gateway protocol (IGP), used by Cisco for IGRP
17	UDP

Table 9-2 *IP Protocol Numbers (Continued)*

Protocol Number	Protocol
88	Enhanced IGRP (EIGRP)
89	Open Shortest Path First (OSPF)
103	Protocol Independent Multicast (PIM)

- **Header checksum**—This field is 16 bits in length. The checksum does not include the data portion of the packet. It is recomputed and verified at each point the IP header is processed.

- **Source address**—This field is 32 bits in length. It is the IP address of the sender.

- **Destination address**—This field is 32 bits in length. It is the IP address of the receiver.

- **IP options**—This field is variable in length. The options provide for control functions that are useful in some situations but unnecessary for the most common communications. Specific options are security, loose source routing, strict source routing, record route, and timestamp.

- **Padding**—This field is variable in length. It ensures the IP header ends on a 32-bit boundary.

Table 9-3 summarizes the fields of the IP header.

Table 9-3 *IPv4 Header Fields*

Field	Length	Description
Version	4 bits	Indicates the format of the IP header, based on the version number. Set to 0100 for IPv4.
IHL	4 bits	Length of the header in 32-bit words.
ToS	8 bits	QoS parameters.
Total length	16 bits	Length of the packet in bytes, including header and data.
Identification	16 bits	Identifies a fragment.
Flags	3 bits	Indicates whether a packet is fragmented and whether more fragments follow.
Fragment offset	13 bits	Location of the fragment in the total packet.
Time to live	8 bits	Decremented by 1 by each router. When this is 0, the router discards the packet.
Protocol	8 bits	Indicates the upper-layer protocol.

continues

Table 9-3 *IPv4 Header Fields (Continued)*

Field	Length	Description
Header checksum	16 bits	Checksum of the IP header; does not include the data portion.
Source address	32 bits	IP address of the sending host.
Destination address	32 bits	IP address of the destination host.
IP options	Variable	Options for security, loose source routing, record route, and timestamp.
Padding	Variable	Added to ensure header ends in a 32-bit boundary.

ToS

The ToS field indicates QoS parameters. The ToS service has undergone several definitions since RFC 791. Figure 9-2 shows the format of this field.

Figure 9-2 *IPv4 ToS Field*

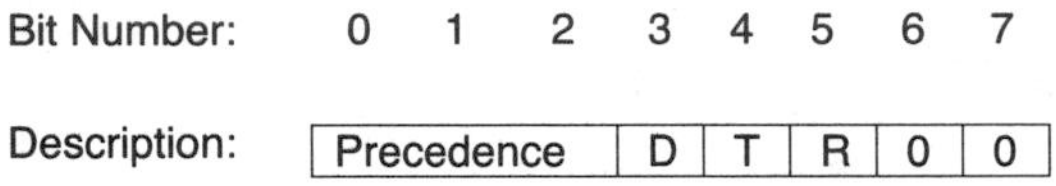

The first three (leftmost) bits are the IP precedence bits. These bits define values that are used by QoS methods. The precedence bits especially help in marking packets to give them differentiated treatment with different priorities. For example, Voice over IP (VoIP) packets can get preferential treatment over regular data packets. The RFC describes the precedence bits as shown in Table 9-4.

Table 9-4 *IP Precedence Bit Values*

Decimal	Binary	Description
0	000	Routine
1	001	Priority
2	010	Immediate
3	011	Flash
4	100	Flash override
5	101	Critical
6	110	Internetwork control
7	111	Network control

All default traffic is set with 000 in the precedence bits. Voice traffic is usually set to 101 (critical) to give it priority over normal traffic.

The D bit is the delay bit. It indicates normal (0) or low (1) delay. The T bit is the throughput bit. The T bit indicates normal (0) or high (1) throughput. The R bit can indicate normal (0) or high (1) reliability. RFC 791 reserved Bits 6 and 7 for future use.

RFC 1349 redefined Bits 3 and 6 to reflect a desired type of service optimization. But RFC 1349 is superceded by RFC 2474, which redefines the ToS field.

RFC 2474 redefines the ToS octet as the Differentiated Services (DS) field and further specifies Bits 0 through 5 as the Differentiated Services Code Point (DSCP) to support differentiated services. The DS field takes the format shown in Figure 9-3. The CU field, currently unused, is reserved for future use.

Figure 9-3   *DS Field*

Bit Number:	0	1	2	3	4	5	6	7
Description:			DSCP				CU	

The DS field provides more granular levels of packet classification by using 6 bits for packet marking. There are $2^6 = 64$ levels of classification with DS, which is significantly higher than the 8 levels of the IP precedence bits.

IPv4 Fragmentation

One of the key characteristics of IPv4 is fragmentation and reassembly. Although the maximum length of an IP packet is 65,536 bytes, many lower-layer protocols do not support such large MTUs. For example, the MTU for Ethernet is approximately 1518 bytes. When the IP layer receives a packet to send, it first queries the outgoing interface to get its MTU. If the size of the packet is greater than the MTU of the interface, it fragments the packet.

When a packet is fragmented, it is not reassembled until it reaches the destination IP layer. The destination IP layer performs the reassembly. Any router in the path can fragment a packet, and any router in the path can fragment a fragmented packet again. Each fragmented packet receives its own IP header and is routed independently from other packets. Routers and switches in the path do not perform the reassembly of the fragments. The destination host performs the reassembly and places the fragments in the correct order by looking at the identification and fragment offset fields.

If one or more fragments are lost, the entire packet must be retransmitted. Retransmission is the responsibility of the higher-layer protocol (such as TCP). Also, you can set the Flags field in the IP header to Do Not Fragment the packet. If the field indicates Do Not Fragment, the packet is discarded if the outgoing MTU is smaller than the packet.

IPv4 Addressing

This section covers the IP address classes, private addressing, and NAT. The IP address space was initially divided into five classes identified by the initial bits of the address. Class A, B, and C are unicast IP addresses. IP Class D addresses are multicast, and IP Class E addresses are reserved. Private addresses are selected address ranges that are reserved for use by companies in their private networks. These private addresses are not routed in the Internet. NAT translates between private and public addresses. IP addresses assign an unique logical number to a network device or interface. The number is 32 bits in length. To make the number easier to read, use the dotted-decimal format. The bits are combined into four 8-bit groups, each converted into decimal numbers. Appendix B, "The OSI Reference Model and Numeric Conversion," contains a review of binary and hexadecimal number manipulation.

The following example shows an IP address in binary and decimal formats:

Binary IP address: 01101110 00110010 11110010 00001010
Convert each byte into decimal.
For the first octet:

128	64	32	16	8	4	2	1	
0	1	1	0	1	1	1	0	
0	+64	+32	+0	+8	+4	+2	+0	= 110

01101110 = 110

For the second octet:

128	64	32	16	8	4	2	1	
0	0	1	1	0	0	1	0	
0	+0	+32	+16	+0	+0	+2	+0	= 50

00110010 = 50

For the third octet:

128	64	32	16	8	4	2	1	
1	1	1	1	0	0	1	0	
128	+64	+32	+16	+0	+0	+2	+0	= 242

11110010 = 242

For the fourth octet:

128	64	32	16	8	4	2	1
0	0	0	0	1	0	1	0
0	+0	+0	+0	+8	+0	+2	+0 = 10

00001010 = 10

The IP address is 110.50.242.10.

IPv4 Address Classes

IPv4 addresses have five classes—A, B, C, D, and E. In classful addressing, the most significant bits of the first byte determine the address class of the IP address. Table 9-5 shows the high-order bits of each IP address class.

Table 9-5 *High-Order Bits of IPv4 Address Classes*

Address Class	High-Order Bits
A	0*xxxxxxx*[*]
B	10*xxxxxx*
C	110*xxxxx*
D	1110*xxxx*
E	1111*xxxx*

[*]   x can be either 1 or 0, regardless of the address class.

The IP Classes A, B, and C are unicast addresses. Unicast addresses represent a single destination. Class D is for multicast addresses. Multicast addresses are a group of hosts. Class E addresses are reserved for experimental use. IANA allocates the IPv4 address space. IANA delegates regional assignments to Regional Internet Registries (RIR). The four RIRs are

- ARIN (American Registry for Internet Numbers)
- RIPE NCC (Reseaux IP Europeens Network Control Center)
- APNIC (Asia Pacific Network Information Center)
- LACNIC (Latin America and Caribbean Network Information Center)

The following sections discuss each of these classes in detail.

Class A Addresses

Class A addresses range from 0 (00000000) to 127 (01111111) in the first byte. Network numbers available for assignment to organizations are from 1.0.0.0 to 126.0.0.0, with networks 0 and 127 reserved. For example, 127.0.0.1 is reserved for localhost. A packet sent to a localhost address is sent to the local machine. Furthermore, network 10.0.0.0 is reserved for private addresses.

By default, for Class A addresses, the first byte is the network number and the three remaining bytes are the host number. The format is *N.H.H.H* with *N* being the network part and *H* the host part. With 24 bits available, there are $2^{24} - 2 = 16,777,214$ IP addresses for host assignment per Class A network. Subtract two for the network number (all 0s) and broadcast address (all 1s). A network with this many hosts will surely not work with so many hosts attempting to broadcast on the network. This section discusses subnetting later as a method for defining smaller networks within a larger network address.

Class B Addresses

Class B addresses range from 128 (10000000) to 191 (10111111) in the first byte. Network numbers assigned to companies or other organizations are from 128.0.0.0 to 191.255.0.0. This section discusses the 16 networks reserved for private use later.

By default, for Class B addresses, the first two bytes are the network number and the remaining two bytes are the host number. The format is *N.N.H.H*. With 16 bits available, there are $2^{16} - 2 = 65,534$ IP addresses for host assignment per Class B network. As with Class A addresses, having a segment with more than 65,000 hosts broadcasting will surely not work; you resolve this issue with subnetting.

Class C Addresses

Class C addresses range from 192 (11000000) to 223 (11011111) in the first byte. Network numbers assigned to companies are from 192.0.0.0 to 223.255.255.0. The format is *N.N.N.H*. With 8 bits available, there are $2^8 - 2 = 254$ IP addresses for host assignment per Class C network. H=0 is the network number; H=255 is the broadcast address.

Class D Addresses

Class D addresses range from 224 (11100000) to 239 (11101111) in the first byte. Network numbers assigned to multicast groups range from 224.0.0.1 to 239.255.255.255. These addresses do not have a host or network part. Some multicast addresses are already assigned; for example, 224.0.0.10 is used by routers running EIGRP.

Class E Addresses

Class E addresses range from 240 (11110000) to 254 (11111110) in the first byte. These addresses are reserved for experimental networks. Network 255 is reserved for the broadcast address, such as 255.255.255.255. Table 9-6 summarizes the IPv4 address classes.

Table 9-6 *IPv4 Address Classes*

Address Class	High-Order Bits	Network Numbers
A	0*xxxxxxx*	1.0.0.0 to 126.0.0.0[*]
B	10*xxxxxx*	128.0.0.0 to 191.255.0.0
C	110*xxxxx*	192.0.0.0 to 223.255.255.0
D	1110*xxxx*	224.0.0.1 to 239.255.255.255
E	1111*xxxx*	240.0.0.0 to 254.255.255.255

[*] Networks 0.0.0.0 and 127.0.0.0 are reserved as special-use addresses, per the IP specifications.

IPv4 Private Addresses

Some network numbers within the IPv4 address space are reserved for private use. These numbers are not routed on the Internet. Many organizations today use private addresses in their internal networks with network NAT to access the Internet. (NAT is covered later in this chapter.) Private addresses are explained in RFC 1918, *Address Allocation for Private Internets*, published in 1996. Private addresses were one of the first steps dealing with the concern that globally unique IPv4 address space would become exhausted. The availability of private addresses combined with NAT reduces the need for organizations to carefully define subnets to minimize the waste of assigned, public, global IP addresses.

The IP network address space reserved for private Internets is 10/8, 172.16/12, and 192.168/16. It includes one Class A network, 16 Class B networks, and 256 Class C networks. Table 9-7 summarizes private address space.

Table 9-7 *IPv4 Private Address Space*

Class Type	Start Address	End Address
Class A	10.0.0.0	10.255.255.255
Class B	172.16.0.0	172.31.255.255
Class C	192.168.0.0	192.168.255.255

NAT

NAT devices convert internal IP address space into globally unique IP addresses. NAT was originally specified by RFC 1631, which was made obsolete by RFC 3022. Companies use NAT to translate internal private addresses to public addresses.

The translation can be from many private addresses to a single public address or from many private addresses to a range of public addresses. When NAT performs many-to-one, the process is called port address translation (PAT) because different port numbers identify translations.

As shown in Figure 9-4, the source address for outgoing IP packets are converted to globally unique IP addresses. The conversion can be configured statically or it can dynamically use a global pool of addresses.

Figure 9-4   *Network Address Translation*

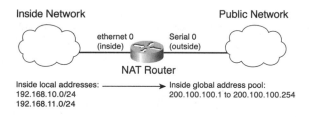

There are several forms of NAT, such as those described in the following list:

- **Static NAT**—Maps an unregistered IP address to a registered IP address, configured manually.
- **Dynamic NAT**—Dynamically maps an unregistered IP address to a registered IP address from a pool (group) of registered addresses. There are two subsets of dynamic NAT: overloading and overlapping.
  - **Overloading**—Maps multiple unregistered IP addresses to a single registered IP address by using different ports. It is also known as PAT, single-address NAT, or port-level multiplexed NAT.
  - **Overlapping**—Maps registered internal IP addresses to outside registered IP addresses. It can also map external addresses to internal registered addresses.

When designing for NAT, you should understand the following terminology:

- **Stub domain**—The internal network that might be using private IP addresses.
- **Public network**—Outside the stub domain, it resides in the Internet. Addresses in the public network are reachable from the Internet.

- **Inside local address**—The real IP address of the device that resides in the internal network. This address is used in the stub domain.

- **Inside global address**—The translated IP address of the device that resides in the internal network. This address is used in the public network.

- **Outside global address**—The real IP address of a device that resides in the Internet, outside of the stub domain.

- **Outside local address**—The translated IP address of the device that resides in the Internet. This address is used inside the stub domain.

Figure 9-5 illustrates the terms described in the list. The real IP address of the host in the stub network is 192.168.10.100; it is the inside local address. The NAT router translates the inside local address into the inside global address (200.100.10.100). Hosts located in the Internet have their real IP address (outside global address) translated; in the example, 30.100.2.50 is translated into the outside local address of 192.168.100.50.

Figure 9-5 *Terminology Example*

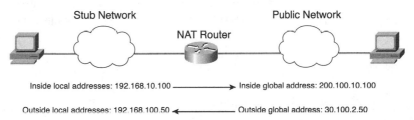

Inside local addresses: 192.168.10.100 ⟶ Inside global address: 200.100.10.100

Outside local addresses: 192.168.100.50 ⟵ Outside global address: 30.100.2.50

IP Address Subnets

Subnetting plays an important part in IP addressing. The subnet mask helps determine the network, subnetwork, and host part of an IP address. The network architect uses subnetting to manipulate the default mask to create subnetworks for LAN and WAN segments. These subnetworks provide enough addresses for LANs of different sizes. Point-to-point WAN links usually get a subnet mask for two hosts because only two routers are present in the point-to-point WAN link. You should become familiar with determining subnetwork numbers, broadcast addresses, and host-address ranges given an IP address and mask.

Subnet masks are used for Class A, B, and C addresses only. Multicast addresses do not use subnet masks. A subnet mask is a 32-bit number where bits are set to 1 to establish the network portion of the address, and a 0 is the host part of the address. The mask's bits set to 1 are contiguous from the left portion of the mask; the bits set to 0 are contiguous to the right portion of the mask. Table 9-5 shows the default masks for Class A, B, and C addresses. This section addresses various ways to represent IP subnet masks. Understanding these ways is significant because the representation of a network and its mask can appear differently in Cisco documentation or on the command-line interface.

Table 9-8 *IPv4 Default Network Address Masks*

Class	Binary Mask	Dotted Decimal Mask
A	11111111 00000000 00000000 00000000	255.0.0.0
B	11111111 11111111 00000000 00000000	255.255.0.0
C	11111111 11111111 11111111 00000000	255.255.255.0

Mask Nomenclature

There are several ways to represent IP subnet masks. The mask can be binary, hexadecimal, or dotted-decimal or a prefix "bit mask." Historically, the most common representation is the dotted-decimal format (255.255.255.0). The prefix bit mask format is now more popular. This format represents the mask by using a slash followed by the number of leading address bits that must be set to 1 for the mask. For example, 255.255.0.0 is represented as /16. Table 9-9 shows some mask representations.

Table 9-9 *Subnet Masks*

Dotted Decimal	Bit Mask	Hexadecimal
255.0.0.0	/8	FF000000
255.192.0.0	/10	FFC00000
255.255.0.0	/16	FFFF0000
255.255.224.0	/19	FFFFE000
255.255.240.0	/20	FFFFF000
255.255.255.0	/24	FFFFFF00
255.255.255.224	/27	FFFFFFE0
255.255.255.240	/28	FFFFFFF0
255.255.255.248	/29	FFFFFFF8
255.255.255.252	/30	FFFFFFFC
255.255.255.255	/32	FFFFFFFF

IP Address Design Example

Say a company of 200 hosts is assigned the Class C network of 195.10.1.0/24. The 200 hosts are in 6 different LANs. You can subnet the Class C network using a mask of 255.255.255.224. Looking at the mask in binary (11111111 11111111 11111111 11100000), the first three bytes are the network part, the first three bits of the fourth byte determine the subnets, and the five remaining 0 bits are for host addressing.

Table 9-10 shows the subnetworks created with a mask of 255.255.255.224. Using this mask, 2^n subnets are created, where n is the number of the bits taken from the host part for the subnet mask. This example uses 3 bits, so $2^3 = 8$ subnets. With Cisco routers, you can use the all 1s subnet (LAN 7) for a subnet. You cannot use the 0s subnet by default, but with Cisco routers, you can use it by configuring the **ip subnet-zero** command.

Table 9-10 *Subnets for Network 195.1.1.0.*

LAN	Fourth Byte	Subnet Number	First Host	Broadcast Address
LAN 0	00000000	195.10.1.0	195.10.1.1	195.10.1.31
LAN 1	00100000	195.10.1.32	195.10.1.33	195.10.1.63
LAN 2	01000000	195.10.1.64	195.10.1.65	195.10.1.95
LAN 3	01100000	195.10.1.96	195.10.1.97	195.10.1.127
LAN 4	10000000	195.10.1.128	195.10.1.129	195.10.1.159
LAN 5	10100000	195.10.1.160	195.10.1.161	195.10.1.191
LAN 6	11000000	195.10.1.192	195.10.1.193	195.10.1.223
LAN 7	11100000	195.10.1.224	195.10.1.225	195.10.1.255

Use the following formula to calculate the number of hosts per subnet: $2^n - 2$, where n is the number of bits for the host portion. The preceding example has 5 bits in the fourth byte for host addresses. With $n = 5$, then $2^5 - 2 = 30$ hosts. For LAN 1, host addresses range from 195.10.1.33 to 195.10.1.62 (30 addresses).

The example uses a fixed-length subnet mask. The whole Class C network has the same subnet mask, 255.255.255.224. Routing protocols such as RIPv1 and IGRP can only use fixed-length subnet masks; they do not support VLSMs in which masks of different lengths identify subnets within network. VLSMs are covered later in this chapter.

Determining the Network Portion of an IP Address

Given an address and mask, you can determine the classful network, the subnetwork, and the broadcast number of the subnetwork. You do so with a logical AND operation between the IP address and subnet mask. Obtain the broadcast address by taking the subnet number and making the host portion all 1s. Table 9-11 shows the logical AND operation. Notice that the AND operation is similar to multiplying Bit 1 and Bit 2; if any 0 is present, the result is 0.

Table 9-11   *The AND Logical Operation*

Bit 1	Bit 2	AND
0	0	0
0	1	0
1	0	0
1	1	1

As an example, take the IP address 150.85.1.70 with a subnet mask of 255.255.255.224, as shown in Table 9-12. Notice the three bold bits in the subnet mask. These bits extend the default Class C prefix (/24) 3 bits to a mask of /27. As shown in Table 9-12, perform an AND operation of the IP address with the subnet mask to obtain the subnetwork. You obtain the broadcast number by making all the host bits 1.

Table 9-12   *Subnetwork of IP Address 150.85.1.70*

	Binary First, Second, and Third Octets	Binary Fourth Octet		Dotted Decimal IP
IP address	10010110 01010101 00000001	010	00110	150.85.1.70
Subnet mask	11111111 11111111 11111111	**111**	00000	255.255.255.224
Subnetwork	10010110 01010101 00000001	010	**00000**	150.85.1.64
	Major network portion	Subnet	Host	
Broadcast address	10010110 01010101 00000001	010	**11111**	150.85.1.95

VLSMs

VLSMs divide a network into subnets of various sizes to prevent wasting IP addresses. If a Class C network uses 255.255.255.240 as a subnet mask, there will be 16 subnets, each with 14 IP addresses. If there is a point-to-point link that needs only two IP addresses, 12 IP addresses are wasted. This problem scales further with Class B and Class A address space. With VLSMs, small LANs can use

/28 subnets with 14 hosts, and larger LANs can use /23 or /22 masks with 510 and 1022 hosts. Point-to-point networks use a /30 mask, which supports two hosts.

VLSM Address-Assignment Example

Take Class B network 110.20.0.0/16 as an example. Using a /20 mask produces 16 subnetworks. Table 9-13 shows the subnetworks. With the /20 subnet mask, the first 4 bits of the third byte determine the subnets.

Table 9-13 *Subnets with /20 Mask*

Third Byte	Subnetwork
00000000	110.20.0.0/20
00010000	110.20.16.0/20
00100000	110.20.32.0/20
00110000	110.20.48.0/20
01000000	110.20.64.0/20
01010000	110.20.80.0/20
01100000	110.20.96.0/20
01110000	110.20.112.0/20
10000000	110.20.128.0/20
10010000	110.20.144.0/20
10100000	110.20.160.0/20
10110000	110.20.176.0/20
11000000	110.20.192.0/20
11010000	110.20.208.0/20
11100000	110.20.224.0/20
11110000	110.20.240.0/20

With fixed-length subnet masks, the network would support only 16 networks. Any LAN or WAN link would have to use a /20 subnet. This scenario is a waste of address space—not efficient. With VLSMs, you can further subnet the /20 subnets.

For example, take 110.20.64.0/20 and subdivide it to support LANs with around 500 hosts. With a /23 mask, there are 9 bits for hosts, producing $2^9 - 2 = 510$ IP addresses for hosts. Table 9-14 shows the subnetworks for LANs within a specified subnet.

Table 9-14   *Subnetworks for 110.20.64.0/20*

Third Byte	Subnetwork
01000000	110.20.64.0/23
01000010	110.20.66.0/23
01000100	110.20.68.0/23
01000110	110.20.70.0/23
01001000	110.20.72.0/23
01001010	110.20.74.0/23
01001100	110.20.76.0/23
01001110	110.20.78.0/23

With VLSMs, you can even further divide these subnetworks of subnetworks. Take subnetwork 110.20.76.0/23 and use it for two LANs that have fewer than 250 hosts. It produces subnetworks 110.20.76.0/24 and 110.20.77.0/24. Also, subdivide 110.20.78.0/23 for serial links. Because each point-to-point serial link needs only two IP addresses, use a /30 mask. Table 9-15 shows the subnetworks produced.

Table 9-15   *Serial-Link Subnetworks*

Third Byte	Fourth Byte	Subnetwork
01001110	00000000	110.20.78.0/30
01001110	00000100	110.20.78.4/30
01001110	00001000	110.20.78.8/30
01001110	00001100	110.20.78.12/30
. . .	. . .	. . .
01001111	11110100	110.20.79.244/30
01001111	11111000	110.20.79.248/30
01001111	11111100	110.20.79.252/30

Each /30 subnetwork includes the subnetwork number, two IP addresses, and a broadcast address. Table 9-16 shows the bits for 110.20.78.8/30.

Table 9-16   *Addresses Within Subnetwork 110.20.78.8/30*

Binary Address	IP Address	Function
1010110 00010000 01001110 00001**000**	110.20.78.8	Subnetwork
1010110 00010000 01001110 00001**001**	110.20.78.9	IP address #1
1010110 00010000 01001110 00001**010**	110.20.78.10	IP address #2
1010110 00010000 01001110 00001**011**	110.20.78.11	Broadcast address

Loopback Addresses

You can also reserve a subnet for router loopback addresses. Loopback addresses provide an always-up interface to use for router-management connectivity. The loopback address can also serve as the router ID for some routing protocols. The loopback address is a single IP address with a 32-bit mask. In the previous example, network 110.20.75.0/24 could provide 255 loopback addresses for network devices starting with 110.20.75.1/32 and ending with 110.20.75.255/32.

IP Telephony Networks

You should reserve separate subnets for LANs using IP phones. IP phones are normally placed in an auxiliary VLAN that is in a separate logical segment from that of the user workstations. Separating voice and data on different subnets or VLANs also aids in providing QoS for voice traffic in regards to classifying, queuing, and buffering. This design rule facilitates troubleshooting.

CIDR and Summarization

CIDR permits the address aggregation of classful networks. It does so by using the common bits to join networks. The network addresses need to be contiguous and have a common bit boundary.

With CIDR, ISPs assign groups of Class C networks to enterprise customers. This arrangement eliminates the problem of assigning too large of a network (Class B) or assigning multiple Class C networks to a customer and having to maintain an entry for each Class C network in the routing tables. It reduces the size of the Internet routing tables.

You can summarize four contiguous Class C networks at the /22 bit level. For example, networks 200.1.100.0, 200.1.101.0, 200.1.102.0, and 200.1.103.0 share common bits, as shown in Table 9-17. The resulting network is 200.1.100.0/22, which you can use for a 1000-node network.

Table 9-17   *Common Bits Within Class C Networks*

Binary Address	IP Address
11001000 00000001 01100100 00000000	200.1.100.0
11001000 00000001 01100101 00000000	200.1.101.0
11001000 00000001 01100110 00000000	200.1.102.0
11001000 00000001 01100111 00000000	200.1.103.0

It is important for an Internet network designer to assign IP networks in a manner that permits summarization. It is preferred that a neighboring router receive one summarized route, rather than 8, 16, 32, or more routes, depending on the level of summarization. This setup reduces the size of the routing tables in the network.

For route summarization to work, the multiple IP addresses must share the same leftmost bits and routers must base their routing decisions on the IP address and prefix length.

Figure 9-6 shows an example of route summarization. All the edge routers send network information to their upstream routers. Router E summarizes its two LAN networks by sending 192.168.16.0/23 to Router A. Router F summarizes its two LAN networks by sending 192.168.18.0/23. Router B summarizes the networks it receives from Router C and D. Routers B, E, and F send their routes to Router A. Router A sends a single route (192.168.16.0/21) to its upstream router, instead of sending eight routes. This process reduces the number of networks that upstream routers need to include in routing updates.

Figure 9-6   *Route Summarization*

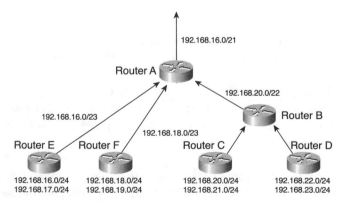

Notice on Table 9-17 that all the Class C networks share a bit boundary with 21 common bits. The networks are different on the 22nd bit and thus cannot be summarized beyond the 21st bit. All these networks are summarized with 192.168.16.0/21.

Table 9-18 *Summarization of Networks*

Binary Address	IP Network
11000000 10101000 00010000 00000000	192.168.16.0
11000000 10101000 00010001 00000000	192.168.17.0
11000000 10101000 00010010 00000000	192.168.18.0
11000000 10101000 00010011 00000000	192.168.19.0
11000000 10101000 00010100 00000000	192.168.20.0
11000000 10101000 00010101 00000000	192.168.21.0
11000000 10101000 00010110 00000000	192.168.22.0
11000000 10101000 00010111 00000000	192.168.23.0

Address Assignment and Name Resolution

IP addresses, subnet masks, default gateways, and DNS servers can be assigned statically or dynamically. You should statically assign most shared network systems, such as routers and servers, but dynamically assign most client systems. This section covers the protocols you use to dynamically assign IP address parameters to a host, which are the Bootstrap Protocol (BOOTP) and the Dynamic Host Configuration Protocol (DHCP). This section also covers DNS and ARP, which are two significant protocols in IP networks. DNS maps domain names to IP addresses, and ARP resolves IP addresses to MAC addresses. These protocols are important in TCP/IP networks because they simplify the methods for address assignment and resolution.

Static and Dynamic IP Address Assignment

Assign the IP addresses of routers, switches, printers, and servers statically. You need to manage and monitor these systems, so you must access them via a stable IP address.

You should dynamically assign end client workstations to reduce the configuration tasks required to connect these systems to the network. When you assign client workstation characteristics dynamically, the system automatically learns which network segment it is assigned to and how to reach its default gateway as the network is discovered. One of the first methods used to dynamically assign IP addresses was BOOTP. The current method to assign IP addresses is DHCP.

BOOTP

The basic BOOTP was first defined in RFC 951. It has been updated by RFC 1497 and RFC 1542. It is a protocol that allows a booting host to configure itself by dynamically obtaining its IP address, IP gateway, and other information from a remote server. You can use a single server to centrally manage numerous network hosts without having to configure each host independently.

BOOTP is an application-layer protocol that uses UDP/IP protocols for transport. UDP Port 67 sends BOOTP request to the BOOTP server, and the server uses UDP Port 68 to send messages to the UDP client. The destination IP of the BOOTP requests uses the all-hosts address (255.255.255.255), which is not forwarded by the router. If the BOOTP server is one or more router hops from the subnet, you must configure the local default gateway router to forward the BOOTP requests.

BOOTP requires that you build a MAC-address-to-IP-address table on the server. You must obtain the MAC address of every device, which is a time-consuming effort. BOOTP has been replaced by the more sophisticated DHCP.

DHCP

DHCP provides a way to dynamically configure hosts on the network. Based on BOOTP, it is defined in RFC 2131 and adds the capability of reusing network addresses and additional configuration options. DHCP improves on BOOTP by using a "lease" for IP addresses and providing the client with all of the IP configuration parameters needed to operate in the network.

DHCP servers allocate network addresses and deliver configuration parameters dynamically to hosts. With DHCP, the computer can obtain its configuration information—IP address, subnet mask, IP default gateway, DNS servers, WINS servers, and so on—when needed. DHCP also includes other optional parameters that you can assign to clients. The configuration information is managed centrally on a DHCP server.

Routers act as relay agents by passing DHCP messages between DHCP clients and servers. Because DHCP is an extension of BOOTP, it uses the message format defined in RFC 951 for BOOTP. It uses the same ports as BOOTP: DHCP messages to a server use UDP Port 67, and DHCP messages sent to a client use UDP Port 68. Because of these similarities, the configuration to support DHCP in the routers is the same described for BOOTP.

DHCP supports permanent allocation, where the DHCP server assigns a IP address to the client and the IP address is never reallocated to other clients. With a lease, DHCP can also assign IP addresses for a limited period of time. This dynamic-allocation mechanism can reuse the IP address after the lease expires.

An IP address is assigned as follows:

1. The client sends a **DHCPDISCOVER** message to the local network using a 255.255.255.255 broadcast.

2. BOOTP relay agents (routers) can forward the **DHCPDISCOVER** message to the DHCP server in another subnet.

3. The server sends a **DHCPOFFER** message to respond to the client, offering IP address, lease expiration, and other DHCP option information.

    Other DHCP messages include

    — **DHCPREQUEST**—The client can request additional options or an extension on its lease of an IP address.

    — **DHCPRELEASE**—The client relinquishes the IP address and cancels the remaining lease.

4. If the server is out of addresses or it determines that the client request is invalid, it sends a **DHCPNAK** message to the client.

DNS

DNS servers return destination IP addresses given a domain name. DNS is a distributed database. Separate, independent organizations administer their assigned domain name spaces and can break their domains into a number of subdomains. For example, given www.cisco.com, DNS returns the IP address 198.133.219.25. DNS was first specified by RFCs 882 and 883. The current specifications are specified in RFCs 1034 and 1035.

DNS was implemented to overcome the limitations of managing a single text-host table. Imagine creating and maintaining text files with the names and IP addresses of all the hosts in the Internet! DNS scales host-name-to-IP-address translation by distributing responsibility for the domain name space. DNS follows a reversed tree structure for domain name space. IANA (http://www.iana.org) manages the root of the tree. The tree looks like Figure 9-7.

DNS uses TCP and UDP Port 53. UDP is the recommended transport protocol for DNS queries. TCP is the recommended protocol for zone transfers between DNS servers. A zone transfer occurs when you place a secondary server in the domain and transfer the DNS information from the primary DNS server to the secondary server. A DNS query searches for the IP address of a FQDN, such as www.cnn.com.

Figure 9-7   *DNS Tree*

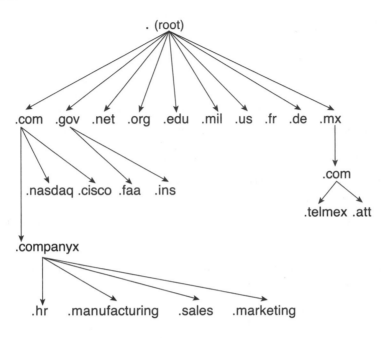

ARP

When a router needs to send an IP packet over an Ethernet network, it needs to find out what 48-bit MAC physical address to send the frame to. Given the destination IP, ARP obtains the destination MAC. The destination MAC can be a local host or the gateway router's MAC address if the destination IP is across the routed network. ARP is described in RFC 826. The local host maintains an ARP table with a list relating IP address to MAC address.

ARP operates by having the sender broadcast an ARP request. Suppose a workstation with the IP address 192.168.1.22 has a packet to send to 192.168.1.17 but does not have the destination MAC address in its ARP table. It broadcasts an ARP request to all hosts in a subnet. The ARP request contains the sender's IP and MAC address as well as the target IP address. All nodes in the broadcast domain receive the ARP request and process it. The device with the target IP address sends an ARP reply back to the sender with its MAC address information; the ARP reply is a unicast message sent to 192.168.1.22. The sender now has the target MAC address in its ARP cache and sends the frame out.

Foundation Summary

The "Foundation Summary" section of each chapter lists the most important facts from the chapter. Although this section does not list every fact from the chapter that will be on your CCDA exam, a well-prepared CCDA candidate should at a minimum know all the details in each "Foundation Summary" before going to take the exam.

This chapter covered the following topics that you will need to master for the CCDA exam:

- **IPv4 header**—Know each field of the IPv4 header.

- **IPv4 addressing**—Know IPv4 address classes, private addressing, and NAT.

- **IPv4 address subnets**—Know VLSMs with a design example.

- **Address assignment and resolution**—Know dynamic IP assignment and address-resolution protocols such as BOOTP, DHCP, DNS, and ARP.

Table 9-19 outlines the IPv4 address classes.

Table 9-19 *IPv4 Address Classes*

Address Class	High-Order Bits	Network Numbers
A	0*xxxxxxx*	1.0.0.0 to 126.0.0.0
B	10*xxxxxx*	128.0.0.0 to 191.255.0.0
C	110*xxxxx*	192.0.0.0 to 223.255.255.0
D	1110*xxxx*	224.0.0.0 to 239.255.255.255
E	1111*xxxx*	240.0.0.0 to 254.255.255.255

Table 9-20 summarizes the IPv4 private address space.

Table 9-20 *IPv4 Private Address Space*

Class Type	Start Address	End Address
Class A	10.0.0.0	10.255.255.255
Class B	172.16.0.0	172.31.255.255
Class C	192.168.0.0	192.168.255.255

Table 9-21 shows subnet mask representations.

Table 9-21 *Subnet Mask Representations*

Dotted Decimal	Prefix	Hexadecimal
255.0.0.0	/8	FF000000
255.128.0.0	/9	FFA00000
255.192.0.0	/10	FFC00000
255.224.0.0	/11	FFE00000
255.240.0.0	/12	FFF00000
255.248.0.0	/13	FFFA0000
255.252.0.0	/14	FFFC0000
255.254.0.0	/15	FFFE0000
255.255.0.0	/16	FFFF0000
255.255.128.0	/17	FFFFA000
255.255.192.0	/18	FFFFC000
255.255.224.0	/19	FFFFE000
255.255.240.0	/20	FFFFF000
255.255.248.0	/21	FFFFFA00
255.255.252.0	/22	FFFFFC00
255.255.254.0	/23	FFFFFE00
255.255.255.0	/24	FFFFFF00
255.255.128.0	/25	FFFFFFA0
255.255.192.0	/26	FFFFFFC0
255.255.255.224	/27	FFFFFFE0
255.255.255.240	/28	FFFFFFF0
255.255.255.248	/29	FFFFFFF8
255.255.255.252	/30	FFFFFFFC
255.255.255.254	/31	FFFFFFFE
255.255.255.255	/32	FFFFFFFF

The following list reviews the various IPv4 address types:

- **Unicast**—IP address of an interface on a single host. It can be a source or destination address.
- **Multicast**—IP address that reaches a group of hosts. It is only a destination address.
- **Broadcast**—IP logical address that reaches all hosts in an IP subnet. It is only a destination address.

Table 9-22 summarizes the fields of the IP header.

Table 9-22 *IPv4 Header Fields*

Field	Length	Description
Version	4 bits	Indicates the format of the IP header, based on the version number. Set to 0100 for IPv4.
IHL	4 bits	Length of the header in 32-bit words.
ToS	8 bits	QoS parameters.
Total length	16 bits	Length of the packet in bytes, including header and data.
Identification	16 bits	Identifies a fragment.
Flags	3 bits	Indicates whether a packet is fragmented and whether more fragments follow.
Fragment offset	13 bits	Location of the fragment in the total packet.
Time to live	8 bits	Decremented by 1 by each router. When this is 0, the router discards the packet.
Protocol	8 bits	Indicates the upper-layer protocol.
Header checksum	16 bits	Checksum of the IP header; does not include the data portion.
Source address	32 bits	IP address of the sending host.
Destination address	32 bits	IP address of the destination host.
IP options	Variable	Options for security, loose source routing, record route, and timestamp.
Padding	Variable	Added to ensure header ends in a 32-bit boundary.

Q&A

As mentioned in the introduction, you have two choices for review questions. Some of the questions that follow give you a bigger challenge than the exam itself by using a short-answer question format. By reviewing now with more difficult question format, you can exercise your memory better and prove your conceptual and factual knowledge of this chapter. The answers to these questions appear in Appendix A.

For more practice with exam-like question formats, use the exam engine on the CD-ROM.

1. List the RFC 1918 private address space.

2. What is the difference between VLSM and CIDR?

3. Fill in the blank. _____ maps FQDN to IP addresses.

4. True or false? You can use DHCP to specify the TFTP host's IP address to a client PC.

5. True or false? The following are two representations of the same IP mask: 255.255.255.248 and /28.

6. True or false? Upper-layer protocols are identified in the protocol field of the IP header. TCP is protocol 6 and UDP is protocol 17.

7. Fill in the blank. Without any options, the IP header is _____ bytes in length.

8. The ToS field of the IP header is redefined as the DS field. How many bits does DSCP use for packet classification, and how many levels of classification are possible?

9. True or false? NAT uses different IP addresses for translations. PAT uses different port numbers to identify translations.

10. True or false? The header checksum field of the IP header performs the checksum of the IP header and data.

11. Calculate the subnet, the address range within the subnet, and the subnet broadcast of the following address.

    172.56.5.245/22

12. When packets are fragmented at the network layer, where are the fragments reassembled?

13. Which protocol can you use to configure a default gateway?

   a. ARP

   b. DHCP

   c. DNS

   d. RARP

14. How many host addresses are available with a Class B network with the default mask?

   a. 63,998

   b. 64,000

   c. 65,534

   d. 65,536

15. Which of the following is a dotted-decimal representation of a /26 prefix mask?

   a. 255.255.255.128

   b. 255.255.255.192

   c. 255.255.255.224

   d. 255.255.255.252

16. Which is the network specification that summarizes both the 192.170.20.16/30 and the 192.170.20.20/30 networks?

   a. 192.170.20.0/24

   b. 192.170.20.20/28

   c. 192.170.20.16/29

   d. 192.170.20.0/30

17. How many bits are used for IP precedence in the IP header?

   a. 1

   b. 2

   c. 3

   d. 4

18. What is true about fragmentation?

    a. Routers between source and destination hosts can fragment IPv4 packets.

    b. Only the first router in the network can fragment IPv4 packets.

    c. IPv4 packets cannot be fragmented.

    d. IPv4 packets are fragmented and reassembled at each link through the network.

19. A packet sent to a multicast address reaches what destinations?

    a. The nearest destination in a set of hosts.

    b. All destinations in a set of hosts.

    c. Broadcasts to all hosts.

    d. Reserved global destinations.

20. What are three types of IPv4 addresses?

Answer the following questions based on the given scenario and figure.

Company VWX has a network, as shown in Figure 9-8. The main site has three LANs with 100, 29, and 60 hosts. The remote site has two LANs each with 100 hosts. The network uses private addresses. The Internet provider assigned the company the network 210.200.200.8/26.

Figure 9-8 *Scenario Diagram*

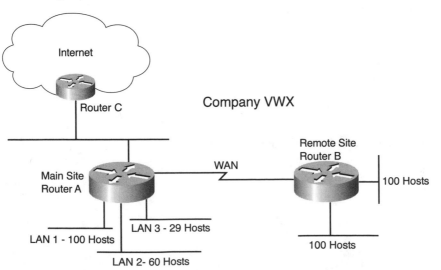

21. The remote site uses the network prefix 192.168.10.0/24. What subnets and masks can you use for the LANs at the remote site and conserve address space?

    a. 192.168.10.64/26 and 192.168.10.192/26

    b. 192.168.10.0/25 and 192.168.10.128/25

    c. 192.168.10.32/28 and 192.168.10.64/28

    d. 192.168.10.0/30 and 192.168.10.128/30

22. The main site uses the network prefix 192.168.15.0/24. What subnets and masks can you use to provide sufficient addresses for LANs at the main site and conserve address space?

    a. 192.168.15.0/25 for LAN1, 192.168.15.128/26 for LAN2, and 172.16.192.0/27 for LAN3

    b. 192.168.15.0/27 for LAN1, 192.168.15.128/26 for LAN2, and 172.16.192.0/25 for LAN3

    c. 192.168.15.0/100 for LAN1, 192.168.15.128/60 for LAN2, and 172.16.192.0/29 for LAN3

    d. 192.168.15.0/26 for LAN1, 192.168.15.128/26 for LAN2, and 172.16.192.0/29 for LAN3

23. What is the network and mask that you can use for the WAN link which would save the most address space?

    a. 192.168.11.240/27

    b. 192.168.11.240/28

    c. 192.168.11.240.29

    d. 192.168.11.240.30

24. What networks does Router C announce to the provider's Internet router?

    a. 210.200.200.8/26

    b. 192.168.10.0/24 and 192.168.11.0/24

    c. 192.168.10.0/25 summary address

    d. 201.200.200.8/29 and 192.168.10.0/25

25. What technology does Router C use to convert private addresses to public addresses?

   a. DNS

   b. NAT

   c. ARP

   d. VLSMs

26. What mechanism supports the ability to divide a given subnet into smaller subnets based on need?

   a. DNS

   b. NAT

   c. ARP

   d. VLSMs

This chapter covers the following subjects:

- Introduction to IPv6

- IPv6 Header

- IPv6 Address Representation

- IPv6 Address Types

- IPv6 Mechanisms

- IPv4 to IPv6 Transition Strategies and Deployments

- IPv6 Comparison with IPv4

CHAPTER 10

Internet Protocol Version 6

This chapter reviews the Internet Protocol Version 6 (IPv6) address structures, address assignments, representations, and mechanisms used to deploy IPv6. The CCDA must understand how an IPv6 address is represented and the different types of IPv6 addresses. This chapter also covers the benefits of IPv6 over IPv4 to provide a comparison of the protocols.

As IPv6 matures, different deployment models will implement the new protocol with existing IPv4 networks. This chapter does not cover these models at a high level. This chapter does not discuss the configuration of IPv6 because it is not a requirement for CCDA certification.

"Do I Know This Already?" Quiz

The purpose of the "Do I Know This Already?" quiz is to help you decide whether you need to read the entire chapter. If you intend to read the entire chapter, you do not necessarily need to answer these questions now.

The 10-question quiz, derived from the major sections in the "Foundation Topics" portion of the chapter, helps you determine how to spend your limited study time.

Table 10-1 outlines the major topics discussed in this chapter and the "Do I Know This Already?" quiz questions that correspond to those topics.

Table 10-1   *"Do I Know This Already?" Foundation Topics Section-to-Question Mapping*

Foundation Topics Section	Questions Covered in This Section
IPv6 Header	1
IPv6 Address Representation	5, 8, 9
IPv6 Address Types	2, 3, 4, 7
IPv6 Mechanisms	10
IPv4 to IPv6 Transition Strategies and Deployments	6

> **CAUTION**   The goal of self assessment is to gauge your mastery of the topics in this chapter. If you do not know the answer to a question or you are only partially sure of the answer, you should mark this question wrong for purposes of the self assessment. Giving yourself credit for an answer you correctly guess skews your self-assessment results and might provide you with a false sense of security.

1. IPv6 uses how many more bits for addresses than IPv4?

    a. 32

    b. 64

    c. 96

    d. 128

2. What is the hierarchy for IPv6 aggregatable addresses?

    a. Public, site, interface

    b. Global, site, loop

    c. Internet, site, interface

    d. Multicast, anycast, unicast

3. What address type is the following IPv6 address?

    FE80::300:34BC:123F:1010

    a. Aggregatable global

    b. Site-local

    c. Link-local

    d. Multicast

4. What are three types of IPv6 addresses?

    a. Unicast, multicast, broadcast

    b. Unicast, anycast, broadcast

    c. Unicast, multicast, endcast

    d. Unicast, anycast, multicast

5. What is a compact representation of the following address?

3f00:0000:0000:a7fb:0000:0000:b100:0023

   a. 3f::a7fb::b100:0023

   b. 3f00::a7fb:0000:0000:b100:23

   c. 3f::a7fb::b1:23

   d. 3f00:0000:0000:a7fb::b1:23

6. What is NAT-PT?

   a. Network address translation–port translation; translates RFC 1918 addresses to public IPv4 addresses

   b. Network addressable transparent-port translation; translates network addresses to ports

   c. Network address translation-protocol translation; translates between IPv4 and IPv6 addresses

   d. Next address translation–port translation

7. What IPv6 address type replaces the IPv4 broadcast address?

   a. Unicast

   b. Multicast

   c. Broadcast

   d. Anycast

8. What is the IPv6 equivalent to 127.0.0.1?

   a. 0:0:0:0:0:0:0:0

   b. 0:0:0:0:0:0:0:1

   c. 127:0:0:0:0:0:0:1

   d. FF::1

9. Which is an "IPv4-compatible" IPv6 address?

   a. ::180.10.1.1

   b. f000:0:0:0:0:0:180.10.1.1

   c. 180.10.1.1::

   d. 2010::180.10.1.1

10. Which protocol maps names to IPv6 addresses?

   a. Address Resolution Protocol (ARP)

   b. Neighbor discovery (ND)

   c. Domain Name System (DNS)

   d. DNSv2

The answers to the "Do I Know This Already?" quiz appear in Appendix A, "Answers to Chapter 'Do I Know This Already?' Quizzes and Q&A Sections." The suggested choices for your next step are as follows:

■ **8 or less overall score**—Read the entire chapter. It includes the "Foundation Topics," "Foundation Summary," and "Q&A" sections.

■ **9–10 overall score**—If you want more review on these topics, skip to the "Foundation Summary" section and then go to the "Q&A" section. Otherwise, move to the next chapter.

Foundation Topics

The following sections cover topics that you need to master for the CCDA exam. The section "IPv6 Header" covers each field of the IPv6 header, which helps you understand the protocol. The section "IPv6 Address Representation" covers the hexadecimal representation of IPv6 addresses and the compressed representation. The section "IPv6 Address Types" covers unicast, multicast, and anycast IPv6 addresses and the current allocations of IPv6 addresses.

The section "IPv6 Mechanisms" covers Internet Control Message Protocol Version 6 (ICMPv6), ND, address assignment and resolution, and IPv6 routing protocols. The section "IPv4 to IPv6 Transition Strategies and Deployments" covers dual-stack backbones, IPv6 over IPv4 tunnels, dual-stack hosts, and network address translation-protocol translation (NAT-PT).

Introduction to IPv6

You should become familiar at a high level with IPv6 specifications, addressing, and design. The driving motivation for the adoption of a new version of IP is the limitation imposed by the 32-bit address field in IPv4. In the 1990s, there was concern that the IP address space would be depleted soon. Although classless interdomain routing (CIDR) and NAT have slowed down the deployment of IPv6, its standards and deployments are becoming mature. IPv6 is playing a significant role in the deployment of IP services for wireless phones; also, some countries such as Japan will have directed IPv6 compatibility by 2005. Several IPv6 testbeds include the 6bone and the 6ren. The 6bone is an IPv6 testbed that focuses on testing standards, implementations, and transition and operational procedures. Under a new phase-out plan, the 6bone will cease to operate by July 2006. The 6ren is a IPv6 network that serves research and educational institutions.

The IPv6 specification provides 128 bits for addressing, a significant increase from 32 bits. The overall specification of IPv6 is in RFC 2460. Other RFCs describing IPv6 specifications are 2373, 2374, 2461, 1886, and 1981.

IPv6 includes the following enhancements over IPv4:

- **Expanded address space**—IPv6 uses 128-bit addresses instead of the 32-bit addresses in IPv4.
- **Fixed header length**—The IPv6 header length is fixed, allowing for vendors to improve switching performance.
- **Improved option mechanism**—IPv6 options are placed in separate optional headers that are located between the IPv6 header and the transport-layer header. The option headers are not required.

- **Address autoconfiguration**—This capability provides for dynamic assignment of IPv6 addresses. IPv6 hosts can automatically configure themselves, with or without a Dynamic Host Configuration Protocol (DHCP) server.

- **Support for labeling traffic flows**—Instead of the type-of-service field in IPv4, IPv6 enables the labeling of packets belonging to a particular traffic class for which the sender requests special handling. This support aids specialized traffic, such as real-time video.

- **Security capabilities**—IPv6 includes features that support authentication and privacy.

- **Maximum transmission unit (MTU) path discovery**—IPv6 eliminates the need for fragmenting packets by implementing MTU path discovery before sending packets to a destination.

IPv6 Header

This section covers each field of the IPv6 header. The IPv6 header is simpler than the IPv4 header. Some IPv4 fields have been eliminated or changed to optional fields. The fragment offset fields and flags in IPv4 have been eliminated from the header. IPv6 adds a flow label field for quality-of-service (QoS) mechanisms to use.

The use of 128 bits for source and destination addresses provides a significant improvement over IPv4. With 128 bits, there are 3.4×10^{38} or 34 billion billion billion billion IPv6 addresses, compared to only 4.3 billion IPv4 addresses.

IPv6 improves over IPv4 by using a fixed-length header. The IPv6 header appears in Figure 10-1.

Figure 10-1 *IPv6 Header Format*

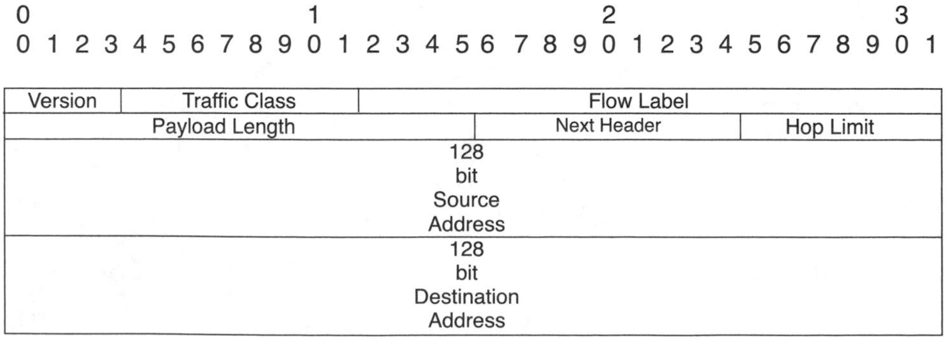

The following is a description of each field in the IP header:

- **Version**—This field is 4 bits long. It indicates the format, based on the version number, of the IP header. These bits are set to 0110 for IPv6 packets.

- **Traffic class**—This field is 8 bits in length. It describes the class or priority of the IPv6 packet and provides similar functionality to the IPv4 type-of-service field.

- **Flow label**—This field is 20 bits in length. It indicates a specific sequence of packets between a source and destination that requires special handling, such as real-time data (voice and video).

- **Payload length**—This field is 16 bits in length. It indicates the size in bytes of the payload. Its length includes any extension headers.

- **Next header**—This field is 8 bits in length. It indicates the type of header that follows this IPv6 header. It uses values defined by the Internet Assigned Numbers Authority (IANA).

- **Hop limit**—This field is 8 bits in length. It is decremented by 1 by each router that forwards the packets. If this field is 0, the packet is discarded.

- **Source address**—This field is 128 bits in length. It indicates the IPv6 address of the sender.

- **Destination address**—This field is 128 bits in length. It indicates the IPv6 address of the destination host.

Notice that although the IPv6 address is four times the length of an IPv4 address, the IPv6 header is only twice the length. Optional network-layer information is not included in the IPv6 header; instead it is included in separate extended headers.

Two important extended headers are the Authentication Header (AH) and the Encapsulating Security Payload (ESP) header. These headers are covered later in the chapter.

IPv6 Address Representation

RFC 2373 specifies the IPv6 addressing architecture. IPv6 addresses are 128 bits in length. For display, the IPv6 addresses have eight 16-bit groups. The hexadecimal value is x:x:x:x:x:x:x:x, where each x represents four hexadecimal digits.

An example of a full IPv6 address is 1111111000011010 0100001010110111 0000000000011011 0000000000000000 0000000000000000 0001001011010000 0000000001011011 0000011010110000.

The hexadecimal representation of the preceding IPv6 binary number is

> FE1A:42B9:001B:0000:0000:12D0:005B:06B0

Groups with a value of zero can be represented with a single zero. For example, you can also represent the preceding number as

> FE1A:42B9:001B:0:0:12D0:005B:06B0

You can represent multiple groups of 16-bit zeros with ::, which might appear only once in the number. Also, you do not need to represent leading zeros in a 16-bit piece. The preceding IPv6 address can be further shortened to

> FE1A:42B9:1B::12D0:5B:6B0

> **TIP** Remember that there are eight blocks in the fully expanded address and that the double colon represents only zeros. You can use the double colon only once.

You expand a compressed address following the same rules used earlier. For example, the IPv6 address 2001:4C::50:0:0:741 expands as follows:

> 2001:004C::0050:0000:0000:0741

Because there should be eight blocks of addresses and you have six, you can expand the double colon to two blocks as follows:

> 2001:004C:0000:0000:0050:0000:0000:0741

In a mixed IPv6/IPv4 environment, the IPv4 portion of the address requires the last two 16-bit blocks or 32 bits of the address, which is represented in IPv4 dotted-decimal notation. The remaining portion of the IPv6 address is all zeros. Six hexadecimal 16-bit blocks are concatenated with the dotted-decimal format. The first 96 bits are zero, and the last 32 bits are used for the IPv4 address. This form is $x:x:x:x:x:x:d.d.d.d$, where each x represents the hexadecimal digits and $d.d.d.d$ is the dotted-decimal representation.

An example of a mixed full address is 0000:0000:0000:0000:0000:0000:100.1.1.1; this example can be shortened to 0:0:0:0:0:0:100.1.1.1 or ::100.1.1.1.

IPv6 Prefix Representation

IPv6 prefixes are represented similar to IPv4 with the following format:

> IPv6-address/prefix

The IPv6-address portion is a valid IPv6 address. The prefix portion is the number of contiguous bits that represent the prefix. You use the double colon only once in the representation. An example of an IPv6 prefix is 200C:001b:1100:0:0:0:0:0/40 or 200C:1b:1100::/40.

For another example, look of the representations of the 60-bit prefix 2001000000000ab0:

> 2001:0000:0000:0ab0:0000:0000:0000:0000/60
> 2001:0000:0000:0ab0:0:0:0:0/60
> 2001:0000:0000:ab0::/60
> 2001:0:0:ab0::/60

The rules for address representation are still valid when using a prefix. The following are not valid representations of the preceding prefix:

> 2001:0:0:ab0/60

The preceding representation is missing the trailing double colon:

> 2001::ab0/60

The preceding representation expands to 2001:0:0:0:0:0:0:0ab0, which is not the prefix 2001:0000:0000:0ab0::/60.

When representing an IPv6 host address with its subnet prefix, you combine the two. For example the IPv6 address 2001:0000:0000:0ab0:001c:1bc0:08ba:1c9a in subnet prefix

2001:0000:0000:0ab0::/60 is represented as the following:

> 2001:0000:0000:0ab0:001c:1bc0:08ba:1c9a/60

IPv6 Address Types

This section covers the major types of IPv6 addresses. IPv4 addresses are unicast, multicast, or broadcast. IPv6 maintains each of these address functions except the IPv6 address types are defined a little differently. A special "all-nodes" IPv6 multicast address handles the broadcast function. IPv6 also introduces the anycast address type.

Also significant to understand are the IPv6 address allocations. Sections of the IPv6 address space are reserved for particular functions, each which are covered in this section. To provide you with a full understanding of address types, the following sections describe each type.

As mentioned earlier, there are three types of IPv6 addresses:

- Unicast
- Anycast
- Multicast

IPv6 Unicast Address

The IPv6 *unicast* address is the logical identifier of a single host interface. It is similar to IPv4 unicast classful (Class A, Class B, and Class C) addresses. Unicast addresses are aggregatable-global, site-local, or link-local. These unicast address types are explained in sections that follow.

IPv6 Anycast Address

The IPv6 *anycast* address identifies a set of devices. An anycast address is built from a set of unicast addresses. You can use it to identify a set of routers within an area. When a packet is sent to the anycast address, it is delivered to the nearest device as determined by the routing protocol.

IPv6 Multicast Address

The IPv6 *multicast* address identifies a set of hosts. The packet is delivered to all the hosts identified by that address. This type is similar to IPv4 multicast (Class D) addresses. IPv6 multicast addresses also supersede the broadcast function of IPv4 broadcasts. You use an "all-nodes" multicast address instead.

IPv6 Address Allocations

The leading bits of an IPv6 address can define the IPv6 address type or other reservations. These leading bits are of variable length and are called the format prefix (FP). Table 10-2 shows the allocation of address prefixes. Many prefixes are still unassigned.

Table 10-2 *IPv6 Prefix Allocation*

Binary Prefix	Hexadecimal/ Prefix	Fraction of Address Space	Allocation
0000 0000	00/8	1/256	Unspecified, loopback, IPv4-compatible
0000 0001	01/8	1/256	Unassigned
0000 001	02/7	1/128	Reserved for network service access point (NSAP) allocation
0000 010	04/7	1/128	Reserved for Internetwork Packet Exchange (IPX) allocation

Table 10-2 *IPv6 Prefix Allocation (Continued)*

Binary Prefix	Hexadecimal/ Prefix	Fraction of Address Space	Allocation
0000 011	06/7	1/128	Unassigned
0000 1	08/5	1/32	Unassigned
0001	1/4	1/16	Unassigned
001	2/3	1/8	Aggregatable-global unicast address
010	4/3	1/8	Unassigned
011	6/3	1/8	Unassigned
100	8/3 or 9	1/8	Reserved for geographical-based unicast addresses
101	A/3	1/8	Unassigned
110	C/3	1/8	Unassigned
1110	E/3	1/16	Unassigned
1111 0	F0/5	1/32	Unassigned
1111 10	F1/6	1/64	Unassigned
1111 110	FC/7	1/128	Unassigned
1111 1110 0	FE0/9	1/512	Unassigned
1111 1110 10	FE8/10	1/1024	Link-local unicast addresses
1111 1110 11	FEC/10	1/1024	Site-local unicast addresses
1111 1111	FF/8	1/256	Multicast addresses

Unspecified Address

An unspecified address is all zeros: 0:0:0:0:0:0:0:0. It signifies that an IPv6 address is not specified for the interface.

Loopback Address

The IPv6 loopback address is 0:0:0:0:0:0:0:1. This address is similar to the IPv4 loopback address of 127.0.0.1.

IPv4-Compatible IPv6 Address

IPv4-compatible IPv6 addresses begin with leading zeros (six 16-bit groups) followed by the IPv4 address, as in 0:0:0:0:0:0:130.100.50.1 or just ::130.100.50.1.

NOTE RFC 2374 has been replaced by RFC 3587, which obsoletes RFC 2374, and documents and makes RFC 2374 and the TLA/NLA structure historic.

IPv6 NSAP Addresses

IPv6 NSAP addresses help transition from an Open Systems Interconnection (OSI) NSAP-addressed network to a native IPv6 network. These addresses support the OSI NSAP addresses within an IPv6 network. IPv6 NSAP addresses are identified by the leading 0000001 bits. Using IPv6 NSAP addresses is not an exam topic and is not covered further in this book.

IPv6 IPX Addresses

IPv6 IPX addresses are identified by the leading 0000010 bits. The usage of these IPv6 addresses has not been defined at this time.

Aggregatable-Global Addresses

IPv6 aggregatable-global addresses connect to the public network. These unicast addresses are globally unique and routable. This address format is defined in RFC 2374.

The address format has a three-layer hierarchy: public topology, site topology, and interface identi-fier. The *public topology* consists of service providers that provide transit services and exchanges of routing information. The *site topology* is local to the company or site and does not provide transit services. The *interface layer* uniquely identifies an interface on the network.

As shown in Figure 10-2, the IPv6 aggregatable-global address format consists of various fields. FP is the format prefix (001) used to identify an aggregatable address. TLA ID is the top-level aggre-gation identifier; it is the top level of the routing hierarchy. The RES field is reserved for future use. The NLA ID field is the next-level identifier; it is used by organizations that have been assigned a TLA ID to assign a hierarchy. The SLA ID is the site-level aggregation identifier; it is used by orga-nizations to assign its own addressing hierarchy. The interface ID uniquely identifies the interface on the link. These identifiers will permit Internet service providers to identify the site allocation of an address and permit organizations to further allocate the address space.

Figure 10-2 *IPv6 Aggregatable-Global Address Format*

3	13	8	24 bits	16 bits	64 bits
FP	TLA ID	RES	NLA ID	SLA ID	Interface ID
Public Topology				Site Topology	Interface Identifier

Link-Local Addresses

IPv6 link-local addresses are significant only to nodes on a single link. Routers do not forward packets with a link-local source or destination address beyond the local link. Link-local addresses are identified by leading FE8 hexadecimal numbers. Link-local addresses are configured automatically or manually.

As shown in Figure 10-3, the format of the link-local address is an FP of 1111111010, followed by 54 zeros and a 64-bit interface identifier (ID). The interface ID is obtained automatically through communication with other nodes in the link. The interface ID is then concatenated with the link-local address prefix of FE80::/64 to obtain the interface link-local address.

Figure 10-3 *IPv6 Link-Local Address Format*

10 bits	54 bits	64 bits
1111111010	0	Interface Identifier

Site-Local Addresses

IPv6 site-local addresses are analogous to IPv4 private addresses (RFC 1918). Site-local addresses are used within an organization and are not globally unique. Site-local addresses are not routable across a public network such as the Internet.

As shown in Figure 10-4, the format of the site-local address is a 10-bit FP of 1111111010, followed by 38 zeros, a 16-bit subnet ID, and a 64-bit interface ID.

Figure 10-4 *IPv6 Site-Local Address Format*

10 bits	38 bits	16 bits	64 bits
1111111011	0	Subnet ID	Interface ID

Multicast Addresses

IPv6 multicast addresses perform the same function as IPv4 multicast addresses. Multicast addresses send packets to all hosts in a group. IPv6 multicast addresses are identified by the leading FF hexadecimal numbers (an FP value of 11111111). RFC 2373 specifies the format for IPv6 multicast addresses.

As shown in Figure 10-5, the fields of the IPv6 multicast address are the FP, a value of 0xFF, followed by a 4-bit flags field, a 4-bit scope field, and 112 bits for the group identifier (ID).

Figure 10-5 *Multicast Address Format*

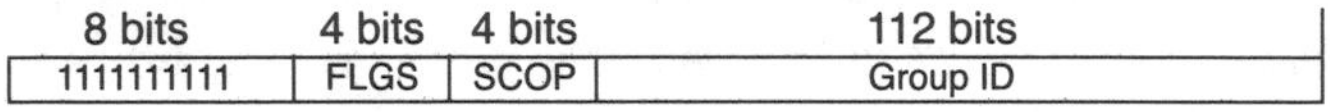

8 bits	4 bits	4 bits	112 bits
1111111111	FLGS	SCOP	Group ID

The FLGS (flags) field consists of three leading zeros followed by a T bit: 000T. If T = 0, the address is a well-known multicast address assigned by the global IANA. If T = 1, the address is not a permanently assigned address.

The SCOP (scope) field limits the scope of the multicast group. Table 10-3 shows the assigned scope values.

Table 10-3 *Multicast Scope Assignments*

SCOP (Binary)	SCOP (Hexadecimal)	Assignment
0000	0	Reserved
0001	1	Node-local scope
0010	2	Link-local scope
0011	3	Unassigned
0100	4	Unassigned
0101	5	Site-local scope
0110	6	Unassigned
0111	7	Unassigned
1000	8	Organization-local scope
1001	9	Unassigned
1010	A	Unassigned
1011	B	Unassigned
1100	C	Unassigned
1101	D	Unassigned
1110	E	Global scope
1111	F	Reserved

The group ID identifies the multicast group within the given scope. The group ID is independent of the scope. A group ID of 0:0:0:0:0:0:1 identifies nodes, whereas a group of ID of 0:0:0:0:0:0:2 identifies routers. Some well-known multicast addresses appear in Table 10-4 associated with a variety of scope values.

Table 10-4 *Well-Known Multicast Addresses*

Multicast Address	Multicast Group
FF01:0:0:0:0:0:0:1	All nodes (node-local)
FF02:0:0:0:0:0:0:1	All nodes (link-local)
FF01:0:0:0:0:0:0:2	All routers (node-local)
FF02:0:0:0:0:0:0:2	All routers (link-local)
FF05:0:0:0:0:0:0:2	All routers (site-local)
FF02:0:0:0:0:0:0:5	Open Shortest Path First (OSPF)
FF02:0:0:0:0:0:0:6	OSPF-designated routers
FF02:0:0:0:0:0:0:9	Routing Information Protocol (RIP)

IPv6 Mechanisms

The changes of the 128-bit address length and IPv6 header format modified the underlying protocols that support IP. This section covers ICMPv6, IPv6 ND, address resolution, address assignment, and IPv6 routing protocols. These protocols must now support 128-bit addresses; for example, DNS adds a new record locator for resolving fully qualified domain names (FQDNs) to IPv6 addresses. IPv6 also replaces ARP with the IPv6 ND protocol. IPv6 ND uses ICMPv6.

ICMPv6

The ICMP needed some modifications to support IPv6. RFC 2463 describes the use of ICMPv6 for IPv6 networks. All IPv6 nodes must implement ICMPv6 to perform network-layer functions. ICMPv6 performs diagnostics (ping), reports errors, and provides reachability information.

Informational messages are

■ Echo request

■ Echo reply

Some error messages are

- Destination unreachable
- Packet too big
- Time exceeded
- Parameter problem

The destination-unreachable messages also provide further detail as follows:

- No route to destination
- Destination administratively prohibited
- Address unreachable
- Port unreachable

Other IPv6 mechanisms use ICMPv6 to determine neighbor availability, path MTU, or destination address or port reachability.

IPv6 ND

IPv6 does not implement the ARP that is used in IPv4. Instead, IPv6 implements the ND protocol described in RFC 2461. Hosts use ND to discover all other nodes in the same link, check for duplicate addresses, and find routers in the link. The protocol also searches for alternative routers if the primary fails.

The address-resolution process uses neighbor-solicitation messages to obtain the link-layer address of a neighbor. Nodes respond with a neighbor-advertisement message that contains the link-layer address.

IPv6 Name Resolution

IPv4 uses ARP for resolving IP addresses to MAC addresses. IPv6 uses ND to map IPv6 addresses to MAC addresses. DNS adds a resource record to support name-to-IPv6-address resolution. RFC 3596 describes the addition of a new DNS resource record type to support IPv6 name resolution. The new record type is AAAA, commonly known as "quad-A." Given a domain name, the AAAA record returns an IPv6 address to the requesting host. DNS A records return an IPv4 address. The node's DNS resolver must be able to handle both A and AAAA records with dual-stacks.

Path MTU Discovery

IPv6 does not allow fragmentation of packets throughout the internetwork. Only sending hosts are allowed to fragment. Routers are not allowed to perform fragmentation of packets. RFC 2460 specifies that the MTU of every link in an IPv6 must be 1280 bytes or greater. RFC 1981 recommends that nodes should implement IPv6 path MTU discovery to determine whether there are paths greater than 1280 bytes. ICMPv6 packet-too-big error messages determine the path MTU. Nodes along the path send the ICMPv6 packet-too-big message to the sending host if the packet is larger than the outgoing interface MTU.

Figure 10-6 shows a host sending a 2000-byte packet. Because the outgoing interface MTU is 1500 bytes, Router A sends an ICMPv6 packet-too-big error message back to Host A. The sending host then sends a 1500-byte packet. The outgoing interface MTU at Router B is 1300 bytes. Router B sends a ICMPv6 packet-too-big error message to Host A. Host A then sends the packet with 1300 bytes.

Figure 10-6 *ICMPv6 Packet-Too-Big Message*

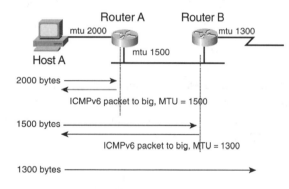

IPv6 Address-Assignment Strategies

An IPv6 host can obtain its address through autoconfiguration or from the DHCP. DHCP is a stateful method of address assignment. IPv6 nodes might or might not use DHCP to acquire IP address information.

Autoconfiguration

IPv6 hosts can use a stateless autoconfiguration method, without DHCP, to acquire their own IP address information. Hosts obtain their link-local addresses automatically as an interface is initialized. First, the host performs a duplicate address-detection process. The host joins the all-nodes multicast group to receive neighbor advertisements from other nodes. The neighbor advertisements include the subnet or prefix associated with the link. The host then sends a neighbor-solicitation message with the tentative IP address (interface identifier) as the target. If there is a host already using the tentative IP address, that host replies with a neighbor advertisement. If the host receives no neighbor advertisement, the target IP address becomes the link-local address of the originating host.

IPv6 Security

IPv6 has two integrated mechanisms to provide security for communications. It natively supports IPSecurity (IPSec). IPSec is mandated at the operating-system level for all IPSec hosts. RFC 2401 describes IPSec. Extension headers carry the IPSec AH and ESP header. The AH provides authentication and integrity. The ESP header provides confidentiality by encrypting the payload. For IPv6, the AH defaults to message digest algorithm 5 (MD5), and the ESP encryption defaults to data encryption standard-cipher block chaining (DES-CBC).

A description of the mechanisms of IPSec appear in Chapter 8, "VPN and DSL WAN Design." More information also appears in RFC 2402, *IP Authentication Header* and RFC 2406, *IP Encapsulating Security Payload (ESP)*.

IPv6 Routing Protocols

New routing protocols are being developed to support IPv6, such as RIPng, Integrated/ Intermediate System-to-Intermediate System (i/IS-IS), and OSPFv3. The Border Gateway Protocol (BGP) also includes changes that support IPv6. In the future, a newer version of Enhanced Interior Gateway Routing Protocol (EIGRP) will support IPv6.

RIPng for IPv6

RFC 2080 describes changes to the RIP to support IPv6 networks, called RIP next generation (RIPng). RIP mechanisms remain the same. RIPng still has a 15-hop limit, counting to infinity, and uses User Datagram Protocol (UDP) port 521. RIPng version supports IPv6 addresses and prefixes. Cisco IOS Software currently supports RIPng.

OSPFv3 for IPv6

RFC 2740 describes OSPF Version 3 to support IPv6 networks. OSPF algorithms and mechanisms (flooding, designated router [DR] election, areas, short path first [SFP] calculations) remain the same. Changes are made for OSPF to support IPv6 addresses and address hierarchy. Cisco IOS Software currently supports OSPFv3.

IS-IS for IPv6

Specifications for routing IPv6 with integrated IS-IS is currently an Internet draft of the IETF. The draft specifies new type, length, and value (TLV) objects, reachability TLVs, and an interface address TLV to forward IPv6 information in the network. IOS currently supports IS-IS for IPv6 as currently described in the draft standard.

BGP4 Multiprotocol Extensions for IPv6

RFC 2545 specifies the use of BGP attributes for passing on IPv6 route information. The MP_REACH_NLRI (multiprotocol-reachable) attribute describes reachable destinations. It includes the next-hop address and a list of Network Layer Reachability Information (NLRI) prefixes of reachable networks. The MP_UNREACH_NLRI (multiprotocol-unreachable) attribute conveys unreachable networks. IOS currently supports these BGP4 multiprotocol attributes to communicate reachability information for IPv6 networks.

IPv4 to IPv6 Transition Strategies and Deployments

Several deployment models exist to migrate from an IPv4 network to IPv6. During a transition time, both protocols can coexist in the network. The deployment models are

- IPv6 over dedicated WAN links
- IPv6 over IPv4 tunnels
- IPv6 using dual-stack backbones
- Protocol translation

Each model provides several advantages and disadvantages with which you should become familiar. The sections that follow describe each model.

IPv6 over Dedicated WAN Links

In this deployment model, all nodes and links use IPv6 hierarchy, addressing, and protocols. The WAN in this model uses IPv6. The disadvantage of this model is that there are additional costs when using separate links for IPv6 WAN circuits during the transition to using IPv6 exclusively. As shown in Figure 10-7, a company needs both IPv6 and IPv4 networks in sites A and B during the IPv6 deployment and transition. The networks are connected using separate WANs.

Figure 10-7 *Dedicated IPv6 WAN*

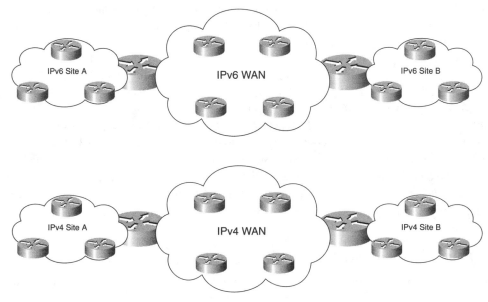

IPv6 over IPv4 Tunnels

In this deployment model, pockets of IPv6-only networks are connected using IPv4 tunnels. With tunneling, IPv6 traffic is encapsulated within IPv4 packets so that they are sent over the IPv4 WAN. The advantage of this method is that you do not need separate circuits to connect the IPv6 networks. A disadvantage of this method is the increased protocol overhead of the encapsulated IPv6 headers. Figure 10-8 shows a network using IPv4 tunnels. Site A and Site B both have IPv4 and IPv6 networks. The IPv6 networks are connected using an IPv4 tunnel in the WAN.

Figure 10-8 *IPv6 over IPv4 Tunnels*

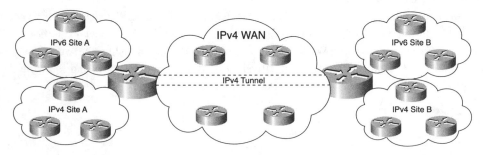

Dual-Stack Backbones

In this model, all routers in the backbone are dual-stack, capable of routing both IPv4 and IPv6 packets. The IPv4 protocol stack is used between IPv4 hosts, and the IPv6 protocol stack is used between IPv6 hosts. This deployment model works for organizations with a mixture of IPv4 and IPv6 applications. Figure 10-9 shows a network with a dual-stack backbone. All the WAN routers run both IPv4 and IPv6 routing protocols. The disadvantages are that the WAN routers require dual addressing, run two routing protocols, and might require additional CPU and memory resources. Another disadvantage is that IPv4-only and IPv6-only hosts cannot communicate with each other directly; dual-stack hosts or network translation is required (covered next) for IPv4 and IPv6 hosts to communicate.

Figure 10-9   *Dual-Stack Backbone*

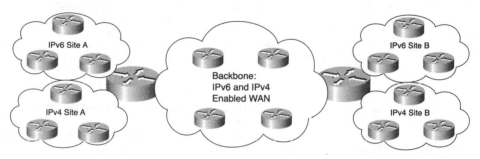

Hosts require dual stacks (IPv4 and IPv6) to communicate with both IPv4 and IPv6 hosts. When using dual stacks, a host uses DNS to determine which stack to use to reach a destination. If DNS returns an IPv6 (AAAA record) address to the host, the host uses the IPv6 stack. If DNS returns an IPv4 (A record) address to the host, the host uses the IPv4 stack.

Protocol Translation Mechanisms

One of the mechanisms for an IPv6-only host to communicate with an IPv4-only host without using dual stacks is protocol translation. RFC 2766 describes NAT-PT, which provides translation between IPv6 and IPv4 hosts. NAT-PT operates similarly to the NAT mechanisms to translate IPv4 private addresses to public address space. NAT-PT binds addresses in the IPv6 network to addresses in the IPv4 network and vice versa. Figure 10-10 shows a network using NAT-PT.

Figure 10-10   *Network Address Translation-Protocol Translation*

IPv6 Comparison with IPv4

This section provides a summary comparison of IPv6 to IPv4. Become knowledgeable about the characteristics summarized in Table 10-5. The use of 128 bits over 32 bits is an obvious change. The upper-layer protocol is identified with the next header field in IPv6, which was the protocol type field used in IPv4. ARP is replaced by IPv6 ND. Site-local addresses provide the function that IPv4 RFC 1918 private addresses provide.

Table 10-5   *IPv6 and IPv4 Characteristics*

Characteristic	IPv6	IPv4
Address length	128 bits	32 bits
Address representation	Hexadecimal	Dotted-decimal
Header length	Fixed (40 bytes)	Variable
Upper-layer protocols	Next header field	Protocol type field
Address resolution	ND	ARP
Address configuration	Stateless autoconfiguration or stateful DHCP	Stateful DHCP
DNS (name-to-address resolution)	AAAA records	A records
Interior routing protocols	OSPFv3, RIPng, IS-IS for IPv6	OSPFv2, RIPv2, IS-IS
Classification and marking	Traffic class and flow label fields, Differentiated Service Code Point (DSCP)	IP precedence bits, type-of-service field, DSCP
Private addresses	Site-local addresses	RFC 1918 private address space
Fragmentation	Sending host only	Sending host and intermediate routers
Loopback address	0:0:0:0:0:0:0:1	127.0.0.1
Address types	Unicast, anycast, multicast	Unicast, multicast, broadcast

Foundation Summary

The "Foundation Summary" section of each chapter lists the most important facts from the chapter. Although this section does not list every fact from the chapter that will be on your CCDA exam, a well-prepared CCDA candidate should at a minimum know all the details in each "Foundation Summary" before going to take the exam.

The CCDA exam requires that you be familiar with the three types of IPv6 addresses:

- **Unicast**—The logical identifier of a single host. Unicast addresses are aggregatable-global, site-local, or link-local.
- **Anycast**—Identifies a set of devices. The packet is delivered to the nearest device as determined by the routing protocol.
- **Multicast**—Identifies a set of hosts. The packet is delivered to all the hosts.

Table 10-6 provides a quick look of the current IPv6 allocations. Be able to identify the allocation based on the leading binary or hexadecimal numbers.

Table 10-6 *IPv6 Prefix Allocations*

Binary Prefix	Hexadecimal/ Prefix	Fraction of Address Space	Allocation
0000 0000	00/8	1/256	Unspecified, loopback, IPv4-compatible
0000 0001	01/8	1/256	Unassigned
0000 001	02/7	1/128	Reserved for network service access point (NSAP) allocation
0000 010	04/7	1/128	Reserved for Internetwork Packet Exchange (IPX) allocation
0000 011	06/7	1/128	Unassigned
0000 1	08/5	1/32	Unassigned
0001	1/4	1/16	Unassigned
001	2/3	1/8	Aggregatable-global unicast address
010	4/3	1/8	Unassigned

continues

Table 10-6   *IPv6 Prefix Allocations (Continued)*

Binary Prefix	Hexadecimal/ Prefix	Fraction of Address Space	Allocation
011	6/3	1/8	Unassigned
100	8/3 or 9	1/8	Reserved for geographical-based unicast addresses
101	A/3	1/8	Unassigned
110	C/3	1/8	Unassigned
1110	E/3	1/16	Unassigned
1111 0	F0/5	1/32	Unassigned
1111 10	F1/6	1/64	Unassigned
1111 110	FC/7	1/128	Unassigned
1111 1110 0	FE0/9	1/512	Unassigned
1111 1110 10	FE8/10	1/1024	Link-local unicast addresses
1111 1110 11	FEC/10	1/1024	Site-local unicast addresses
1111 1111	FF/8	1/256	Multicast addresses

Table 10-7 is actually a review of Table 10-5. It is presented again in this section because it is essential for the exam. It provides a quick summary of IPv6 characteristics as they are compared with IPv4. Study this table in detail.

Table 10-7   *IPv6 and IPv4 Characteristics*

Characteristic	IPv6	IPv4
Address length	128 bits	32 bits
Address representation	Hexadecimal	Dotted-decimal
Header length	Fixed (40 bytes)	Variable
Upper-layer protocols	Next header field	Protocol type field
Address resolution	ND	ARP
Address configuration	Stateless autoconfiguration or stateful DHCP	Stateful DHCP

Table 10-7 *IPv6 and IPv4 Characteristics (Continued)*

Characteristic	IPv6	IPv4
DNS (name-to-address resolution)	AAAA records	A records
Interior routing protocols	OSPFv3, RIPng, IS-IS for IPv6	OSPFv2, RIPv2, IS-IS
Classification and marking	Traffic class and flow label fields, DSCP	IP precedence bits, type-of-service field, DSCP
Private addresses	Site-local addresses	RFC 1918 private address space
Fragmentation	Sending host only	Sending host and intermediate routers
Loopback address	0:0:0:0:0:0:0:1	127.0.0.1
Address types	Unicast, anycast, multicast	Unicast, multicast, broadcast

Table 10-8 provides a description of each field in the IP header.

Table 10-8 *IPv6 Header Fields*

IPv6 Header Field	Description
Version	This field is 4 bits long. It indicates the format, based on the version number, of the IP header. These bits are set to 0110 for IPv6 packets.
Traffic class	This field is 8 bits in length. It describes the class or priority of the IPv6 packet and provides similar functionality to the IPv4 type-of-service field.
Flow label	This field is 20 bits in length. It indicates a specific sequence of packets between a source and destination that requires special handling, such as real-time data (voice and video).
Payload length	This field is 16 bits in length. It indicates the size in bytes of the payload. Its length includes any extension headers.
Next header	This field is 8 bits in length. It indicates the type of header that follows this IPv6 header.
Hop limit	This field is 8 bits in length. It is decremented by 1 by each router that forwards the packets. If this field is 0, the packet is discarded.
Source address	This field is 128 bits in length. It indicates the IPv6 address of the sender.
Destination address	This field is 128 bits in length. It indicates the IPv6 address of the destination host.

Q&A

As mentioned in the introduction, you have two choices for review questions. Some of the questions that follow give you a bigger challenge than the exam itself by using a short-answer question format. By reviewing now with more difficult question format, you can exercise your memory better and prove your conceptual and factual knowledge of this chapter. The answers to these questions appear in Appendix A.

For more practice with exam-like question formats, use the exam engine on the CD-ROM.

1. True or false? OSPFv2 supports IPv6.

2. True or false? DNS AAAA records are used in IPv6 networks for name-to-IPv6-address resolution.

3. Fill the blank. IPv6 ND is similar to what _____ does for IPv4 networks.

4. What is the top layer of the hierarchy of IPv6 aggregatable addresses?

5. IPv6 multicast addresses begin with what hexadecimal numbers?

6. IPv6 link-local addresses begin with what hexadecimal prefix?

7. IPv6 site-local addresses begin with what hexadecimal prefix?

8. True or false? The IPv6 address 2001:0:0:1234:0:0:0:abcd can be represented as 2001::1234:0:0:0:abcd and 2001:0:0:1234::abcd.

9. What is the subnet prefix of 2001:1:0:ab0:34:ab1:0:1/64?

10. The IPv6 address has 128 bits. How many hexadecimal numbers does an IPv6 address have?

11. What type of IPv6 address is the following address?

    FF01:0:0:0:0:0:0:2

    _____

12. True or false? You can use RIPv2 to route IPv6 networks.

13. What is the compact format of the following address?

    2102:0010:0000:0000:0000:fc23:0100:00ab

    a. 2102:10::fc23:01:ab

    b. 2102:001::fc23:01:ab

    c. 2102:10::fc23:100:ab

    d. 2102:0010::fc23:01:ab

14. When using the dual-stack backbone, which statement is correct?

    a. The backbone routers have IPv4/IPv6 dual stacks and end hosts do not.

    b. The end hosts have IPv4/IPv6 dual stacks and backbone routers do not.

    c. Both the backbone routers and end hosts have IPv4/IPv6 dual stacks.

    d. Neither the backbone routers or end hosts have IPv4/IPv6 dual stacks.

15. How does a dual-stack host know which stack to use to reach a destination?

    a. It performs an ND, which returns the destination host type.

    b. It performs a DNS request that returns the IP address. If the returned address is IPv4, the host uses the IPv4 stack. If the returned address is IPv6, the host uses the IPv6 stack.

    c. The IPv6 stack makes a determination. If the destination is IPv4, the packet is sent to the IPv4 stack.

    d. The IPv4 stack makes a determination If the destination is IPv6, the packet is sent to the IPv6 stack.

16. Name at least two transition methods or technologies used to migrate from IPv4 to IPv6.

17. What is the IPv6 equivalent to IPv4 private addresses?

    a. Aggregatable-global

    b. Site-local

    c. Link-local

    d. Multicast

18. What is true about fragmentation?

    a. Routers between source and destination hosts can fragment IPv4 and IPv6 packets.

    b. Routers between source and destination hosts cannot fragment IPv4 and IPv6 packets.

    c. Routers between source and destination hosts can fragment IPv6 packets only. IPv4 packets cannot be fragmented.

    d. Routers between source and destination hosts can fragment IPv4 packets only. IPv6 packets cannot be fragmented.

19. A packet sent to an anycast address reaches what?

    a. The nearest destination in a set of hosts

    b. All destinations in a set of hosts

    c. Broadcasts to all hosts

    d. Aggregatable-global destinations

20. Regarding IPv6 and IPv4 headers, what is true?

    a. The IPv6 header is of fixed length, and the next-header field describes the upper-layer protocol.

    b. The IPv4 header is of variable length, and the protocol-type field describes the upper-layer protocol.

    c. The IPv6 header is of fixed length, and the protocol-type field describes the upper-layer protocol.

    d. Answers a and b.

    e. Answer b and c.

Answer the following questions based on the scenario and figure.

A company has an existing WAN that uses IPv4. Sites A and B also use IPv4. As shown in Figure 10-11, the company plans on adding two new locations (Sites C and D). The new sites will implement IPv6. The company does not want to lease more WAN circuits.

Figure 10-11   *Company Adds Sites C and D*

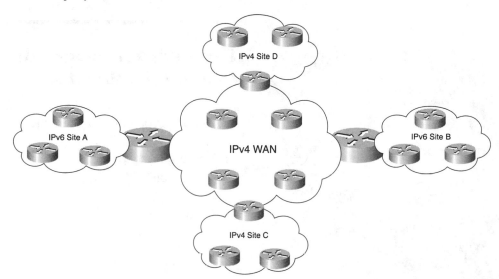

Answer the following questions.

21. What options does the company have to connect Site C to Site D?

22. What mechanism needs to be implemented so that IPv6 hosts can communicate with IPv4 hosts and vice versa?

23. If the company uses RFC 1918 addresses in its IPv4 network, what IPv6 addresses should it use at the new sites?

24. If a dual-stack backbone is implemented, do all WAN routers and all hosts need an IPv6-IPv4 dual stack?

25. If a IPv4 tunnel is implemented between Sites C and D, do all WAN routers require an IPv6-IPv4 dual stack?

This chapter covers the following subjects:

- Routing Protocol Characteristics

- Routing Protocol Metrics and Loop Prevention

- ODR

CHAPTER 11

Routing Protocol Selection Criteria

This chapter covers the metrics used and other characteristics of routing protocols. The CCDA must understand how each routing protocol is classified to select the one that meets the customer's requirements. This chapter covers only the routing protocols at a high level. The chapters that follow dive into more detail on the operations and algorithms used in each routing protocol.

"Do I Know This Already?" Quiz

The purpose of the "Do I Know This Already?" quiz is to help you decide whether you need to read the entire chapter. If you intend to read the entire chapter, you do not necessarily need to answer these questions now.

The 8-question quiz, derived from the major sections in the "Foundation Topics" portion of the chapter, helps you determine how to spend your limited study time.

Table 11-1 outlines the major topics discussed in this chapter and the "Do I Know This Already?" quiz questions that correspond to those topics.

Table 11-1 *"Do I Know This Already?" Foundation Topics Section-to-Question Mapping*

Foundation Topics Section	Questions Covered in This Section
Routing Protocol Characteristics	1, 2, 3, 4, 7, 8
Routing Protocol Metrics and Loop Prevention	6
On-Demand Routing	5

CAUTION The goal of self assessment is to gauge your mastery of the topics in this chapter. If you do not know the answer to a question or you are only partially sure of the answer, you should mark this question wrong for purposes of the self assessment. Giving yourself credit for an answer you correctly guess skews your self-assessment results and might provide you with a false sense of security.

1. Which of the following routing protocols are classful?

    a. Routing Information Protocol Version 1 (RIPv1) and RIPv2

    b. Enhanced Interior Gateway Routing Protocol (EIGRP) and Open Shortest Path First (OSPF)

    c. Intermediate System-to-Intermediate System (IS-IS) and OSPF

    d. IGRP and RIPv1

2. Which type of routing protocol would you use when connecting to an Internet service provider?

    a. Classless routing protocol

    b. Interior gateway protocol

    c. Exterior gateway protocol

    d. Classful routing protocol

3. Which routing protocol is distance-vector and classless?

    a. RIPv2

    b. EIGRP

    c. OSPF

    d. IS-IS

4. Which type of routing protocol sends periodic routing updates?

    a. Static

    b. Distance-vector

    c. Link-state

    d. Hierarchical

5. What is ODR?

    a. Optical demand routing

    b. On-demand routing

    c. Open dedicated routing

    d. Open default routing

6. Which answer is true regarding routing metrics?

   a. If the metric is bandwidth, the path with the lowest bandwidth is selected.

   b. If the metric is bandwidth, the path with the highest bandwidth is selected.

   c. If the metric is bandwidth, the highest sum of the bandwidth is used to calculate the highest cost.

   d. If the metric is cost, the path with the highest cost is selected.

7. Both OSPF and EIGRP are enabled on a router with default values. Both protocols have a route to a destination network in their databases. Which route is entered into the routing table?

   a. The OSPF route.

   b. The EIGRP route.

   c. Both routes are entered with load balancing.

   d. Neither routes is entered; an error has occurred.

8. Which are classless routing protocols?

   a. RIPv1 and RIPv2

   b. EIGRP and RIPv2

   c. IS-IS and OSPF

   d. Answers b and c

The answers to the "Do I Know This Already?" quiz appear in Appendix A, "Answers to Chapter 'Do I Know This Already?' Quizzes and Q&A Sections." The suggested choices for your next step are as follows:

- **6 or less overall score**—Read the entire chapter. It includes the "Foundation Topics," "Foundation Summary," and "Q&A" sections.

- **7–8 overall score**—If you want more review on these topics, skip to the "Foundation Summary" section and then go to the "Q&A" section. Otherwise, move to the next chapter.

Foundation Topics

This chapter covers the high-level characteristics of routing protocols and their metrics. You should become familiar with the different categories of routing protocols and their characteristics for the test. Understand how each metric is used and, based on the metric, which path is preferred. For example, you need to know that a path with the highest bandwidth is preferred over a path with lower bandwidth. This chapter also covers on-demand routing (ODR).

Routing Protocol Characteristics

This section discusses the different types and characteristics of routing protocols.

Characteristics in routing-protocol design are

- **Distance-vector, link-state, or hybrid**—How routes are learned
- **Interior or exterior**—For use in private networks or the public Internet
- **Classless (classless interdomain routing (CIDR) support) or classful**—Enables aggregation of network advertisements (supernetting) between routers
- **Fixed-length or variable-length subnet masks (VLSMs)**—Conserves addresses within a network
- **Flat or potentially hierarchical**—Addresses scalability in large internetworks

This section also covers the default administrative distance assigned to routes learned from each routing protocol or from static assignment. Routes are categorized as statically (manually) configured or dynamically learned from a routing protocol. The sections that follow cover all these characteristics.

Static Versus Dynamic Route Assignment

Static routes are manually configured on a router. They do not react to network outages. The one exception is when the static route specifies the outbound interface: If the interface goes down, the static route is removed from the routing table. Because static routes are unidirectional, they must be configured for each outgoing interface the router will use. The size of today's networks makes it impossible to manually configure and maintain all the routes in all the routers in a timely manner. Human configuration can involve many mistakes, which is why routing protocols exist. They use algorithms to advertise and learn about changes in the network topology.

The main benefit of static routing is that a router generates no routing protocol overhead. Because no routing protocol is enabled, no bandwidth is consumed by route advertisements between network devices. Static routing is recommended for hub-and-spoke topologies with a low-speed remote connection. A default static route is configured at each remote site because the hub is the only route used to reach all other sites. Figure 11-1 shows a hub-and-spoke WAN where static routes are defined in the remote WAN routers because no routing protocols are configured. This setup eliminates routing-protocol traffic on the low-bandwidth WAN circuits.

Figure 11-1   *Static Routes in a Hub-and-Spoke Network*

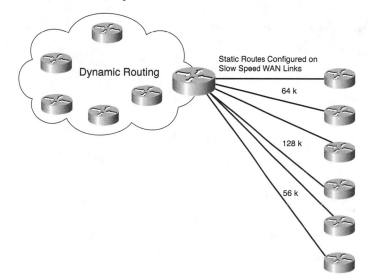

Routing protocols dynamically determine the best route to a destination. When the network topology changes, the routing protocol adjusts the routes without administrative intervention. Routing protocols use a metric to determine the best path toward a destination network. Some use a single measured value such as hop count. Others compute a metric value using one or more parameters. Routing metrics are discussed later in this chapter. The following is a list of dynamic routing protocols:

- RIPv1
- RIPv2
- IGRP
- EIGRP
- OSPF
- IS-IS
- Border Gateway Protocol (BGP)

Interior Versus Exterior Routing Protocols

Routing protocols are interior gateway protocols (IGPs) or exterior gateway protocols (EGPs). IGPs are meant for routing within an organization's administrative domain—in other words, the organization's internal network. EGPs are routing protocols used to communicate with exterior domains. Figure 11-2 shows where an internetwork uses IGPs and EGPs with multiple autonomous administrative domains. BGP exchanges routing information between the internal network and an ISP. IGPs appear in the internal private network.

Figure 11-2   *Interior and Exterior Routing Protocols*

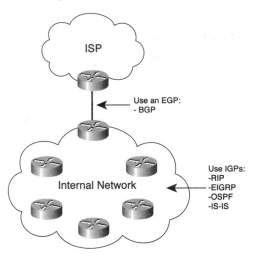

One of the first EGPs was called exactly that, Exterior Gateway Protocol. Today, BGP is the de facto, and the only available, exterior gateway protocol.

Potential IGPs for a network are

- RIPv1
- RIPv2
- OSPF
- IS-IS
- EIGRP
- IGRP

Distance-Vector Routing Protocols

The first IGP routing protocols introduced were distance-vector routing protocols. They used the Bellman-Ford algorithm to build the routing tables. With distance-vector routing protocols, routes are advertised as vectors of distance and direction. The distance metric is usually router hop count. The direction is the next-hop router (IP address) toward which to forward the packet. For RIP, the maximum number of hops is 15, which can be a serious limitation, especially in large nonhierarchical internetworks.

Distance-vector algorithms call for each router to send all its routing table to only its immediate neighbors. The table is sent periodically (30 seconds for RIP and 60 seconds for IGRP). In the period between advertisements, each router builds a new table to send to its neighbors at the end of the period. Having to wait half a minute for a new routing table with new routes is too long for today's networks. RIP and IGRP send triggered updates, full routing table updates sent before the update timer has expired. A router can receive a routing table with 500 routes with only one route change, which creates serious overhead on the network—another drawback.

The following is a list of IP distance-vector routing protocols:

- RIPv1 and RIPv2
- IGRP
- EIGRP (which could be considered a hybrid)

EIGRP

EIGRP is a hybrid routing protocol. It is a distance-vector protocol that implements some link-state routing protocol characteristics. Although using similar metrics as its predecessor, IGRP, EIGRP sends partial updates and maintains neighbor state information just as link-state protocols do. EIGRP does not send periodic updates as other distance-vector routing protocols do. The important thing to consider for the test is that EIGRP could be presented as a hybrid protocol. EIGRP metrics and mechanisms are discussed in Chapter 12, "RIP, IGRP, and EIGRP Characteristics and Design."

Link-State Routing Protocols

Link-state routing protocols address some of the limitations of distance-vector protocols. When running a link-state routing protocol, routers originate information about themselves (IP addresses), their connected links (the number and type of links), and the state of those links (up or down). The information is flooded to all routers in the network as changes in the link state occur. Each router makes a copy of the information received and forwards it without change. Each router independently calculates the best paths to each destination network, using a spanning tree with itself as the root, and maintains a map of the network.

The following is a list of link-state routing protocols (including non-IP routing protocols):

- OSPF
- IS-IS
- IPX NetWare Link-Services Protocol (NLSP)
- DECnet Phase V

OSPF and IS-IS are covered in Chapter 13, "OSPF and IS-IS."

Distance-Vector Routing Protocols Versus Link-State Protocols

When choosing a routing protocol, consider that distance-vector routing protocols use more network bandwidth than link-state protocols. Distance-vector protocols generate more bandwidth overhead because of the large periodic routing updates. Link-state routing protocols do not generate significant routing update overhead but do use more router CPU and memory resources than distance-vector protocols. Generally, WAN bandwidth is a more expensive resource than router CPU and memory in modern devices.

Hierarchical Versus Flat Routing Protocols

Some routing protocols require a network topology that must have a backbone network defined. This network contains some, or all, of the routers in the internetwork. When the internetwork is defined hierarchically, the backbone consists of only some devices. Backbone routers service and coordinate the routes and traffic to or from routers not in the local internetwork. The supported hierarchy is relatively shallow. Two levels of hierarchy are generally sufficient to provide scalability. Selected routers forward routes into the backbone. OSPF and IS-IS are examples of hierarchical routing protocols.

Flat routing protocols do not allow a hierarchical network organization. Carefully designing network addressing to naturally support aggregation within routing-protocol advertisements can provide many of the benefits offered by hierarchical routing protocols. Every router is a peer of any other router in flat routing protocols; no router has a special role in the internetwork. RIP is an example of a flat routing protocol.

Classless Versus Classful Routing Protocols

Routing protocols can be classified based on their support for VLSM and CIDR. Classful routing protocols do not advertise subnet masks in their routing updates; therefore, the configured subnet mask for the IP network must be the same throughout the entire internetwork. Further, the subnets must, for all practical purposes, be contiguous within the larger internetwork. For example, if you use a classful routing protocol for network 130.170.0.0, you must use the chosen mask (such as

255.255.255.0) on all router interfaces using the 130.170.0.0 network. You must configure serial links with only two hosts and LANs with tens or hundreds of devices with the same mask of 255.255.255.0. The grand disadvantage with classful routing protocols is that the network designer cannot take advantage of address summarization across networks (CIDR) or allocation of smaller or larger subnets within an IP network (VLSM). For example, with a classful routing protocol that uses a default mask of /25 for the entire network, you cannot assign a /30 subnet to a serial point-to-point circuit. Classful routing protocols are

- RIPv1
- IGRP

Classless routing protocols advertise the subnet mask with each route. You can configure subnetworks of a given IP network number with different subnet masks (VLSM). You can configure large LANs with a smaller subnet mask and configure serial links with a larger subnet mask, thereby conserving IP address space. Classless routing protocols also allow flexible route summarization and supernetting (CIDR). You create supernets by aggregating classful IP networks. For example, 200.100.100.0/23 is a supernet of 200.100.100.0/24 and 200.100.101.0/24. Classless routing protocols are

- RIPv2
- OSPF
- EIGRP
- IS-IS
- BGP

Administrative Distance

On Cisco routers running more than one routing protocol, it is possible for two different routing protocols to have a route to the same destination. Cisco routers assign each routing protocol an administrative distance. When multiple routes exist for a destination, the router selects the longest prefix. In the event that two or more routing protocols offer the same route (with same prefix length) for inclusion in the routing table, the Cisco IOS router selects the route with the lowest administrative distance. The administrative distance is a rating of the trustworthiness of a routing information source. Table 11-2 shows the default administrative distance for configured (static) or learned routes. In the table, you can see that static routes are trusted over dynamically learned routes. Within IGP routing protocols, EIGRP internal routes are trusted over OSPF, ISIS, and RIP routes.

Table 11-2 *Default Administrative Distances for IP Routes*

IP Route	Administrative Distance
Connected interface	0
Static route directed to a connected interface	0
Static route directed to an IP address	1
EIGRP summary route	5
External BGP route	20
Internal EIGRP route	90
IGRP route	100
OSPF route	110
IS-IS route	115
RIP route	120
EGP route	140
External EIGRP route	170
Internal BGP route	200
Route of unknown origin	255

The administrative distance establishes the precedence used among routing algorithms. Suppose a router has an EIGRP route to network 172.20.10.0/24 with the best path out Ethernet 0 and an OSPF route for the same network out Ethernet 1. Because EIGRP has an administrative distance of 90 and OSPF has an administrative distance of 110, the router will enter the EIGRP route in the routing table and send packets with destinations of 172.20.10.0/24 out Ethernet 0.

Static routes have a default administrative distance of 1. There is one exception. If the static route points to a connected interface, it inherits the administrative distance of connected interfaces, which is 0. You can configure static routes with a different distance by appending the distance value to the end of the command.

Routing Protocol Metrics and Loop Prevention

Routing protocols use a metric to determine best routes to a destination. Some routing protocols use a combination of metrics to build a composite metric for best path selection. This section describes metrics and also covers routing loop-prevention techniques. You must understand each metric for the CCDA.

Some routing metric parameters are

- Hop count
- Bandwidth
- Cost
- Load
- Delay
- Reliability
- Maximum transmission unit (MTU)

Hop Count

The hop-count parameter counts the number of links between routers the packet must traverse to reach a destination. The RIP routing protocols use hop count as the metric for route selection. If all links were the same bandwidth, this metric would work well. The problem with routing protocols that use only this metric is that the shortest hop count is not always the most appropriate path. For example, between two paths to a destination network, one with two 56 Kbps links and another with four T1 links, the router chooses the first path because of the lower number of hops (see Figure 11-3). However, it is not necessarily the best path. You would prefer to transfer a 20 MB file via the T1 links instead of the 56 Kbps links.

Figure 11-3 *Hop Count Metric*

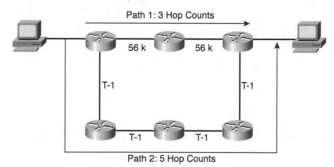

Bandwidth

The bandwidth parameter uses the interface bandwidth to determine a best path to a destination network. When bandwidth is the metric, the router prefers the path with the highest bandwidth to a destination. For example, a Fast Ethernet (100 Mbps) is preferred over a DS-3 (45 Mbps). As shown in Figure 11-3, a router using bandwidth to determine a path would select Path 2 because of the larger bandwidth, 1.5 Mbps over 56 Kbps.

If a routing protocol uses only bandwidth as the metric and there are several different speeds in the path, it can use the lowest speed in the path to determine the bandwidth for the path. EIGRP and IGRP use the minimum path bandwidth, inverted and scaled, as one part of the metric calculation. In Figure 11-4, Path 1 has two segments, each with 256 kbps and 512 kbps of bandwidth. Because the smaller speed is 256 kbps, this speed is used as Path 1's bandwidth. The smallest bandwidth in Path 2 is 384 kbps. When the router has to choose between Path 1 and Path 2, it selects Path 2 because 384 kbps beats 256 kbps.

Figure 11-4 *Bandwidth Metric Example*

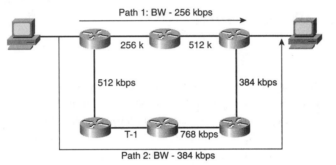

Cost

Cost is the name of the metric used by OSPF and IS-IS. In OSPF on a Cisco router, the default cost of a link is derived from the bandwidth of the interface.

IS-IS assigns a default cost of 10 for all interfaces.

The formula to calculate cost in OSPF is

$$10^8/BW$$

where BW is the default or configured bandwidth of the interface.

For Ethernet, cost is calculated as follows:

$$BW = 10 \text{ Mbps} = 10 \times 10^6 = 10,000,000 = 10^7$$
$$Cost \text{ (Ethernet)} = 10^8 / 10^7 = 10$$

The sum of all the costs to reach a destination is the metric for that route. The lowest cost is the preferred path.

Figure 11-5 shows an example of how the path costs are calculated. The path cost is the sum of all costs in the path. The cost for Path 1 is 350 + 180 = 530. The cost for Path 2 is 15 + 50 + 100 + 50 = 215.

Because the cost of Path 2 is less than that for Path 1, Path 2 is selected as the best route to the destination.

Figure 11-5 *Cost Metric Example*

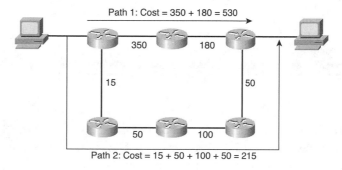

Path 1: Cost = 350 + 180 = 530

350   180

15   50

50   100

Path 2: Cost = 15 + 50 + 100 + 50 = 215

Load

The load parameter refers to the degree to which the interface link is busy. The router keeps track of interface utilization; routing protocols can use this metric in the calculation of a best route. Load is one of the five parameters included in the definition of the IGRP and EIGRP metric. By default, it is not used in the calculation of the composite metric. If you have 512 kbps and 256 kbps links to reach a destination, but the 512 Kbps circuit is 99 percent busy and the 256 kbps is only 5 percent busy, the 256 kbps link would be the preferred path. On Cisco routers, the percentage of load is shown as a fraction over 255. Utilization at 100 percent is shown as 255/255 and utilization at 0 percent is shown as 0/255. Example 11-1 shows the load of a serial interface at 5/255 (1.9 percent).

Example 11-1 *Interface Load*

```
router3>show interface serial 1
Serial1 is up, line protocol is up
  Hardware is PQUICC Serial
  Internet address is 10.100.1.1/24
  MTU 1500 bytes, BW 1544 Kbit, DLY 20000 usec, rely 255/255, load 5/255
```

Delay

The delay parameter refers to the length in time to move a packet to the destination. Delay depends on many factors, such as link bandwidth, utilization, port queues, and physical distance traveled. Total delay is one of the five parameters included in the definition of the IGRP and EIGRP composite metric. By default, it is used in the calculation of the composite metric. You can configure the delay of an interface with the **delay** tens-of-microseconds command, where tens-of-microseconds specifies the delay in tens of microseconds for an interface or network segment. As shown in Example 11-2, the delay of the interface is 20,000 microseconds.

Example 11-2 *Interface Delay*

```
router3> show interface serial 1
Serial1 is up, line protocol is up
  Hardware is PQUICC Serial
  Internet address is 10.100.1.1/24
  MTU 1500 bytes, BW 1544 Kbit, DLY 20000 usec, rely 255/255, load 1/255
```

Reliability

The reliability parameter is the dependability of a network link. Some WAN links tend to go up and down throughout the day. These links get a small reliability rating. Reliability is measured by factors such as the expected received keepalives of a link and the number of packet drops and interface resets. If the ratio is high, the line is reliable. The best rating is 255/255, which is 100 percent reliability. Reliability is one of the five parameters included in the definition of the IGRP and EIGRP metric. By default, it is not used in the calculation of the composite metric. As shown in Example 11-3, you can verify the reliability of an interface using the **show interface** command.

Example 11-3 *Interface Reliability*

```
router4# show interface serial 0
Serial0 is up, line protocol is up
  Hardware is PQUICC Serial
  MTU 1500 bytes, BW 1544 Kbit, DLY 20000 usec, rely 255/255, load 1/255
```

Maximum Transmission Unit (MTU)

The MTU parameter is simply the maximum size of bytes a unit can have on an interface. If the outgoing packet is larger than the MTU, the IP protocol might need to fragment it. If a packet larger that the MTU has the "do not fragment" flag set, the packet is dropped. As shown in Example 11-4, you can verify the MTU of an interface using the **show interface** command.

Example 11-4 *Example 11-4 Interface MTU*

```
router4# show interface serial 0
Serial0 is up, line protocol is up
  Hardware is PQUICC Serial
  MTU 1500 bytes, BW 1544 Kbit, DLY 20000 usec, rely 255/255, load 1/255
```

Routing Loop-Prevention Schemes

Some routing protocols employ schemes to prevent the creation of routing loops in the network. These schemes are

- Split horizon
- Split horizon with poison reverse
- Counting to infinity

Split Horizon

Split horizon is a technique used by distance-vector routing protocols to prevent routing loops. Routes that are learned from a neighboring router are not sent back to that neighboring router, thus suppressing the route. If the neighbor is already closer to the destination, it already has a better path.

In Figure 11-6, Routers 1, 2, and 3 learn about Networks A, B, C, and D. Router 2 learns about A from Router 1 and has Networks B and C in its routing table also. Router 3 advertises Network D to Router 2. Now, Router 2 knows about all networks. Router 2 will send its routing table to Router 3 without the route for Network D because it learned that route from Router 3.

Figure 11-6 *Simple Split-Horizon Example*

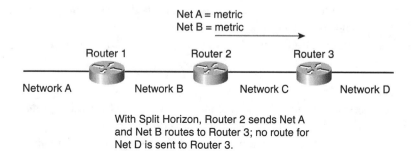

Split Horizon with Poison Reverse

Split horizon with poison reverse is a route update sent out an interface with an infinite metric for routes learned (received) from the same interface. Poison reverse simply indicates that the learned route is unreachable. It is more reliable that split horizon alone. Examine Figure 11-7. Instead of suppressing the route for Network D, Router 2 will send that route in the routing table marked as unreachable. In RIP, the poison-reverse route is marked with a metric of 16 (infinite) to prevent that path from being used.

Figure 11-7   *Split Horizon with Poison Reverse*

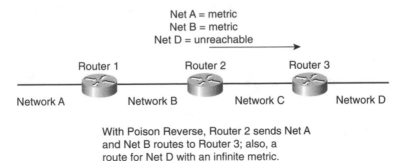

With Poison Reverse, Router 2 sends Net A
and Net B routes to Router 3; also, a
route for Net D with an infinite metric.

Counting to Infinity

Some routing protocols keep track of router hops as the packet travels through the network. In large networks where a routing loop might not be present because of a network outage, routers might forward a packet without it reaching its destination.

Counting to infinity is a loop prevention technique where the router discards a packet when it reaches a maximum limit. It assumes that the network diameter is smaller than the maximum allowed hops. The router uses the Time-To-Live (TTL) field for counting to infinity. The TTL starts at a set number and is decremented at each router hop. When the TTL equals 0, the packet is discarded. For IGRP and EIGRP, the TTL of routing updates are 100 by default.

Triggered Updates

Another loop-prevention and fast-convergence technique used by routing protocols is triggered updates. When a router interface changes state (up or down), the router is required to send an update message, even if it is not time for the periodic update message. Immediate notification about a network outage is key to maintaining valid routing entries within all routers in the network. Some distance-vector protocols, including RIP, specify a small time delay to avoid having triggered updates generate excessive network traffic. The time delay is variable for each router.

Summarization

Another characteristic of routing protocols is the ability to summarize routes. Protocols that support CIDR have the ability to perform summarization outside of IP class boundaries. By summarizing, the routing protocol can reduce the size of the routing table, and there are fewer routing updates on the network.

ODR

ODR is a mechanism for reducing the overhead with routing. Only Cisco routers can use ODR. With ODR, there is no need to configure dynamic routing protocols or static routes at a stub router. ODR eliminates the need to manage static route configuration at the hub router.

Figure 11-8 shows a hub-and-spoke network where you can configure ODR. The stub router is the spoke router in the hub-and-spoke network. The stub network consists of small LAN segments connected to the stub router and a WAN connection to the hub. Because all outgoing traffic travels via the WAN, no external routing information is necessary.

Figure 11-8 *ODR Hub-and-Spoke Network*

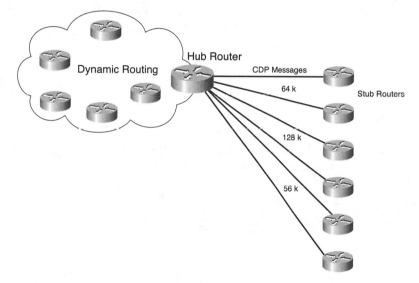

ODR simplifies the configuration of IP with stub networks in which the hub routers dynamically maintain routes to the stub networks. With ODR, the stub router advertises the IP prefixes of its connected networks to the hub router. It does so without requiring the configuration of an IP routing protocol at the stub routers.

ODR uses the Cisco Discovery Protocol (CDP) for communication between hub and stub routers. CDP must be enabled for ODR to work. CDP updates every 60 seconds. Because ODR route prefixes are carried in CDP messages, a change is not reported until the CDP message is sent.

The hub router receives the prefix routes from its stub routers. You can configure the hub router to redistribute these prefixes into a dynamic routing protocol to propagate those routes to the rest of the internetwork.

The benefits of ODR follow:

- Less routing overhead than dynamic routing protocols
- No configuration or management of static routes
- Reduced circuit utilization

Foundation Summary

The "Foundation Summary" section of each chapter lists the most important facts from the chapter. Although this section does not list every fact from the chapter that will be on your CCDA exam, a well-prepared CCDA candidate should at a minimum know all the details in each "Foundation Summary" before going to take the exam.

The CCDA exam requires that you be familiar with the following topics that were covered in this chapter:

- **Routing protocol characteristics**—Characteristics such as static, dynamic, distance-vector, link-state, and interior and exterior protocols

- **Routing protocol metrics**—The metrics used by routing protocols and loop-prevention schemes

- **On-demand routing**—Where to use ODR

Ensure that you know and understand default administrative distances for IP routes. For your convenience in this summary, Table 11-3 lists the default administrative distances for IP routes.

Table 11-3 *Default Administrative Distances for IP Routes*

IP Route	Administrative Distance
Connected interface	0
Static route directed to a connected interface	0
Static route directed to next-hop IP address	1
EIGRP summary route	5
External BGP route	20
Internal EIGRP route	90
IGRP route	100
OSPF route	110
IS-IS route	115
RIP route	120
EGP route	140

continues

Table 11-3 *Default Administrative Distances for IP Routes (Continued)*

IP Route	Administrative Distance
External EIGRP route	170
Internal BGP route	200
Route of unknown origin	255

Table 11-4 summarizes routing protocol characteristics.

Table 11-4 *Routing Protocol Characteristics*

Routing Protocol	Distance-Vector or Link-State	Interior or Exterior	Classful or Classless	Administrative Distance
RIPv1	DV	Interior	Classful	120
RIPv2	DV	Interior	Classless	120
IGRP	DV	Interior	Classful	100
EIGRP	DV (hybrid)	Interior	Classless	90
OSPF	LS	Interior	Classless	110
IS-IS	LS	Interior	Classless	115
BGP	n/a	Both	Classless	20

Q&A

As mentioned in the introduction, you have two choices for review questions. Some of the questions that follow give you a bigger challenge than the exam itself by using an open-ended question format. By reviewing now with this more difficult question format, you can exercise your memory better and prove your conceptual and factual knowledge of this chapter. The answers to these questions appear in Appendix A.

For more practice with exam-like question formats, including questions using a router simulator and multichoice questions, use the exam engine on the CD-ROM.

1. What two routing protocols do not carry mask information in the route updates?

2. True or false? Link-state routing protocols send periodic routing updates.

3. True or false? With ODR, no static routes are configured at remote stub routers.

4. True or false? The path with the lowest cost is preferred.

5. True or false? A link with a reliability of 200/255 is preferred over a link with a reliability of 10/255.

6. True or false? A link with a delay of 200/255 is preferred over a link with a delay of 10/255.

7. On a router, both EIGRP and OSPF have a route to 198.168.10.0/24. Which route is injected into the routing table?

8. On a router, both RIPv2 and IS-IS have a route to 198.168.10.0/24. Which route is injected into the routing table?

9. Which is the best measurement of the reliability and load of an interface?

    a. Rely 255/255, load 1/255

    b. Rely 255/255, load 255/255

    c. Rely 1/255, load 1/255

    d. Rely 1/255, load 255/255

10. Which routing protocols permit an explicit hierarchical topology?

    a. BGP

    b. EIGRP

    c. IS-IS

    d. RIP

    e. OSPF

    f. b and d

    g. c and e

11. What routing protocol parameter is concerned with the time a packet takes to travel from one end to another in the internetwork?

12. For what routing protocol metric is the value of a 10 Mbps Ethernet interface calculated as $10^8/10^7 = 10$?

13. What is the Cisco default OSPF metric for a Fast Ethernet interface?

14. Match the loop-prevention technique with its description:

    i. Split horizon

    ii. Split horizon with poison reverse

    iii. Triggered updates

    iv. Counting to infinity

    a. Sends an infinite metric from which the route was learned

    b. Drops a packet when the hop-count limit is reached

    c. Suppresses a route announcement from which the route was learned

    d. Sends a route update when a route changes

15. True or false? Link-state routing protocols are more CPU and memory-intensive than distance-vector routing protocols.

16. Which routing protocols would you select if you need to take advantage of VLSMs? (Select more than one answer.)

    a. RIPv1

    b. RIPv2

    c. IGRP

    d. EIGRP

    e. OSPF

    f. IS-IS

17. What additional protocol is required for ODR to work?

Answer the following questions based on Figure 11-9.

Figure 11-9 *Scenario Diagram*

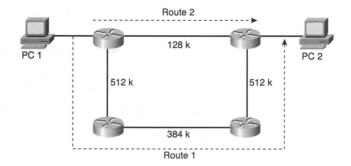

18. A user performs a Telnet from PC 1 to PC 2. If the metric used by the configured routing protocol is the bandwidth parameter, which route will the packets take?

  a. Route 1.

  b. Route 2.

  c. Neither; there is not sufficient information.

  d. One packet will take Route 1, the following packet will take Route 2, and so on.

19. A user performs a Telnet from PC 1 to PC 2. If the metric used by the configured routing protocol is hop count, which route will the packets take?

  a. Route 1.

  b. Route 2.

  c. Neither; there is not sufficient information.

  d. One packet will take Route 1, the following packet will take Route 2, and so on.

20. A user performs a Telnet from PC 1 to PC 2. If the metric used by the configured routing protocol is OSPF cost, which route will the packets take?

  a. Route 1.

  b. Route 2.

  c. Neither; there is not sufficient information.

  d. One packet will take Route 1, the following packet will take Route 2, and so on.

This chapter covers the following subjects:

- RIPv1

- RIPv2

- IGRP

- EIGRP

CHAPTER 12

RIP, IGRP, and EIGRP Characteristics and Design

This chapter reviews distance-vector routing protocols. It covers both versions of the Routing Information Protocol (RIP). It also discusses the Cisco Interior Gateway Routing Protocol (IGRP) and Enhanced Interior Gateway Routing Protocol (EIGRP). The CCDA should understand the capabilities and constraints of each routing protocol.

"Do I Know This Already?" Quiz

The purpose of the "Do I Know This Already?" quiz is to help you decide whether you need to read the entire chapter. If you intend to read the entire chapter, you do not necessarily need to answer these questions now.

The 8-question quiz, derived from the major sections in the "Foundation Topics" portion of the chapter, helps you determine how to spend your limited study time.

Table 12-1 outlines the major topics discussed in this chapter and the "Do I Know This Already?" quiz questions that correspond to those topics.

Table 12-1 *"Do I Know This Already?" Foundation Topics Section-to-Question Mapping*

Foundation Topics Section	Questions Covered in This Section
RIPv1	1, 2, 5
RIPv2	1, 3, 7
IGRP	5
EIGRP	4, 6, 7, 8

CAUTION The goal of self assessment is to gauge your mastery of the topics in this chapter. If you do not know the answer to a question or you are only partially sure of the answer, you should mark this question wrong for purposes of the self assessment. Giving yourself credit for an answer you correctly guess skews your self-assessment results and might provide you with a false sense of security.

1. Which protocol should you select if the network diameter is more than 17 hops?

   a. RIPv1

   b. RIPv2

   c. EIGRP

   d. Answers a and b

   e. Answers b and c

   f. Answers a, b, and c

2. How often does a RIPv1 router broadcast its routing table by default?

   a. Every 30 seconds.

   b. Every 60 seconds.

   c. Every 90 seconds.

   d. RIPv1 does not broadcast periodically.

3. RIPv2 improves RIPv1 with which of the following capabilities?

   a. Multicast updates, authentication, hop count

   b. Multicast updates, authentication, variable-length subnet mask (VLSM)

   c. Authentication, VLSM, hop count

   d. Multicast updates, hop count

4. Which protocol maintains neighbor adjacencies?

   a. RIPv2 and EIGRP

   b. IGRP and EIGRP

   c. RIPv2

   d. EIGRP

5. Which pair of routing protocols does not support VLSM or classless interdomain routing (CIDR)?

   a. EIGRP and IGRP

   b. RIPv1 and RIPv2

   c. RIPv1 and IGRP

   d. Intermediate System-to-Intermediate System (IS-IS) and Open Shortest Path First (OSPF)

6. Which parameters does the computation of the EIGRP composite metric use by default?

   a. Bandwidth and load

   b. Bandwidth and delay

   c. Bandwidth and reliability

   d. Bandwidth and maximum transmission unit (MTU)

7. Which protocols support VLSM?

   a. RIPv1 and RIPv2

   b. EIGRP and IGRP

   c. RIPv1 and IGRP

   d. RIPv2 and EIGRP

8. Which routing protocol implements the diffusing update algorithm (DUAL)?

   a. IS-IS

   b. IGRP

   c. EIGRP

   d. OSPF

The answers to the "Do I Know This Already?" quiz appear in Appendix A, "Answers to Chapter 'Do I Know This Already?' Quizzes and Q&A sections." The suggested choices for your next step are as follows:

■ **6 or less overall score**—Read the entire chapter. This includes the "Foundation Topics," "Foundation Summary," and "Q&A" sections.

■ **7–8 overall score**—If you want more review on these topics, skip to the "Foundation Summary" section and then go to the "Q&A" section. Otherwise, move to the next chapter.

Foundation Topics

"Foundation Topics" covers the characteristics of the distance-vector routing protocols that the CCDA might choose from in a network design. *RIPv1* is a routing protocol developed in the late 1980s; it was the only interior gateway protocol (IGP) at that time. *RIPv2* provides enhancements to RIP, such as support for VLSMs.

The *IGRP* is an IGP developed by Cisco in the early 1990s that was not limited to the 15 router-hop constraint in RIP. EIGRP is a hybrid routing protocol that uses distance-vector metrics and link-state routing protocol characteristics.

RIPv1

RFC 1058 from June 1988 defines RIPv1. RIP is a distance-vector routing protocol that uses router hop count as the metric. RIP is a classful routing protocol that does not support VLSMs or CIDR.

There is no method for authenticating route updates. A RIP router sends a copy of its routing table to its neighbors every 30 seconds. RIP uses split horizon with poison reverse; therefore, route updates are sent out an interface with an infinite metric for routes learned (received) from the same interface.

The RIP standard was based on the popular **routed** program used in UNIX systems since the 1980s. The Cisco implementation of RIP adds support for load balancing. RIP will load-balance traffic if there are several paths with the same metric (equal-cost load balancing) to a destination. Also, RIP sends triggered updates when the metric of a route changes. Triggered updates can help the network converge faster rather than wait for the periodic update. RIP has an administrative distance of 120. Chapter 11, "Routing Protocol Selection Criteria," covers administrative distance.

RIP summarizes to IP network values at network boundaries. A network boundary occurs at a router that has one or more interfaces that do not participate in the specified IP network. The IP address assigned to the interface determines participation. IP class determines the network value. For example, an IP network that uses 24-bit subnetworks from 180.100.50.0/24 to 180.100.120.0/24 is summarized to 180.100.0.0/16 at a network boundary.

RIPv1 Forwarding Information Base

The RIPv1 protocol keeps the following information about each destination:

- **IP address**—IP address of the destination host or network
- **Gateway**—The first gateway along the path to the destination

- **Interface**—The physical network that must be used to reach the destination
- **Metric**—A number indicating the number of hops to the destination
- **Timer**—The amount of time since the entry was last updated

The database is updated with the route updates received from neighboring routers. As shown in Example 12-1, the **show ip rip database** command shows the RIP private database of a router.

Example 12-1   **show ip rip database** *Command*

```
router9# show ip rip database
172.16.0.0/16    auto-summary
172.16.1.0/24    directly connected, Ethernet0
172.16.2.0/24
    [1] via 172.16.4.2, 00:00:06, Serial0
172.16.3.0/24
    [1] via 172.16.1.2, 00:00:02, Ethernet0
172.16.4.0/24    directly connected, Serial0
```

RIPv1 Message Format

As described in RFC 1058, the RIPv1 message format appears in Figure 12-1. The RIP messages are encapsulated using User Datagram Protocol (UDP). RIP uses the well-known UDP port 520.

Figure 12-1   *RIPv1 Message Format*

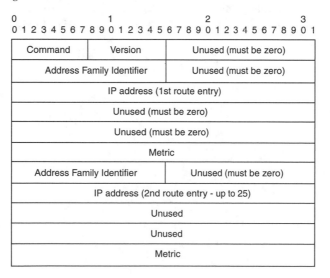

The following is a description of each field:

- **Command**—Describes the purpose of the packet. The RFC describes five commands, two of which are obsolete and one of which is reserved. The two used commands are
  - **request**—Requests all or part of the responding router's routing table.
  - **response**—Contains all or part of the sender's routing table. This message might be a response to a request, or it might be an update message generated by the sender.
- **Version**—Set to the value of 1 for RIPv1.
- **Address Family Identifier (AFI)**—Set to a value of 2 for IP.
- **IP address**—The destination route. It might be a network address, subnet, or host route. Special route 0.0.0.0 is used for the default route.
- **Metric**—A field that is 32 bits in length. It contains a value between 1 and 15 inclusive, specifying the current metric for the destination. The metric is set to 16 to indicate that a destination is not reachable.

Because RIP has a maximum hop count, it implements counting to infinity. For RIP, infinity is 16 hops. Notice in the RIP message that there are no subnet masks accompanying each route. Five 32-bit words are repeated for each route entry: AFI (16 bits); unused, which is 0 (16 bits); IP address; two more 32-bit unused fields; and the 32-bit metric. Five 32-bit words equals 20 bytes for each route entry. Up to 25 routes are allowed in each RIP message. The maximum datagram size is limited to 512 bytes, not including the IP header. Calculating 25 routes by 20 bytes each, plus the RIP header (4 bytes), plus an 8-byte UDP header, you get 512 bytes.

RIPv1 Timers

The Cisco implementation of RIP uses four timers:

- Update
- Invalid
- Flush
- Holddown

RIP sends its full routing table out all configured interfaces. The table is sent periodically as a broadcast (255.255.255.255) to all hosts.

Update Timer

The update timer specifies the frequency of the periodic broadcasts. By default, the update timer is set to 30 seconds. Each route has a timeout value associated with it. The timeout gets reset every time the router receives a routing update containing the route.

Invalid Timer

When the timeout value expires, the route is marked as unreachable because it is marked invalid. The router marks the route invalid by setting the metric to 16. The route is retained in the routing table. By default, the invalid timer is 180 seconds, or six updates periods (30 x 6 = 180).

Flush Timer

A route entry marked as invalid is retained in the routing table until the flush timer expires. By default, the flush timer is 240 seconds, which is 60 seconds longer than the invalid timer.

Holddown Timer

Cisco implements an additional timer for RIP, the holddown timer. The holddown timer stabilizes routes by setting an allowed time for which routing information regarding different paths is suppressed. After the metric for a route entry changes, the router accepts no updates for the route until the holddown timer expires. By default, the holddown timer is 180 seconds.

The output of the show ip protocol command, as shown in Example 12-2, shows the timers for RIP, unchanged from the defaults.

Example 12-2 *RIP Timers Verified with* **show ip protocol**

```
router9> show ip protocol
Routing Protocol is "rip"
  Sending updates every 30 seconds, next due in 3 seconds
  Invalid after 180 seconds, hold down 180, flushed after 240
  Outgoing update filter list for all interfaces is
  Incoming update filter list for all interfaces is
  Redistributing: rip
  Default version control: send version 1, receive any version
    Interface            Send  Recv  Triggered RIP  Key-chain
    Ethernet0            1     1 2
    Serial0              1     1 2
  Automatic network summarization is in effect
  Routing for Networks:
    172.16.0.0
  Routing Information Sources:
    Gateway          Distance      Last Update
    172.16.4.2           120      00:00:00
    172.16.1.2           120      00:00:07
  Distance: (default is 120)
```

RIPv1 Design

Things to remember in designing a network with RIPv1 include that it does not support VLSM and CIDR. The IP addressing scheme with RIPv1 requires the same subnet mask for the entire IP network, a flat IP network. RIPv1 is limited to 15 hops; therefore, the network diameter cannot exceed this limit. RIPv1 also broadcasts its routing table every 30 seconds. RIPv1 is usually limited to accessing networks where it can interoperate with servers running **routed** or with non-Cisco routers. RIP also appears at the edge of larger networks.

As shown in Figure 12-2, when you use RIPv1, all segments must have the same subnet mask.

Figure 12-2 *RIPv1 Design*

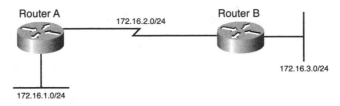

RIPv1 Summary

The characteristics of RIPv1 follow:

- Distance-vector protocol.
- Uses UDP port 520.
- Classful protocol (no support for VLSM or CIDR).
- Metric is router hop count.
- Maximum hop count is 15; unreachable routes have a metric of 16.
- Periodic route updates broadcast every 30 seconds.
- 25 routes per RIP message.
- Implements split horizon with poison reverse.
- Implements triggered updates.
- No support for authentication.
- Administrative distance for RIP is 120.
- Used in small, flat networks or at the edge of larger networks.

RIPv2

RIPv2 was first described in RFC 1388 and RFC 1723 (1994); the current RFC is 2453, written in November 1998. Although current environments use advanced routing protocols such as OSPF and EIGRP, there still are networks using RIP. The need to use VLSMs and other requirements prompted the definition of RIPv2.

RIPv2 improves upon RIPv1 with the ability to use VLSM, with support for route authentication, and with multicasting of route updates. RIPv2 supports CIDR. It still sends updates every 30 seconds and retains the 15-hop limit; it also uses triggered updates. RIPv2 still uses UDP port 520; the RIP process is responsible for checking the version number. It retains the loop-prevention strategies of poison reverse and counting to infinity. On Cisco routers, RIPv2 has the same administrative distance as RIPv1, which is 120. Finally, RIPv2 uses the IP address 224.0.0.9 when multicasting route updates to other RIP routers. As in RIPv1, RIPv2 will, by default, summarize IP networks at network boundaries. You can disable autosummarization if required.

You can use RIPv2 in small networks where VLSM is required. It also works at the edge of larger networks.

Authentication

Authentication can prevent communication with any RIP routers that are not intended to be part of the network, such as UNIX stations running **routed**. Only RIP updates with the authentication password are accepted. RFC 1723 defines simple plain-text authentication for RIPv2.

MD5 Authentication

In addition to plain-text passwords, the Cisco implementation provides the ability to use Message Digest 5 (MD5) authentication, which is defined in RFC 1321. Its algorithm takes as input a message of arbitrary length and produces as output a 128-bit fingerprint or message digest of the input, making it much more secure than plain-text passwords.

RIPv2 Forwarding Information Base

RIPv2 maintains a routing table database as in Version 1. The difference is that it also keeps the subnet mask information. The following list repeats the table information of RIPv1:

- **IP address**—IP address of the destination host or network, with subnet mask
- **Gateway**—The first gateway along the path to the destination
- **Interface**—The physical network that must be used to reach the destination
- **Metric**—A number indicating the number of hops to the destination
- **Timer**—The amount of time since the route entry was last updated

RIPv2 Message Format

The RIPv2 message format takes advantage of the unused fields in the RIPv1 message format by adding subnet masks and other information. Figure 12-3 shows the RIPv2 message format.

Figure 12-3 *RIPv2 Message Format*

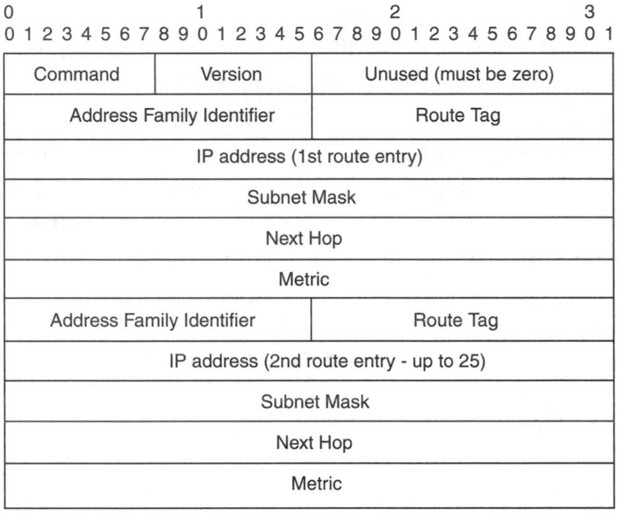

The following is a description of each field:

- **Command**—Indicates whether the packet is a request or a response message. The request message asks that a router send all or a part of its routing table. Response messages contain route entries. The router sends the response periodically or as a reply to a request.

- **Version**—Specifies the RIP version used. It is set to 2 for RIPv2 and set to 1 for RIPv1.

- **AFI**—Specifies the address family used. RIP is designed to carry routing information for several different protocols. Each entry has an AFI to indicate the type of address specified. The AFI for IP is 2. The AFI is set to 0xFFFF for the first entry to indicate that the remainder of the entry contains authentication information.

- **Route tag**—Provides a method for distinguishing between internal routes (learned by RIP) and external routes (learned from other protocols). You can add this optional attribute during the redistribution of routing protocols.

- **IP address**—Specifies the IP address (network) of the destination.

- **Subnet mask**—Contains the subnet mask for the destination. If this field is 0, no subnet mask has been specified for the entry.

- **Next hop**—Indicates the IP address of the next hop where packets are sent to reach the destination.

- **Metric**—Indicates how many router hops to reach the destination. The metric is between 1 and 15 for a valid route or 16 for an unreachable or infinite route.

Again, as in Version 1, the router permits up to 25 occurrences of the last five 32-bit words (20 bytes) for up to 25 routes per RIP message. If the AFI specifies an authenticated message, the router can specify only 24 routing-table entries. The updates are sent to the multicast address of 224.0.0.9.

RIPv2 Timers

RIPv2 timers are the same as in Version 1. They send periodic updates every 30 seconds. The default invalid timer is 180 seconds, the holddown timer is 180 seconds, and the flush timer is 240 seconds. You can write this list as 30/180/180/240 representing the U/I/H/F timers.

RIPv2 Design

Things to remember in designing a network with RIPv2 include that it supports VLSM within networks and CIDR for network summarization across adjacent networks. RIPv2 allows for the summarization of routes in a hierarchical network. RIPv2 is still limited to 16 hops; therefore, the network diameter cannot exceed this limit. RIPv2 multicasts its routing table every 30 seconds to the multicast IP address 224.0.0.9. RIPv2 is usually limited to accessing networks where it can interoperate with servers running **routed** or with non-Cisco routers. RIPv2 also appears at the edge of larger internetworks. RIPv2 further provides for route authentication.

As shown in Figure 12-4, when you use RIPv2, all segments can have different subnet masks.

Figure 12-4 *RIPv2 Design*

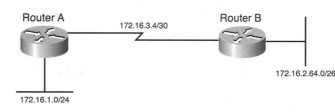

RIPv2 Summary

The characteristics of RIPv2 follow:

- Distance-vector protocol.

- Uses UDP port 520.

- Classless protocol (support for CIDR).

- Supports VLSMs.

- Metric is router hop count.

- Maximum hop count is 15; infinite (unreachable) routes have a metric of 16.

- Periodic route updates sent every 30 seconds to multicast address 224.0.0.9.

- 25 routes per RIP message (24 if you use authentication).

- Supports authentication.

- Implements split horizon with poison reverse.

- Implements triggered updates.

- Subnet mask included in route entry.

- Administrative distance for RIPv2 is 120.

- Used in small, flat networks or at the edge of larger networks.

IGRP

Cisco Systems developed the IGRP to overcome the limitations of RIPv1. IGRP is a distance-vector routing protocol that considers a composite metric which, by default, uses bandwidth and delay as parameters instead of hop count. IGRP is not limited to the 15-hop limit of RIP. IGRP has a maximum hop limit of 100, by default, and can be configured to support a network diameter of 255.

With IGRP, routers usually select paths with a larger minimum-link bandwidth over paths with a smaller hop count. Links do not have a hop count. They are exactly one hop.

IGRP is a classful protocol and cannot implement VLSM or CIDR. IGRP summarizes at network boundaries. As in RIP, IGRP implements split horizon with poison reverse, triggered updates, and holddown timers for stability and loop prevention. Another benefit of IGRP is that it can load-balance over unequal-cost links. As a routing protocol developed by Cisco, IGRP is available only on Cisco routers.

By default, IGRP will load-balance traffic if there are several paths with equal cost to the destination. IGRP will do unequal-cost load balancing if configured with the **variance** command.

IGRP Timers

IGRP sends its routing table to its neighbors every 90 seconds. IGRP's default update period of 90 seconds is a benefit compared to RIP, which can consume excessive bandwidth when sending updates every 30 seconds. IGRP uses an invalid timer to mark a route as invalid after 270 seconds (three times the update timer). As with RIP, IGRP uses a flush timer to remove a route from the routing table; the default flush timer is set to 630 seconds (seven times the update period and more than 10 minutes).

If a network goes down or the metric for the network increases, the route is placed in holddown. The router accepts no new changes for the route until the holddown timer expires. This setup prevents routing loops in the network. The default holddown timer is 280 seconds (three times the update timer plus 10 seconds). Table 12-2 summarizes the default settings for IGRP timers.

Table 12-2 *IGRP Timers*

IGRP Timer	Default Time
Update	90 seconds
Invalid	270 seconds
Holddown	280 seconds
Flush	630 seconds

IGRP Metrics

IGRP uses a composite metric based on bandwidth, delay, load, and reliability. Chapter 11 discussed these metrics. By default, IGRP uses bandwidth and delay to calculate the composite metric, as follows:

$$IGRP_{metric} = \{k1 \times BW + [(k2 \times BW)/(256 - load)] + k3 \times delay\} \times \{k5/(reliability + k4)\}$$

In this formula, BW uses the lowest interface bandwidth in the path, and delay is the sum of all outbound interface delays in the path. The router dynamically measures reliability and load. The values of reliability and load used in the metric computation range from 1 to 255. Cisco IOS routers display a 100 percent reliability as 255/255. They also display load as a fraction of 255. They display an interface with no load as 1/255. By default, k1 and k3 are set to 1, and k2, k4, and k5 are set to 0. With the default values, the metric becomes

$$IGRP_{metric} = \{1 \times BW + [(0 \times BW)/(256 - load)] + 1 \times delay\} \times \{0/(reliability + 0)\}$$
$$IGRP_{metric} = BW + delay$$

The BW is 10,000,000 divided by the smallest of all the bandwidths (in kbps) from outgoing interfaces to the destination. To find delay, add all the delays (in microseconds) from the outgoing interfaces to the destination and divide this number by 10. (The delay is in 10s of microseconds.)

Example 12-3 shows the output interfaces of two routers. For a source host to reach network 172.16.2.0, a path takes the serial link and then the Ethernet interface. The bandwidths are 10,000 and 1544; the slowest bandwidth is 1544. The sum of delays is 20000 + 1000 = 21000.

Example 12-3   **show interface**

```
RouterA> show interface serial 0
Serial0 is up, line protocol is up
  Hardware is HD64570
  Internet address is 172.16.4.1/24
  MTU 1500 bytes, BW 1544 Kbit, DLY 20000 usec,
     reliability 255/255, txload 1/255, rxload 1/255

RouterB> show interface ethernet 0
Ethernet0 is up, line protocol is up
  Hardware is Lance, address is 0010.7b80.bad5 (bia 0010.7b80.bad5)
  Internet address is 172.16.2.1/24
  MTU 1500 bytes, BW 10000 Kbit, DLY 1000 usec,
     reliability 255/255, txload 1/255, rxload 1/255
```

The IGRP metric is calculated as follows:

$$\text{IGRP}_{\text{metric}} = (10,000,000/1544) + (20000 + 1000)/10$$
$$\text{IGRP}_{\text{metric}} = 6476 + 2100 = 8576$$

You can change the default metrics using the **metric weight** *tos k1 k2 k3 k4 k5* subcommand under **router igrp**. Cisco once intended to implement the tos field as a specialized service in IGRP; it was not implemented so the value of tos is always 0. The *k* arguments are the k values used to build the composite metric. For example, if you want to use all metrics, the command is as follows:

```
router igrp n
 metric weight 0 1 1 1 1 1
```

IGRP Design

Something to remember when designing a network with IGRP is that it does not support VLSMs. The IP addressing scheme with IGRP requires the same subnet mask for the entire IP network, a flat IP network. IGRP does not support CIDR and network summarization within the major network boundary. IGRP is not limited to a maximum of 15 hops as RIP is; therefore, the network diameter can be larger than that of networks using RIP. IGRP also broadcasts its routing table every 90 seconds, which produces less network overhead than RIP. IGRP is limited to Cisco-only networks. EIGRP is recommended over IGRP.

As shown in Figure 12-5, when you use IGRP, all segments must have the same subnet mask.

Figure 12-5 *IGRP Design*

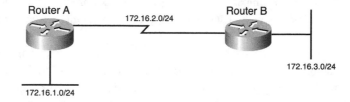

IGRP Summary

The characteristics of IGRP follow:

- Distance-vector protocol.
- Uses IP protocol 9.
- Classful protocol (no support for CIDR).
- No support for VLSMs.
- Composite metric using bandwidth and delay by default.
- You can include load and reliability in the metric.
- Route updates sent every 90 seconds.
- 104 routes per IGRP message.
- Hop count limited to 100 by default, configurable to up to 255.
- No support for authentication.
- Implements split horizon with poison reverse.
- Implements triggered updates.
- By default, equal-cost load balancing. Unequal-cost load-balancing with the **variance** command.
- Administrative distance is 100.
- Previously used in large networks; now replaced by EIGRP.

EIGRP

Cisco Systems released EIGRP in the early 1990s as an evolution of IGRP toward a more scalable routing protocol for large internetworks. EIGRP is a classless protocol that permits the use of VLSMs and that supports CIDR for the scalable allocation of IP addresses. EIGRP does not send routing updates periodically, as does IGRP. EIGRP allows for authentication with simple passwords or with MD5. EIGRP autosummarizes networks at network borders and can load-balance over unequal–cost paths. Packets using EIGRP use IP protocol 88. Only Cisco routers can use EIGRP.

EIGRP is an advanced distance-vector protocol that implements some characteristics similar to those of link-state protocols. Some Cisco documentation refers to EIGRP as a hybrid protocol. EIGRP advertises its routing table to its neighbors as distance-vector protocols do, but it uses hellos and forms neighbor relationships as link-state protocols do. EIGRP sends partial updates when a metric or the topology changes on the network. It does not send full routing-table updates in periodic fashion as do distance-vector protocols. EIGRP uses DUAL to determine loop-free paths to destinations. This section discusses DUAL.

By default, EIGRP load-balances traffic if there are several paths with equal cost to the destination. EIGRP performs unequal-cost load balancing if you configure it with the **variance** $<n>$ command. EIGRP includes routes that are equal to or less that n times the minimum metric route to a destination. As in RIP and IGRP, EIGRP also summarizes IP networks at network boundaries.

EIGRP internal routes have an administrative distance of 90. EIGRP summary routes have an administrative distance of 5, and EIGRP external routes (from redistribution) have an administrative distance of 170.

EIGRP Components

EIGRP has four components that characterize it:

- Protocol-dependent modules
- Neighbor discovery and recovery
- Reliable Transport Protocol (RTP)
- DUAL

Know the role of the EIGRP components, which are described in the following sections.

Protocol-Dependent Modules

EIGRP uses different modules that independently support IP, Internetwork Packet Exchange (IPX), and AppleTalk routed protocols. These modules are the logical interface between DUAL and routing protocols such as IPX RIP, AppleTalk Routing Table Maintenance Protocol (RTMP), and IGRP. The EIGRP module sends and receives packets but passes received information to DUAL, which makes routing decisions.

EIGRP automatically redistributes with IGRP if you configure both protocols with the same autonomous system number. When configured to support IPX, EIGRP communicates with the IPX RIP and forwards the route information to DUAL to select the best paths. AppleTalk EIGRP automatically redistributes routes with AppleTalk RTMP to support AppleTalk networks. AppleTalk is not a CCDA objective and is not covered in this book.

Neighbor Discovery and Recovery

EIGRP discovers and maintains information about its neighbors. It multicasts hello packets (224.0.0.10) every 5 seconds for most networks. The router builds a table with EIGRP neighbor information. The holdtime to maintain a neighbor is three times the hello time: 15 seconds. If the router does not receive a hello in 15 seconds, it removes the neighbor from the table. EIGRP multicasts hellos every 60 seconds on multipoint WAN interfaces (X.25, Frame Relay, ATM) with speeds less than 1544 Mbps, inclusive. The neighbor holdtime is 180 seconds on these types of interfaces. To summarize, hello/holdtime timers are 5/15 seconds for high-speed links and 60/180 seconds for low-speed links.

Example 12-4 shows an EIGRP neighbor database. The table lists the neighbor's IP address, the interface to reach it, the neighbor holdtime timer, and the uptime.

Example 12-4   *EIGRP Neighbor Database*

```
Router# show ip eigrp neighbor
IP-EIGRP neighbors for process 100
H   Address              Interface    Hold Uptime   SRTT   RTO  Q  Seq Type
                                      (sec)         (ms)        Cnt Num
1   172.17.1.1           Se0          11 00:11:27   16     200  0  2
0   172.17.2.1           Et0          12 00:16:11   22     200  0  3
```

RTP

EIGRP uses RTP to manage EIGRP packets. RTP ensures the reliable delivery of route updates and also uses sequence numbers to ensure ordered delivery. It sends update packets using multicast address 224.0.0.10. It acknowledges updates using unicast hello packets with no data.

DUAL

EIGRP implements DUAL to select paths and guarantee freedom from routing loops. J.J. Garcia Luna-Aceves developed DUAL, which is mathematically proven to result in a loop-free topology, providing no need for periodic updates or route-holddown mechanisms that make convergence slower.

DUAL selects a best path and a second best path to reach a destination. The best path selected by DUAL is the *successor*, and the second best path (if available) is the *feasible successor*. The feasible distance is the lowest calculated metric of a path to reach the destination. The topology table in Example 12-5 shows the feasible distance. The example also shows two paths (Ethernet 0 and Ethernet 1) to reach 172.16.4.0/30. Because the paths have different metrics, DUAL chooses only one successor.

Example 12-5 *Feasible Distance as Shown in the EIGRP Topology Table*

```
Router8# show ip eigrp topology
IP-EIGRP Topology Table for AS(100)/ID(172.16.3.1)


Codes: P - Passive, A - Active, U - Update, Q - Query, R - Reply,
       r - reply Status, s - sia Status


P 172.16.4.0/30, 1 successors, FD is 2195456
          via 172.16.1.1 (2195456/2169856), Ethernet0
          via 172.16.5.1 (2376193/2348271), Ethernet1
P 172.16.1.0/24, 1 successors, FD is 281600
          via Connected, Ethernet0
```

The route entries in Example 12-5 are marked **P** as in the "passive" state. A destination is in passive state when the router is not performing any recomputations for the entry. If the successor goes down and the route entry has feasible successors, the router does not need to perform any recomputations and does not go into active state.

DUAL places the route entry for a destination into active state if the successor goes down and there are no feasible successors. EIGRP routers send query packets to neighboring routers to find a feasible successor to the destination. A neighboring router can send a reply packet that indicates it has a feasible successor or a query packet. The query packet indicates that the neighboring router does not have a feasible successor and will participate in the recomputation. A route does not return to passive state until it has received a reply packet from each neighboring router. If the router does not receive all the replies before the "active-time" timer expires, DUAL declares the route as stuck-in-active (SIA). The default active timer is 3 minutes.

EIGRP Timers

EIGRP sends updates only when necessary and sends them only to neighboring routers. There is no periodic update timer.

EIGRP uses hello packets to learn of neighboring routers. On high-speed networks, the default hello packet interval is 5 seconds. On multipoint networks with link speeds of T1 and slower, hello packets are unicast every 60 seconds.

The holdtime to maintain a neighbor adjacency is three times the hello time: 15 seconds. If a router does not receive a hello within the holdtime, it removes the neighbor from the table. Hellos are multicast every 60 seconds on multipoint WAN interfaces (X.25, Frame Relay, ATM) with speeds less than 1544 Mbps, inclusive. The neighbor holdtime is 180 seconds on these types of interfaces. To summarize, hello/holdtime timers are 5/15 seconds for high-speed links and 60/180 seconds for multipoint WAN links less than 1544 Mbps, inclusive.

> **NOTE** EIGRP does not send updates using a broadcast address; instead, it sends them to the multicast address 224.0.0.10 (all EIGRP routers).

EIGRP Metrics

EIGRP uses the same composite metric as IGRP, but the BW term is multiplied by 256 for finer granularity. The composite metric is based on bandwidth, delay, load, and reliability. MTU is not an attribute for calculating the composite metric.

EIGRP calculates the composite metric with the following formula:

$$\text{EIGRP}_{\text{metric}} = \{k1 \times BW + [(k2 \times BW)/(256 - load)] + k3 \times delay\} \times \{k5/(reliability + k4)\}$$

In this formula, BW is the lowest interface bandwidth in the path, and delay is the sum of all outbound interface delays in the path. The router dynamically measures reliability and load. It expresses a 100 percent reliability as 255/255. It expresses load as a fraction of 255. An interface with no load is represented as 1/255.

Bandwidth is the inverse minimum bandwidth (in kbps) of the path in bits per second scaled by a factor of 256×10^7. The formula for bandwidth is

$$(256 \times 10^7)/BW_{\text{min}}$$

The delay is the sum of the outgoing interface delays (in microseconds) to the destination. A delay of all 1s (that is, a delay of hexadecimal FFFFFFFF) indicates that the network is unreachable. The formula for delay is

$$[\text{sum of delays}] \times 256$$

Reliability is a value between 1 and 255. Cisco IOS routers display reliability as a fraction of 255. That is, 255/255 is 100 percent reliability or a perfectly stable link; a value of 229/255 represents a 90 percent reliable link.

Load is a value between 1 and 255. A load of 255/255 indicates a completely saturated link. A load of 127/255 represents a 50 percent saturated link.

By default, k1=k3=1 and k2=k4=k5=0. The default composite metric, adjusted for scaling factors, for EIGRP is

$$EIGRP_{metric} = 256 \text{ x } \{ [10^7/BW_{min}] + [sum\_of\_delays] \}$$

BW_{min} is in kbps, and the sum_of_delays is in 10s of microseconds. The bandwidth and delay for an Ethernet interface are 10 Mbps and 1 ms, respectively.

The calculated EIGRP BW metric is

$256 \text{ x } 10^7/BW$ $= 256 \text{ x } 10^7/10,000$

$= 256 \text{ x } 1000$

$\mathbf{= 256,000}$

The calculated EIGRP delay metric is

$256 \text{ x sum of delay} = 256 \text{ x } 1 \text{ ms}$

$= 256 \text{ x } 100 \text{ x } 10 \text{ microseconds}$

= 25,600 (in tens of microseconds)

Table 12-3 shows some default values for bandwidth and delay.

Table 12-3 *Default EIGRP Values for Bandwidth and Delay*

Media Type	Delay	Bandwidth
Satellite	5120 (2 seconds)	5120 (500 Mbps)
Ethernet	25,600 (1 ms)	256,000 (10 Mbps)
T-1 (1.544 Mbps)	512,000 (20 ms)	1,657,856
64 kbps	512,000	40,000,000
56 kbps	512,000	45,714,176

As with IGRP, you use the **metric weights** subcommand to change EIGRP metric computation. You can change the k values in the EIGRP composite metric formula to select which EIGRP metrics to use. The command to change the k values is the **metric weights** *tos k1 k2 k3 k4 k5* subcommand under **router eigrp** *n*. The tos value is always 0. You set the other arguments to 1 or 0 to alter the composite metric. For example, if you want the EIGRP composite metric to use all the parameters, the command is as follows:

```
router eigrp n
 metric weights 0 1 1 1 1 1
```

EIGRP Packet Types

EIGRP uses five packet types:

- **Hello**—EIGRP uses hello packets in the discovery of neighbors. They are multicast to 224.0.0.10. By default, EIGRP sends hello packets every 5 seconds (60 seconds on WAN links with 1544 Mbps speeds or less).

- **Acknowledgment**—An acknowledgment packet acknowledges the reception of an update packet. It is a hello packet with no data. EIGRP sends acknowledgment packets to the unicast address of the sender of the update packet.

- **Update**—Update packets contain routing information for destinations. EIGRP unicasts update packets to newly discovered neighbors; otherwise, it multicasts update packets to 224.0.0.10 when a link or metric changes. Update packets are acknowledged to ensure reliable transmission.

- **Query**—EIGRP sends query packets to find feasible successors to a destination. Query packets are always multicast.

- **Reply**—EIGRP sends reply packets to respond to query packets. Reply packets provide a feasible successor to the sender of the query. Reply packets are unicast to the sender of the query packet.

EIGRP Design

When designing a network with EIGRP, remember that it supports VLSMs, CIDR, and network summarization. EIGRP allows for the summarization of routes in a hierarchical network. EIGRP is not limited to 16 hops as RIP is; therefore, the network diameter can exceed this limit. EIGRP does not broadcast its routing table periodically so there is no large network overhead. You can use EIGRP for large networks; it is a potential routing protocol for the core of a large network. EIGRP further provides for route authentication.

As shown in Figure 12-6, when you use EIGRP, all segments can have different subnet masks.

Figure 12-6 *EIGRP Design*

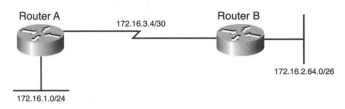

EIGRP Summary

The characteristics of EIGRP follow:

■ Hybrid routing protocol (distance vector that has link-state protocol characteristics).

■ Uses IP protocol 88.

■ Classless protocol (supports VLSMs).

■ Default composite metric uses bandwidth and delay.

■ You can factor load and reliability into the metric.

■ Sends partial route updates only when there are changes.

■ Support for authentication.

■ Uses DUAL for loop prevention.

■ By default, equal-cost load balancing. Unequal-cost load balancing with the **variance** command.

■ Administrative distance is 90 for EIGRP internal routes, 170 for EIGRP external routes, and 5 for EIGRP summary routes.

■ Potential routing protocol for the core of a network; used in large networks.

Foundation Summary

The "Foundation Summary" section of each chapter lists the most important facts from the chapter. Although this section does not list every fact from the chapter that will be on your CCDA exam, a well-prepared CCDA candidate should at a minimum know all the details in each "Foundation Summary" before going to take the exam.

This chapter covered the following topics that you will need to master for the CCDA exam:

- **RIPv1**—The first version of RIP
- **RIPv2**—The enhancements in Version 2 of RIP to support network designs
- **IGRP**—The Cisco proprietary routing protocol IGRP
- **EIGRP**—The enhanced version of IGRP and its uses in network design

Some reviews listings and/or tables that appear in this summary were copied directly from within the chapter to emphasize their significance for exam preparation.

Table 12-5 compares the routing protocols covered in this chapter.

Table 12-4 *Routing Protocols Comparison*

	Routing Protocol			
	RIPv1	RIPv2	IGRP	EIGRP
Distance Vector	Yes	Yes	Yes	Hybrid
VLSMs	No	Yes	No	Yes
Authentication	No	Yes	No	Yes
Update Timer (sec)	30	30	90	n/a
Invalid Timer (sec)	180	180	270	n/a
Flush Timer (sec)	240	240	630	n/a
Holddown Timer (sec)	180	180	280	n/a
Protocol/port	UDP 520	UDP 520	IP 9	IP 88
Admin Distance	120	120	100	90

RIPv1 Summary

The characteristics of RIPv1 follow:

- Distance-vector protocol.
- Uses UDP port 520.
- Classful protocol (no support for VLSMs or CIDR).
- Metric is router hop count.
- Maximum hop count is 15; unreachable routes have a metric of 16.
- Periodic route updates broadcast (255.255.255.255) every 30 seconds.
- 25 routes per RIP message.
- Implements split horizon with poison reverse.
- Implements triggered updates.
- No support for authentication.
- Administrative distance for RIP is 120.
- Used in small, flat networks or at the edge of larger networks.

RIPv2 Summary

The characteristics of RIPv2 follow:

- Distance-vector protocol.
- Uses UDP port 520.
- Classless protocol (support for CIDR).
- Supports VLSMs.
- Metric is router hop count.
- Maximum hop count is 15; infinite (unreachable) routes have a metric of 16.
- Periodic route updates sent every 30 seconds to multicast address 224.0.0.9.
- 25 routes per RIP message (24 if authentication is used).
- Supports authentication.
- Implements split horizon with poison reverse.
- Implements triggered updates.
- Subnet mask included in route entry.
- Administrative distance for RIPv2 is 120.
- Used in small, flat networks or at the edge of larger networks.

IGRP Summary

The characteristics of IGRP follow:

- Distance-vector protocol.

- Uses IP protocol 9.

- Classful protocol (no support for CIDR).

- No support for VLSMs.

- Composite metric of bandwidth and delay.

- You can factor load and reliability into the metric.

- Route updates broadcast every 90 seconds.

- 104 routes per IGRP message.

- No support for authentication.

- Implements split horizon with poison reverse.

- Implements triggered updates.

- By default, equal-cost load balancing. Unequal-cost load balancing with the **variance** command.

- Administrative distance is 100.

- Previously used in large networks; now replaced by EIGRP.

EIGRP Summary

The characteristics of EIGRP follow:

- Hybrid routing protocol (distance vector that has link-state protocol characteristics).

- Uses IP protocol 88.

- Classless protocol (supports VLSMs).

- Default composite metric of bandwidth and delay.

- You can factor load and reliability into the metric.

- Sends route updates to multicast address 224.0.0.10.

- Sends partial route updates only when there are changes.

- Support for authentication.

- Uses DUAL for loop prevention.

- By default, equal-cost load balancing. Unequal-cost load balancing with the **variance** command.

- Administrative distance is 90 for EIGRP internal routes, 170 for EIGRP external routes, and 5 for EIGRP summary routes.

- Potential routing protocol for the core of a network; used in large networks.

Q&A

As mentioned in the introduction, you have two choices for review questions. Some of the questions that follow give you a bigger challenge than the exam itself by using a short-answer question format. By reviewing now with more difficult question format, you can exercise your memory better and prove your conceptual and factual knowledge of this chapter. The answers to these questions appear in Appendix A.

For more practice with exam-like question formats, use the exam engine on the CD-ROM.

1. True or false? RIPv2 broadcasts (255.255.255.255) its routing table every 30 seconds.

2. True or false? By default, EIGRP uses bandwidth, delay, reliability, and load to calculate the composite metric.

3. True or false? EIGRP routers maintain neighbor adjacencies.

4. True or false? EIGRP and RIPv2 support VLSMs and CIDR.

5. True or false? RIPv2 does not have the 15-hop limit of RIPv1.

6. RIP uses _____ port _____.

7. IGRP uses IP protocol number _____.

8. EIGRP uses IP protocol number _____.

9. Between RIP, IGRP, and EIGRP, which protocol would you recommend for use in a large network?

10. Between RIPv2, IGRP, and EIGRP, which protocol would you use in a small network that has both Cisco and non-Cisco routers?

11. Which protocol broadcasts its routing table every 90 seconds by default?

12. Match the protocol with the characteristic:

    i. RIPv1   **a.** No VLSM or CIDR support; default update period of 90 seconds.

    ii. RIPv2   **b.** VLSM and CIDR support; limited to 15 hops

    iii. IGRP   **c.** No VLSM or CIDR support; default update period of 30 seconds

    iv. EIGRP   **d.** Uses triggered updates

13. Why is EIGRP sometimes considered a hybrid protocol?

14. True or False? IGRP is limited to 16 router hops.

15. Which routing protocol can you use to exchange route updates with UNIX workstations running the **routed** process?

16. Match the RIP routing table field with its description:

i. IP address

ii. Gateway

iii. Interface

iv. Metric

v. Timer

a. The number of hops to the destination

b. Next router along the path to the destination

c. Destination network or host, with subnet mask

d. Used to access the physical network that must be used to reach the destination

e. Time since the route entry was last updated

17. Match the EIGRP component with its description:

i. RTP

ii. DUAL

iii. Protocol-dependent modules

iv. Neighbor discovery

a. An interface between DUAL and IPX RIP, IGRP, and AppleTalk

b. Used to deliver EIGRP messages reliably

c. Builds an adjacency table

d. Guarantees a loop-free network

18. With Cisco routers, which protocols use only equal-cost load balancing?

19. With Cisco routers, which protocols allow unequal-cost load balancing?

20. Complete Table 12-6 with the VLSM, authentication, and administrative-distance capabilities of each routing protocol.

Table 12-5 *Distance Capabilities*

Routing Protocol	VLSM	Authentication	Admin Distance
RIPv1			
RIPv2			
IGRP			
EIGRP			

Use the Figure 12-7 to answer the following questions.

Figure 12-7 *Path Selection*

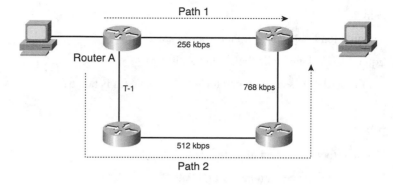

21. By default, if RIPv2 is enabled on all routers, what path is taken?

  a. Path 1

  b. Path 2

  c. Unequal load balance with Path 1 and Path 2

  d. Equal load balance with Path 1 and Path 2

22. By default, if IGRP is enabled on all routers, what path is taken?

  a. Path 1

  b. Path 2

  c. Unequal load balance with Path 1 and Path 2

  d. Equal load balance with Path 1 and Path 2

23. By default, if EIGRP is enabled on all routers, what path is taken?

  a. Path 1

  b. Path 2

  c. Unequal load balance with Path 1 and Path 2

  d. Equal load balance with Path 1 and Path 2

24. EIGRP is configured on the routers. If configured with the variance command, what path is taken?

    a. Path 1

    b. Path 2

    c. Unequal load balance with Path 1 and Path 2

    d. Equal load balance with Path 1 and Path 2

25. By default, if RIPv1 is enabled on all routers, what path is taken?

    a. Path 1

    b. Path 2

    c. Unequal load balance with Path 1 and Path 2

    d. Equal load balance with Path 1 and Path 2

This chapter covers the following subjects:

- OSPF

- IS-IS

CHAPTER 13

OSPF and IS-IS

This chapter reviews the characteristics and design issues of the Open Shortest Path First (OSPF) and Intermediate System-to-Intermediate System (IS-IS) protocols. Both OSPF and IS-IS are link-state routing protocols. They do not broadcast their route tables as distance-vector routing protocols do. Routers using link-state routing protocols send information about the status of their interfaces to all other routers in the area. Then, they perform database computations to determine the shortest paths to destinations.

"Do I Know This Already?" Quiz

The purpose of the "Do I Know This Already?" quiz is to help you decide whether you need to read the entire chapter. If you intend to read the entire chapter, you do not necessarily need to answer these questions now.

The 10-question quiz, derived from the major sections in the "Foundation Topics" portion of the chapter, helps you determine how to spend your limited study time.

Table 13-1 outlines the major topics discussed in this chapter and the "Do I Know This Already?" quiz questions that correspond to those topics.

Table 13-1 *"Do I Know This Already?" Foundation Topics Section-to-Question Mapping*

Foundation Topics Section	Questions Covered in This Section
OSPF	1, 2, 4, 6, 7, 8
IS-IS	2, 3, 5, 9, 10

CAUTION   The goal of self assessment is to gauge your mastery of the topics in this chapter. If you do not know the answer to a question or you are only partially sure of the answer, you should mark this question wrong for purposes of the self assessment. Giving yourself credit for an answer you correctly guess skews your self-assessment results and might provide you with a false sense of security.

1. Which protocol defines an Area Border Router (ABR)?

   a. Enhanced Interior Gateway Routing Protocol (EIGRP)

   b. OSPF

   c. IS-IS

   d. On-Demand Routing (ODR)

2. Which routing protocols support variable-length subnet masks (VLSMs)?

   a. EIGRP

   b. OSPF

   c. IS-IS

   d. Answers a and b

   e. Answers a and c

   f. Answers b and c

   g. Answers a, b, and c

3. Which IGP protocol is a common alternative to EIGRP and OSPF as a routing protocol for large networks?

   a. OSPFv2

   b. RIPv2

   c. IGRP

   d. IS-IS

4. What is an ASBR?

   a. Area Border Router

   b. Autonomous System Boundary Router

   c. Auxiliary System Border Router

   d. Area System Border Router

5. What is the default IS-IS metric for a T1 interface?

   a. 5

   b. 10

   c. 64

   d. 200

6. What is the OSPF link-state advertisement (LSA) type for autonomous system (AS) external LSAs?

   a. Type 1

   b. Type 2

   c. Type 3

   d. Type 4

   e. Type 5

7. What address do you use to multicast to the OSPF designated router (DR)?

   a. 224.0.0.1

   b. 224.0.0.5

   c. 224.0.0.6

   d. 224.0.0.10

8. To where are OSPF Type 1 LSAs flooded?

   a. The OSPF area

   b. The OSPF domain

   c. From the area to the OSPF backbone

   d. Through the virtual link

9. In IS-IS networks, the backup designated router (BDR) forms adjacencies to what routers?

   a. Only to the DR.

   b. To all routers.

   c. The BDR only becomes adjacent when the DR is down.

   d. There is no BDR in IS-IS.

10. What is NET in the context of IS-IS?

   a. Network

   b. Network Edge Translator

   c. Network Entity Title

   d. Network Edge Title

The answers to the "Do I Know This Already?" quiz appear in Appendix A, "Answers to Chapter 'Do I Know This Already?' Quizzes and Q&A Sections." The suggested choices for your next step are as follows:

- **8 or less overall score**—Read the entire chapter. It includes the "Foundation Topics," "Foundation Summary," and "Q&A" sections.
- **9–10 overall score**—If you want more review on these topics, skip to the "Foundation Summary" section and then go to the "Q&A" section. Otherwise, move to the next chapter.

Foundation Topics

This chapter covers the link-state routing protocols OSPF and IS-IS. These two routing protocols are Interior Gateway Protocols (IGP) used within an autonomous system. OSPF is a popular standards-based protocol used in enterprises. IS-IS is commonly used by large Internet service providers (ISPs) in their internal networks.

For the CCDA test, understand the characteristics and design constraints of these routing protocols. You should know the differences between OSPF, IS-IS, and the distance-vector routing protocols covered in Chapter 12, "RIP, IGRP, and EIGRP Characteristics and Design."

OSPF

RFC 2328 defines OSPF, a link-state routing protocol that uses Dijkstra's shortest-path first (SPF) algorithm to calculate paths to destinations. In OSPF, each router sends link-state advertisements about itself and its links to all other routers in the area. Note that it does not send routing tables but link-state information about its interfaces. Then, each router individually calculates the best routes to the destination by running the SPF algorithm. Each OSPF router in an area maintains an identical database describing the area's topology. The routing table at each router is individually constructed using the local copy of this database to construct a shortest-path tree.

OSPF is a classless routing protocol that permits the use of VLSMs and classless interdomain routing (CIDR). With Cisco routers, OSPF also supports equal-cost multipath load balancing and neighbor authentication. OSPF uses multicast addresses to communicate between routers. OSPF uses IP protocol 89.

OSPF Concepts and Design

This section covers OSPF theory and design concepts. It discusses OSPF LSAs, area types, and router types. OSPF uses a two-layer hierarchy with a backbone area at the top and all other areas below. Routers send LSAs informing other routers on the status of their interfaces. The use of LSAs and the limitation of OSPF areas are important concepts to understand for the test.

OSPF Metric

The metric OSPF uses is cost. It is an unsigned 16-bit integer in the range of 1 to 65,535. The default cost for interfaces is calculated based on the bandwidth in the formula $10^8/BW$, with BW being the bandwidth of the interface expressed as a full integer of bps. If the result is smaller than 1, the cost is set to 1. A 10BASE-T (10 Mbps = 10^7 bps) interface has a cost of $10^8/10^7 = 10$. OSPF performs a summation of the costs to reach a destination; the lowest cost is the preferred path. Table 13-2 shows some sample interface metrics.

Table 13-2 *OSPF Interface Costs*

Interface Type	OSPF Cost
10 Gigabit Ethernet	.01 => 1
Gigabit Ethernet	.1 => 1
OC-3 (155 Mbps)	.64516 => 1
Fast Ethernet	$10^8/10^8 = 1$
DS-3 (45 Mbps)	2
Ethernet	$10^8/10^7 = 10$
T1	64
512 kbps	195
256 kbps	390

The default reference bandwidth used to calculate OSPF costs is 10^8 (cost = 10^8/BW). Notice that for technologies that support speeds greater than 100 Mbps, the default metric gets set to 1 without regard for the different capabilities (speed) of the network.

Cisco provides a method to modify the default reference bandwidth. The cost metric can be modified on every interface.

OSPF Adjacencies and Hello Timers

OSPF uses Hello packets for neighbor discovery. The default Hello interval is 10 seconds (30 seconds for nonbroadcast multiple-access (NBMA) networks). Hellos are multicast to 224.0.0.5 (**ALLSPFRouters**). Hello packets include such information as the router ID, area ID, authentication, and router priority.

After two routers exchange Hello packets and set two-way communication, they establish adjacencies.

Figure 13-1 shows a point-to-point network and an NBMA network.

For point-to-point networks, valid neighbors always become adjacent and communicate using multicast address 224.0.0.5. For broadcast (Ethernet) and NBMA networks (Frame Relay), all routers become adjacent to the DR and BDR but not to each other. The section "DRs," later in this chapter, covers the DR concept.

Figure 13-1 *OSPF Networks*

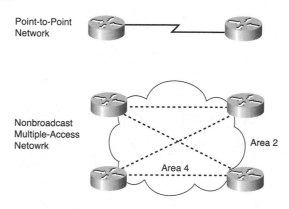

On OSPF point-to-multipoint nonbroadcast networks, it might be necessary to configure the set of neighbors that are directly reachable over the point-to-multipoint network. Each neighbor is identified by its IP address on the point-to-multipoint network. Point-to-multipoint networks do not elect DRs, so the DR eligibility of configured neighbors is undefined. Communication is similar to point-to-point networks using multicast address 224.0.0.5.

OSPF virtual links unicast OSPF packets. Later in this chapter, the section "Virtual Links" discusses virtual links.

OSPF Areas

As a network grows, the initial flooding and database maintenance of LSAs can burden the CPU of a router. OSPF uses areas to reduce these effects. An area is a logical grouping of routers and links that divides the network. Routers share link-state information with only those routers in their areas. This setup reduces the size of the database and the cost of computing the SPF tree at each router.

Each area is assigned a 32-bit integer number. Area 0 (or 0.0.0.0) is reserved for the backbone area. Every OSPF network must have a backbone area. The backbone area is responsible for distributing routing information between areas. It must exist in any internetwork using OSPF over multiple areas as a routing protocol. As you can see in Figure 13-2, communication between Area 1 and Area 2 must flow through Area 0. This communication can be internal to a single router that has interfaces directly connected to Areas 0, 1, and 2.

Figure 13-2 *OSPF Areas*

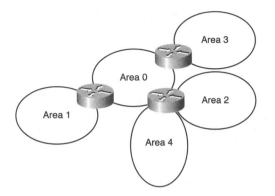

Intra-area traffic is packets passed between routers in a single area.

OSPF Router Types

OSPF classifies participating routers based on their place and function in the area architecture. Figure 13-3 displays a diagram of OSPF router types.

Figure 13-3 *OSPF Router Types*

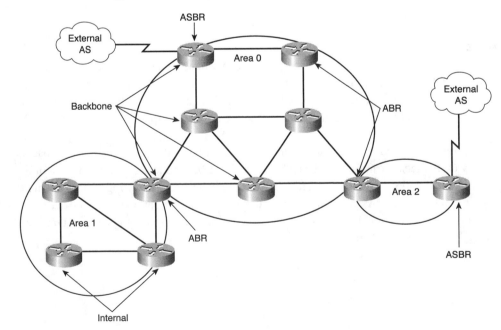

The following list explains each router type in Figure 13-3:

- **Internal router**—Any router whose interfaces all belong to the same OSPF area. These routers keep only one link-state database.

- **ABR**—Routers that are connected to more than one area. These routers maintain a link-state database for each area they belong to. These routers generate summary LSAs.

- **ASBR**—Routers that inject external LSAs into the OSPF database (redistribution). These external routes are learned via either other routing protocols or static routes.

- **Backbone router**—Routers with at least one interface attached to Area 0.

> **TIP** An OSPF router can be an ABR, ASBR, and a backbone router at the same time. The router is an ABR if it has an interface on Area 0 and another interface in another area. The router is a backbone router if it has one or more interfaces in Area 0. The router is an ASBR if it redistributes external routes into the OSPF network.

DRs

On multiaccess networks (such as Ethernet or multipoint Frame Relay), some routers get selected as DRs. The purpose of the DR is to collect all LSAs for the multiaccess network and to forward the LSA to all non-DR routers; this arrangement reduces the amount of LSA traffic generated. A router can be the DR for one multiaccess network and not the DR in another attached multiaccess network.

The DR also floods the network LSAs to the rest of the area. OSPF also selects a BDR; it takes over the function of the DR if the DR fails. Both the DR and BDR become adjacent to all routers in the multiaccess network. All routers that are not DR and BDR are sometimes called DRothers. These routers are only adjacent to the DR and BDR. OSPF routers multicast LSAs only to adjacent routers. DRothers multicast packets to the DR and BDR using the multicast address 224.0.0.6 (**ALLDRouters**). The DR floods updates using **ALLSPFRouters** (224.0.0.5).

DR and BDR selection is based on an OSPF DR interface priority. The default value is 1, and the highest priority determines the DR. In a tie, then OSPF uses the numerically highest router ID. The router ID is the IP address of the configured loopback interface. Routers with a priority of 0 are not considered for DR/BDR selection. The dotted lines in Figure 13-4 show the adjacencies in the network.

In Figure 13-4, Router A is configured with a priority of 10, and Router B is configured with a priority of 5. Assuming these routers are turned on simultaneously, Router A becomes the DR for the Ethernet network. Router C has a lower priority, becoming adjacent to the Router A and Router B but not to Router D. Router D has a priority of 0 and thus is not a candidate to become a DR or BDR.

Figure 13-4 *DRs*

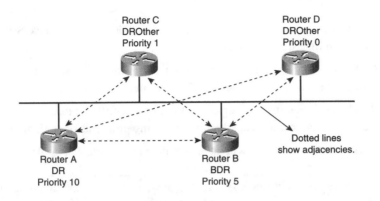

If you introduce a new router to the network with a higher priority than that of the current DR and BDR, it does not become the selected DR unless both the DR and BDR fail. If the DR fails, the current BDR becomes the DR.

LSA Types

OSPF routers generate LSAs that are flooded throughout an area or the entire autonomous system. OSPF defines different LSA types for participating routers, DRs, ABRs, and ASBRs. Understanding the LSA types can help you with other OSPF concepts. Table 13-3 describes the major LSA types. There are other LSA types that are not covered in this book.

Type 1 and Type 2 LSAs are contained within each OSPF area. Routers in different areas pass interarea traffic. ABRs exchange Type 2 and Type 3 LSAs. Type 4 and Type 5 LSAs are flooded throughout all areas.

Table 13-3 *Major LSA Types*

Type Code	Type	Description
1	Router LSA	Produced by every router and includes all the router's links, interfaces, state of links, and cost. This LSA type is flooded within a single area.
2	Network LSA	Produced by every DR on every broadcast or NBMA network. It lists all the routers in the multiaccess network. This LSA type is contained within an area.
3	Summary LSA for ABRs	Produced by ABRs. It is sent into an area to advertise destinations outside the area.

Table 13-3   *Major LSA Types (Continued)*

Type Code	Type	Description
4	Summary LSA for ASBRs	Originated by ABRs. Sent into an area by the ABR to advertise the ASBRs.
5	AS external LSA	Originated by ASBRs. Advertises destinations external to the OSPF AS, flooded throughout the whole OSPF AS.
7	Not-so-stubby area (NSSA) external LSA	Originated by ASBRs in an NSSA. It is not flooded throughout the OSPF autonomous system, only to the NSSA. Similar to the Type 5 LSA.

AS External Path Types

There are two types of AS external paths, Type 1 (E1) or Type 2 (E2), and they are associated with Type 5 LSAs. ASBRs advertise external destinations whose cost can be just a redistribution metric (E2) or a redistribution metric plus the costs of each segment (E1) used to reach the ASBR.

By default, external routes are of Type 2, which is the metric (cost) used in the redistribution. Type 1 external routes have a metric that is the sum of the redistribution cost plus the cost of the path to reach the ASBR.

OSPF Stub Area Types

OSPF provides support for stub areas. The concept is to reduce the number of interarea or external LSAs that get flooded into a stub area. RFC 2328 defines OSPF stub areas. RFC 1587 defines support for NSSAs. Cisco routers use totally stubby areas, as shown in Figure 13-5.

Stub Areas

Consider Area 1 in Figure 13-5. Its only path to the external networks is via the ABR through Area 0. All external routes are flooded to all areas in the OSPF AS. You can configure an area as a stub area to prevent OSPF external LSAs (Type 5) from being flooded into that area. A single default route is injected into the stub area instead. If multiple ABRs exist in a stub area, all inject the default route. Traffic originating within the stub area routes to the closest ABR.

Note that network summary LSAs (Type 3) from other areas are still flooded into the Stub Area 1.

Figure 13-5 *OSPF Stub Networks*

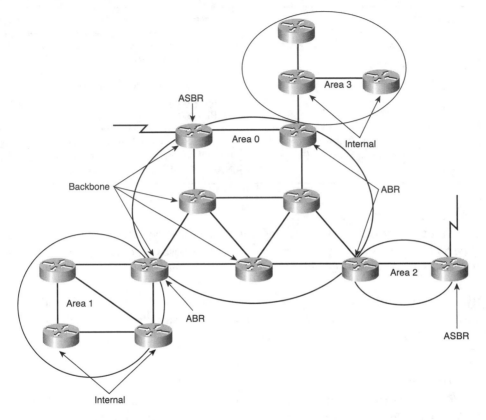

Totally Stubby Areas

Take the Area 1 in Figure 13-5 one step further. The only path for Area 1 to get to Area 0 and other areas is through the ABR. A totally stubby area does not flood network summary LSAs (Type 3). It stifles Type 4 LSAs as well. Like regular stub areas, totally stubby areas do not flood Type 5 LSAs. They send just a single LSA for the default route. If multiple ABRs exist in a totally stubby area, all ABRs inject the default route. Traffic originating within the totally stubby area routes to the closest ABR.

NSSAs

Notice that Area 2 in Figure 13-5 has an ASBR. If this area is configured as an NSSA, it generates the external LSAs (Type 7) into the OSPF system while retaining the characteristics of a stub area to the rest of the AS. The ABR for Area 2 can translate the NSSA external LSAs (Type 7) to AS external LSAs (Type 5) and flood the rest of the internetwork. If the ABR is not configured to convert the NSSA external LSAs to Type 5 external LSAs, the NSSA external LSAs remain within the NSSA.

Virtual Links

OSPF requires that all areas be connected to a backbone router. Sometimes, WAN link provisioning or failures can prevent an OSPF area from being directly connected to a backbone router. You can use virtual links to temporarily connect (virtually) the area to the backbone.

As shown in Figure 13-6, Area 4 is not directly connected to the backbone. A virtual link is configured between Router A and Router B. The flow of the virtual link is unidirectional and must be configured in each router of the link. Area 2 becomes the transit area through which the virtual link is configured. Traffic between Areas 2 and 4 does not flow directly to Router B. Instead, the traffic must flow to Router A to reach Area 0 and then pass through the virtual link.

Figure 13-6 *OSPF Virtual Link*

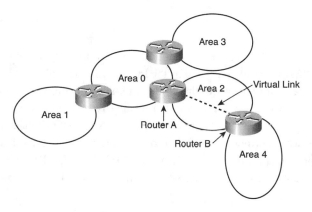

OSPF Router Authentication

OSPF supports the authentication of routes using 64-bit clear text or cryptographic Message Digest 5 (MD5) authentication. Plain-text authentication passwords do not need to be the same for the routers throughout the area, but they must be the same between neighbors.

MD5 authentication provides higher security than plain-text authentication. As with plain-text authentication, passwords don't have to be the same throughout an area, but they do need to be same between neighbors.

OSPF Summary

The characteristics of OSPF follow:

- Link-state routing protocol.
- Uses IP protocol 89.
- Classless protocol (supports VLSMs and CIDR).

- Metric is cost (based on interface bandwidth by default).

- Sends partial route updates only when there are changes.

- Routes labeled as intra-area, interarea, external Type 1, or external Type 2.

- Support for authentication.

- Uses Dijkstra algorithm to calculate SPF tree.

- Default administrative distance is 110.

- Uses multicast address 224.0.0.5 (**ALLSPFRouters**).

- Uses multicast address 224.0.0.6 (**ALLDRouters**).

- Recommended for large networks.

IS-IS

IS-IS is an International Organization for Standardization (ISO) dynamic routing specification. IS-IS is described in ISO/IEC 10589, reprinted by the Internet Engineering Task Force (IETF) as RFC 1142. IS-IS is a link-state routing protocol that floods link-state information throughout the network to build a picture of network topology. IS-IS was primarily intended for routing OSI Connectionless Network Protocol (CNLP) packets but has the capability to route IP packets. IP packet routing uses Integrated IS-IS, which provides the ability to route protocols such as IP. IS-IS is a common alternative to other powerful routing protocols such as OSPF and EIGRP in large networks. Although not seen much in enterprise networks, IS-IS is commonly used for internal routing in large ISP networks.

IS-IS creates two levels of hierarchy with Level 1 for intra-area and Level 2 for interarea routing. IS-IS distinguishes between Level 1 and Level 2 intermediate systems (ISs). Level 1 ISs communicate with other Level 1 ISs in the same area. Level 2 ISs route between Level 1 areas and form an intradomain routing backbone. Hierarchical routing simplifies backbone design because Level 1 ISs only need to know how to get to the nearest Level 2 IS.

> **NOTE** In IS-IS, a router is usually the IS and personal computers, workstations, and servers are end systems (ESs). End Systems to Intermediate System links are Level 0.

IS-IS Metrics

IS-IS as originally defined uses a composite metric with a maximum path value of 1024. The required default metric is arbitrary and typically assigned by a network administrator. By convention, it is intended to measure the capacity of the circuit for handling traffic, such as its throughput in bits per second. Higher values indicate a lower capacity. Any single link can have a maximum value of 64. IS-IS calculates path values by summing link values. The standard set the maximum metric values to provide the granularity to support various link types while at the same time ensuring that the shortest-path algorithm used for route computation is reasonably efficient. In Cisco routers, all interfaces have the default metric of 10. The administrator must configure the interface metric to get a different value. This small metric value range has proved insufficient for large networks and provides too little granularity for new features such as traffic engineering and other applications, especially with high bandwidth links. Cisco IOS Software addresses this issue with the support of a 24-bit metric field, the so-called "wide metric." Wide metrics are also required for route-leaking. Using the new metric style, link metrics now have a maximum value of 16,777,215 ($2^{24} - 1$) with a total path metric of 4,261,412,864 (254 x 2^{24} or 2^{32}). Deploying IS-IS in the IP network with wide metrics is recommended for enabling finer granularity and supporting future applications such as traffic engineering.

IS-IS also defines three optional metrics (costs): delay, expense, and error. Cisco routers do not support the three optional metrics. The wide metric noted earlier uses the octets reserved for these metrics.

IS-IS Operation and Design

This subsection discusses IS-IS areas, designated routers, authentication, and the NET. IS-IS defines areas differently from OSPF; area boundaries are links and not routers. IS-IS has no BDRs. Because IS-IS is an OSI protocol, it uses a NET to identify each router.

NET

To configure the IS-IS routing protocol, you must configure a NET on every router. Although configuring NET is not a CCDA test requirement, this information is included for "extra credit."

Although you can configure IS-IS to route IP, the communication between routers uses OSI PDUs. The NET is the OSI address used for each router to communicate with OSI PDUs. A NET address ranges from 8 to 20 bytes. It consists of a domain, area ID, system ID, and selector (SEL), as shown in Figure 13-7.

Figure 13-7 *NET*

Area ID	System ID	SEL
	6 bytes	00

Level 2 routers use the area ID. The system ID must be the same length for all routers in an area. For Cisco routers, it must be 6 bytes in length. Usually, a router MAC address identifies each unique router. The SEL is configured as 00. You configure the NET with the **router isis** command. In this example, the domain authority and format identifier (AFI) is 49, the area is 0001, the system ID is 00aa.0101.0001, and the SEL is 00:

```
router isis
  net 49.0001.00aa.0101.0001.00
```

DRs

As with OSPF, IS-IS selects DRs on multiaccess networks. It does not choose a backup DR as does OSPF. By default, the priority value is 64. You can change the priority value to a value from 0 to 127. If you set the priority to 0, then the router is not eligible to become a DR for that network. IS-IS uses the highest system ID to select the DR if there is a tie with the priorities. On point-to-point networks, the priority is 0 because no DR is elected. In IS-IS, all routers in a multiaccess network establish adjacencies with all others in the subnetwork, and IS-IS neighbors become adjacent upon the discovery of one another. Both these characteristics are different from OSPF behavior.

IS-IS Areas

IS-IS uses a two-level hierarchy similar to the OSPF area hierarchy developed later. Routers are configured to route Level 1 (L1), Level 2 (L2), or both Level 1 and Level 2 (L1/L2). Level 1 routers are like OSPF internal routers in a Cisco totally stubby area. An L2 router is similar to an OSPF backbone router. A router that has both Level 1 and 2 routes is similar to an OSPF ABR. IS-IS does not define a backbone area, but you can consider the backbone a continuous path of adjacencies among Level 2 ISs.

The L1/L2 routers maintain a separate link-state database for the L1 routes and L2 routes. Also, the L1/L2 routers do not advertise L2 routes to the L1 area. L1 routers do not have information about destinations outside the area and use L1 routes to its L1/L2 router to reach outside destinations.

As shown in Figure 13-8, IS-IS areas are not bounded by the L1/L2 routers but by the links between L1/L2 routers and L2 backbone routers.

IS-IS Authentication

IS-IS supports three types of clear-text authentication: link authentication, area authentication, and domain authentication. All these types support only clear-text password authentication. Recently, an RFC draft has added support for an IS-IS MD5.

Routers in a common subnetwork (Ethernet, private line) use link authentication. The clear-text password must be common only between the routers in the link. Level 1 and Level 2 routes use separate passwords.

With area authentication, all routers in the area must use authentication and must have the same password.

Figure 13-8 *IS-IS Areas and Router Types*

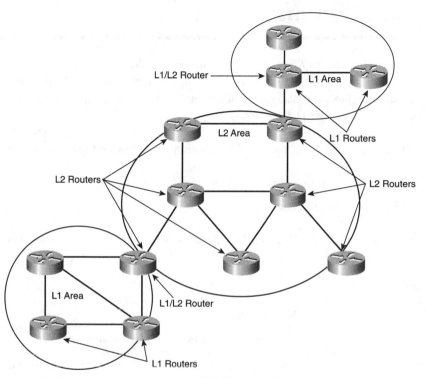

Only L2 and L1/L2 routers use domain authentication. All L2 and L1/L2 routers must be configured for authentication and must use the same password.

IS-IS Summary

The characteristics of IS-IS follow:

- Link-state protocol.
- Uses OSI CNLP to communicate with routers.
- Classless protocol (supports VLSMs and CIDR).
- Default metric is set to 10 for all interfaces.
- Single metric: single link max = 64, path max = 1024.
- Sends partial route updates only when there are changes.
- Authentication with clear-text passwords.
- Administrative distance is 115.
- Used in large networks. Sometimes attractive as compared to OSPF and EIGRP.
- Described in ISO/IEC 10589; reprinted by the IETF as RFC 1142.

Foundation Summary

The "Foundation Summary" section of each chapter lists the most important facts from the chapter. Although this section does not list every fact from the chapter that will be on your CCDA exam, a well-prepared CCDA candidate should at a minimum know all the details in each "Foundation Summary" before going to take the exam.

The CCDA exam requires that you be familiar with the following topics covered in this chapter:

- **OSPF**—The OSPF link-state routing protocol
- **IS-IS**—The ISIS link-state routing protocol

Table 13-4 summarizes the OSPF router types. Know how to identify these routers from a description or a diagram.

Table 13-4 *OSPF Router Types*

OSPF Router Type	Description
Internal router	Router whose interfaces belong to the same OSPF area.
ABR	Router connected to more than one area. It generates summary LSAs.
ASBRs	Routers that inject external routes into the OSPF protocol.
Backbone routers	All routers with at least one interface connected to Area 0.

Table 13-5 summarizes OSPF stub network types. Remember which LSAs are not permitted in each stub type.

Table 13-5 *OSPF Stub Network Types*

OSPF Area Stub Type	Description	LSA Types Not permitted
Stub area	No OSPF external LSAs	Type 5
Totally stubby	No OSPF external and summary LSAs	Type 3, Type 4, and Type 5
NSSA	No OSPF external, Type 7 produced by NSSA	Type 5

Table 13-6 summarizes OSPF LSA types. Understand which routers generate the LSA and what type of information each contains.

Table 13-6 *OSPF Major LSA Types*

Type Code	Type	Description
1	Router LSA	Produced by every router and includes all the router's links, interfaces, state of links, and cost. This LSA type is flooded within a single area.
2	Network LSA	Produced by every DR on every broadcast or NBMA network. It lists all the routers in the multiaccess network. This LSA type is contained within an area.
3	Summary LSA for ABRs	Produced by ABRs. It is sent into an area to advertise destinations outside the area.
4	Summary LSA for ASBRs	Originated by ABRs. Sent into an area by the ABR to advertise the ASBRs.
5	AS external LSA	Originated by ASBRs. Advertises destinations external to the OSPF AS, flooded throughout the whole OSPF AS.
7	NSSA external LSA	Originated by ASBRs in an NSSA. It is not flooded throughout the OSPF AS, only to the NSSA.

OSPF Characteristics

Memorize the characteristics of OSPF. The characteristics of OSPF follow:

- Link-state routing protocol.
- Uses IP protocol 89.
- Classless protocol (supports VLSMs and CIDR).
- Metric is cost (based on interface bandwidth by default).
- Sends partial route updates only when there are changes.
- Routes labeled as intra-area, interarea, external Type 1, or external Type 2.
- Support for authentication.
- Uses Dijkstra algorithm to calculate SPF tree.
- Default administrative distance is 110.
- Uses multicast address 224.0.0.5 (**ALLSPFRouters**).
- Uses multicast address 224.0.0.6 (**ALLDRouters**).
- Recommended for large networks.

IS-IS Summary

Know and understand the characteristics of IS-IS, as summarized in the following list:

- Link-state protocol.

- Uses OSI CNLP to communicate with routers.

- Classless protocol (supports VLSMs and CIDR).

- Default metric is set to 10 for all interfaces.

- Single metric: single link max = 64, path max = 1024.

- Sends partial route updates only when there are changes.

- Authentication with clear-text passwords and MD5.

- Administrative distance is 115.

- Used in large networks. Sometimes attractive as compared to OSPF and EIGRP.

- Described in ISO/IEC 10589; reprinted by the IETF as RFC 1142.

Q&A

As mentioned in the introduction, you have two choices for review questions. Some of the questions that follow give you a bigger challenge than the exam itself by using a short-answer question format. By reviewing now with more difficult question format, you can exercise your memory better and prove your conceptual and factual knowledge of this chapter. The answers to these questions appear in Appendix A.

For more practice with exam-like question formats, use the exam engine on the CD-ROM.

1. True or false? A router needs to have all its interfaces in Area 0 to be considered an OSPF backbone router.

2. True or false? Both OSPF and IS-IS use a designated router in multiaccess networks.

3. Which multicast address do OSPF routers use?

4. What are the Cisco administrative distances of OSPF and IS-IS?

5. True or false? By default, IS-IS assigns a cost metric of 10 to a T1 interface and also 10 to an Ethernet interface.

6. Which OSPF router type generates the OSPF Type 3 LSA?

7. Which OSPF router type generates the OSPF Type 2 LSA?

8. What is included in an OSPF router LSA?

9. True or false? An IS-IS L2 router is analogous to an OSPF backbone router.

10. True or false? The router with the lowest priority is selected as the OSPF DR.

11. Match the routing protocol with the description:

    i.   EIGRP   **a.** Distance-vector protocol used in the edge of the network

    ii. OSPF   **b.** IETF link-state protocol used in the network core

    iii. RIPv2   **c.** Hybrid protocol used in the network core

    iv. IS-IS   **d.** OSI link-state protocol

12. What router produces OSPF Type 2 LSAs?

13. True or false? IS-IS uses the IP layer to communicate between routers.

14. What is the default OSPF cost for a Fast Ethernet interface?

15. Which link-state protocols support VLSMs?

16. Which routing protocol do you use in the core of a large network that supports VLSMs for a network with a mix of Cisco and non-Cisco routers?

17. True or false? An IS-IS L1/L2 router is similar to an OSPF ABR.

18. You use _____ to connect a nondirectly connected OSPF area to the backbone.

19. What is the benefit of designing for stub areas?

20. What constraint does the OSPF network design have for traffic traveling between areas?

21. True or false? The OSPF and IS-IS default costs for Fast Ethernet interfaces are the same.

22. True or false? The OSPF and IS-IS default costs for Ethernet interface are the same.

Use Figure 13-9 to answer the following questions.

Figure 13-9 *Path Selection*

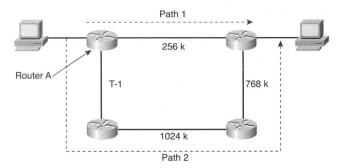

23. If IS-IS is enabled on all routers with the default metrics unchanged, what path is taken?

  a. Path 1

  b. Path 2

  c. Unequal load balance with Path 1 and Path 2

  d. Equal load balance with Path 1 and Path 2

24. If OSPF is enabled on all routers with the default metrics unchanged, what path is taken?

  a. Path 1

  b. Path 2

  c. Unequal load balance with Path 1 and Path 2

  d. Equal load balance with Path 1 and Path 2

This chapter covers the following subjects:

- BGP

- PBR and Route Redistribution

- IP Multicast Review

CHAPTER 14

Border Gateway Protocol, Redistribution, and IP Multicast

This chapter covers the Border Gateway Protocol (BGP), which is used to exchange routes between autonomous systems. It is most frequently used between enterprises and service providers. This chapter also covers the redistribution of route information between routing protocols. The CCDA should know where redistribution occurs when required by the network design. This chapter also reviews policy-based routing (PBR) as a method to change the destination IP address based on policies. Finally, the chapter covers IP multicast protocols.

"Do I Know This Already?" Quiz

The purpose of the "Do I Know This Already?" quiz is to help you decide whether you need to read the entire chapter. If you intend to read the entire chapter, you do not necessarily need to answer these questions now.

The 8-question quiz, derived from the major sections in the "Foundation Topics" portion of the chapter, helps you determine how to spend your limited study time.

Table 14-1 outlines the major topics discussed in this chapter and the "Do I Know This Already?" quiz questions that correspond to those topics.

Table 14-1   *"Do I Know This Already?" Foundation Topics Section-to-Question Mapping*

Foundation Topics Section	Questions Covered in This Section
BGP	1, 2, 7, 8
PBR and Route Redistribution	3, 4
IP Multicast Review	5, 6

CAUTION   The goal of self assessment is to gauge your mastery of the topics in this chapter. If you do not know the answer to a question or you are only partially sure of the answer, you should mark this question wrong for purposes of the self assessment. Giving yourself credit for an answer you correctly guess skews your self-assessment results and might provide you with a false sense of security.

1. What protocol do you use to exchange IP routes between autonomous systems?

    a. IGMP

    b. eBGP

    c. IGRP

    d. OSPF

2. What is the current version of BGP?

    a. BGP Version 2

    b. BGP Version 3

    c. BGP Version 4

    d. BGP Version 1

3. In a network with Enhanced Interior Gateway Routing Protocol (EIGRP) and IGRP using the same autonomous system number, what happens on the router where both protocols are configured?

    a. Redistribution occurs automatically.

    b. Redistribution does not occur automatically.

    c. Redistribution is not necessary.

    d. EIGRP assumes IGRP is a less capable protocol and overtakes it.

4. What is PBR?

    a. Public-Broadcast Routing

    b. Private-Based Routing

    c. Policy-Broadcast Routing

    d. Policy-Based Routing

5. What is IGMP?

    a. Interior Group Management Protocol

    b. Internet Group Management Protocol

    c. Interior Gateway Routing Protocol

    d. Interior Gateway Media Protocol

6. How many bits are mapped from the Layer 3 IP multicast address to a Layer 2 MAC address?

    a. 16 bits

    b. 23 bits

    c. 24 bits

    d. 32 bits

7. What is the administrative distance of eBGP routes?

    a. 20

    b. 100

    c. 110

    d. 200

8. What is CIDR?

    a. Classful Intradomain Routing

    b. Classful Interior Domain Routing

    c. Classless Intradomain Routing

    d. Classless Interdomain Routing

The answers to the "Do I Know This Already?" quiz appear in Appendix A, "Answers to Chapter 'Do I Know This Already?' Quizzes and Q&A Sections." The suggested choices for your next step are as follows:

- **6 or less overall score**—Read the entire chapter. It includes the "Foundation Topics," "Foundation Summary," and "Q&A" sections.

- **7–8 overall score**—If you want more review on these topics, skip to the "Foundation Summary" section and then go to the "Q&A" section. Otherwise, move to the next chapter.

Foundation Topics

The "Foundation Topics" section includes discussions of BGP, PBR, route redistribution, and IP multicast protocols. The "BGP" section covers the characteristics and design of BGP. eBGP exchanges routes between autonomous systems. eBGP is commonly used between enterprises and their service providers.

The section "PBR and Route Redistribution" covers how you use PBR to change the destination address of packets based on policies. This section also covers the redistribution of route information between routing protocols.

The section "IP Multicast Review" covers multicast protocols such as IGMP, Cisco Group Management Protocol (CGMP), and Protocol Independent Multicast (PIM) protocol.

BGP

This section covers BGP theory and design concepts. The current version of BGP, Version 4, is defined in RFC 1771 (March 1995). BGP is an interdomain routing protocol. What this means is that you use BGP to exchange routing information between autonomous systems. The primary function of BGP is to provide and exchange network-reachability information between domains or autonomous systems. It is the de-facto standard for routing between service providers on the Internet due to its rich features. You can also use it to exchange routes in large internal networks. The Internet Assigned Numbers Authority (IANA) reserved TCP port 179 to identify the BGP protocol. BGPv4 was created to provide CIDR, a feature that was not present in the earlier versions. BGP is a path-vector routing protocol; it is neither a distance-vector nor link-state routing protocol.

> **NOTE** RFC 1519 describes CIDR, which provides the capability of forwarding packets based on IP prefixes only, with no concern for IP address class boundaries. CIDR was created as a means to constrain the growth of the routing tables in the Internet core through the summarization of IP addresses across network class boundaries. The early 1990s saw an increase in the growth of the Internet routing tables and a reduction of the Class B address space. CIDR provides a way for service providers to assign address blocks smaller than a Class B network but larger than a Class C network.

BGP Neighbors

BGP is usually configured between two directly connected routers that belong to different autonomous systems. Each autonomous system is under different technical administration. BGP is frequently used to connect the enterprise to service providers and to interconnect service providers, as shown in Figure 14-1. The routing protocol within the enterprise could be any interior gateway protocol (IGP). Common IGP choices include RIPv2, EIGRP, Open Shortest Path First (OSPF), and Intermediate System-to-Intermediate System (IS-IS). BGPv4 is the only deployed exterior gateway protocol (EGP). AS numbers are a managed resource allocated by the IANA. In IP, the AS numbers 64,512 through 65,534 are allocated to IANA and designated for private use.

Figure 14-1 *BGP Neighbors*

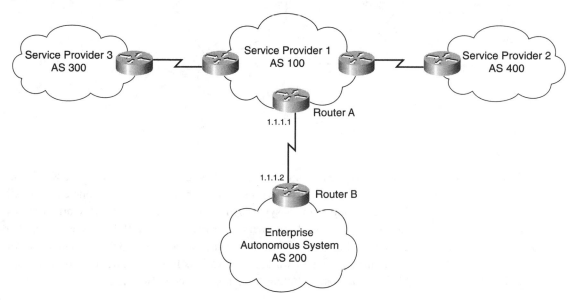

Before two BGP routers can exchange routing updates, the routers must become established neighbors. After BGP routers establish a TCP connection, exchange information, and accept the information, they become established neighbors and start exchanging routing updates. If the neighbors do not reach an established state, they do not exchange BGP updates. The information exchanged before the neighbors are established includes the BGP version number, AS number, BGP router ID, and BGP capabilities.

eBGP

eBGP is the name used to describe BGP peering between neighbors in different autonomous systems. As required by RFC 1771, the eBGP peers share a common subnet. In Figure 14-2, all routers speak eBGP with routers in other autonomous systems. Within AS 500, the routers communicate using iBGP, which is covered next.

Figure 14-2 *eBGP Used Between Autonomous Systems*

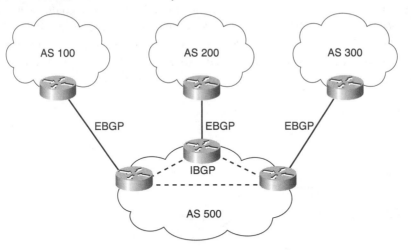

iBGP

iBGP is the name used to describe the peering between BGP neighbors in the same AS. iBGP is used in transit autonomous systems. Transit autonomous systems forward traffic from one external AS to another external AS. If transit autonomous systems did not use iBGP, the eBGP-learned routes would have to be redistributed into an IGP and then redistributed into the BGP process in another eBGP router. iBGP provides a better way to control the routes within the transit AS. With iBGP, the external route information (attributes) is forwarded. The various IGPs that might be used do not understand or forward BGP attributes, including AS paths, between eBGP routers.

Another use for iBGP is in large corporations where the IGP networks are in smaller independent routing domains along organizational or geographic boundaries. In Figure 14-3, a company decided to use three independent IGPs: one for the Americas; another for Asia and Australia; and another for Europe, the Middle East, and Africa. Routes are redistributed into an iBGP core.

Route Reflectors

iBGP requires that all routers be configured to establish a logical connection with all other iBGP routers. The logical connection is a TCP link between all iBGP-speaking routers. The routers in each TCP link become BGP peers. In large networks, the number of iBGP-meshed peers can become very large. Network administrators can use route reflectors to reduce the number of required mesh links between iBGP peers. Some routers are selected to become the route reflectors to serve several other routers that act as route-reflector clients. Route reflectors allow a router to advertise or reflect routes to clients. The route reflector and its clients form a cluster. All client routers in the cluster peer with the route reflectors within the cluster. The route reflectors also peer with all other route reflectors in the internetwork. A cluster can have more than one route reflector.

Figure 14-3   *iBGP in a Large Corporation*

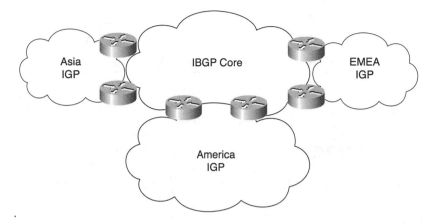

In Figure 14-4, without route reflectors, all iBGP routers are configured in an iBGP mesh as required by the protocol. When Routers A and G become route reflectors, they peer with Routers C and D; Router B becomes a route reflector for Routers E and F. Routers A, B, and G peer among each other.

> **NOTE**   The combination of the route reflector and its clients is called a cluster. In Figure 14-4, Routers A, G, C, and D form a cluster. Routers B, E, and F form another cluster.

Routers A and G are configured to peer with each other and with Routers B, C, and D. The configuration of Routers C and D is different from the rest; they are configured to peer with Routers A and G only. All route reflectors in the same cluster must have the same cluster ID number.

Router B is the route reflector for the second cluster. Router B peers with Routers A and G and with Routers E and F in its cluster. Routers E and F are route-reflector clients and peer only with Router B. If Router B goes down, the cluster on the right goes down because there is no second route reflector configured.

Confederations

Another method to reduce the iBGP mesh within an AS is BGP confederations. With confederations, the AS is divided into smaller, private autonomous systems and the whole group is assigned a confederation ID. The private AS numbers or identifiers are not advertised to the Internet but are contained within the iBGP networks. The routers within each private AS are configured with the full iBGP mesh. Each private AS is configured with eBGP to communicate with other semi-autonomous systems in the confederation. External autonomous systems see only the AS number of the confederation, and this number is configured with the BGP confederation identifier.

Figure 14-4 *Route Reflectors*

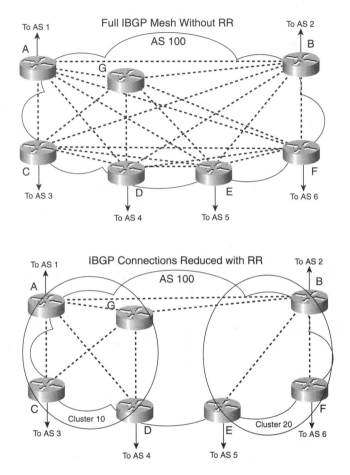

In Figure 14-5, a confederation divides the AS into two.

Routers A, B, and G are configured for eBGP between the private autonomous systems. You configure these routers with the **bgp confederation identifier** command. The confederation identifier number is the same for all routers in the network. You use the **bgp confederation** command to identify the AS number of other private autonomous systems in the confederation. Because Routers A and G are in AS 10, the peer confederation to Router B is AS 20. Router B is in AS 20, and its peer confederation to Routers A and G is AS 10. Routers C and D are part of AS 10 and peer with each other and with Routers A and G. Routers E and F are part of AS 20 and peer with each other and with Router B.

Figure 14-5 *BGP Confederations*

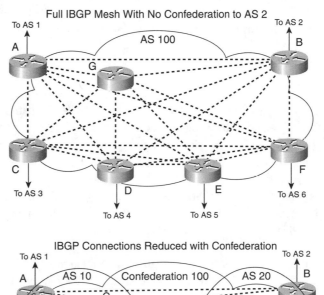

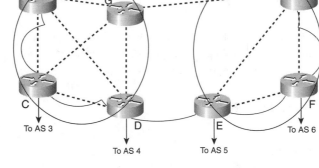

BGP Administrative Distance

The Cisco IOS Software assigns an administrative distance to eBGP and iBGP routes, as it does with other routing protocols. For the same prefix, the route with the lowest administrative distance is selected for inclusion in the IP forwarding table. Because iBGP-learned routes do not have metrics associated with the route as IGPs (OSPF and EIGRP) do, iBGP-learned routes are less trusted. For BGP, the administrative distances are

■ **eBGP routes**— 20

■ **iBGP routes**—200

BGP Attributes, Weight, and the BGP Decision Process

BGP is a protocol that uses route attributes to make a selection for the best path to a destination. This subsection describes BGP attributes, the use of weight to influence path selection, and the BGP decision process.

BGP Path Attributes

BGP uses several attributes for the path-selection process. BGP uses path attributes to communicate routing policies. BGP path attributes include next hop, local preference, AS path, origin, multi-exit discriminator (MED), atomic aggregate, and aggregator. Of these, the AS path is one of the most important attributes: it lists the number of AS paths to reach a destination network.

BGP attributes can be categorized as *well-known* or *optional*. Well-known attributes are recognized by all BGP implementations. Optional attributes do not have to be supported by the BGP process; they are used on a test or experimental basis.

Well-known attributes can be further subcategorized as *mandatory* or *discretionary*. Mandatory attributes are always included in BGP update messages. Discretionary attributes might or might not be included in the BGP update message.

Optional attributes can be further subcategorized as *transitive* or *nontransitive*. Routers must advertise the route with transitive attributes to its peers even if is does not support the attribute locally. If the path attribute is nontransitive, the router does not have to advertise the route to its peers.

The subsections that follow cover each attribute category.

Next-Hop Attribute

The next-hop attribute is the IP address of the next eBGP hop that will be used to reach the destination. The next-hop attribute is a well-known mandatory attribute. With eBGP, the eBGP peer sets the next hop when it announces the route. Multiaccess networks use the next-hop attribute where there is more than one BGP router.

Local Preference Attribute

The local preference attribute indicates which path to use to exit the AS. It is a well-known discretionary attribute used between iBGP peers and not passed on to external BGP peers. In Cisco IOS Software, the default local preference is 100. The higher local preference is preferred.

The default local preference is configured on the BGP router with an external path; it then advertises its local preference to internal iBGP peers. Figure 14-6 shows an example of the local preference attribute where Routers B and C are configured with different local preference values. Router A and other iBGP routers then receive routes from both Router B and Router C. Router A prefers using

Router C to route Internet packets because it has a higher local preference (400) than Router B (300). The arrows represent the paths taken to go out of the AS.

Figure 14-6 *BGP Local Preference*

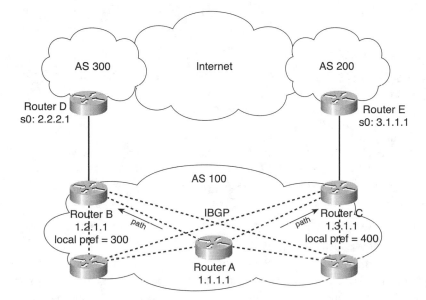

Origin Attribute

Origin is a well-known mandatory attribute that defines the source of the path information. Do not confuse the origin with comparing whether the route is external (eBGP) or internal (iBGP). The origin attribute is received from the source BGP router. There are three types:

■ **IGP**—Indicated by an i in the BGP table. Present when the route is learned by way of the **network** statement.

■ **EGP**—Indicated by an e in the BGP table. Learned from EGP.

■ **Incomplete**—Indicated by a ? in the BGP table. Learned from static redistribution of the route.

In terms of choosing a route based on origin, BGP prefers routes that have been verified by an IGP over routes that have been learned from EGP peers, and BGP prefers routes learned from eBGP peers over incomplete paths.

AS Path Attribute

The AS path is a well-known mandatory attribute that contains a list of AS numbers in the path to the destination. Each AS prepends its own AS number to the AS path. The AS path describes all the autonomous systems a packet would have to travel to reach the destination IP network. It is used to ensure that the path is loop-free. When the AS path attribute is used to select a path, the route with the least number of AS hops is preferred. In the case of a tie, other attributes, such as MED, break the tie. Example 14-1 shows the AS path for network 200.50.32.0/19. To reach the destination, a packet must pass autonomous systems 3561, 7004, and 7418. The command **show ip bgp 200.50.32.0** displays the AS path information.

Example 14-1 *AS Path Attribute*

```
Router# show ip bgp 200.50.32.0
BGP routing table entry for 200.50.32.0/19, version 93313535
Paths: (1 available, best #1)
  Not advertised to any peer
  3561 7004 7418
    206.24.241.181 (metric 490201) from 165.117.1.219 (165.117.1.219)
      Origin IGP, metric 4294967294, localpref 100, valid, internal, best
      Community: 2548:182 2548:337 2548:666 3706:153
```

MED Attribute

The MED attribute, also known as metric, tells external BGP peers the preferred path into the AS when there are multiple paths into the AS. In other words, MED influences which one of many paths a neighboring AS will use to reach destinations within the AS. It is an optional nontransitive attribute carried in eBGP updates. The MED attribute is not used with iBGP peers. The lowest MED value is preferred, and the default value is 0. Paths received with no MED are assigned a MED of 0. The MED is not compared for paths received from two separated autonomous systems. The MED is carried into an AS but does not leave the AS.

Consider the diagram in Figure 14-7. With all attributes considered equal, Router C will select Router A as its best path into AS 100 based on Router A's lower router ID (RID). Router A is configured with a MED of 200 to make Router C select Router B as the best path to AS 100. No additional configuration is required on Router B because the default MED is 0.

Community Attribute

Although not an attribute used in the routing-decision process, the community attribute groups routes and applies policies or decisions (accept, prefer) to those routes. It is a group of destinations that share some common property. The community attribute is an optional transitive attribute of variable length.

Atomic Aggregate and Aggregator Attributes

The atomic aggregate attribute informs BGP peers that the local router used a less specific (aggregated) route to a destination without using a more specific route.

Figure 14-7 *MED Attribute*

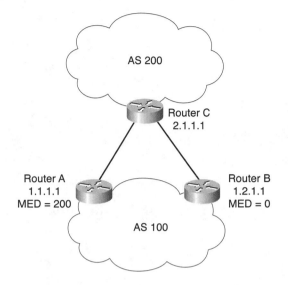

If a BGP router selects a less specific route when there is a more specific route available, it must attach the atomic aggregate attribute when propagating the route. The atomic aggregate attribute lets the BGP peers know that the BGP router used an aggregated route. A more specific route must be in the advertising router's BGP table before it will propagate an aggregate route.

When the atomic aggregate attribute is used, the BGP speaker has the option to send the aggregator attribute. The aggregator attribute includes the AS number and the IP address of the router that originated the aggregated route. In Cisco routers, the IP address used is the RID of the router that performs the route aggregation. Atomic aggregate is a well-known discretionary attribute, and aggregator is an optional transitive attribute.

Weight

Weight is assigned locally on a router to specify a preferred path if multiple paths exist out of a router for a destination. Weights can be applied to individual routes or to all routes received from a peer. Weight is specific to Cisco routers and is not propagated to other routers. The weight value ranges from 0 to 65,535. Routes with a higher weight are preferred when multiple routes exist to a destination. Routes that are originated by the local router have a default weight of 32,768.

You can use weight instead of local preference to influence the selected path to external BGP peers. The difference is that weight is configured locally and not exchanged in BGP updates. On the other hand, the local preference attribute is exchanged between iBGP peers and is configured at the gateway router.

Figure 14-8 shows an example of the use of weight to influence the preferred route.

Figure 14-8 *BGP Weight*

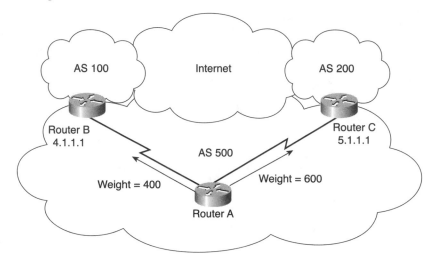

When the same destinations are advertised from both Router B and Router C in Figure 14-8, Router A prefers the routes from Router C over Router B because the routes received from Router C have a larger weight (600) locally assigned.

BGP Decision Process

By default, BGP will select only a single path to reach a specific destination (unless you specify maximum paths). The Cisco implementation of BGP uses a simple decision process. When the path is selected, BGP puts the selected path in its routing table and propagates the path to its neighbors.

To select the best path to a destination, Cisco routers running BGP use the following algorithm in the following order:

1. If the specified next hop is inaccessible, drop the path.

2. If the path is internal, synchronization is enabled, and the path is not in the IGP, drop the path.

3. Prefer the path with the largest weight. (This step is Cisco specific and weight is localized to the router.)

4. Prefer the path with the largest local preference. iBGP uses this path only to reach the preferred external BGP router.

5. Prefer the path that was locally originated via a **network** or **aggregate** BGP subcommand or through redistribution from an IGP. Local paths sourced by **network** or **redistribute** commands are preferred over local aggregates sourced by the **aggregate-address** command. (This step is Cisco specific.)

6. If no route was originated, prefer the route that has the shortest AS path. (This step is Cisco specific.)

7. If all paths have the same AS path length, prefer the path with the lowest origin type. Paths with origin type of IGP are (lower) preferred over paths originated from an EGP like BGP, and EGP origin is preferred over a route with an incomplete origin. (This step is Cisco specific.)

8. If the origin codes are the same, prefer the path with the lowest MED attribute. An eBGP peer uses this attribute to select a best path to AS. (This step is a tie-breaker described in the RFC that defines the BGP.)

9. If the paths have the same MED, prefer the external path (eBGP) over the internal (iBGP) path. (This step is Cisco specific.)

10. If the paths are still the same, prefer the path through the closest IGP neighbor (best IGP metric). (This step is a tie-breaker described in the RFC that defines the BGP.)

11. Prefer the path with the BGP neighbor with the lowest router ID. (The RFC that defines the BGP describes the router ID.)

After BGP decides on a best path, it marks it with a > sign in the **show ip bgp** table and adds it to the IP routing table.

BGP Summary

The characteristics of BGP follow:

- Interdomain routing protocol.
- Uses TCP port 179 to establish connections with neighbors.
- BGPv4 implements CIDR.
- eBGP for external neighbors; used between autonomous systems.
- iBGP for internal neighbors; used within an AS.
- Uses several attributes in the routing-decision algorithm.
- Uses confederations and route reflectors to reduce BGP peering overhead.
- MED (metric) attribute used between autonomous systems to influence inbound traffic.
- Weight used to influence the path of outbound traffic from a single router, configured locally.

PBR and Route Redistribution

This section covers PBR and route redistribution. You can use PBR to modify the next hop of packets from what is selected by the routing protocol. PBR is useful when the traffic engineering of paths is required. Redistribution between routing protocols is required to inject route information from one routing protocol to another. The CCDA must understand the issues with the redistribution of routes.

PBR

You can use PBR to modify the next-hop address of packets or mark packets to receive differential service. Routing is based on destination addresses; routers look at the routing table to determine the next-hop IP address based on a destination lookup. PBR is commonly used to modify the next-hop IP address based on the source address. You can also use PBR to mark the IP precedence bits in outbound IP packets so that you can apply quality-of-service (QoS) policies. In Figure 14-9, Router A exchanges routing updates with routers in the WAN. The routing protocol might select Serial 0 as the preferred path for all traffic because of the higher bandwidth. The company might have business-critical systems that use the T1 but does not want systems on Ethernet 1 to affect WAN performance. You can configure PBR on Router A to force traffic from Ethernet 1 out on Serial 1.

Figure 14-9 *PBR*

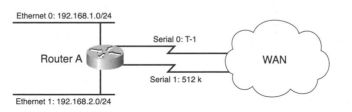

Redistribution

You configure the redistribution of routing protocols on routers that reside at the Service Provider Edge of the network that also communicate with other autonomous systems or on routers that run more than one routing protocol. The redistribution of routes might be required when two companies merge: One might be running EIGRP and the other OSPF.

Figure 14-10 shows an example of the exchange of routes between two autonomous systems. Routes from AS 100 are redistributed into BGP on Router A. Routes from AS 200 are redistributed into BGP on Router B. Then, Routers A and B exchange BGP routes. Router A and Router B also implement filters to redistribute only the desired networks.

Figure 14-10 *Redistribution of BGP Routes*

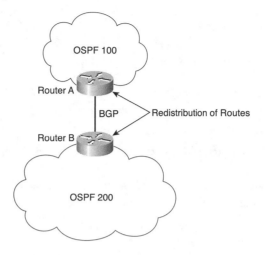

Companies might also acquire another company that might be running another routing protocol. Figure 14-11 shows an example of a network that has both OSPF and EIGRP routing protocols. Routers A and B perform redistribution between OSPF and EIGRP. Both routers must filter routes from OSPF before redistributing them into EIGRP and filter routes from EIGRP before redistributing them into OSPF. This setup prevents route feedback.

Route feedback occurs when a routing protocol learns routes from another routing protocol and then announces the routes back to the other routing protocol. In Figure 14-11, OSPF should not announce the routes it learned from EIGRP, and EIGRP should not announce the routes it learned from OSPF.

Figure 14-11 *Redistribution Between IGPs*

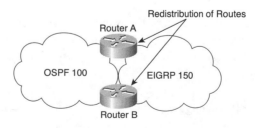

You can use access lists, distribution lists, and route maps when redistributing routes; you can use these methods to specify (select) routes for redistribution, to set metrics, or to set other policies to the routes.

Default Metric

When redistributing routes into RIP, IGRP, IS-IS, and EIGRP, you must also configure the metric of the redistributed routes. You can configure the metric in the **redistribution** command or configure a default metric. You can also use the command in OSPF. IS-IS does not use the **default-metric** command. The **default-metric** command has the following syntax for IGRP and EIGRP:

```
default-metric bandwidth delay reliability load mtu
```

EIGRP-IGRP Redistribution

For routers that run both IGRP and EIGRP, the network designer must be aware of the following:

- If EIGRP and IGRP have the same system number, the router automatically redistributes between the routing protocols without your having to configure redistribution.

- If EIGRP and IGRP have a different number, then you must configure redistribution to have EIGRP and IGRP exchange routes.

NOTE   eBGP and iBGP also automatically redistribute if the BGP configuration for BGP peers uses the same AS number.

OSPF Redistribution

This subsection reviews a few things you need to remember when designing a network that will be redistributing with OSPF.

When redistributing routes into OSPF, use the **subnets** keyword to permit subnetted routes to be received. If you do not use it, only the major network route will be redistributed, without any subnetworks. In other words, OSPF performs automatic summarization to IP classful network values.

By default, redistributed routes are classified as external Type 2 (E2) in OSPF. You can use the **metric-type** keyword to change the external route to an external Type 1 (E1). The network design can take into account the after-redistribution cost (Type 2) or the after-redistribution cost plus the cost of the path (Type 1).

In Figure 14-12, Router B is configured to perform mutual redistribution between EIGRP and OSPF. In this example, you can use route maps and access lists to prevent routing loops. The route maps permit or deny the networks that are listed in the access lists. The **subnets** keyword redistributes every subnet in EIGRP into OSPF. This book does not cover exact configurations.

Figure 14-12 *OSPF and EIGRP Redistribution*

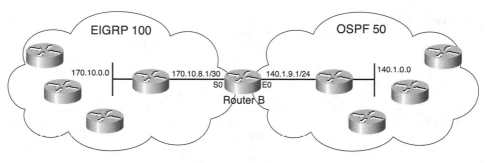

IP Multicast Review

With multicast, packets are sent to a multicast group, which is identified with an IP multicast address. Multicast supports the transmission of IP packets from one source to multiple hosts. Packets with unicast addresses are sent to one device, and broadcast addresses are sent to all hosts; packets with multicast addresses are sent to a group of hosts.

Multicast Addresses

Multicast addressing uses Class D addresses from the IPv4 protocol. Class D addresses range from 224.0.0.1 to 239.255.255.255. IANA manages multicast addresses.

Routing protocols (RIPv2, EIGRP, and OSPF) use multicast addresses to speak to their neighbors. For example, OSPF routers use 224.0.0.6 to speak to the designated router (DR) in a multiaccess network. Class D multicast address range from 224.0.0.0 to 239.255.255.255. Multicast addresses in the range of 224.0.0.1 to 224.255.255.255 are reserved for special addresses or network protocol on a multiaccess link. RFC 2365 reserves multicast addresses in the range of 239.192.000.000 to 239.251.255.255 for organization-local scope. Similarly, 239.252.000.000 to 239.252.255.255, 239.254.000.000 to 239.254.255.255, and 239.252.000.000 to 239.252.0.0 are reserved for site-local scope.

Table 14-2 contains some well-known and multicast address blocks.

Table 14-2 *Multicast Addresses*

Multicast Address	Description
224.0.0/24	Local network control block
224.0.0.1	All hosts or all systems on this subnet
224.0.0.2	All multicast routers
224.0.0.4	Distance-Vector Multicast Routing Protocol (DVMRP) routers
224.0.0.5	All OSPF routers
224.0.0.6	All OSPF DR routers
224.0.0.9	RIPv2 routers
224.0.0.10	EIGRP routers
224.0.0.13	All PIM routers
224.0.1/24	Internetwork control block
224.0.1.39	Rendezvous point (RP) announce
224.0.1.40	RP discovery
224.0.2.0 to 224.0.255.0	Ad hoc block
239.0.0.0 to 239.255.255.255	Administratively scoped
239.192.0.0 to 239.251.255.255	Organization-local scope
239.252.0.0 to 239.254.255.255	Site-local scope

Layer 3 to Layer 2 Mapping

Multicast-aware Ethernet, Token Ring, and Fiber Distributed Data Interface (FDDI) network interface cards use the reserved IEEE 802 address 0100.5e00.0000 for multicast addresses at the MAC layer. Notice that for the address, the high-order byte 0x01 has the low-order bit set to 1. This bit is the Individual/Group (I/G) bit. It signifies whether the address is an individual address (0) or a group address (1). Hence, for multicast addresses, this bit is set to 1.

Ethernet interfaces map the lower 23 bits of the IP multicast address to the lower 23 bits of the MAC 0100.5e00.0000. As an example, the IP multicast address 224.0.0.2 is mapped to the MAC layer as 0100.5e00.0002. Figure 14-13 shows another example looking at the bits of multicast IP 239.192.44.56. The IP address in hexadecimal is EF:C0:2C:38. The lower 23 bits get mapped into the lower 23 bits of the base multicast MAC to produce the multicast MAC address 01:00:5E:40:2C:38.

Figure 14-13 *Mapping of Multicast IP Addressing to MAC Addresses*

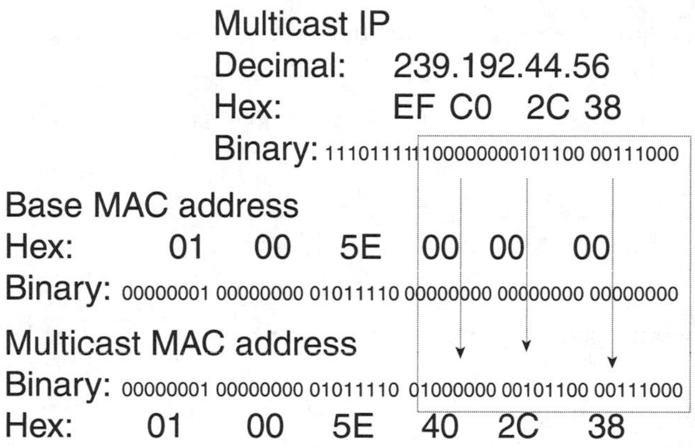

Multicast IP
Decimal: 239.192.44.56
Hex: EF C0   2C 38
Binary: 11101111 10000000 101100 00111000

Base MAC address
Hex: 01   00   5E   00   00   00
Binary: 00000001 00000000 01011110 00000000 00000000 00000000

Multicast MAC address
Binary: 00000001 00000000 01011110 01000000 00101100 00111000
Hex: 01   00   5E   40   2C   38

IGMP

IGMP is the protocol used in multicast implementations between the end hosts and the local router. RFC 2236 describes IGMP Version 2 (IGMPv2). RFC 3376 describes IGMP Version 3 (IGMPv3). RFC 1112 describes the first version of IGMP.

IP hosts use IGMP to report their multicast group memberships to routers. IGMP messages use IP protocol number 2. IGMP messages are limited to the local interface and are not routed.

IGMP v1

The first RFC describing IGMP (RFC 1112), written in 1989, describes the host extension of multicasting. IGMPv1 provides simple message types for communication between hosts and routers. These messages are

- **Membership query**—Sent by the host to request to join a multicast group
- **Membership report**—Sent by the router to check whether there are still hosts in multicast groups in the segment

The problem with IGMPv1 is the latency involved for a host to leave a group. With IGMPv1, the router sends out membership reports periodically; a host must wait for the membership-report message to leave a group. The query interval is 60 seconds, and it takes three query intervals (3 minutes) for a host to leave the group.

IGMP v2

IGMPv2 improves over IGMPv1 by allowing faster termination or leaving of multicast groups.

IGMPv2 has three message types, plus one for backward-compatibility:

- **Membership query**—Sent to indicate that a host wants to join a group.

- **Version 2 membership report**—Message sent to the group address with the multicast group members (IP addresses). It is sent to verify whether there are still hosts in multicast groups on the segment.

- **Version 2 leave group**—Sent by the hosts to indicate that a host will leave a group, to destination 224.0.0.2. The message is sent without having to wait for the IGMPv2 membership-report message.

- **Version 1 membership report**—For backward-compatibility with IGMPv1 hosts.

You enable IGMP on an interface when you configure a multicast routing protocol, such as PIM. You can configure the interface for IGMPv1 or IGMPv2.

IGMP v3

IGMPv3 provides the extensions required to support source-specific multicast (SSM). It is designed to be backward-compatible with both prior versions of IGMP.

IGMPv3 has two message types, plus three for backward-compatibility:

- **Membership query**—Sent to indicate that a host wants to join a group.

- **Version 3 membership report**—Message sent to the group address with the multicast group members (IP addresses). It is sent to verify whether there are still hosts in multicast groups on the segment.

- **Version 2 membership report**—Message sent to the group address with the multicast group members (IP addresses). It is sent to verify whether there are still hosts in multicast groups on the segment. This message is used for backward-compatibility with IGMPv2 hosts.

- **Version 2 leave group**—Sent by the hosts to indicate that a host will leave a group, to destination 224.0.0.2. The message is sent without having to wait for the IGMPv2 membership-report message. This message is used for backward-compatibility with IGMPv2 hosts.

- **Version 1 membership report**—This message is used for backward-compatibility with IGMPv1 hosts.

You enable IGMP on an interface when you enable a multicast routing protocol, such as PIM. You can configure the interface for IGMPv1, IGMPv2, or IGMPv3.

CGMP

CGMP is a Cisco proprietary protocol implemented to control multicast traffic at Layer 2. Because a Layer 2 switch is not aware of Layer 3 IGMP messages, it cannot restrain multicast packets from being sent to all ports.

As shown in Figure 14-14, with CGMP the LAN switch can speak with the IGMP router to find out the MAC addresses of the hosts that want to receive the multicast packets. With CGMP, switches distribute multicast sessions only to the switch ports that have group members.

Figure 14-14   *CGMP*

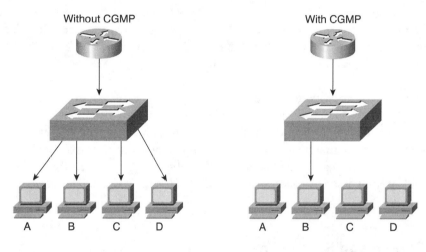

When a router receives an IGMP report, it processes the report and then sends a CGMP message to the switch. The switch can then forward the multicast messages to the port with the host receiving multicast traffic. CGMP fast-leave processing allows the switch to detect IGMP Version 2 leave messages sent by hosts on any of the switch ports. When a host sends the IGMPv2 leave message, the switch can then disable multicasting for the port.

IGMP Snooping

IGMP snooping is another way for switches to control multicast traffic at Layer 2. It listens to IGMP messages between the hosts and routers. If a host sends an IGMP query message to the router, the switch adds the host to the multicast group and permits that port to receive multicast traffic. The port is removed from multicast traffic if the host sends an IGMP leave message to the router. The disadvantage of IGMP snooping is that it has to process every IGMP control message, which can impact the CPU utilization of the switch.

Sparse Versus Dense Multicast Routing Protocols

IP multicast traffic for a particular (source, destination group) multicast pair is transmitted from the source to the receivers using a spanning tree from the source that connects all the hosts in the group. Each destination host registers itself as a member in interesting multicast groups through the use of IGMP. Routers keep track of these groups dynamically and build distribution trees that chart paths from each sender to all receivers. IP multicast routing protocols follow two approaches.

The first approach assumes that the multicast group members are densely distributed throughout the network (many of the subnets contain at least one group member) and that bandwidth is plentiful. The approach with dense multicast routing protocols is to flood the traffic throughout the network and then, at the request of receiving routers, stop the flow of traffic on branches of the network that have no members of the multicast group. Multicast routing protocols that follow this technique of flooding the network include DVMRP, Multicast Open Shortest Path First (MOSPF), and Protocol Independent Multicast-Dense Mode (PIM-DM).

The second approach to multicast routing assumes that multicast group members are sparsely distributed throughout the network and that bandwidth is not necessarily widely available. Sparse mode does not imply that the group has few members, just that they are widely dispersed. The approach with sparse multicast routing protocols is to not send traffic until it is requested by the receiving routers or hosts. Multicast routing protocols of this type are Core Based Trees (CBT) and Protocol Independent Multicast-Sparse Mode (PIM-SM). CBT is not widely deployed and is not discussed in this guide.

Multicast Source and Shared Trees

Multicast distribution trees control the path multicast packets take to the destination hosts. The two types of distribution trees are source and shared. With *source* trees, the tree roots from the source of the multicast group and then expands throughout the network in spanning-tree fashion to the destination hosts. Source trees are also called shortest-path trees (SPT) because they create paths without having to go through a rendezvous point (RP). The drawback is that all routers through the path must use memory resources to maintain a list of all multicast groups. PIM-DM uses a source-based tree.

Shared trees create the root of the distribution tree somewhere between the source and the receivers of the network. The root is called the RP. The tree is created from the RP in spanning-tree fashion with no loops. The advantage of shared trees is that they reduce the memory requirements of routers in the multicast network. The drawback is that initially the multicast packets might not take the best paths to the receivers because they need to pass through the RP. After the data stream begins to flow from sender to RP to receiver, the routers in the path optimize the path automatically to remove any unnecessary hops. The RP function consumes significant memory on the assigned router. PIM-SM uses an RP.

PIM

PIM comes in two flavors: *sparse mode* (PIM-SM) and *dense mode* (PIM-DM). The first uses shared trees and RPs to reach widely dispersed group members with reasonable protocol bandwidth efficiency. The second uses source trees and reverse path forwarding (RPF) to reach relatively near group members with reasonable processor and memory efficiency in the network devices of the distribution trees.

With RPF, received multicast packets are forwarded out all other interfaces, allowing the data stream to reach all segments. If no hosts are members of a multicast group on any of the router's attached or downstream subnets, the router sends a prune message up the distribution tree (the reverse path) to inform the upstream router to not send packets for the multicast group. So, the analogy for PIM-DM is the push method for sending junk mail, and the intermediate router must tell upstream devices to stop sending it.

PIM-SM

PIM-SM is defined in RFC 2362 (experimental). PIM-SM assumes that no hosts want to receive multicast traffic unless specifically requested. In PIM-SM, a router is selected as the RP. The RP has the task of gathering the information from senders and making the information available to receivers. Routers with receivers have to register with the RP. The end-host systems request multicast group membership using IGMP with their local routers. The routers serving the end systems then register as traffic receivers with the RPs for the specified group in the multicast network.

Joining PIM-SM

With PIM-SM, DRs on end segments receive IGMP query messages from hosts wanting to join a multicast group. The router checks whether it is already receiving the group for another interface. If it is receiving the group, the router adds the new interface to the table and sends membership reports periodically on the new interface.

If the multicast group is not in the multicast table, the router adds the interface to the multicast table and sends a join message to the RP with multicast address 224.0.0.13 (all PIM routers) requesting the multicast group.

Pruning PIM-SM

When a PIM-SM does not have any more multicast receiving hosts or receiving routers out any of its interfaces, it sends a prune message to the RP. The prune message includes the group to be pruned or removed.

PIM DR

A designated router is selected in multiaccess segments running PIM. The PIM DR is responsible for sending join, prune, and register messages to the RP. The PIM router with the highest IP address is selected as the DR.

Auto-RP

Another way to configure the RP for the network is to have the RP announce its services to the PIM network. This process is called auto-RP. Candidate RPs send their announcements to RP mapping agents with multicast address 224.0.1.39 (**cisco-rp-announce**). RP mapping agents are also configured. In smaller networks, the RP can be the mapping agent. Configured RP mapping agents listen to the announcements. The RP mapping agent then selects the RP for a group based on the highest IP address of all the candidate RPs. The RP mapping agents then send RP-discovery messages to the rest of the PIM-SM routers in the internetwork with the selected RP-to-group mappings.

PIMv2 Bootstrap Router

Instead of using auto-RP, you can configure a PIMv2 bootstrap router (BSR) to automatically select an RP for the network. The RFC for PIM Version 2, RFC 2362, describes BSR. With BSR, you configure BSR candidates (C-BSRs) with priorities from 0 to 255 and a BSR address. C-BSRs exchange bootstrap messages. Bootstrap messages are sent to multicast IP 224.0.0.13 (all PIM routers). If a C-BSR receives a bootstrap message, it compares it with its own. The largest priority C-BSR is selected as the BSR.

After the BSR is selected for the network, it collects a list of candidate RPs. The BSR selects RP-to-group mappings, which is called the RP set, and distributes the selected RPs using bootstrap messages sent to 224.0.0.13 (all PIM routers).

DVMRP

RFC 1075 describes DVMRP. It is the primary multicast routing protocol used in the multicast backbone (MBONE). The MBONE is used in the research community.

DVMRP operates in the dense mode using RPF by having routers send a copy of a multicast packet out all paths. Routers that receive the multicast packets then send prune messages back to their upstream neighbor router to stop a data stream if there are no downstream receivers of the multicast group (either receiving routers or hosts on connected segments). DVMRP implements its own unicast routing protocol, similar to RIP, based on hop counts. DVMRP has a 32 hop-count limit. DVMRP does not scale suboptimally. The Cisco support of DVMRP is partial; DVMRP networks are usually implemented on UNIX machines running the **mrouted** process. A DVMRP tunnel is typically used to connect to the MBONE DVMRP network.

Foundation Summary

The "Foundation Summary" section of each chapter lists the most important facts from the chapter. Although this section does not list every fact from the chapter that will be on your CCDA exam, a well-prepared CCDA candidate should at a minimum know all the details in each "Foundation Summary" before going to take the exam.

This chapter covered the following topics that you need to master for the CCDA exam:

- **BGP**—The characteristics and design of the BGP.
- **PBR and route redistribution**—How you use PBR to change the destination address of packets based on policies. This section also covers the redistribution of routes between routing protocols.
- **IP multicast protocols**—Multicast protocols such as IGMP, CGMP, and PIM.

The material summarized in this section can help you review some of these topical areas.

BGP Summary

The characteristics of BGP follow:

- Interdomain routing protocol.
- Uses TCP port 179 to establish connections with neighbors.
- BGPv4 implements CIDR.
- eBGP for external neighbors; used between autonomous systems.
- iBGP for internal neighbors; used within an AS.
- Uses several attributes in the routing-decision algorithm.
- Uses confederations and route reflectors to reduce BGP peering overhead.
- MED (metric) attribute used between autonomous systems to influence inbound traffic.
- Weight used to influence the path of outbound traffic from a single router, configured locally.

Table 14-3 summarizes IP multicast protocols.

Table 14-3 *IP Multicast Protocols*

Multicast Protocol	Description
IGMP	Internet Group Management Protocol. Used by IP hosts to report their multicast group memberships to routers.
CGMP	Cisco Group Management Protocol. Used to control multicast traffic at Layer 2.
IGMP snooping	Another method used to control multicast traffic at Layer 2.
PIM	Protocol Independent Multicast. IP multicast routing protocol.
DVMRP	Distance-Vector Multicast Routing Protocol. Primary multicast routing protocol used in the MBONE.

Table 14-4 summarizes IP multicast addresses.

Table 14-4 *IP Multicast Addresses*

Multicast Address	Description
224.0.0.0/24	Local network control block
224.0.0.1	All hosts or all systems on this subnet
224.0.0.2	All routers on this subnet
224.0.0.4	DVMRP routers
224.0.0.5	All OSPF routers
224.0.0.6	All OSPF DR routers
224.0.0.9	RIPv2 routers
224.0.0.10	EIGRP routers
224.0.0.13	All PIM routers
224.0.1/24	Internetwork control block
224.0.1.39	RP announce
224.0.1.40	RP discovery
224.0.2.0 to 224.0.255.0	Ad hoc block
239.000.000.000 to 239.255.255.255	Administratively scoped
239.192.000.000 to 239.251.255.255	Organization-local scope
239.252.000.000 to 239.254.255.255	Site-local scope

Q&A

As mentioned in the introduction, you have two choices for review questions. Some of the questions that follow give you a bigger challenge than the exam itself by using an open-ended question format. By reviewing now with this more difficult question format, you can exercise your memory better and prove your conceptual and factual knowledge of this chapter. The answers to these questions appear in Appendix A.

For more practice with exam-like question formats, use the exam engine on the CD-ROM.

1. True or false? You use iBGP to exchange routes between different autonomous systems.

2. True or false? BGP Version 4 includes support for CIDR.

3. True or false? EIGRP and IGRP redistribute automatically on a router if the two protocols are configured with the same AS number.

4. Use _____ to modify the next hop of packets based on source IP address.

5. eBGP routes have an administrative distance of _____ and iBGP routes have an administrative distance of _____.

6. True or false? IGMP snooping and CGMP are methods to reduce the multicast traffic at Layer 2.

7. True of false? PIM has a 32 hop-count limit.

8. True or false? PIM-SM routers use the multicast 224.0.0.13 address to request a multicast group to the RP.

9. True or false? AS path is the only attribute BGP uses to determine the best path to the destination.

10. List three IP routing protocols that use multicast addresses to communicate with their neighbors.

11. Match the IP multicast address with its description:

    i.   224.0.0.1   **a.** All OSPF routers

    ii. 224.0.0.2   **b.** All routers

    iii. 224.0.0.5   **c.** EIGRP routers

    iv. 224.0.0.10   **d.** All hosts

12. Match the BGP attribute with the description:

    i. Local preference   **a.** An IP address

    ii. MED   **b.** Indicates path used to exit the AS

    iii. AS path   **c.** Tells external BGP peers the preferred path into the AS

    iv. Next hop   **d.** List of AS numbers

13. Which Cisco feature can you use instead of local preference to influence the selected path to external BGP routers?

14. What is the purpose of route reflectors?

15. When using BGP confederations, which number do external peers see?

16. With _____ all routers peer with each other within the private AS, and with _____ client routers only peer with the reflector.

17. Which of the following shows the correct order that BGP uses to select a best path?

    a. Origin, lowest IP, AS path, weight, local preference

    b. Weight, local preference, AS path, origin, MED, lowest IP

    c. Lowest IP, AS path, origin, weight, MED, local preference

    d. Weight, origin, local preference, AS path, MED, lowest IP

18. What feature did BGPv4 implement to provide forwarding of packets based on IP prefixes?

Refer to Figure 14-15 to answer the questions that follow.

Figure 14-15 *Network Scenario*

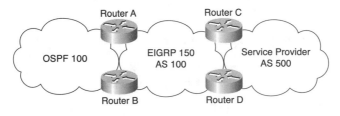

19. Where should you configure BGP?

    a. Routers A and B

    b. Routers C and D

    c. Answers a and b

    d. Routers A and C

20. On which router should you configure redistribution for OSPF and EIGRP?

    a. Router A only.

    b. Router B only.

    c. Routers A and B.

    d. Redistribution will occur automatically.

21. To announce the networks from AS 100 to AS 500, which routing protocols should you redistribute into BGP?

    a. OSPF only

    b. EIGRP only

    c. OSPF and EIGRP

    d. iBGP

22. Where should you use filters?

    a. Routers A and B

    b. Routers C and D

    c. Routers A and C

    d. Answers a and b

PART IV: Security, Convergence, and Network Management

This part covers the following CCDA exam objectives (to view the CCDA exam outline, visit http://www.cisco.com/go/training):

- Gather and evaluate information regarding a network owner's current voice network and future needs.

- Given a network design or a set of requirements, evaluate a solution that meets network-management needs.

- Evaluate solutions addressing the issues of delivering voice traffic over a data network.

- Evaluate solutions for compliance with SAFE.

This chapter covers the following subjects:

- Introduction to Threats

- Network Reconnaissance

- Packet Sniffing

- Man-in-the-Middle Attacks

- IP Spoofing

- DoS

- Password Attacks

- Port Redirection

- Trust Exploitation

- Unauthorized Access

- Application-Layer Attacks

- Virus and Trojan-Horse Applications

- Secure Monitoring and Management

- Secure Management Communications

- Out-of-Band Management

- In-Band Management

CHAPTER 15

Common Security Flaws and Monitoring

A major emphasis of SAFE is understanding the types of attacks that are common to various parts of the architecture. This chapter discusses the modularity principles in designing network-security services and how each module addresses the security threats. The chapter goes on to describe individual network modules and lists the solutions within a module and across modules. Also, this chapter discusses security monitoring and management, as well as the communication between the building blocks.

"Do I Know This Already?" Quiz

The purpose of the "Do I Know This Already?" quiz is to help you decide whether you need to read the entire chapter. If you intend to read the entire chapter, you do not necessarily need to answer these questions now.

The 10-question quiz, derived from the major sections in the "Foundation Topics" portion of the chapter, helps you determine how to spend your limited study time.

Table 15-1 outlines the major topics discussed in this chapter and the "Do I Know This Already?" quiz questions that correspond to those topics.

Table 15-1 *"Do I Know This Already?" Foundation Topics Section-to-Question Mapping*

Foundation Topics Section	Questions Covered in This Section
Introduction to Threats	6
Man-in-the-Middle Attacks	1
Packet Sniffing	2
Unauthorized Access	3
Password Attacks	4
Application-Layer Attacks	5

continues

Foundation Topics Section	Questions Covered in This Section
Virus and Trojan Horse Applications	7
Secure Monitoring	8
Out-of-Band Management	9
In-Band Management	10

CAUTION The goal of self assessment is to gauge your mastery of the topics in this chapter. If you do not know the answer to a question or you are only partially sure of the answer, you should mark this question wrong for purposes of the self assessment. Giving yourself credit for an answer you correctly guess skews your self-assessment results and might provide you with a false sense of security.

1. Which method would you use to secure a network against man-in-the-middle attack?

    a. Firewall

    b. Encryption

    c. Management module

    d. Two-factor authentication

2. True or false? Even encrypted packets can be compromised.

3. Filtering Layer 3 traffic of specific subnets to protect server modules is a mitigation strategy for which type of attack?

    a. Password attack

    b. Trojan horse

    c. Application-layer attacks

    d. Unauthorized access

4. A brute-force attack is associated with what type of threat?

    a. Denial of service (DoS)

    b. Trojan horse

    c. Password attack

    d. Unauthorized access

5. What types of attacks should you expect on segments that have many servers for some well-known applications?

   a. Application-layer attacks

   b. Trojan horses

   c. Password attacks

   d. DoS attacks

6. A common response to an attack by this device can be either to send an alert or to take corrective action. What type of device is it?

   a. Intrusion-detection system (IDS)

   b. Vulnerability assessment

   c. Firewall

   d. Router

7. An infected host that actively scans for other hosts to infect is called what type of attack?

   a. DoS

   b. Trojan horse

   c. Password attack

   d. Worm

8. What is the name of the Cisco product that provides centralized, policy-based security management?

   a. IDS

   b. AAA

   c. CSPM

   d. Out-of-band management

9. What method of network management will allow you to access devices if the network is down?

   a. IDS

   b. In-band management

   c. CSPM

   d. Out-of-band management

10. Which of the following terms is a secure alternative to Telnet access to devices?

    a. IDS

    b. Secure Shell (SSH)

    c. Penetration testing

    d. Secure Sockets Layer (SSL)

The answers to the "Do I Know This Already?" quiz appear in Appendix A, "Answers to Chapter 'Do I Know This Already?' Quizzes and Q&A Sections." The suggested choices for your next step are as follows:

- **8 or less overall score**—Read the entire chapter. It includes the "Foundation Topics," "Foundation Summary," and "Q&A" sections.

- **9–10 overall score**—If you want more review on these topics, skip to the "Foundation Summary" section and then go to the "Q&A" section. Otherwise, move to the next chapter.

Foundation Topics

Before designing network-security services and comprehending how each module of the SAFE blueprint addresses security threats, it is critical to understand the different types of attacks that are common to various parts of the architecture. After you install the security-based solution, security management and monitoring, as for all other systems, is a requirement.

Introduction to Threats

This section is devoted to listing the threats that are defined for SAFE. Remember that anticipating the threats for each of the modules of SAFE is the basis for designing the solution. Cisco starts you on this process by providing you a list of the common threats and the associated solutions. The threats appear with a description of how they function. This arrangement helps you categorize new attacks as they appear. Understanding the basic principles of an attack and its mitigation is a foundational strategy for SAFE.

You can use two common techniques to detect attacks and record details of the episode. The first involves (automated) inspection of the device logs, which most devices can generate. The second is using an IDS, which recognizes patterns of activity (signatures) that reflect known attacks.

You analyze logs to recognize the "m.o." of an attack. The *modus operandi* of an attack is the offender's action while committing the crime. Logs can be helpful in identifying early warning signs that do not always trigger an alarm. Reviewing logs is a daunting task, however; some applications have a subscription service with preprogrammed patterns to review logs. The subscription ensures that the log review coordinates with current patterns. More importantly, it enables you to review a large quantity of logs with efficiency. The section "Secure Monitoring" later in the chapter provides more details.

There are two categories of IDS, which can trigger an alarm when it detects an attack that it recognizes; sometimes, it is also capable of countering the attack. A network-based IDS (NIDS) can scan a particular segment, or you can get a host-based IDS (HIDS).

Human diligence is necessary to thwart new attacks as well as technological efforts by IDSs. Subscribing to mailing lists and checking various security sites must be part of the daily management routine. Common sources for security information are

- Vendor sites for patches and bug fixes
- Bugtraq (http://www.securityfocus.com)

- CERT (http://www.cert.org)

- SANS (http://www.sans.org)

Before discussing the specific attacks, review the following diagrams of the different functional areas as defined in SAFE and their associated modules. Figure 15-1 shows the functional area called the Enterprise Campus.

Figure 15-1 *Enterprise Campus and Detail of Modules*

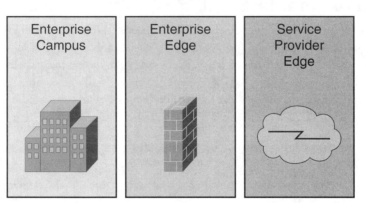

Figure 15-2 is the functional area called the Enterprise Edge. Note the positioning and the modules that make up the Enterprise Edge. By understanding its functions, you can accurately identify the types of attacks it is vulnerable to.

Figure 15-2 *Enterprise Edge and Detail of Modules*

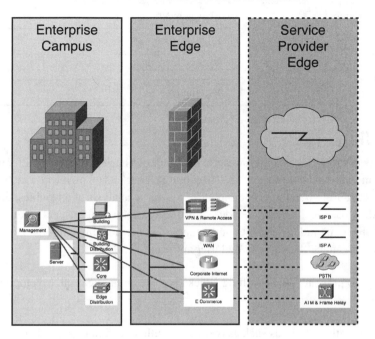

Three SAFE Functional Areas and Modules

Network Reconnaissance

Network reconnaissance refers to learning information about a target network using publicly available information and applications such as Domain Name System (DNS) queries, ping sweeps, and port scans.

IDSs at the network and host levels can usually notify an administrator when a reconnaissance attack is underway. This alert allows the administrator to better prepare for the coming attack or to notify the ISP that is hosting the system that is launching the reconnaissance attack.

Table 15-2 lists the most commonly affected modules in the SAFE blueprint that are targeted by reconnaissance attacks.

Table 15-2   *Modules Affected by Reconnaissance*

Functional Area	Module
Enterprise Campus	Management
	Edge distribution
Enterprise Edge	Corporate Internet
	E-commerce

Packet Sniffing

Useful network tools can become threats in the hands of a hacker. A packet sniffer provides an example of how someone can exploit a tool used to capture all packets on physical wire (promiscuous mode). A packet-sniffer application is common tool for traffic analysis and troubleshooting by capturing and decoding packets. You can use packet sniffers to capture and inspect all unencrypted data (clear text), which can include usernames and passwords or critical information. Hackers can use this information to attack the network and user applications.

Some ways to prevent packet-sniffing attacks include authentication, cryptography, and network segmenting:

■   Authentication methods such as two-factor authentication (using token cards that generate a random password, which is used in conjunction with a user password), which uses a one-time password, mitigate subsequent attacks using false credentials for authentication and some replay attacks.

■   Cryptography is the most common and effective method of securing data against sniffers because it scrambles the clear text. IP Security (IPSec), SSH, and SSL are common encryption protocols.

■   Segmenting the network using switches can help to localize the sniffer's activity.

Table 15-3 lists the most commonly affected modules in the SAFE blueprint that are targeted by packet sniffing.

Table 15-3 *Modules Affected by Sniffing*

Functional Area	Module
Enterprise Campus	Management
	Core
	Building distribution
	Building
	Server
	Edge distribution
Enterprise Edge	Corporate Internet
	E-commerce

Man-in-the-Middle Attacks

By using packet sniffers or type products, it is possible to capture information as it is transferred from one network to another. This type of attack requires access to the network media or devices between the source and destination. Wireless LAN technologies are particularly susceptible to this kind of attack. Rogue employees responsible for the enterprise or service-provider networks can also conduct them. Attackers can use the information captured to launch other attacks that deny service, obtain vital information, subvert applications, or corrupt data stores.

Use strong encryption so that if packets are sniffed, they are useless to the attacker. Mandatory use of encrypted VPN connections mitigates the inherent vulnerability of wireless LANs. It is possible to thwart encryption methods if the hacker obtains information about the encryption process, such as keys.

Table 15-4 lists the most commonly affected modules in the SAFE blueprint that are targeted by man-in-the-middle attacks.

Table 15-4 *Modules Affected by a Man-in-the-Middle*

Functional Area	Module
Enterprise Campus	Management
	Building access
Enterprise Edge	VPN and remote access

IP Spoofing

IP spoofing is a technique in which the attacker sends packets with the source IP address modified to match that of a trusted host. IP spoofing can also disguise the source of packets launched as part of a DoS attack.

Some ways to prevent IP spoofing attacks are authentication and filtering:

- Authentication prevents access to systems based solely on IP address.
- With filtering (see RFC 2827), you can prevent a network's users from spoofing other networks from your networks by preventing any outbound traffic on your network that does not have a source address in your organization's own IP range.

Table 15-5 lists the most commonly affected modules in the SAFE blueprint that are targeted by IP spoofing attacks.

Table 15-5 *Modules Affected by Spoofing*

Functional Area	Module
Enterprise Campus	Management
	Building distribution
	Server
	Edge distribution
Enterprise Edge	Corporate Internet
	E-commerce
	WAN

DoS

DoS attacks deny legitimate users access to services. DoS attacks are characterized by disrupting connectivity between devices, preventing access to specific services, halting processes on devices by sending bad packets, and flooding networks.

Some ways to prevent DoS attacks follow:

- Properly configure firewalls and routers to prevent DoS attacks. You can find these configurations on vendor and security websites.
- Prevent spoofing.
- Prevent traffic rates from getting out of control.

Table 15-6 lists the most commonly affected modules in the SAFE blueprint that are targeted by DoS attacks.

Table 15-6 *Modules Affected by DoS*

Functional Area	Module
Enterprise Edge	E-commerce
	WAN
	Corporate Internet

Password Attacks

Password attacks can use information "sniffed" from a network or gained through user inattention or carelessness. Another password attack is the brute-force attack. The attacker uses known, or inferred, usernames and a sequence of guessed passwords against each username until she gains access, she abandons the attack as too difficult, or something counters the attack. These attacks often succeed because administrators and users have not changed documented default passwords. When an attacker determines a username and password, he can use the same information to attack multiple systems or applications—because individuals frequently reuse passwords. When an exploit has gained access to a system or application, the attacker might be able to create a backdoor, which gives him network access at a later time.

Some ways to prevent password attacks follow:

- Use a password format that is not easy to guess or decipher:
    - Avoid using personal information such as child, spouse, or pet names, birthdates, anniversary dates, etc.
    - Avoid using names, dates, or words that appear in a standard dictionary.
    - Include a mixture of alphabetic and numeric characters with at least one special character (such as !, @, and $) in the middle of the password.
- Do not post passwords on your workstation, bulletin board, or any other conspicuous place.
- Do not store the password and ID together.

Table 15-7 lists the most commonly affected modules in the SAFE blueprint that are targeted by password attacks.

Table 15-7 *Modules Affected by Password Attacks*

Functional Area	Module
Enterprise Campus	Management
	Building access
Enterprise Edge	VPN and remote access
	Corporate Internet

Port Redirection

Port-redirection attacks use a compromised host to pass traffic through a firewall that would otherwise be dropped. An example of an application that can provide this type of access is Netcat. For more information, refer to the website http://insecure.org/tools.html.

Mitigation strategies include using trust models, as described in the next section on "Trust Exploitation," or deploying IDSs in the network.

Table 15-8 lists the most commonly affected modules in the SAFE blueprint that are targeted by port-redirection attacks.

Table 15-8 *Modules Affected by Port Redirection*

Functional Area	Module
Enterprise Campus	Server
Enterprise Edge	Corporate Internet
	E-commerce

Trust Exploitation

Trust exploitation is not a name of an attack, but it is a description of how an attack works. As its name suggests, it is when a trusted source on a network takes advantage of its position. This vulnerability applies to systems as well so that if one device on a segment is compromised, it can lead to other systems being compromised on the same segment. This vulnerability is a key reason that SAFE divides the network into logical groups based on access needs.

By managing system access with assigned trust levels, you can make sure that systems on the outside of a firewall are never trusted by systems inside the firewall.

Table 15-9 lists the most commonly affected modules in the SAFE blueprint that are targeted by trust exploitation.

Table 15-9 *Modules Affected by Trust Exploitation*

Functional Area	Module
Enterprise Campus	Management
	Server
Enterprise Edge	Corporate Internet
	E-commerce

Unauthorized Access

Although this attack doesn't have a fancy name, it is often the first breach that occurs. The best way to prevent attacks is to prevent access to possible entry points. This prevention includes securing ports, passwords, and applications. Unauthorized access frequently follows a successful password attack.

You should secure access to a module with a firewall. The filtering on this firewall will secure all inbound traffic and outbound traffic from this module to others.

Table 15-10 lists the most commonly affected modules in the SAFE blueprint that are targeted by unauthorized access.

Table 15-10 *Modules Affected by Unauthorized Access*

Functional Area	Module
Enterprise Campus	Management
	Building distribution
	Building
	Server
	Edge distribution
Enterprise Edge	Corporate Internet
	E-commerce
	WAN module
	VPN and remote access

Application-Layer Attacks

Application-layer attacks often use port access through firewalls to gain entry to your systems, using the same ports opened to enable you to access the services you need, such as web servers that use port 80. Once the hacker exploits an opening, she can gain access to systems. Many application-layer attacks are launched against security holes in the software. Many platforms required advance configuration to "lock down" access methods so that the user can define his own level of security. Another common attack method is to gain access using an administrator-level account. This access would allow unrestricted use of the servers, applications and utilities. The administrator-level account is used to verify warnings in log files and to provide fixes for these applications, but it means that the hacker has access to the same information.

Some ways to prevent application-layer attacks follow:

- Keep applications, utilities, and servers current with the latest supported patches and fixes.
- Restrict access to applications using strong authentication.
- Use logging to capture data and access information.
- Secure traffic access to applications.
- Block inbound access using filters.

Table 15-11 lists the most commonly affected modules in the SAFE blueprint that are targeted by application-layer attacks.

Table 15-11   *Modules Affected by Application-Layer Attacks*

Functional Area	Module
Enterprise Campus	Server
Enterprise Edge	Corporate Internet
	E-commerce

Virus and Trojan-Horse Applications

There are two common end-user host attacks. A virus is malicious code that is attached to another program. You activate the virus by running the infected program or opening the infected file, and it performs its intended tasks. These tasks can range from relatively benign distractions to the catastrophic destruction of local system capabilities. The virus can propagate itself to other devices. The only difference in a Trojan horse is that it disguises itself as an application that looks like something else. Worms are self-replicating malicious code that exploit a vulnerability on servers.

You can contain these kinds of applications through the effective use of antivirus software at the user level and potentially at the network level. Antivirus software can detect most viruses and many Trojan applications and prevent them from spreading in the network. Keeping up-to-date with the latest developments in these sorts of attacks is the only way to ensure that you will be protected against new attacks. The only problem you will encounter is if the applications do not know how to manage newer types of attacks.

Table 15-12 lists the most commonly affected modules in the SAFE blueprint that are targeted by virus and Trojan applications.

Table 15-12 *Modules Affected by Viruses and Trojans*

Functional Area	Module
Enterprise Campus	Building
Enterprise Edge	Corporate Internet

Introduction to Secure Monitoring and Management

The security-based solution that you install requires management and monitoring just like all other systems. This section addresses the requirements for establishing security management. You can apply these suggestions to other systems as well.

You can use products such as IDSs to continuously monitor systems and alert security managers to breaches. The Cisco IDS also can perform mitigation tasks to stop the breach in progress to minimize the damage. In addition, you can use regular vulnerability and penetration assessments to test your security solution to identify possible security holes. These tests ensure that changes to your network and your security solutions work the way you expect them to work.

Secure Monitoring

A component of secure monitoring is reviewing log information for the security devices. As discussed in the beginning of the chapter, logs play an important role, but knowing how to manage them is key. Logs can be generated quickly over a short period of time. If you multiply large quantities of logs by the number of devices, you can feel overwhelmed by the task of reviewing them. In addition, you have to know what you are looking for in the logs; just having them is not enough. If you are not going to use the logs or manage them correctly, don't bother collecting them. However, you can use these logs as evidence if legal action is required. If you do not organize the logs, it will be extremely difficult to locate the proper logs if required.

Syslog is a common way to collect and store logs. Syslog lets you collect messages from devices to a server running a syslog daemon. In general, the syslog daemon runs on UNIX servers. Using network-management tools, you can collect the syslogs from various devices and analyze them together. There is more to this practice than logging activity; logging changes to devices can be a valuable tool. Have you ever experienced a situation where you made changes to a system, and when the changes caused issues, you should have written down the changes? Change management can help you retrace your steps for troubleshooting, but having a log of configurations before and after you institute changes is even more useful. Good change-management practices should be part of your security strategy.

Collecting logs is not the only management process you can use to support security devices. Polling (pulling) logs from devices is one issue, but what about pushing data and applications to servers? How will you manage the push of data so that it isn't compromised in transit? What if you have to manage a device that you can't access?

Secure Management

Just as the security solution began with a security policy, secure management should begin with managing the security policy once it is in place. The policies that govern your solutions require maintenance. As the policies that guide the security solution change, you must make changes to the corporate security policy and to the configurations on the security devices that enforce this policy.

Cisco has a product called the Cisco Secure Policy Manager (CSPM) used to specify, manage, and audit the state of a security policy through browser-based user interfaces. This process enables the security manager to control large numbers of security elements in the network. Distributing security policy from a central management system increases the consistency of the policy implementation across multiple devices. Policies implemented centrally tend to be more comprehensive and effective because they consider the entire information system rather than just individual components.

Secure Management Communications

Network-device management requires that a communications channel be available to the network devices. Devices can support out-of-band management, in-band management, or both. In-band management consumes bandwidth that could otherwise be used by network traffic. Out-of-band management increases bandwidth available for network traffic and typically improves the privacy and security of network-management communications. You achieve the benefits at the possible cost of designing, provisioning, and managing the management network itself. In any case, the management channel should be robust, private, and secure.

Out-of-Band Management

Preparing for the worst-case network-management scenario includes ensuring that there is a way to reach the devices when the usual access channel is unavailable. Out-of-band management using modem access through a management port is an attractive option when combined with authentication and access controls. When supported, secured VPN access in-band can provide access if you lose a management network. Directly connecting to management ports using serial communication cables is a final, labor-intensive option.

Out-of-band management offers many significant advantages and becomes more desirable as the managed network grows. In this case, you can perform real-time monitoring and access over a protected channel, which does not impact transport bandwidth availability. In a large network, the costs of provisioning and maintaining the management network are less proportionally than in a small network. Out-of-band management is a part of the Enterprise Composite Network Model and SAFE as applied to large enterprises.

In-Band Management

In-band management is appropriate in smaller networks and in networks with sufficient link capacities to support both application traffic and management activity. Securing access to the devices and management applications is an important consideration. Mechanisms to secure the management command and data stream include IPSec tunnels, SSH, and SSL.

Auto Update Security

A repeating theme throughout the discussion of the SAFE Architecture is the wide range of devices that are needed to secure the enterprise. That is all well and good until it is time to discuss how to manage all the different security devices.

The reasons for having large quantity of security devices varies—such as the need for multiples of devices due to the size of the enterprise or the need to deploy several different types of security devices. Whatever the reason, Cisco included as part of their SAFE architecture, tools and a methodology to effectively manage and maintain these systems—automatically.

This central configuration management system is a part of the CiscoWorks VPN/Security Management Solution (VMS) suite of products. It is called the Auto Update Server Software, which allows the security administrator to initially configure, change and update configurations, and verify configurations remotely.

It is important to note that the central objective of CiscoWorks VMS is to tie together management of various security products such as the PIX Firewalls, the IDS systems, and the VPN routers. These systems required separate management in the past even though their functions were tightly integrated. With this new product, the security can be viewed holistically, thereby organizing the security configurations that would need to be applied to these disparate components. The CiscoWorks VMS product at the time of this publication is on version 2.2 and includes the following components:

- CiscoWorks Management Center for Firewalls
- CiscoWorks Auto Update Server Software
- CiscoWorks Management Center for IDS Sensors
- CiscoWorks Management Center for Cisco Security Agents
- CiscoWorks Management Center for VPN Routers
- CiscoWorks Monitoring for Security
- CiscoWorks VPN Monitor
- CiscoWorks Resource Manager Essentials
- CiscoWorks Common Services Software

This product contains the Auto Update Server at version 1.1. This type of product is ideal in today's enterprise environments where security is not managed locally but from a central office. Today, many companies have several small remote offices and a growing number of telecommuting users. This community has posed a new challenge to IT departments because they are often labor-intensive because you often have a single user per location. In this situation, many IT cycles can be consumed by a small security rule change due to the multiple devices. On a more serious note, many companies that cannot maintain these types of devices often resort to implementing lower security in order to minimize the need for change. This product enables an administrator to successfully and efficiently manage those users and still maintain a secure and robust corporate network.

Foundation Summary

The "Foundation Summary" section of each chapter lists the most important facts from the chapter. Although this section does not list every fact from the chapter that will be on your CCDA exam, a well-prepared CCDA candidate should at a minimum know all the details in each "Foundation Summary" before going to take the exam.

The CCDA exam requires that you be familiar with the objectives of the most commonly affected modules in the SAFE blueprint that are targeted by security threats.

It will be important to understand how these attacks function and which modules are commonly affected. This understanding will ensure that you keep current information for your design regarding these types of attacks.

Following is a list of the different threats and their relation to the SAFE blueprint modules.

Table 15-13 lists the modules commonly affected by some of the different threats.

Table 15-13 *Modules Affected by the Different Threats (Part 1)*

Functional Area	Module	Reconnaissance Attacks	Packet Sniffing	Man-in-the-Middle	IP Spoofing	DoS
Enterprise Campus	Management	X	X	X	X	
	Server		X		X	
	Building		X	X		
	Building distribution		X		X	
	Core					
	Edge distribution	X	X		X	

continues

Table 15-13 *Modules Affected by the Different Threats (Part 1) (Continued)*

Functional Area	Module	Reconnaissance Attacks	Packet Sniffing	Man-in-the-Middle	IP Spoofing	DoS
Enterprise Edge	E-commerce	X	X		X	X
	Corporate Internet	X	X		X	X
	VPN and remote access			X		
	WAN				X	X

Table 15-14 lists the modules commonly affected by the other threats.

Table 15-14 *Modules Commonly Affected by the Different Threats (Part 2)*

Functional Area	Module	Password Attacks	Port Redirection	Trust Exploitation	Unauthorized Access	Application-Layer Attacks
Enterprise Campus	Management	X		X	X	
	Server		X	X	X	X
	Building	X			X	
	Building distribution				X	
	Core					X
	Edge distribution				X	
Enterprise Edge	E-commerce		X	X	X	X
	Corporate Internet	X	X	X	X	X
	VPN and remote access	X			X	
	WAN				X	

It will be important to know how these attacks function and which modules are commonly affected. The descriptions here are not extensive, and it is recommended that you do additional review. The security-based solution that you install requires a secure management and monitoring system, which can be either in-band or out-of-band.

Q&A

As mentioned in the introduction, you have two choices for review questions. Some of the questions that follow give you a bigger challenge than the exam itself by using an open-ended question format. By reviewing now with this more difficult question format, you can exercise your memory better and prove your conceptual and factual knowledge of this chapter. The answers to these questions appear in Appendix A.

For more practice with exam-like question formats, use the exam engine on the CD-ROM.

1. You can use private IP addresses to prevent which types of attacks?

    a. DoS

    b. Trojan horses

    c. IP spoofing

    d. Unauthorized access

2. What is a backdoor?

    a. A type of attack

    b. Another name for a Trojan

    c. An automatic result of a hacker gaining access to the network

    d. A method left by the hacker to gain access at a later time

3. What does HIDS refer to?

    a. Host-based intrusion-detection system

    b. Host intrusion-detection sources

    c. Hacker information-data system

    d. Hacker intrusion-detection system

4. Port-redirection attacks are associated with which type of attack?

    a. Password attack

    b. Trust exploitation

    c. Application-layer attacks

    d. Unauthorized access

5. Packet sniffing is most common in which type of functional area?

   a. E-commerce module

   b. Enterprise Edge

   c. VPN and remote access

   d. ISP

6. Which of the following mitigation tactics can you use to thwart a man-in-the-middle attack?

   a. Encrypt traffic

   b. Switched infrastructure

   c. IDS

   d. Firewall

7. In which module should you place content filtering on applications such as e-mail?

   a. Corporate module

   b. Management module

   c. Server module

   d. Corporate Internet module

8. A TCP SYN flood is categorized as which type of attack?

   a. Password attack

   b. Man-in-the-middle

   c. DoS

   d. Network reconnaissance

9. What is the most common method used to prevent IP spoofing?

   a. Encryption

   b. Operating-system upgrades

   c. IP address management

   d. Access control lists (ACLs)

10. True or false? Host-based IDSs are a viable solution in the server module of the Enterprise Campus functional area.

11. What is a secure method for remotely accessing applications?

12. How would you achieve remote access to a device for remote management when the network is not available?

13. What type of management does the Cisco Security Policy Manager application provide?

14. What other advantage aside from historical information can logging provide?

15. What does the abbreviation NIDS stand for?

16. Which application can serve as a secure alternative to Telnet access to devices?

17. True or false? Packet encryption is a good mitigation strategy for man-in-the-middle attacks, which sniff packets to obtain information.

18. Which are the most commonly affected modules in the SAFE blueprint that are targeted by reconnaissance attacks?

   a. Management module

   b. Edge distribution module

   c. WAN module

   d. Corporate Internet module

19. Which are the most commonly affected modules in the SAFE blueprint that are targeted by man-in-the-middle attacks?

   a. Management module

   b. Edge distribution module

   c. Building access module

   d. Corporate Internet module

20. Which are the most commonly affected modules in the SAFE blueprint that are targeted by DoS attacks?

   a. Management module

   b. E-commerce module

   c. WAN module

   d. Corporate Internet module

21. Which type of attack is common to core modules in the Enterprise Campus?

   a. Unauthorized access

   b. Packet sniffing

   c. IP spoofing

   d. Trust exploitation

22. An attacker who connects to multiple devices because an authorized user has set all his access codes the same has used what type of attack?

   a. DoS

   b. Trojan

   c. Password attack

   d. Unauthorized access

23. An attack that tries to access your data phone numbers might use what type of device?

   a. IDS

   b. War dialer

   c. Terminal server

   d. Modem

This chapter covers the following subjects:

- SAFE Blueprint Overview

- Achieving the Balance

- Defining Customer Expectations

- Design Objectives

- Security Ecosystem

CHAPTER 16

SAFE Blueprint and the Security Ecosystem

Cisco developed a design guideline called SAFE. Understanding this architecture can enable you to develop a network with layers of security. Using layers, you can halt malicious attacks with different security implementations throughout the network. The essence of SAFE requires you to understand which parts of the network are vulnerable to specific types of attacks.

Using SAFE can help you determine whether your security solution complies with industry best practices. This chapter addresses such topics.

"Do I Know This Already?" Quiz

The purpose of the "Do I Know This Already?" quiz is to help you decide whether you need to read the entire chapter. If you intend to read the entire chapter, you do not necessarily need to answer these questions now.

The 10-question quiz, derived from the major sections in the "Foundation Topics" portion of the chapter, helps you determine how to spend your limited study time.

Table 16-1 outlines the major topics discussed in this chapter and the "Do I Know This Already?" quiz questions that correspond to those topics.

Table 16-1 *"Do I Know This Already?" Foundation Topics Section-to-Question Mapping*

Foundation Topics Section	Questions Covered in This Section
SAFE Blueprint Overview	3, 4, 6
Achieving the Balance	2
Defining Customer Expectations	8
Design Objectives	1, 5, 7, 10
Security Ecosystem	9

> **CAUTION** The goal of self assessment is to gauge your mastery of the topics in this chapter. If you do not know the answer to a question or you are only partially sure of the answer, you should mark this question wrong for purposes of the self assessment. Giving yourself credit for an answer you correctly guess skews your self-assessment results and might provide you with a false sense of security.

1. The corporate Internet is part of which functional area?

    a. Enterprise

    b. Service Provider (SP) Edge

    c. Enterprise Campus

    d. Enterprise Edge

2. What does Cisco recommend as the foundation of any deployed security solution?

    a. Customer needs

    b. Corporate security policy

    c. Security audit

    d. Service-level agreement

3. The Cisco security architecture called SAFE stands for

    a. Security Architecture for Enterprise

    b. Security Analysis for Enterprise

    c. Standard Architecture for Enterprise

    d. Standard Assessment for Enterprise

4. SAFE employs a "defense-in-depth" approach to designing security solutions. How does this approach handle a security breach?

    a. The process would launch an alert to the intrusion-detection system (IDS).

    b. A secondary security mechanism would attempt to halt the breach.

    c. It will minimize the effect of the breach on the network using a defense-in-depth authorized product.

    d. Standard Assessment for Enterprise.

5. SAFE defines modules. What is the first layer of these modules called?

  a. Layers

  b. Hierarchical areas

  c. Functional areas

  d. Security areas

6. You can achieve secure connectivity from the corporate network to a remote location using which security method?

  a. IDS

  b. Filtered traffic

  c. Virtual private networks (VPNs)

  d. Dial-up

7. Which functional areas compose the Enterprise network?

  a. Enterprise ISP

  b. Enterprise Module

  c. Enterprise Campus

  d. Enterprise Access

  e. Enterprise Edge

8. What is the common point from which most attacks are launched?

  a. Internal users

  b. Remote access

  c. War-dialing

  d. Internet

  e. Hackers

9. What is the advantage of security systems that are part of the Cisco ecosystem?

  a. The Cisco ecosystem ensure that partners can implement the solution.

  b. There is a suite of products to choose from.

  c. Various partners as well as supporting products increase the effectiveness of security systems.

  d. There are no advantages.

10. What is the basis on which SAFE recommends the deployment of security capabilities within the functional modules?

   a. Using an assessment

   b. Mitigation strategies required to thwart anticipated security threats

   c. Appropriate placement of security devices

   d. Using the SAFE blueprint

   e. Determining which modules to implement

The answers to the "Do I Know This Already?" quiz appear in Appendix A, "Answers to Chapter 'Do I Know This Already?' Quizzes and Q&A sections." The suggested choices for your next step are as follows:

■ **8 or less overall score**—Read the entire chapter. It includes the "Foundation Topics," "Foundation Summary," and "Q&A" sections.

■ **9–10 overall score**—If you want more review on these topics, skip to the "Foundation Summary" section and then go to the "Q&A" section. Otherwise, move to the next chapter.

Foundation Topics

This chapter teaches a methodology, how you can check proposed security solutions for compliance with the SAFE blueprint.

SAFE Blueprint Overview

Cisco developed a security methodology called SAFE that you can use as a guide to design and implement network security. It takes into account implementing products, detecting breaches, and employing mitigation strategies.

SAFE is based on Cisco and partner products and uses a defense-in-depth and modular approach to security design.

The SAFE blueprint that is discussed in this chapter applies to large enterprise environments. There are modifications to the SAFE blueprint for smaller or more specialized environments. Table 16-2 lists the environment and the corresponding documentation that describes how to implement a SAFE blueprint in those environments.

Table 16-2 *SAFE White Papers*

Environment	Document Name
Large enterprise	SAFE: A Security Blueprint for Enterprise Networks
Small, medium, and remote-user networks	SAFE: Extending the Security Blueprint to Small, Midsize, and Remote-User Networks
VPN	SAFE VPN: IPSec Virtual Private Networks in Depth
Wireless LAN	SAFE: Wireless LAN Security in Depth
IP telephony	SAFE: IP Telephony Security in Depth

Cisco describes SAFE as a defense-in-depth approach. Defense in depth means that a system has multiple security measures in place—in other words, layers—so that if one defense is breached, another is in place to prevent further damage. The concept is similar to all the booby traps that Indiana Jones had to get past before he could get to the treasure.

The SAFE blueprint discourages having only one device performing a security function. It means that you mitigate threat throughout the network. Security capabilities can be hosted on dedicated appliances, such as firewalls; incorporated in the Cisco IOS on routers and switches; or running in the background on end systems. The choice depends on the amount of activity to be monitored, the location of the device within the network, the threat being mitigated, and the available residual capacity of the existing devices. The blueprint guidelines encourage you to make security decisions based on the dangers to be avoided, rather than solely on security devices. Often, security devices that are not correctly configured are considered robust until someone breaks into them. How do you know which configuration is going to work unless you design it against a known threat? You have to understand your enemy if you are going to defend against attacks from that enemy.

Achieving the Balance

The area of network security has always projected a mysterious aura because it is commonly thought that a network cannot be totally secure. If absolute security is not achievable, then doesn't the task of securing it seem futile? Of course, denying access to the network would secure it—but then who would use it?

The SAFE method clears some of the mystery behind designing and implementing a secure network. It is essentially a blueprint, a guide to help network designers develop security solutions.

The essence of defining network security is achieving an acceptable balance between accessibility and usability. The network security policy defines this balance. Before beginning a security design, you must have a security policy to reference. If you do not have access to one, you should create a policy prior to beginning a security design.

> **NOTE** Although developing a security policy is beyond the scope of this book, it is important to understand the contents of the security policy. Cisco has a white paper on security-policy development best practices at http://www.cisco.com/warp/public/126/secpol.pdf. The network security-policy document discusses how to identify the security needs, which underlie the security policy, to establish a structure for security-policy management and to respond to threats, attacks, and breaches. Other sources for security policy development aids appear at the following websites:
>
> http://www.sans.org
>
> http://www.cert.org

You should develop the security policy with the participation and agreement of the highest levels of an organization's management. This process can help build the required support for the creation, acceptance, and adaptation of the security design. The process of developing a security policy is complex. You must tailor it to the target environment.

In a real-life situation, you might be required to develop a security design without a corporate policy. Begin by setting clear expectations. This step ensures that you write a policy that supports the organization's needs and encourages the development of a security policy. It is critical to document these expectations prior to developing the design.

If you encounter this type of situation, don't be shy about taking your time to work through this expectation-defining process.

Defining Customer Expectations

The key to establishing a secure network is to first define what network security means to the organization. Organizations have different requirements for security. For example, a library might not restrict network access to the Internet, but a bank will have a much stricter policy. As a matter of fact, separate segments on the network can have different security requirements. If you apply the example of Internet access, you can imagine that a research department of a marketing company might have fewer restrictions to the Internet than the back office does.

The Cisco SAFE assumes that a security policy is already in place. You already learned that this policy might not exist. Remember that designing and implementing security can be challenging exercises. Organizations have been known to carry unrealistic expectations regarding security implementations and the results. Take the opportunity to discuss those expectations prior to beginning a security design project. The following sections address some common customer expectations and misunderstandings.

Complete Security Is Not Achievable

A key expectation to set is that complete security is not achievable. Only by diligence and proactive maintenance can you protect a network. Often, people have an "install it and leave it" attitude with security systems. Unless a breach occurs, the security systems are considered to be "working." Unfortunately, this type of reasoning is dangerous. New, debilitating attacks occur on a regular basis, so the company must adapt a proactive regime to keep the security systems robust.

Where Most Breaches Occur (or Not)

Another important expectation centers on which side of the network most threats exist. It is commonly accepted that network-security breaches occur inside the network. Therefore, a firewall that protects a network from the outside is not sufficient. You need security measures that also can detect and reduce risks that begin on a "secured" segment.

Discuss these expectations and others throughout the security-design phase to ensure alignment with the organization's expectations. Although SAFE is not the cure-all for security issues, it can offer a strong defense along with sound administrative practices. Ultimately, addressing such expectations provides both you and the organization with a clear vision of how to assess the existing network.

Design Objectives

This approach focuses on how vulnerabilities are exploited. The blueprint enables you to assess the existing network to understand the nature of threats and determine how to mitigate these threats.

The following are the design objectives of the SAFE blueprint:

■ Security and attack mitigation based on policy

■ Security implementation throughout the infrastructure (not just on specialized security devices)

■ Secure management and reporting

■ Authentication and authorization of users and administrators to critical network resources

■ Intrusion detection for critical resources and subnets

■ Support for emerging networked applications

TIP A good understanding of these design objectives is required for the exam.

The SAFE blueprint emphasizes the defining modules within a network. The first level of modules are functional areas. Figure 16-1 illustrates the SAFE functional areas.

Figure 16-1 *Three SAFE Functional Areas*

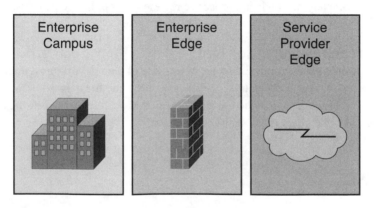

Three SAFE Functional Areas

Table 16-3 shows the second layer of SAFE components. They are also defined functionally. Each of the three functional areas has its own components or modules. The table lists these modules with the associated SAFE functional area.

Table 16-3 *Included Modules*

Functional Areas	Included Modules
Enterprise Campus	Management
	Server
	Building
	Building distribution
	Core
	Edge distribution
Enterprise Edge	E-commerce
	Corporate Internet
	VPN and remote access
	WAN
SP Edge	ISP B
	ISP A
	Public Switched Telephone Network (PSTN)
	Frame/ATM

Not all actual enterprise networks have specific devices, blades, cards, or ports clearly assigned to all the modules mentioned. It is still useful to the designer to identify where all the functions occur and the interactions between the functions. Changes in function that mark the component boundaries offer natural opportunities for specialization and hierarchy as a network grows. This understanding also assists in identifying the quality of service (QoS) and security treatments that the network traffic might require. Figure 16-2 is an illustration of the different modules within each functional area.

Figure 16-2 *SAFE Functional Areas and Modules*

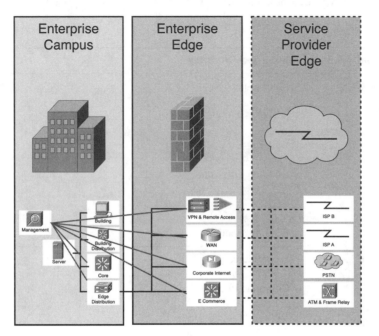

Three SAFE Functional Areas and Modules

Significance of Areas and Modules

The definition of areas or modules each with a specific function helps to layer the protection because there will be a different security measure in place at different points in the network. This layering makes the security solution more resilient and scalable. The modules, as built, become templates for the modifications to the network required by the addition of users and applications. Modularization also reduces security issues caused by growth because the security capabilities are considered in the module implementation.

The following are the benefits of using SAFE in network design and implementation:

■ Provides a proven, detailed blueprint to securely compete in the Internet economy

■ Provides the foundation for migrating to secure, cost-effective converged networks

■ Enables organizations to stay within their budgets by deploying a modular, scalable security framework in stages

■ Delivers integrated network protection by offering best-in-class security products and services

In conclusion, this modular approach allows the network designer to address the security relationship between the various functional blocks of the network. This approach also permits you to evaluate and implement security on a module-by-module basis.

Security Ecosystem

What is an ecosystem?

Cisco envisions a community dedicated to providing customers the best solution by giving them access to the following resources:

- Best-of-breed consulting and vendor partners
- SAFE blueprint-based solutions such as managed services and vulnerability assessments

The security ecosystem includes solutions from vendors of supplemental products; partners to provide assessment, planning, and integration capabilities; and providers of monitoring and management services. This web of partner-provided services and products enables the design and implementation of solutions that build on the capabilities of Cisco and the partners.

Essential Elements for Comprehensive Network Security

A comprehensive design for network security includes five elements, each addressed by a variety of products:

- **Identity**—Ensure the accurate and positive identification of network users, hosts, applications, services, and resources. These systems allow authorized users access only to the resources they are entitled to use by policy.
- **Perimeter security**—Control access to critical network applications, data, and services so that only legitimate users and information can pass through the network. Firewalls are generally the first perimeter solutions companies implement. Complementary tools include virus scanners and content filters.
- **Secure connectivity**—Protect confidential information by implementing VPNs to establish private, secure communications across a public network and extend corporate networks to remote offices, mobile users, and partners.
- **Security monitoring**—Proactively identify areas of weakness with network-vulnerability scanners and monitor and respond to security events as they occur with IDSs.
- **Policy management**—Specify, manage, and audit the state of a security policy.

Concentrating on these five elements in conjunction with the modular approach provides maximum flexibility, enabling organizations to adopt the modules that are appropriate for their businesses. This process guarantees that the existing security infrastructure meets the network security-policy requirements while staying within security budgets on new e-business projects.

Foundation Summary

The "Foundation Summary" section of each chapter lists the most important facts from the chapter. Although this section does not list every fact from the chapter that will be on your CCDA exam, a well-prepared CCDA candidate should at a minimum know all the details in each "Foundation Summary" before going to take the exam.

The SAFE blueprint from Cisco layers security solutions based on modeling functional areas in the network. This type of layering implements a defense-in-depth approach. This approach ensures that your security systems are resilient because you have more than one security measure protecting your network. If one system is compromised, other security systems protect the network.

The CCDA exam requires that you be familiar with the objectives of the SAFE blueprint:

- Security and attack mitigation based on policy
- Security implementation throughout the infrastructure (not just on specialized security devices)
- Secure management and reporting
- Authentication and authorization of users and administrators to critical network resources
- Intrusion detection for critical resources and subnets
- Support for emerging networked applications

In addition to the SAFE objectives, the blueprint focuses on five key areas to ensure that the security solutions are comprehensive, all of which are critical to understanding SAFE:

- Identity
- Perimeter security
- Secure connectivity
- Security monitoring
- Policy management

Cisco extended its ability to provide best-in-breed solutions to its customers by establishing a security ecosystem consisting of consulting partners, product vendors, and managed service providers. This partnership works to provide the full range of services needed to establish and maintain an enterprise's network using the SAFE blueprint.

Q&A

As mentioned in the introduction, you have two choices for review questions. Some of the questions that follow give you a bigger challenge than the exam itself by using an open-ended question format. By reviewing now with this more difficult question format, you can exercise your memory better and prove your conceptual and factual knowledge of this chapter. The answers to these questions appear in Appendix A.

For more practice with exam-like question formats, use the exam engine on the CD-ROM.

1. Cisco defines five elements that are key to providing network security. Which of these choices are not one of the five elements?

   a. Secure connectivity

   b. Intrusion detection

   c. Security monitoring

   d. Identity

   e. Perimeter security

2. Support for emerging network appliances is an objective of the SAFE blueprint. What is the result of achieving this objective?

   a. Resilience

   b. Performance

   c. Protection

   d. Management

   e. Scalability

3. Using vendor partners and consulting firms to create a best-of-breed solution is part of what strategy?

   a. SAFE

   b. Cisco network assurance

   c. Cisco Security ecosystem

   d. Cisco channel

4. Which of the following modules is not a part of the SP Edge functional area?

   a. ISP

   b. Frame Relay

   c. Corporate Internet

   d. ATM

5. True or false? Layering network solutions in the SAFE blueprint provides resilience in a network.

6. True or false? Most attacks are launched by hackers.

7. Which of the following is a module part of the Enterprise Edge functional area?

   a. WAN

   b. ISP A

   c. Core

   d. PSTN

8. Which of the following is not part of the five key areas that are used as a basis for the development of SAFE?

   a. Perimeter security

   b. Identity

   c. Secure management and reporting

   d. Policy management

9. Which of the following statements describes SAFE's focus on identity?

   a. Use encryption.

   b. Authorized users have access to specific systems.

   c. Use network-security scanners.

   d. Manage the state of a security policy.

10. True or false? Corporate Internet is part of the functional area Enterprise Campus.

11. A _____ is recommended by Cisco as the foundation of any deployed security solution.

12. The Cisco security architecture called SAFE stands for what?

13. Which functional areas compose the Enterprise Edge?

   a. Enterprise ISP

   b. E-commerce

   c. Corporate Internet

   d. Enterprise access

   e. WAN

14. True or false? The Cisco ecosystem increases the effectiveness of security systems by using various partners as well as supporting products.

Exam Topics in This Chapter

- Traditional Voice Architectures

- Integrated Multiservice Networks

- QoS Mechanisms for VoIP Networks

CHAPTER 17

Traditional Voice Architectures and Integrated Voice Design

The designs of enterprise voice networks are migrating from the traditional use of Private Branch Exchange (PBX) switches to the use of IP telephony architectures such as AVVID. Enterprise networks still connect to the Public Switched Telephone Network (PSTN) to communicate globally. This chapter reviews PSTN and PBX voice networks, integrated IP telephony, and quality of service (QoS) for IP telephony networks.

"Do I Know This Already?" Quiz

The purpose of the "Do I Know This Already?" quiz is to help you decide whether you need to read the entire chapter. If you intend to read the entire chapter, you do not necessarily need to answer these questions now.

The 10-question quiz, derived from the major sections in the "Foundation Topics" portion of the chapter, helps you determine how to spend your limited study time.

Table 17-1 outlines the major topics discussed in this chapter and the "Do I Know This Already?" quiz questions that correspond to those topics.

Table 17-1 *"Do I Know This Already?" Foundation Topics Section-to-Question Mapping*

Foundation Topics Section	Questions Covered in This Section
Traditional Voice Architectures	5, 9
Integrated Multiservice Networks	1, 2, 3, 4, 6, 7, 10
QoS Mechanisms for VoIP Networks	8

CAUTION The goal of self assessment is to gauge your mastery of the topics in this chapter. If you do not know the answer to a question or you are only partially sure of the answer, you should mark this question wrong for purposes of the self assessment. Giving yourself credit for an answer you correctly guess skews your self-assessment results and might provide you with a false sense of security.

1. Which International Telecommunication Union (ITU) standard provides a framework for multimedia protocols for the transport of voice, video, and data over packet-switched networks?

    a. Session Initiation Protocol (SIP)

    b. Voice over IP (VoIP)

    c. H.323

    d. Weighted fair queuing (WFQ)

2. What is the default coder-decoder (codec) used with VoIP dial peers?

    a. G.711

    b. G.723

    c. G.728

    d. G.729

3. Real-Time Transport Protocol (RTP) operates in what layer of the OSI model?

    a. Application

    b. Session

    c. Transport

    d. Network

4. Which H.323 protocol is responsible for call setup and signaling?

    a. H.245

    b. G.711

    c. H.225

    d. RTCP

5. What unit measures the number of voice calls in one hour?

    a. Kbps

    b. Erlang

    c. DS0

    d. FXS

6. Which feature does not transmit packets when there is silence?

    a. Ear and mouth (E&M)

    b. Voice Activity Detection (VAD)

    c. Dial peers

    d. Digital Silence Suppressor (DSS)

7. Compressed Real-Time Transport Protocol (CRTP) compresses what?

    a. RTP headers

    b. RTP, TCP, and IP headers

    c. RTP, User Datagram Protocol (UDP), and IP headers

    d. Real-Time Transport Control Protocol (RTCP) headers

8. Which QoS mechanism is recommended for VoIP networks?

    a. Custom queuing

    b. Low-latency queuing (LLQ)

    c. Fast queuing

    d. Switched-based queuing

9. Where is the local loop located?

    a. Between phones and the central office (CO) switch

    b. Between two PBXs

    c. Between the loopback interfaces of two VoIP routers

    d. Between two PSTN switches

10. What is jitter?

    a. The echo caused by mismatched impedance

    b. The loss of packets in the network

    c. The variable delay of received packets

    d. The fixed delay of received packets

The answers to the "Do I Know This Already?" quiz appear in Appendix A, "Answers to Chapter 'Do I Know This Already?' Quizzes and Q&A Sections." The suggested choices for your next step are as follows:

- **8 or less overall score**—Read the entire chapter. It includes the "Foundation Topics," "Foundation Summary," and "Q&A" sections.

- **9–10 overall score**—If you want more review on these topics, skip to the "Foundation Summary" section and then go to the "Q&A" section. Otherwise, move to the next chapter.

Foundation Topics

The "Foundation Topics" section covers traditional voice architectures, integrated voice design, and QoS in voice networks. The section "Traditional Voice Architectures" covers the architecture of time-division multiplexing (TDM) voice networks. It also discusses PSTN technologies and limitations.

The section "Integrated Multiservice Networks" covers IP telephony design and the Cisco Architecture for Voice, Video, and Integrated Data (AVVID). The section "QoS Mechanisms for VoIP Networks" covers the effects of QoS mechanisms in integrated networks.

Traditional Voice Architectures

This section reviews the technologies and concepts to help you understand traditional voice networks.

The PSTN is the global voice network that provides voice services. The PSTN is a variety of networks and services that are in place worldwide; it provides a circuit-switched service using Signaling System 7 (SS7) for out-of-band call provisioning through the network. CO switches exchange SS7 messages to place and route voice calls throughout the network. The PSTN uses TDM facilities for calls within the network. From the CO to the customer premises, the call can be analog, ISDN, or TDM digital. Each call consumes 64 Kbps of bandwidth, called a digital service zero (DS0).

Local Loop and Trunks

Depending on the dialed digits, a call will route through the local loop, one or more trunks, and the destination local loop to reach the destination phone. The local loop is the pair of wires that runs from the CO to the home or business office.

Trunks connect two switches. The type of trunk depends on the function of the switches the trunk is connecting. Tie-line is frequently used to describe a dedicated line connecting two telephone switches within a single organization. Another name for trunk is tie-line. The following is a list of trunk types:

- **Interoffice trunk**—Connects two CO switches
- **Tandem trunks**—Connects central offices within a geographical area
- **Toll-connecting trunk**—Connects the CO to the long-distance office
- **Intertoll trunk**—Connects two long-distance offices
- **Private trunk**—Connects two privately owned switches

Figure 17-1 shows an example of the PSTN. All phones connect to their local CO via the local loop. Calls between Phones 1 and 2 and between Phones 4 and 5 go through interoffice trunks. Calls between Phones 2 and 3 go through tandem trunks within a region. When you place calls between Texas and Massachusetts, calls are forwarded to the long-distance toll provider via a toll-connecting trunk and are routed through intertoll trunks.

Figure 17-1   *Local Loops and Trunks*

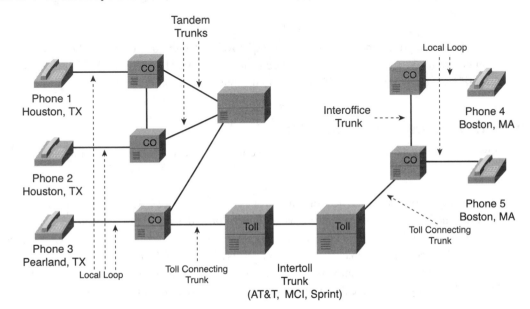

Ports

You can use several ports to connect to voice end stations (phones) and private voice switches:

- **Foreign Exchange Station (FXS)**—Connects to an end device such as an analog phone or fax machine; it provides dial tone and ring voltage.

- **Foreign Exchange Office (FXO)**—Connects to the PSTN. It is an RJ-11 connector that allows an analog connection to be directed at the PSTN's central office or to a station interface on a PBX. The FXO sits on the switch end of the connection. It plugs directly into the line side of the switch so the switch thinks the FXO interface is a telephone.

- **Ear and mouth (E&M)**—Connects private switches. It is an analog trunk used to connect to a voice switch; it supports tie-line facilities or signaling between phone switches. E&M can be connected with 2-wire and 4-wire. E&M is also known as Earth and Magnet.

- **Channelized T1 (or E1)**—Commonly used as a digital trunk line to connect to a phone switch where each DS0 supports an active phone call connection. Provides 24 (for T1) or 30 (for E1) channels or DS0 for voice calls.

- **ISDN Primary Rate Interface (PRI)**—Digital trunk link used to connect to a phone switch. A separate channel is used for common channel-signaling messages.

Major Analog and Digital Signaling Types

The signaling type depends on the type of connection. The five major areas are

- CO to phone (loop and ground start)
- PBX to PBX (E&M)
- T1/E1 Channel Associated Signaling (CAS)
- ISDN PRI Common Channel Signaling (CCS)
- SS7 Interswitch PSTN signaling

Loop-Start Signaling

Loop-start signaling is an analog signaling technique used to indicate on-hook and off-hook conditions on the network. It is commonly used between the telephone set and the CO, PBX, or FXS module. As shown in Figure 17-2, with loop-start the local loop is open when the phone is on-hook. When the phone is taken off-hook, a –48 direct current (DC) voltage loops from the CO through the phone and back.

Figure 17-2 *Loop-Start Signaling*

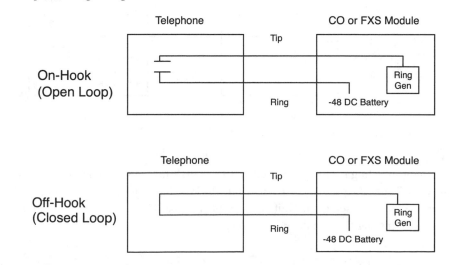

Ground-Start Signaling

Ground-start signaling is an analog signaling technique used to indicate on-hook and off-hook conditions. Ground-start is commonly used in switch-to-switch connections. The difference between ground-start and loop-start is that ground-start requires the closing of the loop at both locations. The standard way to transport voice between two telephone sets is to use tip and ring lines. Tip and ring lines are the twisted pair of wires that connect to your phone via an RJ-11 connector. As shown in Figure 17-3, the CO switch grounds the tip line. The PBX detects that the tip line is grounded and closes the loop by removing ground from the ring line.

Figure 17-3 *Ground-Start Signaling*

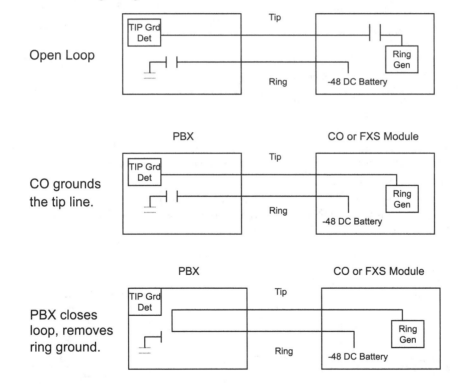

E&M Signaling

E&M analog signaling is most often used in PBX to PBX tie-lines. Cisco routers support four E&M signal types: Type I, Type II, Type III, and Type V. Type I and II are most popular on the American continents. Type V is used in the United States and Europe. There are also three forms of E&M dial-supervision signaling to seize the E&M trunk:

- **Immediate start**—This is the most basic protocol. In this technique, the originating switch goes off-hook, waits for a finite period of time (for example, 200 ms), and then sends the dial digits without regard to the far end.

- **Wink start**—Wink is the most commonly used protocol. In this technique, the originating switch goes off-hook, waits for a temporary off-hook pulse from the other end (which is interpreted as an indication to proceed), and then sends the dial digits.

- **Delay dial**—In this technique, the originating side goes off-hook and waits for about 200 ms and then checks whether the far end is on-hook. If the far end is on-hook, it outputs dial digits. If the far end is off-hook, it waits until it goes on-hook and then outputs dial digits.

T1/E1 CAS

Digital T1 CAS uses selected bits within a selected channel to transmit signaling information. CAS is also referred as robbed-bit signaling or in-band signaling in the T1 implementation. Robbed-bit CAS works with digital voice because losing an occasional voice sample does not affect the voice quality. The disadvantage with robbed-bit CAS is that it cannot be used on channels that might carry voice or data without reducing the data rate to 56 Kbps to ensure that signaling changes do not damage the data stream. E1, which uses a separate channel in the shared media for CAS, does not have this disadvantage. The E1 signaling bits are channel associated, but they are not in-band.

ISDN PRI

ISDN T1 PRI provides 23 channels for voice with a separate channel for signaling. The ISDN E1 PRI provides 30 channels. The use of messages in a separate channel, rather than preassigned bits, is also referred to as common-channel signaling. Any bit in the signaling channel is common to all of the channels sharing the media rather than dedicated to a particular single channel. ISDN provides the advantage of not changing bits in the channels and is thus useful for data traffic in addition to voice traffic.

SS7

SS7 is a global ITU standard for telecommunications control that allows voice-network calls to be routed and controlled by call-control centers. SS7 implements call setup, routing, and control, ensuring that intermediate and far-end switches are available when a call is placed. With SS7, telephone companies are able to implement modern consumer-telephone services such as caller ID, toll-free numbers, call forwarding, and so on.

SS7 provides mechanisms for exchanging control, status, and routing messages on public telephone networks. SS7 messages pass over a separate channel than that used for voice communication. You use common channel signaling (CCS7) when speaking about SS7 signaling. CCS7 controls call signaling, routing, and connections between CO, inter-exchange carrier, and competitive local exchange carrier switches. Figure 17-4 shows the connectivity between SS7 components.

Figure 17-4 *SS7 Signaling Components*

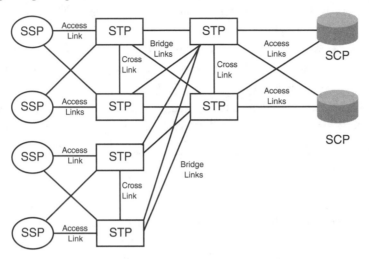

As shown in Figure 17-4, SS7 has the following system components:

- **Signaling Control Point (SCP)**—Databases that provide the necessary information for special call processing and routing, including 800 and 900 call services, credit-card calls, local number portability, cellular roaming services, and advanced call-center applications.

- **Signaling Transfer Point (STP)**—Receives and routes incoming signaling messages toward their destinations. STPs are deployed in mated pairs and share the traffic between them.

- **Signaling Switching Point (SSP)**—Telephone switches equipped with SS7 software and signaling links. Each SSP is connected to both STPs in a mated pair.

Addressing Digit Signaling

There are two methods for submitting analog address digits to place a call:

- Pulse or rotary dialing
- Dual-tone multifrequency (DTMF) dialing

Pulse dialing uses the opening and closing of a switch at the telephone set. A rotary register at the CO detects the opening and closing of the loop. When dialing the number 5 on the rotary phone, the dial mechanism opens and closes 5 times, each 1/10 of a second apart.

DTMF uses two tones simultaneously to indicate the dialed number. Table 17-2 shows the phone keypad and the frequencies used. When dialing the number 5, both frequencies 770 Hz and 1336 Hz are sent to the CO.

Table 17-2 *DTMF Frequencies*

Frequency	1209 Hz	1336 Hz	1477 Hz
697 Hz	1	ABC 2	DEF 3
770 Hz	GHI 4	JKL 5	MNO 6
852 Hz	PRS 7	TUV 8	WXYZ 9
941 Hz	*	OPER 0	#

PSTN Numbering Plan

The PSTN uses the ITU E.164 standard for public network addressing. The E.164 standard uses a maximum of 15 digits. Examples of E.164 addresses are the residential, business, and cell phones that you use everyday. Each country is assigned a country code to identify it. The country codes can be one to three digits in length. Some examples of country codes are

- United States of America and Canada: 1
- Brazil: 55
- Italy: 39
- China: 86
- Egypt: 20
- India: 91
- Germany: 49
- Ukraine: 380

One website that lists country codes is http://www.countrycallingcodes.com/countrylist.htm.

Each country divides its network into area codes that identify a geographical region or city. The United States uses three digits for area codes, and other countries might use codes from one to four digits in length. The areas are further divided into office codes and prefixes. In the United States, the office code is three digits, and the prefix is four digits in length. The prefix identifies the phone.

An example of a PSTN address in the United States is 1-713-781-0300. The 1 identifies the United States; the 713 identifies an area code in the Houston, Texas, geographical region. The 781 identifies a CO in west Houston. The 0300 identifies the phone.

Another example of a PSTN address is 52-55-8452-1110. The country code 52 identifies Mexico. The area code 55 identifies the geographical area of Mexico City. The office code 8452 and prefix 1110 follow.

PBX Switches

PBXs are customer-owned voice switches. Enterprise companies install and configure their own PBXs to provide telephony service, four-digit dialing, remote-office extensions, voicemail, and private-line routing within other features. Organizations can reduce toll charges by using private tie-lines between their switches. Calls that are placed between offices through the private voice network are called on-net. If a user needs to place a call outside the private network, the call is routed to the local PSTN. If the call is forwarded to the PSTN, it is called off-net.

Figure 17-5 shows a PBX network for an enterprise. Callers use the PBX network when they place calls from San Diego to Chicago, Atlanta, or Houston. The enterprise reduces toll charges by using its private voice network. A separate private network is in place for data traffic. If a user places a call from San Diego to Los Angeles, it is routed out to the PSTN from the San Diego PBX. Then, toll charges are incurred for the call.

Another issue in the design is the limitation of the number of calls per private line. If the private lines are T1s, they are each limited to carrying 24 concurrent calls at a time.

Grade of Service and Erlangs

You must consider voice traffic requirements when designing a network. Grade of service and erlangs are two parameters used in the design of voice networks.

Grade of Service

Grade of service (GoS) is the probability of a call being blocked when attempting to seize a circuit. If a network defines P.02 GoS, the probability is that two percent of all attempted calls will be blocked.

Figure 17-5 *PBX Network*

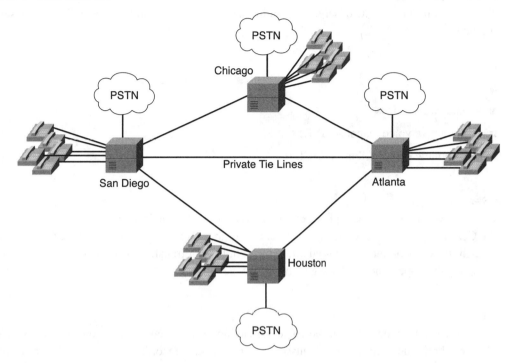

Erlangs

An erlang is a unit of telecommunications traffic measurement representing the continuous use of one voice path for one hour. It describes the total traffic volume of one hour. Erlangs determine voice-call usage for bandwidth requirements for voice network designs, including VoIP.

If a group of users makes 20 calls in an hour and each call lasts 10 minutes, the erlangs are calculated as follows:

20 calls/hour * 10 minutes/call = 200 minutes/hour
Traffic volume = (200 min/hour) / (60 minutes/hour)
= 3.33 erlangs

Other PSTN Services

The PSTN provides a suite of services in addition to just call setup and routing. Other PSTN services include

- Centrex
- Voicemail
- Database services
- Interactive voice response (IVR)
- Automatic call distribution (ACD)

Centrex Services

Companies can use the local phone company to handle all of their internal and external calls from the CO. In this voice model, the CO acts as the company's voice switch with PBX features such as four-digit extension dialing, voicemail, and call holds and transfers. The Centrex service gives the company the appearance of having its own PBX network.

Voicemail

PSTN service providers can enable voice messaging for those customers requesting the service. Voicemail provides automated call answering and message recording. Users can then retrieve the message and forward it to other extensions.

Database Services

The PSTN must keep call detail records (CDR) in the database systems. CDR information includes all types of call information, such as called party, caller, time, duration, locations, and user service plans. This information is used for billing and reporting.

IVR

IVR systems connect incoming calls to an audio playback system that queues the calls, provides pre-recorded announcements, prompts the caller for key options, provides the caller with information, and transfers the call to another switch extension or agent. IVR is used in call centers run by financial, retail, and transportation companies to gather and provide information for the customers before transferring them to agents.

ACD

ACD routes calls to a group of agents. ACD keeps statistics on each agent, such as the number of calls and their duration. Based on the statistics, the ACD system then can evenly distribute the calls to the agents or to the appropriate agent skill group. ACD is used by airline reservation systems, customer service departments, and other call centers.

Integrated Multiservice Networks

The introduction of packet-voice technology allows the convergence of data and voice networks—which lets companies save toll charges on voice telephone calls and reduce their total cost of ownership by not having to build and operate separate networks for voice, video, and data.

In multiservice networks, digitized (coded) voice is packaged into packets, cells, or frames; sent as data throughout the networks; and converted back to analog voice. The underlying protocols used for these converged services are

- Voice over Frame Relay (VoFR)
- Voice over Asynchronous Transfer Mode (VoATM)
- Voice over Internet Protocol (VoIP)

Of these, VoIP, also referenced as IP telephony when integrated with IP-based signaling and call control, is how almost all new deployments are being implemented.

VoFR

VoFR permits enterprise customers with existing Frame Relay networks to implement packetized voice. Access devices or cards access the Frame Relay network. PBX vendors provide VoFR cards for their switches to support call routing over the Frame Relay network. Figure 17-6 shows an example of three PBXs connected with trunks using VoFR. The PSTN is used for backup if the Frame Relay circuit goes down. The disadvantage with VoFR is that it provides only convergence in the WAN; it still requires local dedicated telephony equipment and networks. It cannot provide convergence to LANs without a network protocol that can span the data link technologies, such as IP.

One standard for VoFR is Frame Relay Forum (FRF) 11.1. It establishes specifications for call setup, coding types, and packet formats for VoFR service. It provides the basis for interoperability between vendors.

Figure 17-6 *VoFR Trunks Between PBXs*

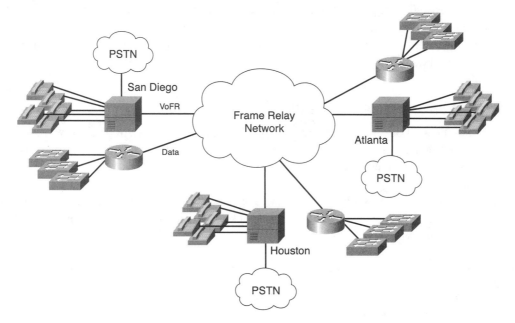

A number of mechanisms can minimize delay and the variable delay (jitter) on a Frame Relay network. The presence of long data frames on a low-speed Frame Relay link can cause unacceptable delays for time-sensitive voice frames. To reduce this problem, some vendors implement smaller frame sizes to help reduce delay and delay variation. FRF.12 is an industry-standard approach to doing this, so products from different vendors can interoperate and consumers will know what type of voice quality to expect. To ensure voice quality, you should set the committed information rate (CIR) of each permanent virtual circuit (PVC) to ensure that voice frames are not discarded.

VoATM

VoATM permits enterprise customers to use their existing ATM networks for voice traffic. ATM inherently provides guaranteed QoS for voice traffic that IP protocols alone cannot provide. ATM can provide the service levels and functionality required to support voice traffic for the WAN. For those enterprise networks with ATM, VoATM provides a mechanism to connect enterprise PBXs via ATM and other VoATM applications.

With ATM, constant bit rate (CBR) or variable bit rate-real time (VBR-rt) classes of service (CoSs) provide levels of bandwidth and delay guarantees for voice. Chapter 5, "Wide-Area Networking Technologies," covers ATM.

PBX vendors provide VoATM cards for their switches to support call routing over the ATM network. Figure 17-7 shows an example of three PBXs that are connected via trunks using VoATM. The PSTN is used for backup if the ATM circuit goes down. As with VoFR, the disadvantage with VoATM is that it provides only convergence in the WAN. It cannot provide convergence within the LAN without a network protocol that can span the data link technologies, such as IP.

Figure 17-7 *VoATM Trunks Between PBXs*

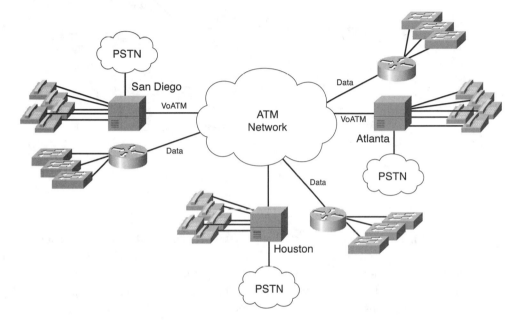

VoIP Introduction

VoIP provides transport of voice over the IP protocol family. IP makes voice globally available regardless of the data link (Ethernet, ATM, Frame Relay) protocol in use. With VoIP, enterprises do not have to build separate voice and data networks. Integrating voice and data into a single converged network reduces the costs of owning and managing separate networks.

Figure 17-8 shows a company that has separate voice and data networks. Phones connect to local PBXs, and the PBXs are connected using TDM trunks. Off-net calls are routed to the PSTN. The data network uses LAN switches connected to WAN routers. The WAN for data uses Frame Relay. Separate operations and management systems are required for these networks.

Figure 17-8 *Separate Voice and Data Networks*

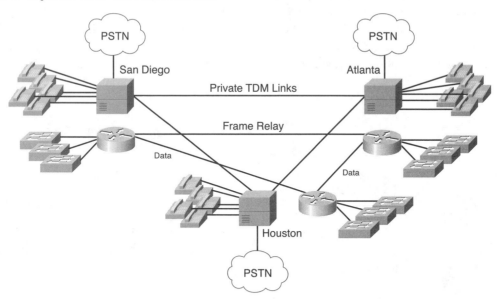

With IP telephony, you can reduce the number of systems, circuits, and support personnel. Figure 17-9 shown a multiservice IP telephony network that employs Ethernet-based phones with server-based call processing with gateway routers. Survivable Remote Site Telephony (SRST) is used for failover or backup to the PSTN if there is a WAN failure. On-net calls travel through the Frame Relay network and off-net calls are forwarded to the PSTN.

Figure 17-9 *Converged VoIP Network*

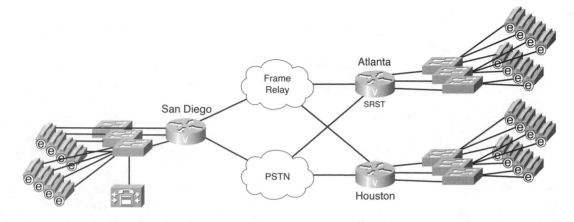

AVVID Components

Cisco's AVVID divides voice systems architecture into four major functional areas. As shown in Figure 17-10, the four areas are

- Service applications
- Call processing
- Clients or endpoints
- Infrastructure

Figure 17-10 *AVVID Functional Areas*

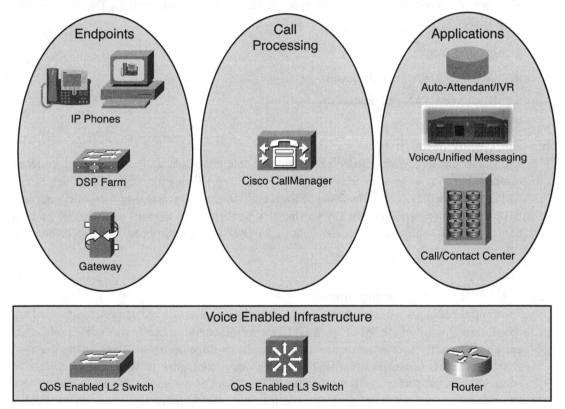

Client endpoints include the IP phones, analog and digital gateways, and digital signal processor (DSP) farms. You can use gateways to access PBXs, analog phones, other IP telephony deployments, or the PSTN.

The Cisco Call Manager (CM) fulfills the role of call processing. The CM servers have the "brains" of the voice dial plan.

Service applications include IVR, Unity Unified Messaging System for voicemail, and Intelligent Contact Management (ICM) for allowing the enterprise to better control contact routing to call centers. There is also a standards-based Telephony Application Program Interface (TAPI) interface.

The infrastructure includes QoS-enabled devices such as L2 switches, L3 switches, and routers.

AVVID Deployment Models

This subsection covers the three AVVID call-processing deployment models. The deployment models are

- Single-site deployment
- Centralized WAN call processing
- Distributed WAN call processing

Single-Site Deployment

The single-site deployment model is a solution for enterprises located in a single large building or campus area with no voice on the WAN links. Figure 17-11 shows the single-site model. A single CM cluster is deployed for redundancy in the server farm, and Unity is used for unified messaging. IP phones are deployed from the LAN switches. CM Version 3.3 supports up to 30,000 users in a cluster. You can configure high-end switches with gateway cards for access to the PSTN for off-net calls.

Centralized WAN Call-Processing Model

The centralized WAN call-processing model is a solution for medium enterprises with one large location and many remote sites. Figure 17-12 shows the centralized call-processing model. A CM cluster with multiple servers is deployed for redundancy at the large site. Remote sites use voice-enabled gateways or routers with SRST for redundancy. In the event of WAN failure, SRST-configured routers forward calls through the PSTN. With CM 3.3, each CM supports up to 7500 users. In this model, admission control is configured on the CM to impose a limit on the number of calls permitted per site.

Figure 17-11 *Single-Site Deployment Model*

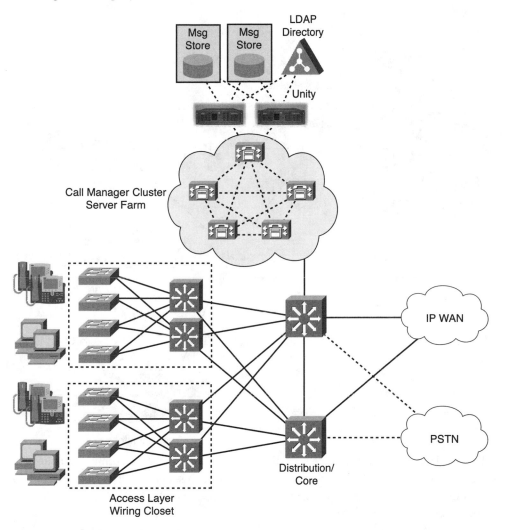

Distributed WAN Call-Processing Model

The distributed WAN call-processing model is a solution for large enterprises with several large locations. Figure 17-13 shows the distributed WAN model. Up to 30,000 users are supported per CM cluster with CM Version 3.3. Several CM clusters are deployed at the large sites for redundancy and Unity servers for messaging. Intercluster trunks establish communication between clusters. IP phones are deployed on LAN switches.

Figure 17-12 *Centralized WAN CM Deployment Model*

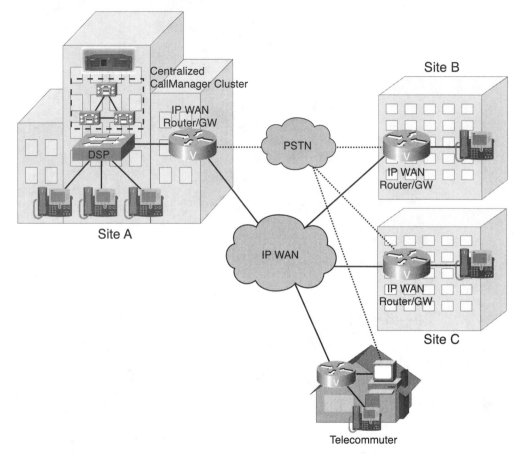

This model also supports remote sites distributed off the large sites. Admission control between the CM and Cisco IOS gateway with gatekeeper (GK) is supported. The Cisco IOS Gatekeeper is required for admission control. Also, this model supports multiple WAN codecs. Compression of VoIP is done between sites.

Codecs

Speech is an analog signal. Speech must be converted into digital signals for transmission over digital systems. The first basic modulation and coding technique was Pulse Code Modulation (PCM). The international standard for PCM is G.711. With PCM, analog speech is sampled 8000 times a second. Each speech sample is mapped onto 8 bits. Thus, PCM produces (8000 samples/second) $*$ (8 bits/sample) = 64,000 bits/second = 64 Kbps coded bit rate. Other coding schemes have been developed to further compress the data representation of speech. Most voice compression codes, like G.729, begin with a G.711-coded voice stream.

Figure 17-13 *Distributed WAN CM Deployment Model*

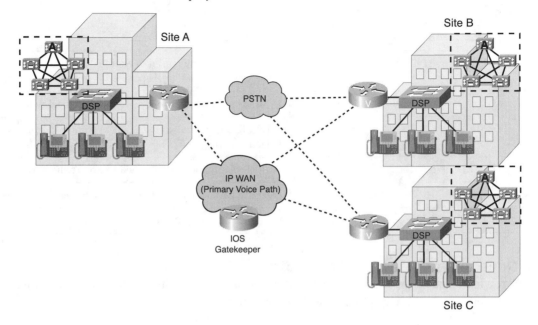

Codec Standards

Codecs transform analog signals into a digital bit stream and digital signals back into analog signals. Figure 17-14 shows that an analog signal is digitized with a coder for digital transport. The decoder converts the digital signal into analog form.

Figure 17-14 *Codec*

Each codec provides a certain quality of speech. A measure used to describe the quality of speech is the Mean Opinion Score (MOS). With MOS, a large group of listeners judges the quality of speech from 5 (best) to 1 (bad). The scores are then averaged out to provide the MOS score for each sample. G.711 has a MOS score of 4.1 and G.729 has a MOS score of 3.92. The default codec setting for VoIP dial peers in Cisco IOS Software is G.729 (g729r8). Some other codec standards appear in Table 17-3. An explanation of the compression techniques is beyond the scope of the CCDA test.

Table 17-3 *Codec Standards*

Codec	Bit Rate	MOS Score	Description
G.711u	64 Kbps	4.1	PCM. Mu-law version used in North America and Japan. Samples speech 8000 times per second represented in 8 bits.
G.711a	64 Kbps	4.1	PCM. A-law used in Europe and in international routes.
G.723.1	6.3 Kbps	3.9	MPE-MLQ (Multipulse Excitation-Maximum Likelihood Quantization).
G.723.1	5.3 Kbps	3.65	ACELP (Algebraic Code-Excited Linear Prediction).
G.726	16/24/ 32/40 Kbps	3.85	Adaptive Differential Pulse-Code Modulation (AD-PCM).
G.729	8 Kbps	3.92	CS-ACELP (Conjugate Structure ACELP).

VoIP Control and Transport Protocols

You use a number of protocols to set up IP telephony clients, calls, and the transport of voice packets. Some of the most significant protocols are

- **Dynamic Host Control Protocol (DHCP)**—To establish IP configuration parameters
- **Domain Name System (DNS)**—To obtain IP addresses of the Trivial File Transfer Protocol (TFTP) server
- **TFTP**—To obtain configurations
- **Skinny Station Control Protocol (SSCP)**—For call establishment
- **RTP**—For voice stream (VoIP) station-to-station traffic in an ongoing call
- **RTCP**—For call control
- **Media Gateway Control Protocol (MGCP)**—For call establishment with gateways
- **H.323**—For call establishment with gateways from the ITU
- **SIP**—For call establishment with gateways, defined by the Internet Engineering Task Force (IETF)

DHCP, DNS, and TFTP

IP phones use DHCP to obtain their IP addressing information: IP address, mask, and default gateway. DHCP also provides the IP address of the DNS server and the name or IP address of the TFTP server. You use TFTP to download the phone operating system and configuration. Both DHCP and TFTP run over UDP.

SSCP

SSCP is a Cisco proprietary signaling protocol for call setup and control. SSCP runs over TCP. SSCP is referred to as a "skinny" protocol because it uses less overhead than the call-setup protocols used by H.323.

RTP and RTCP

In VoIP, RTP transports audio streams. RTP is a transport layer protocol that carries digitized voice in its payload. RTP is defined in RFC 1889. RTP runs over UDP, which has a lower delay than TCP. Because of the time sensitivity of voice traffic and the delay incurred in retransmissions, UDP is used instead of TCP. Real-time traffic is carried over UDP ports ranging from 16,384 to 16,624. The only requirement is that the RTP data is transported on an even port and that RTCP is carried on the next odd port. RTCP is also defined in RFC 1889. RTCP is a session layer protocol that monitors the delivery of data and provides control and identification functions. Figure 17-15 shows a VoIP packet with the IP, UDP, and RTP headers. Notice that the sum of the header lengths is 20 + 8 + 12 = 40 bytes.

Figure 17-15 *IP, UDP, and RTP Headers of a VoIP Packet*

WAN links use RTP header compression to reduce the size of voice packets. It is also referred as Compressed RTP (CRTP). As shown in Figure 17-16, CRTP reduces the IP/UDP/RTP header from 40 bytes to 2 or 4 bytes in length—a significant decrease in overhead. CRTP happens on a hop-by-hop basis with compression and decompression occurring on every link. It must be configured on both ends of the link.

Figure 17-16 *CRTP*

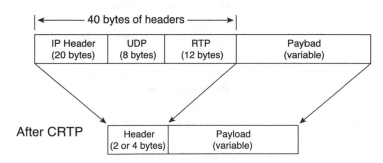

MGCP

MGCP is a gateway protocol used for controlling gateways in VoIP networks. MGCP is defined by the IETF's RFC 2705. MGCP's primary function is to control and supervise connection attempts between different media gateways.

H.323

H.323 is a standard published by the ITU that works as a framework document for multimedia protocols that include voice, video, and data conferencing for use over packet-switched networks. H.323 describes terminals and other entities (such as gatekeepers) to provide multimedia applications. Cisco IOS gateways use H.323 to communicate with the Cisco CM.

H.323 includes the following elements:

- **Terminals**—Telephones, video phones, and voicemail systems
- **Multipoint Control Units (MCU)**—Responsible for managing multipoint conferences
- **Gateways**—Composed of a media gateway controller for call signaling and a media gateway to handle media
- **Gatekeeper**—Optional component used for admission control and address resolution

H.323 terminals must support the following standards:

- H.245
- Q.931
- H.225
- RTP/RTCP

H.245 specifies messages for opening and closing channels for media streams and other commands, requests, and indications. It is a conferencing control protocol.

Q.931 is a standard for call signaling used within the context of H.225 by H.323.

H.225 specifies messages for call control, including signaling between endpoints, registration and admissions, and packetization and synchronization of media streams.

RTP is the transport layer protocol used to transport VoIP packets. RCTP is a session layer protocol.

H.323 includes a series of protocols for multimedia that are listed in Table 17-4.

Table 17-4 *H.323 Protocols*

	Video	Audio	Data	Transport
H.323 protocol	H.261	G.711	T.122	RTP
	H.263	G.722	T.124	H.225
		G.723.1	T.125	H.235
		G.728	T.126	H.245
		G.729	T.127	H.450.1
				H.450.2
				H.450.3
				X.224.0

SIP

SIP is a protocol defined by the IETF and specified in RFC 2543. It is an alternative multimedia framework to H.323, developed specifically for IP telephony. Cisco is now supporting SIP protocol on its phones and gateways.

SIP is an application layer control (signaling) protocol for creating, modifying, and terminating Internet multimedia conferences, Internet telephone calls, and multimedia distribution. Communication between members in a session can be via a multicast, a unicast mesh, or a combination.

SIP is designed as part of the overall IETF multimedia data and control architecture that incorporates protocols such as the following:

- Resource Reservation Protocol (RSVP) (RFC 2205) for reserving network resources
- RTP (RFC 1889) for transporting real-time data and providing QoS feedback
- Real-Time Streaming Protocol (RTSP) (RFC 2326) for controlling delivery of streaming media
- Session Announcement Protocol (SAP) (RFC 2974) for advertising multimedia sessions via multicast
- Session Description Protocol (SDP) (RFC 2327) for describing multimedia sessions

SIP supports user mobility by using proxy and redirect servers to redirect requests to the user's current location. Users can register their current locations, and SIP location services provide the location of user agents.

SIP uses a modular architecture that includes the following components:

■ **SIP user agent**—Endpoints that create and terminate sessions, SIP phones, SIP PC clients, or gateways

■ **SIP proxy server**—Routes messages between SIP user agents

■ **SIP redirect server**—Call-control device used to provide routing information to user agents

■ **SIP registrar server**—Stores the location of all user agents in the domain or subdomain

■ **SIP location services**—Provide logical location of user agents; used by the proxy, redirect, and registrar servers

■ **Back-to-back user agent**—Call-control device that allows centralized control of network call flows

Voice Design Issues

VoIP calls need to meet bandwidth and delay parameters. The amount of bandwidth required depends on the codec used, the Layer 2 protocols, and whether VAD is enabled. For the purpose of call control, you can use the following bandwidth requirements for VoIP design:

■ G.729 calls use 24 Kbps

■ G.723 calls use 24 Kbps

■ G.711 calls use 80 Kbps

When designing for VoIP networks, the total bandwidth for voice, data, and video should not exceed 75 percent of the provisioned link capacity. Use the following formula to provision interface speeds:

Link capacity = [req BW for voice] + [req BW for video] + [req BW for data]

The remaining bandwidth is used by routing, multicast, and management protocols.

VAD

As we listen and pause between sentences, typical voice conversations can contain up to 60 percent silence in each direction. In circuit-switched telephone networks, all voice calls use fixed-bandwidth, 64 Kbps links regardless of how much of the conversation is speech and how much is silence. In multiservice networks, all conversation and silence is packetized. Using VAD, you can suppress packets of silence. Silence suppression at the source IP telephone or VoIP gateway increases the number of calls or data volumes that can be carried over the links, more effectively utilizing network bandwidth. Bandwidth savings are at least 35 percent in conservative estimates. VAD is enabled by default for all VoIP calls.

Table 17-5 shows how much bandwidth is required based on different parameters. Notice that for G.729, bandwidth is reduced from 26.4 Kbps to 17.2 Kbps with VAD and to 7.3 Kbps with VAD and CRTP enabled.

Table 17-5   *VoIP Bandwidth Requirements with CRTP and VAD*

Technique Codec Bit Rate	Payload Size	Bandwidth Multilink PPP (MLP) or FRF.12	Bandwidth with CRTP MLP or FRF.12	Bandwidth with VAD MLP or FRF.12	Bandwidth with CRTP and VAD MLP or FRF.12
Kbps	Bytes	Kbps	Kbps	Kbps	Kbps
G.711 (64)	240	76	66	50	43
G.711 (64)	160 (default)	83	68	54	44
G.726 (32)	120	44	34	29	22
G.726 (32)	80 (default)	50	35	33	23
G.726 (24)	80	38	27	25	17
G.726 (24)	60 (default)	42	27	27	18
G.728 (16)	80	25	18	17	12
G.728 (16)	40 (default)	35	19	23	13
G.729 (8)	40	17.2	9.6	11.2	6.3
G.729 (8)	20 (default)	26.4	11.2	17.2	7.3
G.723.1 (6.3)	48	12.3	7.4	8.0	4.8
G.723.1 (6.3)	24 (default)	18.4	8.4	12.0	5.5
G.723.1 (5.3)	40	11.4	6.4	7.4	4.1
G.723.1 (5.3)	20 (default)	17.5	7.4	11.4	4.8

Delay Components

The ITU's G.114 recommendation specifies that the one-way delay between endpoints should not exceed 150 ms to be acceptable commercial voice quality. In private networks, somewhat longer delays might be acceptable for economic reasons. Delay components are one of two major types: fixed delay and variable delay.

Fixed delay includes

- Propagation delay
- Processing delay
- Serialization delay
- De-jitter delay

Propagation delay is the time it takes for a packet to travel between two points. It is based on the distance between the two endpoints. You cannot overcome this delay component. The speed of light is the theoretical limit. A reasonable planning figure is approximately 10 ms per 1000 miles, or 6 ms per 1000 Km. This figure allows for media degradation and devices internal to the transport network.

Processing delay includes coding and compression delays. G.729 has a delay of 15 ms, and G.711 PCM has a delay of 0.75 ms.

Serialization delay is the time it takes to place bits on the circuit. Faster circuits have less serialization delay. Serialization delay is calculated with the following formula:

Serial delay = frame size (bits)/link BW (bps)

A 1500 byte packet takes (1500 * 8 / 64,000) = 187 ms of serialization delay on a 64 Kbps circuit. If the circuit is increased to 512 Kbps, the serialization delay changes to (1500 * 8/512,000) = 23.4 ms. Data-link fragmentation using Link Fragmentation and Interleaving (LFI) or FRF 12 mechanisms reduces the serialization delay by reducing the size of the larger data packets. This arrangement reduces the delay experienced by voice packets as data packet fragments are serialized and voice packets are interleaved between the fragments. A reasonable design goal is to keep the serialization delay experienced by the largest packets or fragments on the order of 10 ms at any interface.

Packets can take different, redundant paths to reach the destination. Packets might not arrive at a constant rate because they take different paths and they might experience congestion in the network. This variable delay is called jitter. The receiving end uses de-jitter buffers to smooth out the variable delay of received VoIP packets. De-jitter buffers change the variable delay to fixed delay.

The variable-delay component includes queuing delay. As packets cross a network, they pass through several devices. At every output port of these devices is the probability that other voice and data traffic is sharing the link. Queuing delay is the delay experienced as a result of other traffic sharing the link. It is the sum of the serialization delays of all the packets scheduled ahead of delayed packet. As the traffic load on a network increases, both the probability of delay and the length of the probable delay increase. The actual queuing delay depends on the number of queues, queue lengths, and queue algorithms. Queuing effects in VoIP networks are covered in the next section.

QoS Mechanisms for VoIP Networks

Cisco provides different QoS tools that you should use on edge and backbone routers to support VoIP networks. This section covers several QoS mechanisms and their impact on VoIP networks. The covered QoS mechanisms are

- CRTP
- LFI
- Priority Queuing (PQ)
- WFQ
- Priority Queue-WFQ (PQ-WFQ)
- LLQ
- Auto QoS

CRTP

CRTP was covered in an earlier section. It compresses the IP/UDP/RTP headers from 40 bytes to 2/4 bytes. It is configured on a link-to-link basis. Cisco recommends using CRTP for links lower than 768 Kbps. Do not configure CRTP if the router CPU is above 75 percent utilization.

LFI

LFI is a QoS mechanism used to reduce the serialization delay. In a multiservice network, small VoIP packets have to compete with large data traffic packets for outbound interfaces. If the large data packet arrives at the interface first, the VoIP packet has to wait until the large data packet is serialized. When the large packet is fragmented into smaller packets, the VoIP packets can be interleaved in between the data packets. Figure 17-17 shows an example of how LFI works. With no LFI, all VoIP packets and other small packets must wait for the FTP data to be transmitted. With LFI, the FTP data packet is fragmented. The queuing mechanism then can interleave the VoIP packets with the other and send the packets out the interface.

Figure 17-17 *LFI*

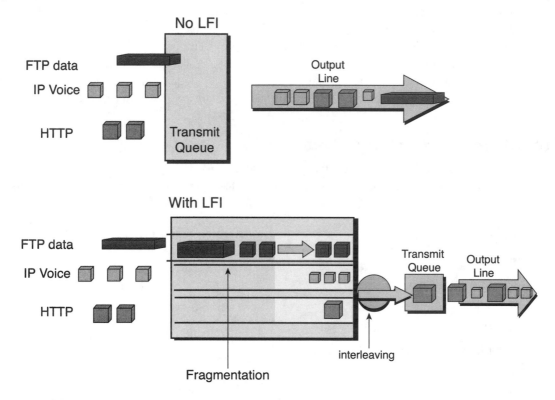

FRF.12 is a fragmentation and interleaving mechanism specific to Frame Relay networks. It is configured on Frame Relay PVCs to fragment large data packets into smaller packets and interleave them with VoIP packets. This process reduces the serialization delay caused by larger packets.

PQ

PQ uses four queues: high, medium, normal, and low. All traffic assigned to the high queue is preferred over the traffic in the other queues. Traffic in lower queues might be discarded if the higher queues always have traffic. This is why PQ is said to be a nonfair queuing scheme.

WFQ

WFQ dequeues packets based on the arrival time of the last bit rather than the first bit, which ensures that applications that use large packets cannot unfairly monopolize the bandwidth. WFQ allows smaller flows to have preferential service over larger bandwidth flows. The disadvantage of WFQ for VoIP networks is that it does not necessary provide service guarantees or priority service to VoIP packets. It is the default queue service for interfaces operating at 2.048 Mbps or less.

PQ-WFQ

PQ-WFQ is also known as IP RTP priority. PQ-WFQ adds a single priority queue to WFQ. The priority queue is used for VoIP packets. All other traffic is queued based on the WFQ algorithm. One variation of PQ-WFQ is Frame Relay RTP priority, which allows strict priority for RTP traffic on Frame Relay PVCs.

With IP RTP priority, the router places VoIP RTP packets in a strict priority queue that is always serviced first. All other (data) traffic is serviced by WFQ. If there is no need for differentiated CoSs for data traffic, use IP RTP priority instead of LLQ. If you require differentiated CoSs for data traffic, use LLQ.

LLQ

LLQ is also known as Priority Queuing-Class Based Weighted Fair Queuing (PQ-CBWFQ). LLQ provides a single priority queue, as does PQ-WFQ, but is preferred for VoIP networks because it can also configure guaranteed bandwidth for different classes of traffic. For example, all voice call traffic would be assigned into the priority queue, VoIP signaling and video would be assigned into a traffic class, FTP traffic would be assigned into a low-priority traffic class, and all other traffic would be assigned to a regular class. With LLQ for Frame Relay, queues are set up on a per-PVC basis. Each PVC has a PQ to support voice traffic. This congestion-management method is considered the most optimal for voice.

If multiple classes are configured for LLQ, they share a single queue but are allocated bandwidth and policed individually. It is recommended that you place only voice in the priority queue because voice traffic is typically well behaved, requiring fixed maximum amounts of bandwidth per call. Introducing video or other variable-rate real-time or nonreal-time traffic types could cause unacceptable jitter for the voice traffic.

Auto QoS

Auto QoS is a recent Cisco IOS feature that uses a simpler command line interface (CLI) to enable QoS for VoIP in WAN and LAN environments. Auto QoS significantly reduces the amount of configuration lines necessary to support VoIP in the network.

For the WAN, Auto QoS provides the following capabilities:

- Automatically classifies RTP and VoIP control packets
- Builds VoIP Modular QoS in the Cisco IOS Software
- Provides LLQ for VoIP bearer traffic
- Provides minimum bandwidth guarantees by using CBWFQ for VoIP control traffic
- Enables WAN traffic shaping, where required
- Enables LFI and RTP, where required

For the LAN, Auto QoS provides the following capabilities:

- Enforces a trust boundary at the Cisco IP Phone
- Enforces a trust boundary on the Catalyst switch access and uplink and downlink ports
- Enables strict priority queuing and weighted round robin for voice and data traffic
- Modifies queue admission criteria by performing CoS to queue mapping
- Modifies queue sizes, as well as queue weights where required
- Modifies CoS to DSCP and IP Precedence to DSCP mappings

AutoQoS is beneficial for small-to-medium size businesses that need to deploy IPT quickly but lack the experience and staffing to plan and deploy IP QoS services.

Auto QoS also benefits large customer enterprises that need to deploy Cisco AVVID on a large scale, while reducing the costs, complexity, and timeframe for deployment and ensuring that the appropriate QoS for voice applications is being set in a consistent fashion.

Foundation Summary

The "Foundation Summary" section of each chapter lists the most important facts from the chapter. Although this section does not list every fact from the chapter that will be on your CCDA exam, a well-prepared CCDA candidate should at a minimum know all the details in each "Foundation Summary" before going to take the exam.

This chapter covered the following topics that you will need to master for the CCDA exam:

- **Traditional voice architectures**—The architecture of TDM voice networks. You must understand PSTN technologies and limitations.

- **Integrated Multiservice Networks**—IP telephony design; AVVID and its components.

- **QoS Mechanisms for VoIP networks**—The effects of QoS mechanisms in integrated networks.

Table 17-6 summarizes technologies or concepts used in voice network design.

Table 17-6   *Voice Technologies*

Technology	Description
FXS	Foreign Exchange Station.
FXO	Foreign Exchange Office.
E&M	Ear and mouth—analog trunk.
Erlang	Measure of total voice traffic volume in one hour.
VAD	Voice activity detection.
RTP	Real-Time Transport Protocol. Carries coded voice; runs over UDP.
RTCP	RTP Control Protocol.
Codec	Coder-decoder. Transforms analog signals into digital bit streams.
H.323	ITU framework for multimedia protocols. Used to control Cisco IOS gateways.
MGCP	Media gateway control protocol. Used to control IOS gateways.
SIP	Session Initiation Protocol. IETF framework for multimedia protocols.

continues

Table 17-6 *Voice Technologies (Continued)*

Technology	Description
SS7	Allows voice and network calls to be routed and controlled by central call controllers; permits modern consumer telephone services. Protocol used in the PSTN.
PSTN	Public Switched Telephone Network.
DTMF	Dual-Tone Multifrequency dialing.
PBX	Private Branch Exchange.
GoS	Grade of service. It is the probability that a call will be blocked when making an attempt.
Centrex	With Centrex services, the CO acts as the company's voice switch, giving the appearance that the company has its own PBX.
IVR	Interactive Voice Response systems provide recorded announcements, prompt callers for key options, and provide information.
ACD	Automatic call distribution systems route calls to a group of agents.

Table 17-7 summarizes the different types of codecs used for voice coding.

Table 17-7 *Codec Standards*

Codec	Bit Rate	MOS Score	Description
G.711u	64 Kbps	4.1	PCM. Mu-law version used in North America and Japan. Samples speech 8000 times per second represented in 8 bits.
G.711a	64 Kbps	4.1	PCM. A-law used in Europe and in international routes.
G.723.1	6.3 Kbps	3.9	MPE-MLQ (Multipulse Excitation-Maximum Likelihood Quantization).
G.723.1	5.3 Kbps	3.65	ACELP (Algebraic Code-Excited Linear Prediction).
G.726	16/24/ 32/40 Kbps	3.85	Adaptive Differential Pulse-Code Modulation (AD-PCM).
G.729	8 Kbps	3.92	CS-ACELP (Conjugate Structure ACELP).

Table 17-8 summarizes the AVVID functional areas.

Table 17-8 *AVVID Functional Areas*

AVVID Functional Area	Description
Applications	Unity, IVR, ICM, TAPI interface
Call processing	Cisco CM
Clients	IP phones, digital and analog gateways
Infrastructure	L2 and L3 switches, routers

Table 17-9 summarizes protocols used in VoIP networks.

Table 17-9 *Significant Protocols in VoIP Networks*

Protocol	Description
DHCP	Dynamic Host Control Protocol. Provides IP address, mask, gateway, DNS address, and TFTP address.
DNS	Domain Name System. Provides IP address of TFTP server.
TFTP	Trivial File Transfer Protocol. Provides the IP phone configuration and operating system.
SSCP	Skinny Station Control Protocol. Establishes calls between IP phones and CM.
RTP	Real-Time Transport Protocol. Carries codec voice streams.
RCTP	Real-Time Transport Control Protocol. Controls RTP streams.
H.323	ITU framework standard. Used for control of Cisco IOS gateways.
SIP	Session Initiation Protocol. An IETF replacement for H.323.

Table 17-10 summarizes the different schemes used for QoS.

Table 17-10 *QoS Scheme Summary*

QoS Scheme	Description
CRTP	RTP Header Compression. Reduces header overhead from 40 bytes to 2 to 4 bytes.
LFI	Link Fragmentation and Interleaving. Fragments large data packets and interleaves VoIP packets between them.
PQ	Priority queuing. Only four queues for services.
WFQ	Weighted fair queuing. Allows smaller flows to have preferential service over larger bandwidth flows.
PQ-WFQ	Also known as IP RTP priority. Uses a single strict queue for RTP traffic. All other traffic in WFQ.
LLC	Also known as PQ-CBWFQ. Uses a single strict queue for RTP traffic. Differentiated CoSs available for all other traffic.

Q&A

As mentioned in the introduction, you have two choices for review questions. Some of the questions that follow give you a bigger challenge than the exam itself by using a short-answer question format. By reviewing now with more difficult question format, you can exercise your memory better and prove your conceptual and factual knowledge of this chapter. The answers to these questions appear in Appendix A.

For more practice with exam-like question formats, use the exam engine on the CD-ROM.

1. True or false? LLQ is recommended for VoIP networks.

2. True or false? H.323 is an IETF standard, and SIP is an ITU standard for multimedia protocols.

3. True or false? An Erlang is a unit that describes the number of calls in a hour.

4. Implement _____ to stop packets from being transmitted when there is silence in a voice conversation.

5. The variable delay of received VoIP packets is corrected with _____ buffers.

6. True or false? Common-channel signaling uses a separate channel for signaling.

7. True or false? FXO ports are used for phones, and FXS ports connect to the PSTN.

8. True or false? SS7 provides mechanisms for exchanging control and routing messages in the PSTN.

9. An organization will use a _____ system to gather and provide information for the customer before transferring her to an agent.

10. An organization will use a _____ system to route calls to agents based on the agent skill group or call statistics.

11. In addition to codec selection, both _____ and _____ can be used to reduce the bandwidth of VoIP calls.

12. Label the delays as fixed or variable:

    a. Processing

    b. De-jitter buffer

    c. Serialization

    d. Queuing

    e. Propagation

13. How can you reduce serialization delay?

14. Which two queuing techniques use a strict priority queue for IP RTP traffic?

15. True or false? The maximum one-way delay in the G.114 recommendation for acceptable voice is 200 ms.

16. True or false? FRF.12 is an LFI standard used in networks with VoFR and VoIP over Frame Relay.

17. Match the protocol with the description:

i.	DHCP	**a.**	Transports coded voice streams
ii.	SSCP	**b.**	Controls Cisco IOS gateways
iii.	RTP	**c.**	Provides call signaling between Cisco IP phones and CM
iv.	H.323	**d.**	Provides IP address
v.	TFTP	**e.**	Provides phone configuration

18. Match the CM deployment model with the description:

i.	Single-site deployment	**a.**	Single CM cluster with SRST at remote sites
ii.	Distributed WAN	**b.**	Single CM cluster implemented in large building
iii.	Centralized WAN	**c.**	Multiple CM clusters

19. Match the component with the AVVID functional area:

i.	CM	**a.**	Service applications
ii.	L3 switch	**b.**	Call processing
iii.	Digital gateway	**c.**	Clients
iv.	Unity	**d.**	Infrastructure

20. The _____ standard establishes specifications for call setup and packet formats for VoFR.

Use both the scenario described in the following paragraph and Figure 17-18 to answer the questions that follow.

The client has an existing Frame Relay network, as shown in Figure 17-18. The network has a large site and 50 small remote sites. The client wants a design for a VoIP network. The client wants to provide differentiated CoSs for the voice, Systems Network Architecture (SNA), FTP, and other traffic.

Figure 17-18 *Client's Current Frame Relay Network*

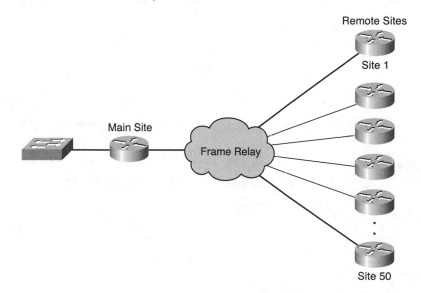

21. Based on the current network diagram, which deployment model should you recommend?

22. What feature should you recommend to provide call processing in the event of a WAN failure?

23. Which queuing technique should you recommend?

24. For Site 1, the current data traffic is 512 kbps and video traffic is 0. What circuit speed should be provisioned if 4 concurrent VoIP G.729 calls will be permitted to the site?

25. Should you implement a CM cluster?

26. What feature can you use to reduce bandwidth over the WAN links?

27. Which LFI technique should you use to reduce the serialization delay?

This chapter covers the following subjects:

- A Sample Roadmap to Network Management

- SNMP

- CDP

CHAPTER 18

Network Management Technologies

This chapter is an introduction to the following network-management protocols: Simple Network Management Protocol (SNMP), Cisco Discovery Protocol (CDP), and Remote Monitoring Protocol (RMON). This chapter is by no means a detailed discussion of each protocol or how to configure it on Cisco equipment. Instead, the chapter introduces them so that a network designer can understand how they function. An awareness of the functionality allows the network designer to accommodate the requirements of these protocols in a network design.

"Do I Know This Already?" Quiz

The purpose of the "Do I Know This Already?" quiz is to help you decide whether you need to read the entire chapter. If you intend to read the entire chapter, you do not necessarily need to answer these questions now.

The 10-question quiz, derived from the major sections in the "Foundation Topics" portion of the chapter, helps you determine how to spend your limited study time.

Table 18-1 outlines the major topics discussed in this chapter and the "Do I Know This Already?" quiz questions that correspond to those topics.

Table 18-1   *"Do I Know This Already?" Foundation Topics Section-to-Question Mapping*

Foundation Topics Section	Questions Covered in This Section
SNMP	1, 2, 6, 7, 8
RMON	3, 4, 9
CDP	5, 10

CAUTION   The goal of self assessment is to gauge your mastery of the topics in this chapter. If you do not know the answer to a question or you are only partially sure of the answer, you should mark this question wrong for purposes of the self assessment. Giving yourself credit for an answer you correctly guess skews your self-assessment results and might provide you with a false sense of security.

1.   Which version or versions of SNMP specify security extensions as part of the protocol definition?

   a.   SNMPv1

   b.   SNMPv2

   c.   SNMPv3

   d.   SNMPv4

2.   What does SNMP stand for?

   a.   Simple Network Monitoring Protocol

   b.   Simple Network Maintenance Procedure

   c.   Sampling Network Management Process

   d.   Simple Network Management Protocol

3.   True or false? RMON is an SNMP command.

4.   RMON architecture consists of which communicating device types?

   a.   Router

   b.   Switch

   c.   Management station

   d.   Monitor

   e.   MIB

5.   CDP is an acronym for which Cisco function?

   a.   Cisco Discovery Protocol

   b.   Collection Device Protocol

   c.   Cisco Device Protocol

   d.   Campus Discovery Protocol

   e.   Cisco Discovery Process

6.   What is the virtual information store used within SNMP called?

   a.   MIB

   b.   Protocol data unit (PDU)

   c.   RMON

   d.   Abstract Syntax Notation One (ASN.1)

7. The device information to be stored by SNMP is defined using what standard language?

   a. Agents

   b. MIBs

   c. ASN.1

   d. SNMPv4

8. Which of the following is not an SNMP operation?

   a. GetNext

   b. Community

   c. Set

   d. Trap

9. What is the remote monitoring agent in the RMON architecture called?

   a. Agent

   b. Probe

   c. Tree

   d. Station

10. SNMP is a request-response architecture; CDP is a _____?

   a. Client/server architecture

   b. Hello protocol

   c. Network management agent

   d. RMON definition

The answers to the "Do I Know This Already?" quiz appear in Appendix A, "Answers to Chapter 'Do I Know This Already?' Quizzes and Q&A sections." The suggested choices for your next step are as follows:

■ **8 or less overall score**—Read the entire chapter. It includes the "Foundation Topics," "Foundation Summary," and "Q&A" sections.

■ **9-10 overall score**—If you want more review on these topics, skip to the "Foundation Summary" section and then go to the "Q&A" section. Otherwise, move to the next chapter.

Foundation Topics

Whether you are going to build a network from scratch or update an existing system, taking the time to assess your network-management architecture is a wise approach. Network management is an essential service in any network, but it is also a complex task requiring planning and design to ensure the integration of the management system with the network.

This chapter reviews selected low-level protocols upon which useful network-management tools have been built. Chapter 19, "Network Management Functionality," explains all five functional areas of network management used in high-level functional models such as Fault-management, Configuration, Accounting, Performance and Security FCAPS and operation, administration, maintenance, and provisioning (OAM&P). Additionally, that chapter explains the service levels that are managed in modern networks and that represent the most comprehensive management solution.

The goal of each protocol section is to provide an overview of the functionality.

A Sample Roadmap to Network Management

For an organization to navigate its way through maintaining day-to-day systems and network availability, it must first chart a course. As separate disciplines, both network management and systems management can be complex to deploy, configure, understand, and administer. This roadmap illustrates the key areas that address issues faced by the organizations that rely heavily on the network and systems infrastructure to complete their daily activities.

Looking at the bigger picture, you can group together the network, systems, and service-management areas as enterprise management.

Organizations require the management tools and processes that give them the ability to monitor a network infrastructure. The network-management server (NMS) must know all the devices on the network to provide an "enterprise view." This view displays overall availability status for all network devices—routers, access servers, switches, and authentication, file, application, and print servers. From this layer, the NMS can conduct periodic status polls of network elements as well as rediscover the network at certain intervals to ensure information is up-to-date on the existence of network elements and their locations. A network node manager (NNM), such as Hewlett-Packard OpenView (HPOV), also provides a good overall network-management backup for all devices, should any or all of the other element managers become unavailable. Custom network-management applications can provide real-time and historical availability information for network elements using SNMP and access to generic data points to monitor server and network equipment.

You perform WAN and LAN element management by configuring and using a central NMS. As is the case for most element-management solutions, the vendor's own management product is best suited for the particular management requirements pertaining to network hardware. The major reasons are three-fold:

- In-depth product knowledge of the desirable features and requirements for managing the various equipment types

- Provision and access to the vendor's enterprise MIBs

- Consolidated technical support and access to caveat information about known implementation issues

With the move to a more robust and "self-healing" network-management model, collection domains are the key to distributing the network-management workload. Collection domains divide the event-collection and polling activities between two logical groups that can, as near as possible, share the load evenly. The logical groups can be by function, geographical area, time zone, machine type, or any one of many other factors. Figure 18-1 illustrates a sample logical diagram of the network design.

Figure 18-1   *Sample Logical Diagram of the Network Design*

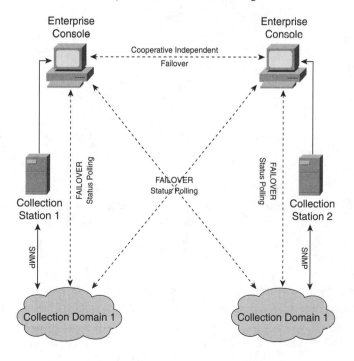

Remember that you should deploy network management, like other network services, using sound security practices. Cisco wrote the SAFE blueprint, in which it describes how you should secure management traffic. The diagram in Figure 18-2 illustrates separating network-management activity into its own modules. For a detailed design, read the white paper "SAFE: A Security Blueprint for Enterprise Networks," http://www.cisco.com/warp/public/cc/so/cuso/epso/sqfr/safe_wp.pdf.

Figure 18-2 *Separating Network-Management Activity*

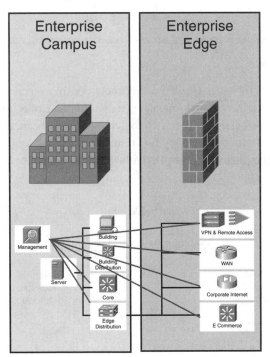

Consider all the elements, the technical, and the process-oriented and human factors that are involved in achieving your network-management goals. Then, imagine building that system without considering the role, functionality, or relationship of the different elements involved before placing them in the network. Imagine you are designing a management system with elements that will be replicated at many locations. Can you afford to replicate a mistake? Think of the assessment of the network-management architecture as a time when you can work out logical issues with the design and make sure your design meets all your objectives. The assessment focuses on identifying functions and their relationships and provides the basis for later design activities.

Evaluate the capabilities during the assessment before you select specific devices or products because they set the requirements that drive later choices of technology and product. Product selection is part of the design phase. Although some have built systems without these considerations, the systems tended to fall short of scalability, security, robustness, or performance expectations.

Identifying network-management solutions requires understanding the network lifecycle. This cycle is an ongoing process of planning, designing, deploying, implementing, optimizing, and operating networks.

You can use several mechanisms to establish the connections of the network-management components within a network. You use SNMP to exchange information between devices and CDP and RMON to monitor the function of remote devices.

SNMP

SNMP supports systems that provide a wide range of functions within the network. SNMP works by using a management and agent model that uses minimal transfer of data; therefore, the agent is very "light," and most of the manager functionality resides on the NMS. The manager applications use SNMP to communicate with the agent software running on the network devices.

Data is passed between an agent and a manager using specially defined SNMP protocol data units (PDUs). You can use SNMP to perform configurations and collect statistics and performance information to manage security and monitor network devices.

SNMP Components

Cisco describes three network-management components: the managed device, the agent that resides in the managed device, and the management server that collects the information. The agent communicates with the management server. The agent packages locally collected management data for transmission to the manager using SNMP. The information collected is device and interface specific.

SNMP MIB

SNMP-compliant devices access remotely stored data using a logical structure called the *MIB*. Organized as a hierarchical tree, the MIB includes data defined by standard or RFC and proprietary data in separate branches. The MIB provides a common structure of definitions used to request, locate, and transmit network-management–related data. Network and end-system equipment manufacturers decide which data they make available through SNMP. Each participating vendor manages a private branch of the MIB tree. The Internet portion of the MIB tree, including vendor private branches, is managed by the Internet Assigned Number Authority (IANA).

Each individual manageable feature in the MIB is referred to as an MIB *variable*. The descriptions of these manageable features, located within an agent, are defined in a document called an MIB *module*. The MIB modules are written in a language called ASN.1. MIB module files are then loaded into the NMS. The primary purpose of the MIB module is to provide a name and description for each of the manageable features a particular agent knows about.

SNMP Commands

SNMP is fundamentally a request-response architecture. The manager issues requests from the NMS to get data values from agents or set control values on agents, and the agent responds with data or confirmation. Additionally, SNMP allows agents to generate unsolicited reports, known as *traps*, when some predefined event occurs. Most frequently, the event involves crossing some threshold value. Basically, the three commands used in SNMP are **get**, **set** and **trap**.

SNMP Design Constraints

The indiscriminate use of SNMP can have an adverse effect on network performance. The messages consume link bandwidth, and the formatting of the responses consumes internal CPU and memory resources on the target network devices. The timeliness of event notification and reporting granularity are network-management design decisions that can affect the infrastructure equipment and bandwidth required in a network.

SNMP References

SNMP is Internet Standard 62. RFC 3411 through RFC 3418, issued in December 2002, define the current standard. Other current Internet standards related to SNMP include Internet Standard 15; the original definition of SNMP in RFC 1157; and Internet Standard 50, which addresses managed objects for Ethernet-like interface types.

SNMP Evolution

The Internet Engineering Task Force (IETF) has defined three versions of SNMP over the years. SNMPv2 extended SNMP to function over networks other than IP networks, such as Novell's Internetwork Packet Exchange (IPX). SNMPv3 retains the data definition language, ASN.1; MIBs; and protocol operations from SNMPv2 and adds more rigorous security and administration. Additionally, SNMPv3 is defined in a modular fashion to allow the evolution of various protocol formats and operations at different times.

For more detailed information on SNMP, refer to the relevant RFCs in Table 18-2.

TIP Table 18-2 is not the complete list of SNMP-relevant RFCs; however, these RFCs are the most pertinent.

Table 18-2 *SNMP RFC Chart*

Protocol	RFC Number	Title
SNMPv1	1155	*Structure and Identification of Management Information for TCP/IP-Based Internets*
	1157	*A Simple Network Management Protocol (SNMP)*
SNMPv2	2578	*Structure of Management Information for Version 2 of the Simple Network Management Protocol (SNMPv2)*
	2579	*Textual Conventions for Version 2 of the Structure of Management Information*
	2580	*Conformance Statements for Version 2 of the Structure of Management Information*
	3416	*Protocol Operations for Version 2 of the Simple Network Management Protocol (SNMPv2)*
	3417	*Transport Mappings for Version 2 of the Simple Network Management Protocol (SNMPv2)*
	3418	*Management Information Base for Version 2 of the Simple Network Management Protocol (SNMPv2)*
	2576	*Coexistence between Version 1, Version 2, and Version 3 of the Internet-Standard Network Management Framework*
SNMPv3	3411	*An Architecture for Describing Internet Management Networks*
	3412	*Message Processing and Dispatching for the Simple Network Management Protocol (SNMP)*
	3414	*User-Based Security Model (USM) for Version 3 of the Simple Network Management Protocol (SNMPv3)*
	3415	*View-Based Access Control Model (VACM) for the Simple Network Management Protocol (SNMP)*

CDP

Cisco developed a proprietary protocol called CDP that informs other devices of their presence on the network as well as receives information of neighboring devices.

CDP Components

Whereas SNMP is fundamentally a request-response architecture, CDP is a "hello-based" protocol, and all devices running CDP periodically advertise their attributes to their neighbors. CDP uses a multicast address to send and receive these advertisements. CDP works at the data link layer, which limits its direct reach to logically adjacent devices. All Cisco infrastructure equipment is CDP compliant. You can use only this protocol to map a network by moving from node to node.

CDP Advantages

Some network-management protocols are limited in multiprotocol environments. Because CDP is independent of any network-layer protocol, two devices that do not have a common network-layer protocol can discover each other. This ability extends connectivity in multiprotocol environments.

CDP Considerations and Constraints

When you use CDP to map a network by moving from node to node, it is a bit chatty. Continuous use of CDP over low-bandwidth connections can result in starving application traffic, and you must take care when enabling CDP in the network. CDP is enabled automatically upon system startup; however, you must explicitly configure all interfaces that need to run CDP.

RMON

RFC 2819 (formerly RFC 1757, formerly RFC 1271) describes specifications for RMON, which is an MIB agent that defines functions for remotely monitoring networked devices. This ability to perform remote management increases the usability of SNMP. RMON-compliant managers and network probes can exchange numerous monitoring, problem detection, and reporting capabilities.

A typical RMON architecture consists of a central NMS and a remote-monitoring capability, which can be a separate device called an RMON probe. The NMS is a network-management station running RMON-capable software. The RMON NMS host can be a dedicated workstation, usually running UNIX or Microsoft Windows, or a blade installed in a central network device. From the management station, you can issue SNMP commands requesting information from the RMON probe.

Foundation Summary

The "Foundation Summary" section of each chapter lists the most important facts from the chapter. Although this section does not list every fact from the chapter that will be on your CCDA exam, a well-prepared CCDA candidate should at a minimum know all the details in each "Foundation Summary" before going to take the exam.

The three versions of SNMP use essentially the same architecture of management and agent components. PDUs pass information from agent to management. CDP is a Cisco protocol on all Cisco devices that advertises and discovers neighboring devices. RMON is an MIB structure that enables the remote management of devices.

The CCDA exam requires that you know and understand the three versions of SNMP described in this chapter. Understand that network management is an essential service in any network but that it is a complex task requiring planning and design to ensure the integration of the management system with the network. You should also understand the low-level protocols described in this chapter.

Q&A

As mentioned in the introduction, you have two choices for review questions. The questions that follow give you a bigger challenge than the exam itself by using an open-ended question format. By reviewing now with this more difficult question format, you can exercise your memory better and prove your conceptual and factual knowledge of this chapter. The answers to these questions appear in Appendix A.

For more practice with exam-like question formats, use the exam engine on the CD-ROM.

1. How are the features available in an MIB branch determined?

2. On which devices is CDP available?

3. What is an MIB variable?

4. Why is the SNMP protocol considered simple?

5. What method does network-management software communicating to managed devices with SNMP use to periodically gather information from agents?

6. What are some examples of information transferred by SNMP using SNMP PDUs?

7. What is the purpose of a trap?

8. How does the managed device communicate with the NMS station?

9. What are the SNMP basic commands?

10. What are the three SNMP management components?

11. Why is CDP not limited in multiprotocol environments?

Exam Topics in This Chapter

- Fault Management

- Configuration Management

- Accounting Management

- Performance Management

- Security Management

- Service Levels

- SLAs

- SLM

CHAPTER 19

Network Management Functionality

This chapter explains a model for defining the network management functionality called FCAPS, which stands for fault, configuration, accounting, performance, and security management. The FCAPS network management model standardized by the International Telecommunication Union Telecommunication Standardization Sector (ITU-T) in Recommendation X.700 is a common basis for developing a comprehensive network management system.

This chapter focuses on identifying the different components of FCAPS and describing some common functions of the different components. Understanding the FCAPS functional model can help you determine the completeness of a network management design.

This chapter also discusses service levels and how to manage them. Service levels are important to understand so you can assess managed network services such as network monitoring.

"Do I Know This Already?" Quiz

The purpose of the "Do I Know This Already?" quiz is to help you decide whether you need to read the entire chapter. If you intend to read the entire chapter, you do not necessarily need to answer these questions now.

The 10-question quiz, derived from the major sections in the "Foundation Topics" portion of the chapter, helps you determine how to spend your limited study time.

Table 19-1 outlines the major topics discussed in this chapter and the "Do I Know This Already?" quiz questions that correspond to those topics.

Table 19-1 *"Do I Know This Already?" Foundation Topics Section-to-Question Mapping*

Foundation Topics Section	Questions Covered in This Section
Introduction	2, 4
Performance Management	1
Accounting Management	5
Fault Management	3
Service Level Manager	6
Service Levels	7
Service Level Contracts	8
Service Level Agreements	9, 10

CAUTION The goal of self assessment is to gauge your mastery of the topics in this chapter. If you do not know the answer to a question or you are only partially sure of the answer, you should mark this question wrong for purposes of the self assessment. Giving yourself credit for an answer you correctly guess skews your self-assessment results and might provide you with a false sense of security.

1. If a network management system could assess network behavior and its effectiveness to deliver packets, which function of FCAPS would it be related to?

   a. Fault management

   b. Security management

   c. Network management

   d. Performance management

2. What is the name of the organization that is responsible for creating the FCAPS architecture?

   a. ISP

   b. IOS

   c. ITU-T

   d. IEEE

3. Which of the FCAPS functions includes finding network problems that reduce availability?

   a. Fault management

   b. Accounting management

   c. Security management

   d. Performance management

4. FCAPS is an acronym for which of the following?

   a. Fault, caching, application, production, security

   b. Fiscal, communication, application, production, security

   c. Fault, consolidation, accounting, performance, security

   d. Fault, configuration, accounting, performance, security

5. Accounting management on a network-management system allows a network manager to perform which function?

   a. Identify problem areas in the network

   b. Assess the network's effectiveness and throughput

   c. Charge back to users for network resources

   d. Performance management

6. What component of the CiscoWorks product allows a network administrator to define and manage service levels?

   a. Service level manager (SLM)

   b. Service assurance agent (SAA)

   c. Service level agreement (SLA)

   d. Collection Manager (CM)

7. Which of the following components is not one of the SLA types defined in the Cisco SLM?

   a. Latency

   b. Failure

   c. Voice over IP (VoIP)

   d. Network services

8. What does SLC stand for?

    a. Service level configuration

    b. Standard level contracts

    c. Service level contracts

    d. Standard level configuration

9. What does the Cisco SLM define as the component that is used to specify expected performance between a pair of devices connected by a network?

    a. SLC

    b. SLA

    c. CM

    d. SAA

10. Service providers often use what mechanism to define their service offerings and to differentiate their services from their competitors?

    a. SLA

    b. SAA

    c. SLC

    d. SLM

The answers to the "Do I Know This Already?" quiz appear in Appendix A, "Answers to Chapter 'Do I Know This Already?' Quizzes and Q&A Sections." The suggested choices for your next step are as follows:

■ **8 or less overall score**—Read the entire chapter. It includes the "Foundation Topics," "Foundation Summary," and "Q&A" sections.

■ **9–10 overall score**—If you want more review on these topics, skip to the "Foundation Summary" section and then go to the "Q&A" section. Otherwise, move to the next chapter.

Foundations Topics

The ITU-T defines five functions expected from the process of network management. You can remember these processes with FCAPS (fault, configuration, accounting, performance, security), each of which is described in this section. These functions represent a comprehensive network-management service. You can use FCAPS to determine the effectiveness of network management based on an assessment of how well the network-management system delivers each of these components. Practically every network-management activity fits into one of these functional areas.

This section also addresses service levels because Internet access and connectivity provided by service providers are critical to customer's business operations and needs.

Fault Management

When you think about network management, fault management usually comes to mind first. Fault management refers to detecting, isolating, and correcting problems (faults) on the network to ensure good network performance. Fault management does not have to reside on a network-management device; fault management is also a function of Cisco IOS Software.

After you identify or discover a fault, you use troubleshooting methods to isolate the network fault and then correct the problem. For fault management on Cisco IOS Software, you can use system monitoring commands such as **show** and **debug** to discover the network problem, system test commands to define the network problem, and configuration commands to resolve them.

Cisco recommends using the following activities for basic fault management for Cisco IOS devices:

- Displaying system information using **show** commands
- Testing network connectivity
- Testing memory and interfaces
- Logging system error messages
- Using field diagnostics on line cards
- Troubleshooting specific line cards
- Storing line-card crash information
- Creating core dumps
- Enabling debug operations
- Enabling conditionally triggered debugging
- Using the environmental monitor

HP OpenView and Tivoli from IBM are common examples of fault-reporting network-management stations. A network-management station identifies faults and facilitates the management of multiple devices. Fault events are reported to the station via Simple Network Management Protocol (SNMP) traps or regular interval polling by the management station. You can configure the station to pop a window or to send an e-mail or page to network analysts. Fault management is the most common element of FCAPS.

Configuration Management

Configuration management refers to baselining, modifying, and tracking configuration changes to network devices. This function also tracks versions of operating systems on the devices. You can use configuration management to gather inventory information instead of going to each device one-by-one. It is also helpful to track changes made to devices when there is more than one administrator with network-management responsibilities.

Just imagine how much easier it is to manage multiple devices and to view the configuration of those devices holistically with one network-management station. The ability to view multiple configurations often accompanies the ability to make template configuration changes. This ability is useful in complex environments that incorporate large amounts of redundancy or in environments where several devices perform the same function.

In case the configurations on the devices go awry, configuration management can save versions of configurations and push those configurations back on to systems. Configuration management systems, with all the stored information as well as a history of changes, can be useful in troubleshooting. This system is a way to manage windows of opportunity for configuration changes; when you face short timeframes, you can always fall back to a known working configuration.

Accounting Management

Accounting management refers to tracking the usage of network segments to determine usage-based billing for services. This management allows IT departments to bill and manage the needs of specific departments based on their usage. It can reduce network-resource issues because the departments that use the most services are billed accordingly.

To begin the accounting process, you must make a baseline to identify the resources to be tracked and to measure the current utilization. This way, the network administrations can analyze the data to determine the current usage patters of important network services. Based on this analysis, they can determine how to "charge" or manage the utilization.

Converged networks increase the bandwidth requirements for the common transport network, which makes bandwidth an important resource to manage. However, it doesn't make sense to deny services to departments that need it. With a tool such as the Cisco NetFlow, you can measure resource utilization to make charge-back decisions and measure the compliance of service providers with the terms of service.

Performance Management

Performance management refers to measuring network behavior and its effectiveness in delivering frames, packets, and segments. In other words, performance management deals with how well a service or a device performs its job. It can include monitoring the behavior of protocols and applications, the ability to reach from point A to point B, and timed responsiveness.

Network-management systems can monitor a defined level of performance against set thresholds. If the network performance passes a threshold, the system triggers an alert. Using performance management can help you maintain network performance at an acceptable level. This maintenance is particularly important in converged networks that have voice, video, and data traffic. Consistent network performance is increasingly important as applications sensitive to both delay and variability share converged transport networks.

You can perform assessments on network performance prior to implementing latency-sensitive applications and use them afterward for monitoring. Examples of performance variables are network throughput, user response times, and line utilization.

Cisco recommends that performance management involve three main steps. First, you gather performance data on the variables determined to be of greatest interest by network administrators. Second, you analyze the data to determine normal (baseline) levels. Finally, you define appropriate performance thresholds for each important variable so that crossing these thresholds indicates a network problem worthy of attention.

Although SLAs are addressed in detail later in this chapter, it is important to note that performance management is often associated with SLAs. This is particularly true regarding the agreement between a service provider and its customers. Just remember that if the agreed-upon metrics are not realistic or measurable, the SLA is meaningless. Statistics such as input queue drops, output queue drops, and ignored packets are useful for diagnosing performance-related problems.

Another interesting use of performance management is in testing pilots to see how a potential network device or system will function. Using performance-management devices and measures allows you to test and measure a new technology for viability. Another example of performance management is using network simulation to project how network growth will affect measured performance. Such simulation can alert administrators to impending problems so they can take counteractive measures. Performance management includes taking proactive steps to identify and, when possible, mitigate possible issues.

Security Management

Security refers to authentication, access control, data confidentiality, data integrity, and nonrepudiation. Security management includes the maintenance and distribution of authentication and authorization information, such as passwords and encryption keys. In other words, security management allows the administrator to control who has access to which resources.

Security management has taken center stage in the past several years and has expanded greatly. Security management also includes configuration and control of intrusion detection systems (IDSs); firewalls; and traffic filtering by URL, address, or protocol to monitor activity and to detect or deflect malicious actions.

Some security is specific to network management, such as SNMP security. Important enhancements in SNMPv3, discussed in Chapter 18, "Network Management Technologies," involved securing that protocol. Central to the security enhancements of SNMPv3 is defining security between the collection device and the agent.

Another common security measure is using logs, whether they are syslogs or logs generated by various devices. Using audit logs to document logins or repeated unsuccessful attempts is also part of security management. Before any security measures are actually implemented, an organization should have a security policy. Cisco offers the Cisco Secure Policy Manager, which assists companies in creating, deploying, and evaluating security policies.

Service Levels

Internet access and connectivity provided by service providers are critical to a customer's business. Business-continuity plans ensure that the network is always available. This view becomes even more important as voice and data networks continue to converge, and the network becomes a possible single point of telecommunications failure.

How do you measure the ability of one service provider or network administration and management team to deliver the services expected? This is a critical question, considering that so much of the success of an organization depends on the network. Customers expect a guaranteed level of service, and service providers might even agree that the customer has to pay only for the levels it receives.

This concept isn't new; Frame Relay networks have used a similar concept to charge for their ability to provide multiple tiers of bandwidth. The customer pays for a guaranteed amount of bandwidth specified in its Committed Information Rate (CIR). It might receive more than that specified bandwidth, but if it receives less, the customer often pays a reduced charge for the period of degraded service.

Service Levels Defined

Because service levels can apply to internal as well as external providers, Cisco developed a way to define and manage these service levels. As discussed previously, service levels must be measurable and reasonable. This charge should sound familiar because corporate security policies should also use the same criteria.

Just one service might have several service agreements that must be managed simultaneously. Cisco developed a method to organize and manage different service levels by defining different components. When managing a service level, the management solution must bring together the metrics from the various service components into a single service view. This idea is similar to event correlation, which organizes multiple events.

It can easily be confusing to have multiple vendors provide several service management applications and contracts. Without an overview for an organization to see how these service levels affect end-to-end service, it is difficult to detect when a service level is not achieved.

The Cisco end-to-end service-level management solution, CiscoWorks Service Management Solution, manages service levels between enterprises and internal or external service providers to ensure high-quality, economic delivery of converged network services. Open XML APIs enable full management of service levels through integration with in-house or third-party analysis and provisioning systems.

SLAs

The most common service-level term is an SLA, which is a contact presented to the end user that defines the level of performance expected for a service. You can use several SLAs to define a service because each SLA can represent a specific metric that can be measured, reported, and monitored. These SLAs should be relevant to the business objectives of the company to which they are presented. Often service levels are used as "icing" on a service contract, and end users have no way of measuring the performance of services they receive against that agreement.

Service Level Contract

SLAs are organized by into SLCs. The SLC specifies connectivity and performance agreements for an end-user service from a provider. The SLC typically includes multiple SLAs. A violation of any particular SLA could create a violation of the overall SLC. The service-level management solution needs to provide a means of managing collections of agreements that constitute a contract with the service provider.

SLM

Cisco developed an SLM that can manage service levels by allowing you to define SLAs and to figure out a method to test these SLAs. In addition, the SLM is an open platform to allow third-party tools from other vendors to enhance its services. This setup enables quicker development of the product with reporting and fault capabilities. The SLM also allows you to view and monitor the services referenced in the SLA.

The SLM enables you to define an SLC, which is either one or several SLAs grouped together based on business objectives. This way, you can monitor several SLAs at one time to assess the overall service delivery. You can also monitor multiple SLCs individually, drill down into SLA details, and monitor the percentage of SLA conformance for a given SLC.

Another component of SLM is the CM, which is an agent that collects and aggregates the performance information needed to assess service levels. You can install CM on servers that meet its software requirements.

Figure 19-1 shows a simple configuration of the CM. It illustrates that the collection of data from remote collection managers can be aggregated into a single device.

> **NOTE** A Service Assurance Agent is residing on a Cisco device (part of IOS 12.l) and communicates to a collection manager. A collection manager can be deployed hierarchically to aggregate information locally to conserve bandwidth to the central CM.

Figure 19-1 *Simple CM Design*

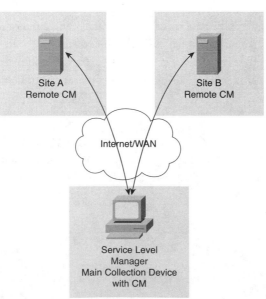

Figure 19-2 shows different SLAs from several network devices or services that form one end-to-end Internet access. This setup is an example of an SLC and how you can logically create the definition of the SLC based on business needs.

Figure 19-2 *Sample End-to-End Internet Access SLC*

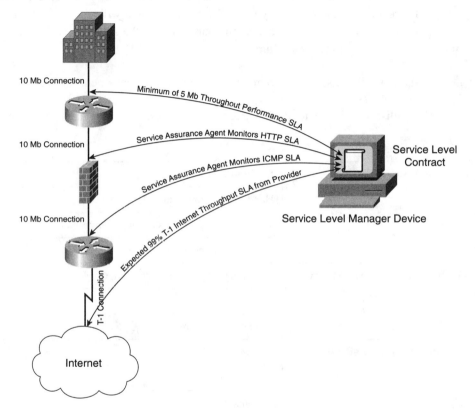

Foundation Summary

The "Foundation Summary" section of each chapter lists the most important facts from the chapter. Although this section does not list every fact from the chapter that will be on your CCDA exam, a well-prepared CCDA candidate should at a minimum know all the details in each "Foundation Summary" before going to take the exam.

A model called FCAPS represents a comprehensive network-management service.

Table 19-2 is a list of activities for each element of the FCAPS network-management model.

Table 19-2 *FCAPS Network-Management Model*

Fault management	Diagnostics
	Handling and correlating alarms based on thresholds
	Threshold-based reports and log management
	Filter management
Configuration management	Managing software upgrades to devices
	Inventory management
	Auto backup and recovery
Accounting management	Managing SLAs
	Reporting usages
	Accounting for billing
Performance management	Collecting and correlating data about network capacity
	Performance monitoring and reporting
Security management	Managing system access and authentication
	Intrusion containment and recovery

Defining service levels and a way to manage these service levels is important because you should establish corporate security policies using the same criteria.

Q&A

As mentioned in the introduction, you have two choices for review questions. Some of the questions that follow give you a bigger challenge than the exam itself by using an open-ended question format. By reviewing now with this more difficult question format, you can exercise your memory better and prove your conceptual and factual knowledge of this chapter. The answers to these questions appear in Appendix A.

For more practice with exam-like question formats, use the exam engine on the CD-ROM.

1. Which FCAPS function would you use to "stress test" a pilot network to determine how well it functions under various conditions?

   a. Fault management

   b. Security management

   c. Network management

   d. Performance management

2. What is a grouping of SLAs called that are created to define an end-to-end service?

   a. Total Service Management (TSM)

   a. CM

   b. SLM

   c. SLC

3. Monitoring logs to assess whether a user has used proper authentication procedures is considered part of which FCAPS function?

   a. Fault management

   b. Accounting management

   c. Security management

   d. Performance management

4. Managing variables that need to be set for a device to function the way you expect it to is included in which FCAPS function?

   a. Security management

   b. Accounting management

   c. Performance management

   d. Configuration management

5. What is the SLM component that you use to collect and aggregate performance data from devices that need to be monitored based on SLA thresholds?

   a. CM

   b. SLC

   c. TSM

   d. SLA

6. Inventory and Cisco IOS Software versions are managed as part of which FCAPS function?

   a. Security management

   b. Accounting management

   c. Performance management

   d. Configuration management

7. Which of the following functions can the Cisco NetFlow product perform to provide accounting management?

   a. Baseline a network

   b. Measure utilization

   c. Detect network faults

   d. Define network services

8. What do you place in Cisco IOS Software to provide Layer 3 and Layer 4 service metrics?

   a. SLA

   b. SLM

   c. SAA

   d. SLC

9. What does Cisco provide to monitor the delivery of services against the terms of an SLA?

   a. SLC

   b. SLM

   c. CM

   d. SAA

10. Intrusion detection can be categorized as part of which FCAPS function?

   a. Fault management

   b. Accounting management

   c. Configuration management

   d. Security management

11. True or false? You can use the performance-management function in FCAPS to assess a network and to determine how well it functions under various conditions.

12. True or false? You can use the accounting-management function in FCAPS to monitor logs to assess whether a user has used proper authentication procedures.

PART V: Comprehensive Scenarios

This part covers the following CCDA exam objectives (to view the CCDA exam outline, visit http://www.cisco.com/go/training):

- Identify possible opportunities for network improvement.
- Given a network design or set of requirements, evaluate a solution that meets IP addressing needs.
- Given a network design or a set of requirements, evaluate a solution to incorporate equipment and technology within an Enterprise Edge design.
- Design solutions to meet network-owner needs applying the Enterprise Composite Network Model.
- Evaluate solutions addressing the issues of delivering voice traffic over a data network.

Exam Topics in This Chapter

- Scenario One: Pearland Hospital

- Scenario Two: Big Oil and Gas

- Scenario Three: Super Consulting

- Scenario Four: Sound Masters Inc.

The case studies and questions in this chapter draw on your knowledge of CCDA exam design objectives. Use these exercises to solidify your mastery of the objectives, as listed in the beginning of this chapter, as well as to identify areas you still need to review for the case-study portion of the exam.

Understand that each scenario presented encompasses several objectives. Each scenario, however, does not necessarily encompass all the objectives. Therefore, you should work through all the scenarios in this chapter to account for all the objectives.

CHAPTER 20

Comprehensive Scenarios

Your CCDA exam will probably contain questions that require review of an accompanying case study. This chapter contains four case studies that are similar in style to the ones you might encounter on the CCDA exam. Read through each case study and answer the corresponding questions. You can find the answers to the case-study questions at the end of each scenario. More than one solution can satisfy the customer's requirements. In these cases, answers presented at the end of the chapter represent recommended solutions developed using good design practices. An explanation accompanies the answer where necessary.

Scenario One: Pearland Hospital

Mr. Robertson, the IT director at Pearland Hospital, is responsible for managing the network. Mr. Robertson has requested your help in proposing a network solution that will meet the hospital's requirements. The hospital is growing and the management has released funds for network improvements.

The medical staff has requested the ability to access medical systems using laptops from any of the patient rooms. Doctors and nurses should be able to access patient medical records, x-rays, prescriptions, and recent patient information. Mr. Robertson purchased and placed new servers in the data center. The wireless LAN (WLAN) has approximately 30 laptops, with approximately 15 more due in six months. The servers must have high availability.

Patient rooms are on Floors 6 through 10 of the hospital building; doctors should be able to roam and access the network from any of the floors. A radio-frequency report mentions that a single access point located in each communication closet can reach all the rooms of each floor. The current network has 10 segments that reach a single router that also serves the Internet. The router is running Routing Information Protocol Version 1 (RIPv1). The backend new servers are located in the same segment as those used on Floor 1. Mr. Robertson mentioned that users have complained of slow access to the servers. He also handed you a table (Table 20-1) with current IP addresses.

Table 20-1   *Current IP Addresses*

Floor	Servers	Clients	IP Network
1	15	40	200.100.1.0/24
2	0	43	200.100.2.0/24
3	0	39	200.100.3.0/24
4	0	42	200.100.4.0/24
5	0	17	200.100.5.0/24
6	0	15	200.100.6.0/24
7	0	14	200.100.7.0/24
8	0	20	200.100.8.0/24
9	0	18	200.100.9.0/24
10	0	15	200.100.10.0/24

Mr. Robertson would like a proposal to upgrade the network with fast switches and provide faster access to the servers. The proposal should also cover secure WLAN access in Floors 6 through 10. Include an IP addressing scheme that will reduce the number of Class C networks the hospital uses. Mr. Robertson wants to reduce the number of networks leased from the Internet service provider (ISP).

Scenario One: Questions

The questions that follow refer to Scenario One:

1. What are the business requirements of Pearland Hospital?

2. Are there any business-cost constraints?

3. What are the technical requirements for the network?

4. What are the technical constraints for the network?

5. Prepare a logical diagram of the current network.

Figure 20-1 *Current Hospital Network*

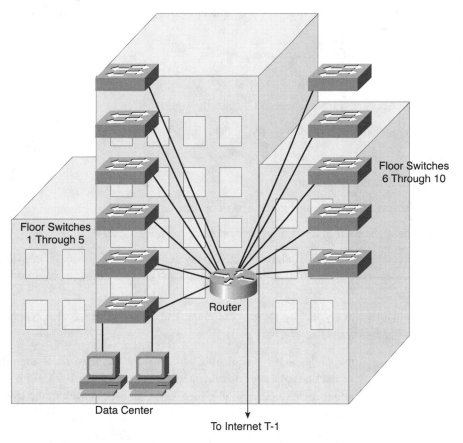

6. Does the hospital use IP addresses effectively?

7. What would you recommend to improve the switching speed between floors?

8. Based on the number of servers and clients provided, what IP addressing scheme would you propose?

9. What routing protocols would you recommend?

10. What solution would you recommend for WLAN access and network upgrade?

11. Draw the proposed network solution.

Answers to Scenario One

1. The hospital needs to provide access to patient records, prescriptions, and information from patient rooms.

2. There were no cost restrictions discussed.

3. The technical requirements are

   — WLAN access from rooms in Floors 6 through 10

   — Redundant access to servers in the data center

   — Fast switching between LAN segments

4. The technical constraints are

   — Servers must be located in the first floor data-center rooms.

5. The logical diagram of the current network appears in Figure 20-1.

6. The hospital does not use IP addresses effectively. It uses Class C networks on each floor. Each floor wastes more than 200 IP addresses because each Class C network provides up to 254 IP addresses.

7. Recommend using a high-speed Layer 3 switch for the building LANs. They can use the router for Internet and WAN access.

8. The primary recommendation is to use private addresses for the network. Using private addresses is a best-practice policy for private internal networks since 1996. With private addresses, the hospital could release eight of the Class C networks back to the ISP, retaining two for ISP connectivity.

   With private addresses, the hospital can choose to use 172.16/16 for private addressing. The addressing scheme in Table 20-2 provides sufficient address space for each network.

Table 20-2 *IP Addressing Scheme Using Private addresses*

Floor	Servers	Clients	IP Network
1	0	40	172.16.1.0/24
1	15		172.16.0.0/24
2	0	43	172.16.2.0/24
3	0	39	172.16.3.0/24
4	0	42	172.16.4.0/24
5	0	17	172.16.5.0/24

Table 20-2 *IP Addressing Scheme Using Private addresses (Continued)*

Floor	Servers	Clients	IP Network
6	0	15	172.16.6.0/24
7	0	14	172.16.7.0/24
8	0	20	172.16.8.0/24
9	0	18	172.16.9.0/24
10	0	15	172.16.10.0/24
WLAN: 6, 7, 8, 9, 10	0	40	172.16.20.0/24

Another solution is to retain the public addresses and use them in their internal network. This solution is less preferred than private addressing. The recommended address scheme that would reduce the number of Class C networks appears in Table 20-3.

Table 20-3 *IP Addressing Scheme Using Public Address Space*

Floor	Servers	Clients	IP Network
1	0	40	200.100.1.0/26
1	15		200.100.1.64/26
2	0	43	200.100.1.128/26
3	0	39	200.100.1.192/26
4	0	42	200.100.2.0/26
5	0	17	200.100.2.64/26
6	0	15	200.100.2.128/26
7	0	14	200.100.2.192/26
8	0	20	200.100.3.0/26
9	0	18	200.100.3.64/26
10	0	15	200.100.3.128/26
WLAN: 6, 7, 8, 9, 10	0	40	200.100.3.192/26

Each subnet has 62 IP addresses for host addressing. Based on the preceding IP address scheme, Pearland Hospital does not need networks 200.100.4.0/24 through 200.100.10.0/24.

9. Recommend routing protocols that support variable-length subnet masks (VLSMs). The network is small. Recommend RIPv2 or Enhanced Interior Gateway Routing Protocol (EIGRP). Do not recommend Open Shortest Path First (OSPF) because of its configuration complexity.

10. Recommend using two access points on each floor for redundancy. Use a VLAN that spans Floors 6 through 10. Change the router to a high-speed Layer 3 switch. Use the router for Internet or WAN access.

11. The diagram appears in Figure 20-2. The router is replaced by the L3 switch to provide high-speed switching between LANs. Each floor has an IP subnet plus a subnet for the WLAN and another for the data center. Each floor has two access points for redundancy. Servers can connect using Fast EtherChannel or Gigabit Ethernet.

Figure 20-2 *Proposed Network Solution*

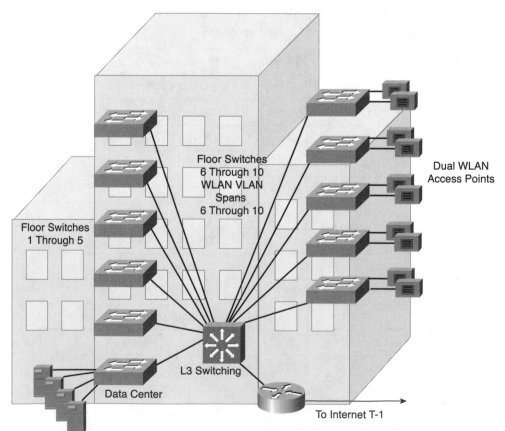

Scenario Two: Big Oil and Gas

Mr. Drew is an IT director at Big Oil and Gas. He is in charge of the network infrastructure, including routers and switches. Mr. Drew's group includes personnel that can install and configure Cisco routers and switches. Big Oil and Gas is a medium-sized petrochemical company based in Houston. It also has operations in the Gulf and in South America.

The Big Oil and Gas CIO wants to begin migrating from the voice network to an IP telephony solution to reduce circuit and management costs. Existing data WAN circuits have 50 percent utilization or less but do spike up to 80 percent when sporadic FTP transfers occur.

Mr. Drew hands you the diagram displayed in Figure 20-3. The exiting data network includes 35 sites with approximately 30 people in each site. The network is hub-and-spoke with approximately 200 people at the headquarters. The WAN links range from 384 Kbps circuits to T1 speeds. Remote-site applications include statistical files and graphical-site diagrams that are transferred using FTP from remote sites to the headquarters.

Figure 20-3 *Big Oil and Gas Current Network*

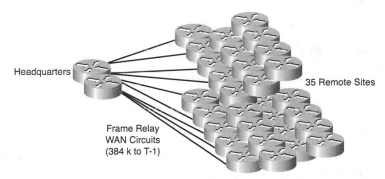

Mr. Drew wants an IP telephony solution that manages the servers at headquarters but still provides redundancy or failover at the remote site. He mentions that he is concerned that the FTP traffic might impact the VoIP traffic. He wants to choose a site to implement a test before implementing IP telephony at all sites.

Scenario Two: Questions

The questions that follow refer to Scenario Two:

1. What are the business requirements of Big Oil and Gas?

2. Are there any business-cost constraints?

3. What are the technical requirements for the network?

4. What are the technical constraints for the network?

5. Approximately how many IP phones should the network support?

6. What type of IP telephony architecture should you propose?

7. What quality-of-service (QoS) features would you propose for the WAN?

8. Would you propose a prototype or a pilot?

9. What solution would you present for voice redundancy at the remote sites?

10. Diagram the proposed solution.

Answers to Scenario Two

1. The company wants to provide voice services in a converged network.

2. Their solution should provide reduced costs over the existing separate voice and data networks.

3. The technical requirements are

   — Provide IP telephony over the data network.

   — Provide voice redundancy or failover for the remote sites.

   — Prevent FTP traffic from impacting the voice traffic.

4. The technical constraints are

   — Call-processing servers need to be located in the headquarters facilities.

5. There are 200 IP phones at headquarters and 35 * 30 = 1050 remote IP phones for a total of 1250 IP phones.

6. Propose the WAN centralized call-processing architecture with a call-manager (CM) cluster at headquarters.

7. Use low-latency queuing (LLQ) on the WAN links to give the highest priority for voice traffic. Then define traffic classes for regular traffic and FTP traffic. Make bandwidth reservations for the voice traffic and maximum bandwidth restrictions for the FTP traffic. Call admission control (CAC) is recommended to limit the number of calls from and to a remote site.

8. To prove that calls can run over the WAN links, implement a pilot site. The pilot would test the functionality of the design over the WAN with or without FTP traffic.

9. Recommend the use of Survivable Remote Site Telephony (SRST) to provide voice services in the event of WAN failure and reroute calls to the Public Switched Telephone Network (PSTN).

10. Figure 20-4 shows a diagram. The diagram shows headquarters and two remote sites for clarity. This architecture is duplicated for all remote sites. Each site uses a voice router that is connected to both the IP WAN and the PSTN. SRST provides voice survivability in the case of WAN failure. A CM cluster is implemented at the headquarters. The CM servers are in the data center in a redundant network.

Figure 20-4 *Headquarters and Two Remote Sites for Clarity*

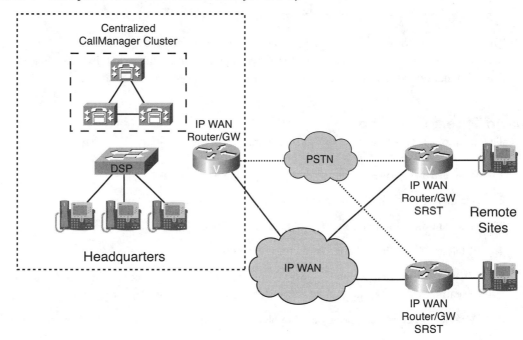

Scenario Three: Super Consulting

Ms. Thompson is the CIO of Super Consulting. Super Consulting is a professional-services company that provides programmers to enterprise clients. The company has a headquarters in Denver and a regional training center in Houston. More than 40 small sales offices are sparsely dispersed throughout the United States and Europe. Field sales representatives, management, and consultants use the network to access back-office applications, e-mail, time and expense systems, and other internal websites.

The sites are connected in a hierarchical mesh using Frame Relay as a WAN technology. They are using EIGRP as a routing protocol. Ms. Thompson mentions that they are looking for ways to reduce local loop and Frame Relay permanent virtual circuit (PVC) WAN costs. She wants a network design that uses a less-cost WAN technology to the remote sales offices. Table 20-4 lists the remote site requirements.

Table 20-4 *Remote Site Requirements*

Number of Sites	Bandwidth Requirements
10	128 Kbps
20	256 Kbps
10	384 Kbps

The Denver and Houston sites would have larger bandwidth speeds to accommodate the remote-site bandwidth. The solution would also need to accommodate home-office and Internet dial-up users. The CIO mentioned that the solution should be verified before implementation.

Scenario Three: Questions

The questions that follow refer to Scenario Three:

1. What are the business requirements of Super Consulting?

2. Are there any business constraints?

3. What are the technical requirements for the network?

4. What are the technical constraints for the network?

5. What remote-access technology would you propose to Ms. Thompson that would enable users to seamlessly access the back-office systems and reduce WAN costs?

6. What local-access technology could you used to reduce access costs at the remote offices?

7. Is the current routing protocol adequate?

8. How should the proposed solution be verified?

9. Diagram the proposed solution.

Answers to Scenario Three

1. The CIO needs to reduce WAN costs.

2. No timelines were specified. The solution should provide a return on investment by reducing recurring WAN costs.

3. The WAN technology should support the bandwidth requirements of 40 remote sites.

4. The solution should support back-office, e-mail, and expense systems. The network hubs are in Denver and Houston.

5. Propose that virtual private network (VPN) technology replace the Frame Relay WAN. Place Cisco VPN concentrators in Denver and Houston and IP Security (IPSec) tunnels through the Internet to connect the remote offices. There are no PVC costs when using VPNs.

6. Where available, recommend the use of business DSL service. DSL would provide local Internet access, which is on average less expensive than other access technologies. DSL providers support the speed requirements of Super Consulting. The remote site would then use a Cisco router to establish the VPN tunnels to the hub sites.

7. The current routing protocol is EIGRP, which supports VLSMs and route summarization and does not send periodic route updates. It is adequate for the current and proposed network.

8. Recommend that a pilot be implemented to verify the solution. A pilot site could ensure that the solution meets the client's requirements and that all applications can run appropriately.

9. As shown in Figure 20-5, the proposed solution uses VPN technology over the Internet to provide WAN connectivity from the hub sites to the remote sites. Redundant tunnels provide redundancy to the hubs. The solution would support home-office users using the Cisco VPN client software.

Figure 20-5 *Super Consulting Proposed Solution*

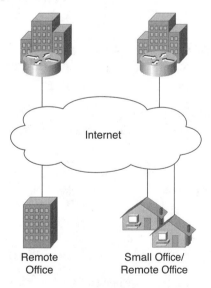

Scenario Four: Sound Masters Inc.

Sound Masters is a retail company that sells car-audio products. The company has expanded from a single store to more than four stores in the regional Miami area. They are now implementing an e-business website to sell products over the Internet. Mr. Bland, the IT manager of Sound Masters, has requested your help in designing a redundant and secure Internet connection.

Currently, they have a single 256 Kbps circuit to ISP1, as shown in Figure 20-6.

Figure 20-6 *Sound Master's Current Network*

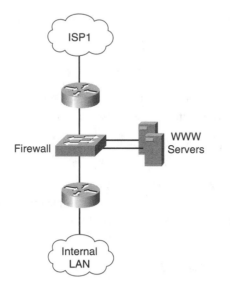

Mr. Bland selected a second ISP and will install a second 256 Kbps circuit in four weeks. You must submit your design in one week to keep the project on track for the website kickoff.

Scenario Four: Questions

The questions that follow refer to Scenario Four:

1. What are the business requirements of Sound Masters?

2. What are the business constraints?

3. What are the technical requirements?

4. Which module of the Enterprise Composite Network model are you designing in this case study?

5. What routing protocol would you use between the Enterprise Edge and SP Edge routers? Would this routing protocol be an interior gateway protocol (IGP) or exterior gateway protocol (EGP)?

6. Diagram a solution if there is only one router in the Enterprise Edge. What are the disadvantages of this solution?

7. Diagram a solution if there are two routers to connect to the ISPs. What are the advantages of this solution?

8. What Cisco solution will meet stateful security requirements of Sound Masters? Diagram the solution.

9. The utilization of the 256 Kbps circuit is averaging more than 85 percent. Should the provisioned bandwidth be increased?

10. If Mr. Bland rejects the use of the PIX Firewall, how can you implement security?

Answers to Scenario Four

1. They want to implement the necessary infrastructure to sell car-audio products over the Internet.

2. The infrastructure needs to be in place before the website kickoff. You must submit the design in a week.

3. Design redundant Internet connections for Sound Masters. Implement security to control access to the business web servers.

4. You are using the Internet connectivity module of the Enterprise Edge. This module contains the Enterprise Edge infrastructure that connects to ISP.

5. Use Border Gateway Protocol (BGP) between the enterprise and SP routers to exchange routes. BGP is an EGP.

6. The solution appears in Figure 20-7. This solution provides for a multihomed solution with two ISPs connected to a single router. There is ISP redundancy with this solution. You can configure exterior BGP (eBGP) to receive routes and let the routing protocol decide which path to take. This is the least-cost solution. The disadvantages of this solution are that there is no router or firewall redundancy. If the enterprise router fails, users lose their connections to the servers.

Figure 20-7 *Single Router Internet Solution*

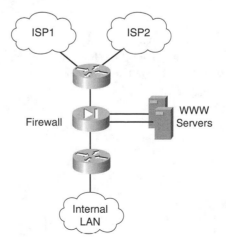

7. A possible solution appears in Figure 20-8. With two routers, each is connected to separate ISPs. The routers use eBGP with the ISPs and interior BGP (iBGP) between the enterprise routers. The advantage of this solution is that it provides for ISP redundancy, circuit redundancy, and router redundancy. There is no firewall redundancy in this solution.

Figure 20-8 *Dual-Router Multihomed Internet Solution*

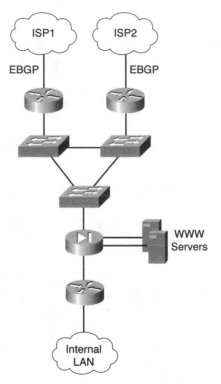

8. Implement a PIX Firewall to provide stateful security to the web servers. The demilitarized zone (DMZ) would be the third leg off the firewall. Figure 20-9 shows the diagram of the network with the DMZ. This design has the advantage of greater device availability, but the disadvantage is greater cost.

Figure 20-9 *Firewall Architecture for Sound Masters*

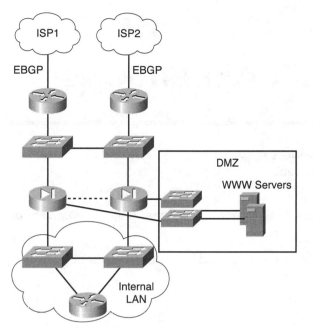

9. Yes. If the utilization of a circuit averages more than 70 percent, it should be increased, even if there will be two circuits. One circuit should be able to handle the utilized bandwidth of both circuits.

10. Use the Cisco IOS Firewall set with access lists in routers or multilayer switches sized to accommodate the additional workload required.

PART VI: Appendixes

Answers to Chapter "Do I Know This Already?" Quizzes and Q&A Sections

Chapter 1

"Do I Know This Already?"

1. **b.** A global network business is a model that leverages the network for competitive advantage by allowing direct access to necessary corporate information by all key constituencies.

2. **d.** Global network businesses are built on customer focus, continuous standardization, and core versus context.

3. **b.** The promise of the global network business model is increased productivity and reduced cost.

4. **a.** The top-down design concept requires the engagement of the top executives during the design process.

5. **c.** Departments using Internet capabilities can be categorized and grouped as either lagging, market parity, leading, or emerging.

6. **a.** Technological, political, social, and economical constraints are limitations in the network-design process.

7. **d.** Processor speed and buffer capacity are among the technical constraints when designing a network.

8. **b.** Partnership agreements are a political constraint when designing a network infrastructure.

9. **a.** Manpower is an economical constraint when designing a network.

10. **a, b, d.** Analyzing network traffic, auditing the network, and simulating network traffic are some of the activities, tools, and techniques used in today's network-design process.

Q&A

1. What is a global network business?

   Answer: A global network business is a model that leverages the network for competitive advantage by opening organizational information to all key constituencies.

2. On what principles are global network businesses built?

   Answer: Global network businesses are built on customer focus, continuous standardization, and core versus context.

3. What does the global network business model achieve?

   Answer: The global networked business model achieves increased productivity and reduced cost.

4. What is critical for the top-down design concept?

   Answer: Engaging the top executives during the design process is critical for top-down design concept.

5. Which levels can you define on how departments are leveraging Internet capabilities?

   Answer: In its Internet capabilities, an organization is either lagging, at market parity, leading, or emerging.

6. What are the four general categories of constraints encountered by a network designer?

   Answer: Technological, political, social, and economical constraints affect network design.

7. What are technological constraints when designing a network infrastructure?

   Answer: Processor speed and buffer capacity are examples of technological constraints.

8. What are social constraints when designing a network infrastructure?

   Answer: Manpower is an example of a social constraint.

9. What are political constraints when designing a network infrastructure?

   Answer: Compulsory use of standards is an example of a political constraint.

10. Define some of the activities supported by the tools used in today's network-design process.

    Answer: In today's network-design process, tools support network audits, traffic analysis, traffic generation, and network simulation.

Chapter 2

"Do I Know This Already?"

1. **c.** Plan, design, implement, operate, and optimize. PDIOO represents the different stages of the network lifecycle.

2. **d.** Network planning begins with understanding abstract requirements for a design, such as the business requirements.

3. False. The top-down process indicates that the network designer will begin with the abstract concepts first before designing the technology to implement.

4. **d.** The CFO typically would read the executive summary to ensure that the project addresses the business needs of the company.

5. **c.** The network diagram appears in the design-solution section of the documentation.

6. **a, c, d.** In total, there are seven steps to prototyping the network.

7. **d.** Hierarchical structured design is used to develop a network design based on layers.

8. **a.** Cisco recommends a Design Requirements section in the network document to discuss performance, scalability, capacity, security, and traffic needs.

9. **d.** Prior to being reviewed by the customer, the prototype is tested during the practice stage of the prototyping process.

10. **a.** Possible problem areas will be determined during the "review requirements" stage of the prototyping process.

Q&A

1. What is the name of the design process that begins with understanding business processes and objectives before creating a network design?

    Answer: The top-down design process.

2. What is the second process in the Cisco network lifecycle?

    Answer: The lifecycle is the PDIOO process, and D stands for design.

3. What is the name of the stage where you perform moves, adds, and changes on the new network?

    Answer: In the PDIOO process, operate follows implementation. Maintenance that you perform on the new network is part of the operate stage of the network lifecycle.

4. After a network is in place, and you need to incorporate new application such as video, what stage of the PDIOO process would this need represent?

   Answer: Optimization.

5. Where would the customer find a description of the network strategy used to address the business issues identified during the design process?

   Answer: The executive summary of a network documentation is where this information appears.

6. A network diagram that uses general icons to represent network functions such as routing and firewalling is called what type of diagram?

   Answer: Logical diagrams.

7. Which step of the network prototype-testing process follows after the develop-and-test-plan step?

   Answer: Step 5 is to purchase and prepare equipment.

8. During which stage of the prototyping process would you order and stage the equipment?

   Answer: Step 5: Purchase and prepare equipment.

9. How many steps are involved in developing a prototype based on Cisco's recommendations?

   Answer: There are seven steps in the prototyping process.

10. What is the first process in the Cisco network lifecycle?

    Answer: The Cisco design lifecycle is PDIOO, and P stands for plan.

11. During which stage of the network prototype-testing phase do you need the proof to demonstrate that your design works?

    Answer: There are seven steps in the prototyping process. The proof required to demonstrate that your design will work happens during the review-the-requirements step.

12. Which tool available to network designers is often described as "one diagram to view the entire network?"

    Answer: The best tool available to network designers is a topology map.

13. For what purposes do you use a network analyzer during the network-design process?

    Answer: You use a network analyzer to simulate traffic and to prove the effectiveness of the network design.

14. Which part of the network document contains the proposed network diagram?

    Answer: The proposed network diagram appears in the design-solution part of the network document.

15. What is the importance of a design assessment during the planning phase for making changes to an existing network?

    Answer: You use a design assessment to understand the state of the existing network. It also provides insight into how the network and the user community operate together.

16. Which part of the network document do you use to summarize the solution and relate specific design details to the project requirements and goals?

    Answer: You include these things in the summary and appendixes part of the network document.

Chapter 3

"Do I Know This Already?"

1. **b.** The core layer of the hierarchical model is responsible for fast transport.

2. **c.** The Enterprise Edge consists of E-commerce, Internet Connectivity, VPN/Remote Access, and WAN modules. The Enterprise Edge modules connect to SPs.

3. **c.** The distribution layer of the hierarchical model is responsible for security filtering, address and area aggregation, and media translation.

4. **d.** The HSRP provides default gateway redundancy. Hosts participating in the RIP can find alternative gateways.

5. **f.** The network-management module monitors all components and functions except the SP Edge.

6. **a.** The SP Edge includes Internet, PSTN, and WAN modules.

7. **c.** The Server Farm hosts campus servers including Cisco Call Manager servers.

8. **d.** The access layer functions are high availability, port security, rate limiting, ARP inspection, virtual access lists, and trust classification.

Q&A

1. True or false? The core layer of the hierarchical model does security filtering and media translation.

   Answer: False.

2. True or false? The access layer provides high availability and port security.

   Answer: True.

3. You add a CM to the network as part of a Voice over IP (VoIP) solution. In which Enterprise Composite Network model module should you place the CM?

   Answer: Server farm.

4. True or false? HSRP provides router redundancy.

   Answer: True.

5. What is the Enterprise Edge module that connects to an ISP?

   Answer: The Internet module.

6. True or false? In the Enterprise Composite Network model, the network-management module does not manage the SP Edge.

   Answer: True.

7. True or false? You can implement a full-mesh network to increase redundancy and reduce the costs of a WAN.

   Answer: False. A full-mesh network will increase costs.

8. How many links are required for a full mesh of six sites?

   Answer: Use $n(n - 1)/2$. n=6: $6(6 - 1)/2 = 30/2 = 15$.

9. List and describe four options for multihoming to the SP between the Enterprise Edge and the SP Edge. Which option provides the most redundancy?

   Answers: Option 1: Single router, dual links to one ISP

   Option 2: Single router, dual links to two ISPs

Option 3: Dual routers, dual links to one ISP

Option 4: Dual router, dual links to two ISPs

Option 4 provides the most redundancy with dual local routers, dual links, and dual ISPs.

10. To what Enterprise Edge module does the SP Edge Internet module connects.

    Answer: The SP Edge Internet module connects to the Enterprise Edge Internet module.

11. What are four benefits of hierarchical network design?

    Answer: Cost savings, ease of understanding, easy network growth (scalability), and improved fault isolation.

12. In an IP telephony network, in which module or layer are the IP phones and CMs located?

    Answer: IP phones reside in the building-access layer of the campus infrastructure. The CMs are placed in the server farm of the Enterprise Campus.

13. Match the redundant model with its description.

i.	Workstation-router redundancy	**a.** Cheap when implemented in the LAN but critical for the WAN.
ii.	Server redundancy	**b.** Provides load balancing.
iii.	Route redundancy	**c.** Host has multiple gateways.
iv.	Media redundancy	**d.** Data is replicated.

    Answer: i = c , ii = d, iii = b, iv = a

14. True or false? Small to medium campus networks must always implement three layers of hierarchical design.

    Answer: False. Small campus networks can have collapsed core and distribution layers and implement a two-layer design. Medium campus networks can have two-tier or three-tier designs.

15. How many full-mesh links do you need for a network with 10 routers?

    Answer: Use the formula $n(n-1)/2$. n=10: $10(10-1)/2 = 90/2 = 45$ links.

Figure 3-16 *Scenario*

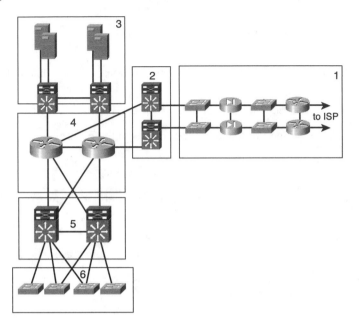

Use Figure 3-16 to answer the following questions:

16. From the diagram in Figure 3-16, which is the enterprise core layer?

    Answer: Block 4.

17. From the diagram in Figure 3-16, which is the Enterprise Edge?

    Answer: Block 1.

18. From the diagram in Figure 3-16, which is the enterprise access layer?

    Answer: Block 6.

19. From the diagram in Figure 3-16, which is the Enterprise Edge distribution?

    Answer: Block 2.

20. From the diagram in Figure 3-16, which is the enterprise infrastructure distribution layer?

    Answer: Block 5.

21.   From the diagram in Figure 3-16, which is the campus data center?

Answer: Block 3.

22.   From the diagram in Figure 3-16, which block does not belong to the enterprise campus of the Enterprise Composite Network model?

Answer: Block 1.

Chapter 4

"Do I Know This Already?"

1.   **f.** The router and Layer 3 switch are Layer 3 devices that control and filter network broadcasts.

2.   **c.** The maximum distance of 100BASE-T is 100 meters.

3.   **g.** Every port of a Layer 2 switch, Layer 3 switch, or LAN port on a router is a collision domain.

4.   **b.** The SSID identifies the network name of wireless LANs.

5.   **b.** Layer 3 switches are recommended for the backbone of campus networks.

6.   **b.** The CGMP controls multicast traffic at Layer 2.

7.   **c.** Marking is also known as coloring. Marking sets class-of-service (CoS) bits at Layer 2 or type-of-service (ToS) bits at Layer 3.

8.   **b.** Each port on a switch is a separate collision or bandwidth domain. All ports on a hub share the same bandwidth domain.

Q&A

1.   True or false? Layer 2 switches control network broadcasts.

Answer: False. Layer 2 switches only limit the collision domain.

2.   What is equivalent to the WLAN network name?

Answer: SSID.

3.   What technology can you use to limit multicasts at Layer 2?

Answer: CGMP.

4.   True or false? Packet marking is also known as coloring.

Answer: True.

5. True or false? The IEEE 802.11a wireless technology is backward-compatible with IEEE 802.11b.

Answer: False. IEEE 802.11g is backward compatible with IEEE 802.11b.

6. What does IEEE 802.1x provide?

Answer: The IEEE 802.1x standard provides port-based authentication for LANs.

7. What IOS feature can you use to provide server redundancy?

Answer: SLB.

8. What are two methods to mark frames to provide CoS?

Answers: - Inter-Switch Link (ISL)

       - IEEE 802.1p/802.1Q

9. Match the LAN media with its original physical specification.

i.	Fast Ethernet	**a.**	IEEE 802.3ab
ii.	Gigabit Ethernet	**b.**	IEEE 802.11b
iii.	WLANs	**c.**	IEEE 802.3u
iv.	Token Ring	**d.**	IEEE 802.5

Answer: i = c, ii = a, iii = b, iv = d.

10. Fill the blank: The _____ interoperability certification exists for IEEE 802.11b WLANs. The certification is governed by _____.

Answer: Wi-Fi, WECA.

11. Match the WLAN mode with its common description:

i.	BSS	**a.**	a. Ad-hoc mode
ii.	IBSS	**b.**	b. Infrastructure mode
iii.	ESS	**c.**	c. Set of BSS

Answer: i = b, ii = a, iii = c.

12. True or false? Layer 3 switches bound Layer 2 collision and broadcast domains.

Answer: True. Layer 3 switches and routers control both the collision and broadcast domains.

13. Match the Enterprise Campus component with its description:

i. Campus infrastructure

ii. Server farm

iii. Edge distribution

a. Consists of backbone, building-distribution, and building-access modules

b. Connects the campus backbone to the Enterprise Edge

c. Provides redundancy access to the servers

Answer: i = a, ii = c, iii = b.

14. Match each LAN device type with the description that best describes it:

i. Hubs

ii. Bridges

iii. Switches

iv. L3 switches

v. Routers

a. Legacy devices that connect 2 data link layer segments

b. Network layer devices that forward packets to serial interfaces connected to the WAN

c. High-speed devices that forward frames between two or more data link layer segments

d. High-speed devices that bound data link layer broadcast domains

e. Devices that amplify the signal between connected segments

Answer: i = e, ii = a, iii = c, iv = d, v = b.

15. True or false? IP phones and LAN switches can reassign the CoS bits of a frame.

Answer: True. IP phones reclassify incoming frames from the PC. Switches can accept or reclassify incoming frames.

16. Name two ways to reduce multicast traffic in the access layer.

Answer: CGMP and IGMP snooping control multicast traffic at Layer 2. The switch and local router exchange CGMP messages. With IGMP snooping, the switch listens to IGMP messages between the host and the router.

17. What are two VLAN methods that you can use to carry marking CoS on frames?

Answer: ISL and IEEE 802.1p/Q are two methods for CoS. ISL was created by Cisco and uses an external tag that contains three bits for marking. IEEE 802.1p specifies three bits for marking that is carried in the internal tag of IEEE 802.1q.

18. True or false? You can configure CGMP c in mixed Cisco switch and non-Cisco router environments.

    Answer: False. You can only configure the CGMP if both the router and the switch are Cisco devices.

19. What security enhancement does the LEAP protocol provide that was missing in WEP?

    Answer: LEAP enables more robust authentication using a authentication server to improve security.

20. Why does the SAFE WLAN architecture pose a potential support problem for a large client deployment base?

    Answer: Using IPSec requires installing a client on every device that wants to connect via the WLAN. It is potentially resource-intensive to support and update the clients on individual devices.

21. What method would you use to manage the issue of LEAP's inability to support OTP?

    Answer: Even though LEAP does not support OTP, using good password-security practices and limiting the number of attempts provides adequate protection.

Use Figure 4-18 to answer the following questions.

Figure 4-18 *Enterprise Campus Diagram*

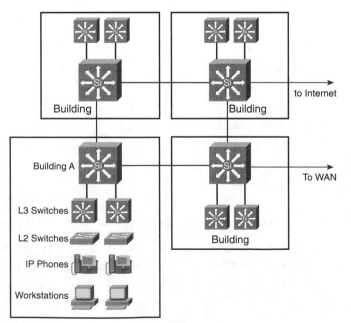

22. What media would you recommend for the campus LAN backbone?

Answer: The campus backbone should have high-speed links. Recommend Gigabit Ethernet links.

23. The workstations send out frames with the CoS set to 5. What should the IP phones do so that the network gives preference to VoIP traffic over data traffic?

Answer: The IP phones should remap the workstation traffic to a value less than the value assigned to voice. Typically, it is recommended that you configure the IP phone to set the CoS to 5 for VoIP traffic.

24. If the Layer 2 switches in Building A do not have the ability to look at CoS and ToS fields, where should these fields be inspected for acceptance or reclassification: in the building L3 switches or in the backbone L3 switches?

Answer: Inspect them at the Layer 3 switches in Building A. Packets should be marked and accepted as close as possible to the source.

25. Does the network have redundant access to the WAN?

Answer: No. There is no redundancy to the WAN module. A separate link to another building would provide that redundancy.

26. Does the network have redundant access to the Internet?

Answer: No. There is no redundancy to the Internet module. A separate link from another building would provide that redundancy.

27. Does the diagram follow recommended devices for networks designed using the Enterprise Composite Network model?

Answer: Yes. The network uses Layer 2 switches at the building-access layer and Layer 3 switches in the building-distribution and campus-backbone layers.

Chapter 5

"Do I Know This Already?"

1. **b.** ISDN and asynchronous serial WAN connections are examples of circuit-switched WAN connections. Legacy voice calls over the Public Switched Telephone Network (PSTN) are circuit-switched as well.

2. **d.** ADSL is a viable home-office solution for wide-area networking. Speeds typically vary upstream from downstream.

3. **d.** LRE allows LAN transmissions to coexist with plain old telephone service (POTS), ISDN, or Private Branch Exchange (PBX) signaling over the same copper.

4. **a.** Frame Relay is similar to X.25, yet it features more throughput thanks to less overhead.

5. **c.** WAN technologies typically function at the lower three layers of the OSI model.

6. **c.** The purpose of the Enterprise Edge is to aggregate connectivity from the edge of the Enterprise Campus.

7. **d.** ATM converts data to cells of a fixed length for transmission over the physical medium.

8. **d.** ISDN is available in almost all areas of the United States and provides a higher-seed and lower-cost connectivity option.

9. **c.** Examples of packet-switched technologies include Frame Relay and SMDS.

10. **c.** p2p links can originate from p2mp hubs and feature maximum speeds of 44 Mbps.

Q&A

1. For each of the following WAN technologies, indicate whether the appropriate category is leased line, circuit-switched, packet-switched, or cell-switched:

    a. ISDN

    b. Frame Relay

    c. ATM

    d. Synchronous serial

    e. X.25

    f. Dial-up

    g. SMDS

    Answer: a. circuit-switched; **b.** packet-switched; **c.** cell-switched; **d.** leased line; **e.** packet-switched; **f.** circuit-switched; **g.** packet-switched.

2. In what part of the Enterprise Composite Network model do WAN technologies best fit?

    _____

    Answer: They operate between the Enterprise Edge and the SP Edge.

3. Match the following WAN technologies with their definitions:

    a. Wireless   i. High bandwidth over telephone local-loop copper lines

    b. LRE   ii. Usually over a hybrid of coaxial and fiber optics

    c. DSL   iii. Electromagnetic waves as opposed to wire or glass fiber

    d. Cable   iv. Utilizes coding and digital modulation techniques from DSL

Answer: a = iii; b = iv; c = i; d = ii.

4. You are designing a WAN solution for a customer that is setting up a small satellite office in New York. The customer needs medium- to high-bandwidth access at this location for downloading constant data streams from the headquarters in Los Angeles. The satellite office also needs to upload large amounts of data frequently to headquarters. The client is interested in a mature and time-tested WAN technology. Which WAN technology should you recommend? Why?

Answer: Frame Relay. Frame Relay offers medium to high bandwidth in both directions and is readily available in almost all areas of the country. Frame Relay is also a mature technology.

5. Describe an ATM cell and explain why cells are well suited for the transmission of voice and video traffic.

Answer: ATM cells consist of 53 octets, or bytes. The first 5 bytes contain cell-header information, and the remaining 48 contain the payload (user information). Small, fixed-length cells are well suited to transferring voice and video traffic because such traffic is intolerant of delays that result from waiting in the interface output queue while a large data packet is transferred.

6. Describe the ISDN options of BRI and PRI, focusing on available bandwidth for each technology.

Answer: ISDN BRI offers two bearer (B) channels and a delta (D) channel. BRI B channels transmit data and operate at 64 Kbps. The BRI D channel handles signaling and operates at 16 Kbps. BRI also provides for framing control and other overhead, thus bringing the total bit rate to 192 Kbps. In North America and Japan, PRI ISDN over T1 media provides 23 B channels and 1 D channel. Unlike BRI, the D channel in PRI operates at 64 Kbps as well, bringing the total bit rate to 1.544 Mbps. In Europe, Australia, and other parts of the world, PRI is provisioned over E1 media and features 30 B channels and one 64 Kbps D channel for a total bit rate of 2.048 Mbps.

7. What is the purpose of FECN and BECN within Frame Relay technology?

   Answer: Frame Relay reduces network overhead by implementing simple congestion-notification mechanisms rather than explicit, per-virtual-circuit flow control. The congestion-notification mechanisms are called FECNs and BECNs, or forward explicit congestion notifications and backward explicit congestion notifications.

8. What is the most common type of virtual circuit used with Frame Relay? With X.25?

   Answer: Frame Relay – PVC; X.25 - SVC.

9. What is the basic Layer 2 technology behind MPLS encapsulation?

   Answer: MPLS functions by "tagging" or "labeling" packets as they arrive at the service provider network. Core routers then forward the traffic appropriately using QoS, traffic engineering, or security mechanisms as required by the traffic.

10. What is the purpose of the ELSR in MPLS technology?

    Answer: Edge Label Switch Routers are located at the ingress point of service provider networks and are responsible for applying (removing) label information from incoming (outgoing) packets.

Chapter 6

"Do I Know This Already?"

1. **b.** Cisco recommends that designers engage in the analysis of customer requirements, the characterization of the existing network, and the design of the new WAN topology.

2. **f.** The most popular DSL option, ADSL, is asymmetric. It allows more bandwidth downstream—from a Network Service Provider's (NSP's) central office to the customer site—than upstream from the subscriber to the central office.

3. **c.** Jitter is a measure of the deviation in delay experienced in a network. Designers often scrutinize this measurement in voice and video networks because they tend to be intolerant of jitter when this value is excessive.

4. **c.** Cisco recommends that designers avoid compression usage if network-equipment CPU utilization levels are at 65 percent or greater.

5. **c.** Larger window sizes allow network equipment to send more data prior to receiving an acknowledgement from the destination system. This has the potential to improve the performance of WAN connections.

6.   **a.** Van Jacobson TCP/IP header compression reduces the size of the TCP/IP headers to as few as three bytes.

7.   **c.** Designers do not require queuing services within WAN designs if links are never congested. If WAN links consistently demonstrate congestion, queuing is not the answer; an upgrade is more appropriate.

8.   **b.** PQ allows designers to give higher priority to certain types of time-sensitive or mission-critical protocols. PQ establishes four interface output queues. The designer assigns each queue a priority and defines traffic types for each queue. PQ then services all traffic in higher-priority queues prior to servicing the lower-priority queues.

9.   **d.** CQ establishes up to 16 interface output queues. CQ cycles through each queue to send some data, sending the amount from each queue specified by the designer.

10. **a.** Traffic shaping delays excess packets by holding them in buffers and then releasing them at preconfigured rates.

Q&A

1.   Describe the Cisco recommended process for designing a WAN solution.

     Answer: Cisco recommends that designers engage in the analysis of customer requirements, the characterization of the existing network, and the design of the new WAN topology as a simple process for designing WAN solutions.

2.   Name three common design factors for creating WAN solutions.

     Answer: Cisco identifies the following design factors: application access, technology, and cost.

3.   Describe the options for WAN media and equipment ownership.

     Answer: WAN ownership falls into three broad categories, private, leased, and shared. With privately owned WAN designs, organizations must purchase all of the physical layer media (copper, fiber, wireless, coaxial) and the terminal equipment that connects it. Leased WAN arrangements involve dedicated bandwidth leased to the organization by a service provider. With shared WAN access, many companies share the bandwidth that the provider has available.

4. Match each of the following queuing options with the appropriate definition:

a. WFQ

b. PQ

c. CQ

i. A queuing method that establishes four interface output queues and allows the designer to assign each queue a priority.

ii. A queuing methodology that prohibits high-volume senders from "crowding out" low-volume senders.

iii. A queuing method that establishes up to 16 interface output queues; CQ cycles through each queue to send data.

Answer: a = ii; b = i; c = iii.

5. Match each of the following compression technologies with the appropriate definition:

a. LZS

b. Predictor

c. Van Jacobson header compression

d. MPPC

e. FRF.9

i. TCP/IP compression that reduces the size of the TCP/IP headers to as few as three bytes.

ii. A scheme used to compress PPP packets between Cisco and Microsoft client devices.

iii. Defines data compression over Frame Relay using the DCP.

iv. A compression algorithm that tries to guess the next sequence of characters in a data stream by using an index to look up a sequence in the compression dictionary.

v. Compression standard for WAN connections also known as STAC.

Answer: a = v; b = iv; c = i; d = ii; e = iii.

6. Of the ownership options for WAN media and equipment, which option provides companies with the highest level of control and predictability?

Answer: Private ownership.

7. Match the WAN access technology option with the appropriate available bandwidth value:

a. Analog modem

b. DSL

c. Cable

d. Frame Relay

i. Less than 2 Mbps

ii. 48 Kbps

iii. 8 Mbps downstream

iv. 27 Mbps downstream; 2.5 Mbps upstream

Answer: a = ii; b = iii; c = iv; d = i.

Chapter 7

"Do I Know This Already?"

1. **b.** A floating static route is a static route with an artificially high administrative distance value. This value ensures that dynamically learned routers are preferable.

2. **c.** With a shadow PVC, a service provider provisions the network with a secondary PVC. Typically, there is no charge for this additional PVC as long as the load on it remains below a defined level. For example, a plan might specify the shadow PVC at no additional charge if load does not exceed one-fourth of the load on the primary PVC—provided, of course, the primary link is available.

3. **c.** Three valid mechanisms for using the Internet as a WAN backup medium include GRE tunnels, IPSec tunnels, and IP routing without constraints.

4. **b.** IPSec enhances the security of the Internet tunnel by providing authentication and antireplay attacks.

5. **d.** A star topology specifies a core router that serves as the hub for the WAN connections. This design can reduce costs and features the simplest configuration and management.

6. **a.** The partial-mesh topology approach features virtual circuits that connect many but not all the routers in the topology. This design reduces the number of routers in the topology that require direct connections to each other.

7. **b.** Advantages of the full-mesh topology include the best possible redundancy and the best possible performance when configured correctly.

8. **a.** The partial-mesh design does have disadvantages. One is that it requires a high level of expertise to implement.

9. **c.** This disadvantage pertains to the star topology.

10. **a.** The star topology features simplified and centralized management of the WAN topology.

Q&A

1. Explain the advantages of IPSec tunneling over GRE tunnels for a backup Internet WAN solution.

    Answer: IPSec features data confidentiality, data integrity, data origin authentication, and antireplay attacks. IPSec utilizes IKE for the automation of security key management and interoperates with the public-key infrastructure (PKI).

2. Match each WAN backup solution with its definition or attribute:

   a. Dial backup

   b. Shadow PVC

   c. Internet

   d. Permanent secondary link

   i. Floating static routes and routing protocols ensure the link is actually a valid path though the network in the event of a failure.

   ii. Options include full IP routing or tunneling solutions.

   iii. The network dynamically engages circuit-switched backups for primary link failures.

   iv. A service provider provisions a backup link.

   Answer: a = iii, b = iv, c = ii, d = i.

3. List the advantages of a packet-switched star topology.

   Answer: The advantages are the simplified and centralized management of the WAN topology.

4. List the advantages of a packet-switched partial-mesh topology.

   Answer: The advantages are improved performance, improved redundancy, and fewer virtual circuits than full-mesh designs.

5. List the advantages of a packet-switched full-mesh topology.

   Answer: The advantages are the best possible redundancy and the best possible performance when configured properly.

   Refer to Figure 7-5 to answer the questions that follow.

Figure 7-5 *Sample WAN Design*

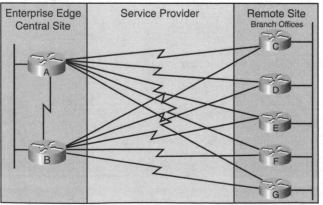

Note: All Connections WAN

   6.   What is the packet-switched WAN topology used in this enterprise network?

         Answer: Full mesh is the packet-switched WAN topology used.

   7.   What are the disadvantages of this packet-switched topology?

         Answer: The disadvantages are large costs, large numbers of packet and broadcast replication, and complex configurations.

Chapter 8

"Do I Know This Already?"

   1.   **c.** The correct spelling of ADSL is Asymmetric Digital Subscriber Line.

   2.   **b.** IPSec uses AH and ESP to provide secure IP communications.

   3.   **d.** Triple DES uses a 3 x 56 = 168-bit key.

   4.   **b.** MPLS is Multiprotocol Label Switching. MPLS can provide VPN service.

   5.   **a.** In ESP transport mode, only the IP data is encrypted. The IP header is not protected in ESP transport mode. ESP tunnel mode encrypts both the IP header and data.

   6.   **b.** ESP and AH use HMAC-MD5 and HMAC-SHA-1 for authentication. They use DES and 3DES for data encryption.

   7.   **c.** SDSL provides symmetric downlink and uplink speeds. It is marketed as business DSL.

   8.   **b.** ADSL provides greater downlink than uplink speeds.

Q&A

   1.   True or false? ADSL provides greater upload than download speeds.

         Answer: False. ADSL provides greater download than upload speeds.

   2.   True or false? IPSec uses AH and ESP to provide secure IP communications.

         Answer: True. Both the Authentication Header (AH) and Encapsulating Security Payload (ESP) protocols are used by IPSec.

   3.   True or false? Triple DES (3DES) uses a 192-bit key.

         Answer: False. 3DES uses a 168-bit key.

4. True or false? Data is encrypted in both ESP transport and tunnel mode.

    Answer: True. In ESP transport mode, data is encrypted for both ESP Tunnel and Transport mode. The IP header is encrypted on ESP Tunnel mode. The IP header is not encrypted in Transport mode.

5. True or false? ADSL is the preferred DSL technology for enterprise sites.

    Answer: False. SDSL is preferred for enterprise sites.

6. True or false? VDSL provides asymmetric DSL services up to 52 Mbps for the downlink.

    Answer: True. VDSL uses a single pair to provide up to 52 Mbps downlink speeds and up to 16 Mbps uplink speeds.

7. True or false? GRE supports tunneling IPX and AppleTalk.

    Answer: True. GRE can tunnel IPX and AppleTalk in addition to IP.

8. True or false? MPLS can provide VPNs with different CoS guarantees.

    Answer: True. MPLS provides VPNs with class of service.

9. Which DSL type do ISDN wired sites use?

    a. IDSL

    b. ADSL

    c. SDSL

    d. VDSL

    Answer: a. IDSL provides DSL service to a location using existing ISDN facilities.

10. Which protocols do Microsoft operating systems use for secure tunneling during the transfer of data between cooperating systems?

    a. GRE and IPSec

    b. VPDN and MPLS

    c. PPTP and MPPE

    d. GRE and MPLS

    Answer: c. MPPE and PPTP are protocols Microsoft operating systems use for the secure transfer of data from clients to servers.

11. True or false? AH does not provide data confidentiality.

    Answer: True. AH does not encrypt the payload data. ESP does encrypt the data, providing confidentiality.

12. What protocol do you use so that you do not have to manually configure IPSec associations?

    Answer: You use the IKE protocol to automatically obtain shared keys between IPSec peers.

13. True or false? VDSL provides symmetric service.

    Answer: False. VDSL provides asymmetric DSL service with speeds up to 52 Mbps.

14. Match the DSL types with the descriptions:

i.	ADSL	**a.** Provides symmetric 144 kbps speed
ii.	IDSL	**b.** Provides up to 1.544 Mbps symmetrical speeds over four wires
iii.	SDSL	**c.** Provides asymmetric speeds up to 8 Mbps
iv.	HDSL	**d.** Provides asymmetric service up to 52 Mbps for the downlink
v.	VDSL	**e.** Provides symmetric service up to 2.3 Mbps

    Answer: i = c , ii = a, iii = e, iv = b, v = d.

15. Match the algorithm with the description:

i.	DES	**a.** Uses 128-bit secret key for authentication
ii.	3DES	**b.** Uses 168-bit secret key for encryption
iii.	HMAC-MD5	**c.** Uses 160-bit secret key for authentication
iv.	HMAC-SHA-1	**d.** Uses 56-bit secret key for data encryption

    Answer: i = d, ii = b, iii = a, iv = c.

16. True or false? In MPLS VPN networks, each router is a peer.

    Answer: True.

17. Which algorithm does IKE Phase 1 use to obtain shared secret keys used by encryption algorithms?

    Answer: IKE Phase 1 uses the Diffie-Hellman key exchange to enable the creation of secure secret keys used by IPSec encryption algorithms.

18. True or false? All routers in a MPLS VPN are peers.

    Answer: True. One characteristic of MPLS VPNs is that each device in the VPN service is a peer.

19. Match the MPLS VPN router types with the descriptions:

    i.   P router   **a.** Provider internal router

    ii. PE router   **b.** Maintains VPN routes

    iii. C router   **c.** Customer internal router

    iv. CE router   **d.** Customer edge router

    Answer: i = b, ii = c, iii = a, iv = d.

20. Match the VPN technology with the description:

    i.   GRE   **a.** Consists of AH and ESP.

    ii. PPTP   **b.** Provides VPNs with guarantees of service.

    iii. VPDN   **c.** Cisco tunneling protocol developed to support tunneled remote access.

    iv. IPSec   **d.** Cisco tunneling protocol. Can tunnel IP, IPX, and AppleTalk.

    v.   MPLS   **e.** Tunneling protocol used by Microsoft operating systems.

    Answer: i = d, ii = e, iii = c, iv = a, v = b.

Chapter 9

"Do I Know This Already?"

1. **b.** IPv4 private addresses are contained within 10.0.0.0/8, 172.16.0.0/12, and 192.168.0.0/16.

2. **b.** There are five hosts bits: $2^5 - 2 = 30$ hosts.

3. **d.** Loopback addresses should have a /32 mask so that address space is not wasted.

4. **c.** The precedence bits are located in the type-of-service field of the IPv4 header.

5. **b.** Multicast addresses range from 224.0.0.1 to 239.255.255.255.

6. **b.** The ARP maps IPv4 addresses to Layer 2 MAC addresses.

7. **d.** Point-to-points links only need two host addresses; use a /30 mask, which provides $2^2 - 2 = 2$ host addresses.

8. **c.** DHCP assigns IP addresses dynamically.

9. **b.** NAT translates between IPv4 private addresses and public addresses.

10.   **c.** The DNS maps FQDNs to IP addresses.

Q&A

1.   List the RFC 1918 private address space.

Answer: 10/8, 172.16/12, and 192.168/16

2.   What is the difference between VLSM and CIDR?

Answer: You use VLSMs to subdivide a network into subnets of various sizes, whereas CIDR permits the aggregation of classful networks.

3.   Fill the blank. _____ maps FQDN to IP addresses.

Answer: DNS

4.   True or false? You can use DHCP to specify the TFTP host's IP address to a client PC.

Answer: True. You can use DHCP to specify several host IP configuration parameters, including IP address, mask, default gateway, DNS servers, and TFTP server.

5.   True or false? The following are two representations of the same IP mask: 255.255.255.248 and /28.

Answer: False. The bit-number representation of 255.255.255.248 is /29. /28 is the same mask as 255.255.255.240.

6.   True or false? Upper-layer protocols are identified in the protocol field of the IP header. TCP is protocol 6 and UDP is protocol 17.

Answer: True.

7.   Fill the blank. Without any options, the IP header is _____ bytes in length.

Answer: 20 bytes.

8.   The ToS field of the IP header is redefined as the DS field. How many bits does DSCP use for packet classification, and how many levels of classification are possible?

Answer: DSCP uses 6 bits, which provides 64 levels of classification.

9.   True or false? NAT uses different IP addresses for translations. PAT uses different port numbers to identify translations.

Answer: True.

10. True or false? The header checksum field of the IP header performs the checksum of the IP header and data.

    Answer: False. The header checksum field only includes a checksum of the IP header; it does not check the data portion.

11. Calculate the subnet, the address range within the subnet, and the subnet broadcast of the following address:

    172.56.5.245/22

    Answer: The subnet is 172.56.4.0/22, the address range is from 172.56.4.1 to 172.56.7.254, and the subnet broadcast is 172.56.7.255.

12. When packets are fragmented at the network layer, where are the fragments reassembled?

    Answer: The IP layer in the destination host.

13. Which protocol can you use to configure a default gateway?

    a. ARP

    b. DHCP

    c. DNS

    d. RARP

    Answer: b. DHCP configures IP address, subnet mask, default gateway, and other optional parameters.

14. How many host addresses are available with a Class B network with the default mask?

    a. 63,998

    b. 64,000

    c. 65,534

    d. 65,536

    Answer: c. Class B networks have 16 bits for hosts addresses with the default mask: $2^{16} - 2 = 65,534$.

15. Which of the following is a dotted-decimal representation of a /26 prefix mask?

    a. 255.255.255.128

    b. 255.255.255.192

    c. 255.255.255.224

    d. 255.255.255.252

    Answer: b. A /26 mask has 26 network bits and 6 host bits.

16. Which is the network specification that summarizes both the 192.170.20.16/30 and the 192.170.20.20/30 networks?

    a. 192.170.20.0/24

    b. 192.170.20.20/28

    c. 192.170.20.16/29

    d. 192.170.20.0/30

    Answer: c. Network 192.170.20.16 with a prefix of /29 summarizes addresses from 192.170.20.16 to 192.170.20.23.

17. How many bits are used for IP precedence in the IP header?

    a. 1

    b. 2

    c. 3

    d. 4

    Answer: c. The ToS field contains 3 bits for IP precedence.

18. What is true about fragmentation?

    a. Routers between source and destination hosts can fragment IPv4 packets.

    b. Only the first router in the network can fragment IPv4 packets.

    c. IPv4 packets cannot be fragmented.

    d. IPv4 packets are fragmented and reassembled at each link through the network.

    Answer: a. IPv4 packets can be fragmented by the sending host and routers.

19. A packet sent to a multicast address reaches what destinations?

    a. The nearest destination in a set of hosts.

    b. All destinations in a set of hosts.

    c. Broadcasts to all hosts.

    d. Reserved global destinations.

    Answer: b. Multicast. Multicast addresses are received to a set of hosts subscribed to the multicast group.

20. What are three types of IPv4 addresses?

    Answer: Unicast, multicast, and broadcast.

Answer the following questions based on the given scenario and figure.

Company VWX has a network as shown in Figure 9-8. The main site has three LANs with 100, 29, and 60 hosts. The remote site has two LANs each with 100 hosts. The network uses private addresses. The Internet provider assigned the company the network 210.200.200.8/26.

Figure 9-8 *Scenario Diagram*

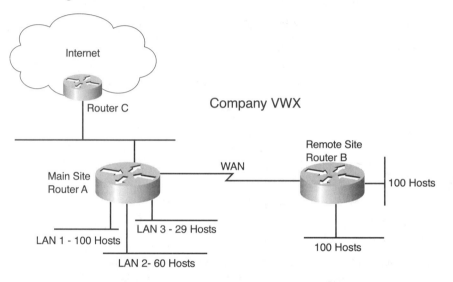

21.   The remote site uses the network prefix 192.168.10.0/24. What subnets and masks can you use for the LANs at the remote site and conserve address space?

   a.   192.168.10.64/26 and 192.168.10.192/26

   b.   192.168.10.0/25 and 192.168.10.128/25

   c.   192.168.10.32/28 and 192.168.10.64/28

   d.   192.168.10.0/30 and 192.168.10.128/30

   Answer: b. The networks in Answer b provide 126 addresses for hosts in each LAN at Site B.

22.   The main site uses the network prefix 192.168.15.0/24. What subnets and masks can you use to provide sufficient addresses for LANs at the main site and conserve address space?

   a.   192.168.15.0/25 for LAN1, 192.168.15.128/26 for LAN2, and 172.16.192.0/27 for LAN3

   b.   192.168.15.0/27 for LAN1, 192.168.15.128/26 for LAN2, and 172.16.192.0/25 for LAN3

   c.   192.168.15.0/100 for LAN1, 192.168.15.128/60 for LAN2, and 172.16.192.0/29 for LAN3

   d.   192.168.15.0/26 for LAN1, 192.168.15.128/26 for LAN2, and 172.16.192.0/29 for LAN3

Answer: a. Network 192.168.15.0/25 provides 126 addresses for LAN1, network 192.168.15.128/26 provides 62 addresses for LAN2, and network 192.168.15.192/27 provides 30 addresses for LAN3.

23. What is the network and mask that you can use for the WAN link which would save the most address space?

    a. 192.168.11.240/27

    b. 192.168.11.240/28

    c. 192.168.11.240.29

    d. 192.168.11.240.30

    Answer: d. You need only two addresses for the WAN link, and the /30 mask provides only two addresses.

24. What networks does Router C announce to the provider's Internet router?

    a. 210.200.200.8/26

    b. 192.168.10.0/24 and 192.168.11.0/24

    c. 192.168.10.0/25 summary address

    d. 201.200.200.8/29 and 192.168.10.0/25

    Answer: a. Private addresses are not announced to Internet service providers.

25. What technology does Router C use to convert private addresses to public addresses?

    a. DNS

    b. NAT

    c. ARP

    d. VLSMs

    Answer: b. NAT translates internal private addresses to public addresses.

26. What mechanism supports the ability to divide a given subnet into smaller subnets based on need?

    a. DNS

    b. NAT

    c. ARP

    d. VLSMs

    Answer: d. VLSMs provide the ability to use different masks throughout the network.

Chapter 10

"Do I Know This Already?"

1. **c.** IPv6 uses 128 bits and IPv4 uses 32 bits for addresses. The difference is 96.

2. **a.** Aggregatable addresses are organized as public topology, site topology, and interface identifier.

3. **c.** The defining first hexadecimal digits for link-local addresses are FE8.

4. **d.** IPv6 addresses can be unicast, anycast, or multicast.

5. **b.** Answers a and c are incorrect because you cannot use the double colons (::)twice. Answers c and d are also incorrect because you cannot reduce b100 to b1.

6. **c.** NAT-PT translates between IPv4 and IPv6 addresses.

7. **b.** The IPv6 multicast address type handles broadcasts.

8. **b.** The IPv6 loopback address is ::1.

9. **a.** IPv4-compatible IPv6 addresses have the format ::d.d.d.d.

10. **c.** The DNS maps fully qualified domain names to IPv4 addresses using (AAAA) records.

Q&A

1. True or false? OSPFv2 supports IPv6.

   Answer: False. OSPFv3 supports IPv6. OSPFv2 is used in IPv4 networks.

2. True or false? DNS AAAA records are used in IPv6 networks for name-to-IPv6-address resolution.

   Answer: True.

3. Fill the blank. IPv6 ND is similar what _____ does for IPv4 networks.

   Answer: ARP.

4. What is the top layer of the hierarchy of IPv6 aggregatable addresses?

   Answer: Public topology.

5. IPv6 multicast addresses begin with what hexadecimal numbers?

   Answer: 0xFF (1111 1111 binary).

6. IPv6 link-local addresses begin with what hexadecimal prefix?

Answer: FE8/10.

7. IPv6 site-local addresses begin with what hexadecimal prefix?

Answer: FEC/10.

8. True or false? The IPv6 address 2001:0:0:1234:0:0:0:abcd can be represented as 2001::1234:0:0:0:abcd and 2001:0:0:1234::abcd.

Answer: True. Both compressed representations are valid.

9. What is the subnet prefix of 2001:1:0:ab0:34:ab1:0:1/64?

Answer: 2001:1:0:ab0::/64.

10. The IPv6 address has 128 bits. How many hexadecimal numbers does an IPv6 address have?

Answer: 32.

11. What type of IPv6 address is the following address?

FF01:0:0:0:0:0:0:2

_____

Answer: It is a multicast address. All IPv6 multicast addresses begin with hexadecimal FF.

12. True or false? You can use RIPv2 to route IPv6 networks.

Answer: False. RIPv2 is used for IPv4 networks. RIPng is used for IPv6 networks.

13. What is the compact format of the following address?

2102:0010:0000:0000:0000:fc23:0100:00ab

   a. 2102:10::fc23:01:ab

   b. 2102:001::fc23:01:ab

   c. 2102:10::fc23:100:ab

   d. 2102:0010::fc23:01:ab

Answer: c. Answers a, b, and d are incorrect because 0100 does not compact to 01. Answer b is also incorrect because 0010 does not compact to 001.

14. When using the dual-stack backbone, which statement is correct?

    a. The backbone routers have IPv4/IPv6 dual stacks and end hosts do not.

    b. The end hosts have IPv4/IPv6 dual stacks and backbone routers do not.

    c. Both the backbone routers and end hosts have IPv4/IPv6 dual stacks.

    d. Neither the backbone routers or end hosts have IPv4/IPv6 dual stacks.

    Answer: a. The dual-stack backbone routers handle packets between IPv4 hosts and IPv6 hosts.

15. How does a dual-stack host know which stack to use to reach a destination?

    a. It performs an ND, which returns the destination host type.

    b. It performs a DNS request that returns the IP address. If the returned address is IPv4, then the host uses the IPv4 stack. If the returned address is IPv6, then the host uses the IPv6 stack.

    c. The IPv6 stack makes a determination. If the destination is IPv4, the packet is sent to the IPv4 stack.

    d. The IPv4 stack makes a determination If the destination is IPv6, the packet is sent to the IPv6 stack.

    Answer: b. DNS indicates which stack to use. DNS A records return IPv4 addresses. DNS AAAA records return IPv6 addresses.

16. Name at least two transition methods or technologies used to migrate from IPv4 to IPv6.

    Answers: 1. IPv6 over dedicated links

    2. IPv6 over IPv4 tunnels

    3. IPv6 using dual-stack backbones

    4. Protocol-translation mechanisms

17. What is the IPv6 equivalent to IPv4 private addresses?

    a. Aggregatable-global

    b. Site-local

    c. Link-local

    d. Multicast

    Answer: b. IPv6 site-local addresses are equivalent to IPv4 private addresses.

18. What is true about fragmentation?

    a. Routers between source and destination hosts can fragment IPv4 and IPv6 packets.

    b. Routers between source and destination hosts cannot fragment IPv4 and IPv6 packets.

    c. Routers between source and destination hosts can fragment IPv6 packets only. IPv4 packets cannot be fragmented.

    d. Routers between source and destination hosts can fragment IPv4 packets only. IPv6 packets cannot be fragmented.

Answer: d. IPv4 packets can be fragmented by the sending host and routers. IPv6 packets are only fragmented by the sending host.

19. A packet sent to an anycast address reaches what?

    a. The nearest destination in a set of hosts

    b. All destinations in a set of hosts

    c. Broadcasts to all hosts

    d. Aggregatable-global destinations

Answer: a. Anycast addresses reach the nearest destination of a group of hosts.

20. Regarding IPv6 and IPv4 headers, what is true?

    a. The IPv6 header is of fixed length, and the next-header field describes the upper-layer protocol.

    b. The IPv4 header is of variable length, and the protocol-type field describes the upper-layer protocol.

    c. The IPv6 header is of fixed length, and the protocol-type field describes the upper-layer protocol.

    d. Answers a and b.

    e. Answer b and c.

Answer: d. Answers a and b are correct.

Answer the following questions based on the scenario and figure.

A company has an existing WAN that uses IPv4. Sites A and B also use IPv4. As shown in Figure 10-11, the company plans on adding two new locations (Sites C and D). The new sites will implement IPv6. The company does not want to lease more WAN circuits.

Figure 10-11 *Company Adds Sites C and D*

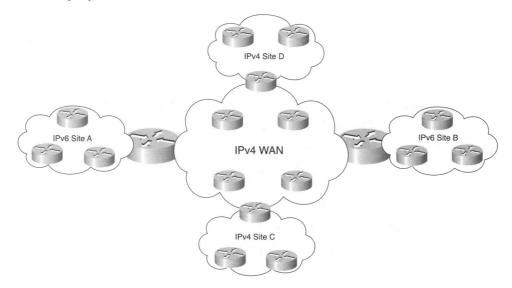

Answer the following questions.

21. What options does the company have to connect Site C to Site D?

    Answer: Implement dual-stack backbone or implement IPv4 tunnels between the sites.

22. What mechanism needs to be implemented so that IPv6 hosts can communicate with IPv4 hosts and vice versa?

    Answer: NAT-PT is required to provide network address translation and protocol translation between IPv6 and IPv4 hosts.

23. If the company uses RFC 1918 addresses in its IPv4 network, what IPv6 addresses should it use at the new sites?

    Answer: The company is using IPv4 private addresses in its existing IPv4 network. Site-local addresses are the IPv6 equivalent to IPv4 private addresses. The company should implement IPv6 site-local addresses.

24. If a dual-stack backbone is implemented, do all WAN routers and all hosts need an IPv6-IPv4 dual stack?

    Answer: If a dual-stack backbone is implemented, only the WAN routers require a IPv6-IPv4 dual stack. End hosts do not need a dual stack.

25. If a IPv4 tunnel is implemented between Sites C and D, do all WAN routers require an IPv6-IPv4 dual stack?

   Answer: No, all WAN routers still run the IPv4 stack with two exceptions: the WAN routers at Site C and Site D. These routers speak IPv6 within their sites and IPv4 to the WAN.

Chapter 11

"Do I Know This Already?"

1. **d.** Only IGRP and RIPv1 are classful routing protocols. EIGRP, OSPF, IS-IS, and RIPv2 are classless routing protocols.

2. **c.** You use an exterior gateway protocol (EGP) to receive Internet routes from a service provider.

3. **a.** RIPv2 is a classless distance-vector routing protocol.

4. **b.** Distance-vector routing protocols send periodic updates.

5. **b.** ODR is on-demand routing used to configure routing for stub sites without having to configure an IP routing protocol on the stubs.

6. **b.** If bandwidth is used, the path with the highest bandwidth is selected. If cost is used, then the path with the lowest cost is selected.

7. **b.** OSPF has an administrative distance of 110. EIGRP has an administrative distance of 90. The route with the lowest administrative distance is selected: EIGRP.

8. **d.** EIGRP, RIPv2, IS-IS, and OSPF are all classless routing protocols.

Q&A

1. What two routing protocols do not carry mask information in the route updates?

   Answer: RIPv1 and IGRP. These protocols are classful.

2. True or false? Link-state routing protocols send periodic routing updates.

   Answer: False. Distance-vector routing protocols send periodic routing updates.

3. True or false? With ODR, no static routes are configured at remote stub routers.

   Answer: True.

4. True or false? The path with the lowest cost is preferred.

   Answer: True.

5. True or false? A link with a reliability of 200/255 is preferred over a link with a reliability of 10/255.

   Answer: True. The more reliable link is preferred.

6. True or false? A link with a delay of 200/255 is preferred over a link with a delay of 10/255.

   Answer: False. The link with the lower delay is preferred.

7. On a router, both EIGRP and OSPF have a route to 198.168.10.0/24. Which route is injected into the routing table?

   Answer: The EIGRP route. EIGRP routes have an administrative distance of 90, and OSPF routes have an administrative distance of 100. The lower administrative distance is preferred.

8. On a router, both RIPv2 and IS-IS have a route to 198.168.10.0/24. Which route is injected into the routing table?

   Answer: The IS-IS route. IS-IS routes have an administrative distance of 115, and RIP routes have an administrative distance of 120. The lower administrative distance is preferred.

9. Which is the best measurement of the reliability and load of an interface?

   a. Rely 255/255, load 1/255

   b. Rely 255/255, load 255/255

   c. Rely 1/255, load 1/255

   d. Rely 1/255, load 255/255

   Answer: a. The best reliability is 255/255 (100 percent) and the best load is 1/255 (~0 percent).

10. Which routing protocols permit an explicit hierarchical topology?

    a. BGP

    b. EIGRP

    c. IS-IS

    d. RIP

    e. OSPF

    f. b and d

    g. c and e

    Answer: g. IS-IS and OSPF permit an explicit hierarchical topology.

11. What routing protocol parameter is concerned with the time a packet takes to travel from one end to another in the internetwork?

Answer: Delay measures the time a packet takes to travel from one end to another in the internetwork.

12. For what routing protocol metric is the value of a 10 Mbps Ethernet interface calculated as $10^8/10^7 = 10$?

Answer: OSPF cost. The Cisco default metric is $10^8/BW$.

13. What is the Cisco default OSPF metric for a Fast Ethernet interface?

Answer: The metric is $10^8/BW$. If BW=100 Mbps = 10^8, then the metric=$10^8/10^8= 1$.

14. Match the loop-prevention technique with its description:

i.   Split horizon

ii. Split horizon with poison reverse

iii. Triggered updates

iv. Counting to infinity

a. Sends an infinite metric from which the route was learned

b. Drops a packet when the hop-count limit is reached

c. Suppresses a route announcement from which the route was learned

d. Sends a route update when a route changes

Answer: i = c, ii =a, iii =d, iv =b.

15. True or false? Link-state routing protocols are more CPU and memory intensive than distance-vector routing protocols.

Answer: True.

16. Which routing protocols would you select if you need to take advantage of VLSMs? (Select more than one answer.)

a. RIPv1

b. RIPv2

c. IGRP

d. EIGRP

e. OSPF

f. IS-IS

Answer: b, d, e, and **f**.

17. What additional protocol is required for ODR to work?

Answer: CDP. The Cisco Discovery Protocol (CDP) provides for communication between hub and stub routers when using ODR.

Answer the following questions based on Figure 11-9.

Figure 11-9 *Scenario Diagram*

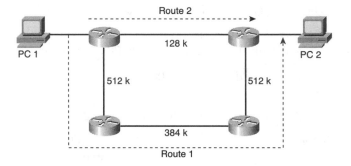

18. A user performs a Telnet from PC 1 to PC 2. If the metric used by the configured routing protocol is the bandwidth parameter, which route will the packets take?

   a. Route 1.

   b. Route 2.

   c. Neither; there is not sufficient information.

   d. One packet will take Route 1, the following packet will take Route 2, and so on.

Answer: a. The minimum bandwidth via Route 1 is 384 Kbps. The minimum bandwidth via Route 2 is 128 Kbps. The route with the higher minimum bandwidth is preferred, so the router chooses Route 1.

19. A user performs a Telnet from PC 1 to PC 2. If the metric used by the configured routing protocol is hop count, which route will the packets take?

   a. Route 1.

   b. Route 2.

   c. Neither; there is not sufficient information.

   d. One packet will take Route 1, the following packet will take Route 2, and so on.

Answer: b. Route 2 has fewer router hops than Route 1.

20. A user performs a Telnet from PC 1 to PC 2. If the metric used by the configured routing protocol is OSPF cost, which route will the packets take?

    a. Route 1.

    b. Route 2.

    c. Neither; there is not sufficient information.

    d. One packet will take Route 1, the following packet will take Route 2, and so on.

Answer: a. Route 2 has a higher cost than Route 1. Route 1 cost = $10^8/128$ Kbps = 781.25. The Route 2 cost = $10^8/512$ Kbps + $10^8/384$ Kbps + $10^8/512$ Kbps = 195.31 + 260.41 + 195.31 = 651.03.

Chapter 12

"Do I Know This Already?"

    1. **c.** RIPv1 and RIPv2 are limited to 15 router hops.

    2. **a.** RIPv1 broadcasts every 30 seconds.

    3. **b.** RIPv2 implements support for VLSMs and an authentication mechanism for route updates and can multicast rather than broadcast updates.

    4. **d.** EIGRP routers maintain adjacencies with their neighboring routers. The adjacencies are kept in a topology table.

    5. **c.** Only RIPv1 and IGRP require a fixed-length subnet mask per network. RIPv2, EIGRP, OSPF, and IS-IS support VLSM and CIDR.

    6. **b.** By default, EIGRP uses bandwidth and delay in its composite metric.

    7. **d.** RIPv2, EIGRP, OSPF, and IS-IS support VLSMs.

    8. **c.** Only EIGRP implements DUAL. DUAL selects the best path and second best path to a destination.

Q&A

    1. True or false? RIPv2 broadcasts (255.255.255.255) its routing table every 30 seconds.

    Answer: False. RIPv2 multicasts its routing table to 224.0.0.9. It does not send a broadcast to all nodes in the segment.

    2. True or false? By default, EIGRP uses bandwidth, delay, reliability, and load to calculate the composite metric.

    Answer: False. By default, EIGRP uses bandwidth and delay to calculate the composite metric.

3. True or false? EIGRP routers maintain neighbor adjacencies.

   Answer: True. EIGRP routers build a table of adjacent EIGRP neighbors.

4. True or false? EIGRP and RIPv2 support VLSMs and CIDR.

   Answer: True.

5. True or false? RIPv2 does not have the 15-hop limit of RIPv1.

   Answer: False. Both RIPv1 and RIPv2 have a 15 router-hop limit.

6. RIP uses _____ port _____.

   Answer: RIP uses UDP port 520.

7. IGRP uses IP protocol number _____.

   Answer: IGRP uses IP protocol 9.

8. EIGRP uses IP protocol number _____.

   Answer: EIGRP uses IP protocol 88.

9. Between RIP, IGRP, and EIGRP, which protocol would you recommend for use in a large network?

   Answer: EIGRP is preferred for large networks.

10. Between RIPv2, IGRP, and EIGRP, which protocol would you use in a small network that has both Cisco and non-Cisco routers?

    Answer: You would use RIPv2 because IGRP and EIGRP are only available on Cisco devices.

11. Which protocol broadcasts its routing table every 90 seconds by default?

    Answer: IGRP.

12. Match the protocol with the characteristic:

i.	RIPv1	**a.**	No VLSM or CIDR support; default update period of 90 seconds.
ii.	RIPv2	**b.**	VLSM and CIDR support; limited to 15 hops
iii.	IGRP	**c.**	No VLSM or CIDR support; default update period of 30 seconds
iv.	EIGRP	**d.**	Uses triggered updates

Answer: i = c, ii = b, iii = a, iv = d.

13. Why is EIGRP sometimes considered a hybrid protocol?

Answer: EIGRP combines characteristics commonly associated with both distance-vector and link-state routing protocols.

14. True or false? IGRP is limited to 16 router hops.

Answer: False. IGRP is not limited to 16 router hops. The default limit of 100 hops is configurable up to 255 hops.

15. Which routing protocol can you use to exchange route updates with UNIX workstations running the **routed** process?

Answer: You can use RIP to exchange routing information with UNIX workstations running routed.

16. Match the RIP routing table field with its description:

i.	IP address	**a.**	The number of hops to the destination
ii.	Gateway	**b.**	Next router along the path to the destination
iii.	Interface	**c.**	Destination network or host, with subnet mask
iv.	Metric	**d.**	Used to access the physical network that must be used to reach the destination
v.	Timer	**e.**	Time since the route entry was last updated

Answer: i = c, ii = b, iii = d, iv = a, v = e.

17. Match the EIGRP component with its description:

    i. RTP

    ii. DUAL

    iii. Protocol-dependent modules

    iv. Neighbor discovery

    a. An interface between DUAL and IPX RIP, IGRP, and AppleTalk

    b. Used to deliver EIGRP messages reliably

    c. Builds an adjacency table

    d. Guarantees a loop-free network

    Answer: i = b, ii = d, iii = a, iv = c.

18. With Cisco routers, which protocols use only equal-cost load balancing?

    Answer: Equal-cost load balancing is a feature of RIPv1 and RIPv2 with Cisco routers.

19. With Cisco routers, which protocols allow unequal-cost load balancing?

    Answer: Unequal-cost load balancing is a feature of IGRP and EIGRP with Cisco routers.

20. Complete Table 12-6 with the VLSM, authentication, and administrative-distance capabilities of each routing protocol.

    Answer:

Table 12-6 *Distance Capabilities*

Routing Protocol	VLSM	Authentication	Admin Distance
RIPv1	No	No	120
RIPv2	Yes	Yes	120
IGRP	No	No	100
EIGRP	Yes	Yes	90

Use the Figure 12-7 to answer the following questions.

Figure 12-7 *Path Selection*

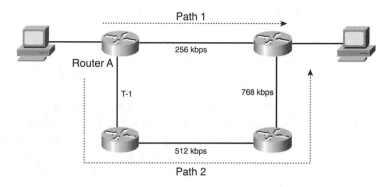

21. By default, if RIPv2 is enabled on all routers, what path is taken?

    a. Path 1

    b. Path 2

    c. Unequal load balance with Path 1 and Path 2

    d. Equal load balance with Path 1 and Path 2

    Answer: a. From Router A, Path 1 is one router hop, Path 2 is three router hops. RIPv2 selects Path 1 because of the lower metric.

22. By default, if IGRP is enabled on all routers, what path is taken?

    a. Path 1

    b. Path 2

    c. Unequal load balance with Path 1 and Path 2

    d. Equal load balance with Path 1 and Path 2

    Answer: b. From Router A, the lowest bandwidth in Path 1 is 256 kbps, the lowest bandwidth in Path 2 is 512 kbps. With default delay values, the IGRP metric calculation would be more sensitive to the bandwidth component of the metric calculation. IGRP selects the path with the greatest minimum bandwidth.

23. By default, if EIGRP is enabled on all routers, what path is taken?

    a. Path 1

    b. Path 2

    c. Unequal load balance with Path 1 and Path 2

    d. Equal load balance with Path 1 and Path 2

    Answer: b. From Router A, the lowest bandwidth (BW_{min1}) in Path 1 is 256 kbps; the lowest bandwidth in Path 2 (BW_{min2}) is 512 kbps. With default delay values, the EIGRP metric calculation would be more sensitive to the bandwidth component of the metric calculation. EIGRP selects the path with the greatest minimum bandwidth.

24. EIGRP is configured on the routers. If configured with the **variance** command, what path is taken?

    a. Path 1

    b. Path 2

    c. Unequal load balance with Path 1 and Path 2

    d. Equal load balance with Path 1 and Path 2

    Answer: c. By default, EIGRP will load-balance using equal-cost paths. EIGRP will do unequal load balancing when you use the **variance** command.

25. By default, if RIPv1 is enabled on all routers, what path is taken?

    a. Path 1

    b. Path 2

    c. Unequal load balance with Path 1 and Path 2

    d. Equal load balance with Path 1 and Path 2

    Answer: a. From Router A, Path 1 is one router hop, and Path 2 is three router hops. RIPv1 selects Path 1 because of the lower metric.

Chapter 13

"Do I Know This Already?"

1. **b.** OSPF defines ABRs that connect areas to the OSPF backbone.

2. **g.** EIGRP, OSPF, and IS-IS support VLSMs.

3. **d.** IS-IS is a common alternative to EIGRP and OSPF for certain large networks.

4.   **b.** OSPF defines the (ASBR as the router that injects external routes into the OSPF autonomous system.

5.   **b.** The default IS-IS cost metric for any interface type is 10.

6.   **e.** OSPF Type 5 LSAs are AS external LSAs.

7.   **c.** OSPF routers use 224.0.0.6 to communicate to DRs.

8.   **a**. Type 1 LSAs (router LSAs) are forwarded to all routers within an OSPF area.

9.   **d.** IS-IS does not define BDRs.

10.   **c.** NET is Network Entity Title; it is the Open System Interconnection (OSI) address used by IS-IS to communicate using OSI protocol data units (PDUs).

Q&A

1.   True or false? A router needs to have all its interfaces in Area 0 to be considered an OSPF backbone router.

     Answer: False. A router with one or more interfaces in Area 0 is considered an OSPF backbone router.

2.   True or false? Both OSPF and IS-IS use a designated router in multiaccess networks.

     Answer: True.

3.   Which multicast address do OSPF routers use?

     Answer: 224.0.0.5 for ALLSPFRouters and 224.0.0.6 for ALLDRouters.

4.   What are the Cisco administrative distances of OSPF and IS-IS?

     Answer: The administrative distance of OSPF is 110, and the administrative distance of IS-IS is 115.

5.   True or false? By default, IS-IS assigns a cost metric of 10 to a T1 interface and also 10 to an Ethernet interface.

     Answer: True. By default, IS-IS assigns a cost metric of 10 to all interfaces.

6.   Which OSPF router type generates the OSPF Type 3 LSA?

     Answer: OSPF ABRs generate the Type 3 summary LSA for ABRs.

7.   Which OSPF router type generates the OSPF Type 2 LSA?

     Answer: OSPF DRs generate Type 2 network LSAs.

8. What is included in an OSPF router LSA?

Answer: Included are the router's links, interfaces, state of links, and cost.

9. True or false? An IS-IS L2 router is analogous to an OSPF backbone router.

Answer: True.

10. True or false? The router with the lowest priority is selected as the OSPF DR.

Answer: False. The router with the highest priority is selected as the OSPF designated router.

11. Match the routing protocol with the description:

i. EIGRP	**a.**	Distance-vector protocol used in the edge of the network
ii. OSPF	**b.**	IETF link-state protocol used in the network core
iii. RIPv2	**c.**	Hybrid protocol used in the network core
iv. IS-IS	**d.**	OSI link-state protocol

Answer: i = c, ii = b, iii = a, iv = d.

12. What router produces OSPF Type 2 LSAs?

Answer: OSPF DRs produce OSPF network LSAs for every NBMA network.

13. True or false? IS-IS uses the IP layer to communicate between routers.

Answer: False. IS-IS uses Layer 2 OSI PDUs to communicate between routers.

14. What is the default OSPF cost for a Fast Ethernet interface?

Answer: 1 Cost is calculated as 10^8/BW, and BW=100 Mbps = 10^8 bps for Fast Ethernet. Cost = $10^8/10^8$.

15. Which link-state protocols support VLSMs?

Answer: OSPF and IS-IS are the only link-state routing protocols, and they both support VLSMs.

16. Which routing protocol do you use in the core of a large network that supports VLSMs for a network with a mix of Cisco and non-Cisco routers?

Answer: OSPF. Although RIPv2 and EIGRP support VLSMS, you should use RIPv2 only on the edge, and EIGRP is not supported on non-Cisco routers.

17.   True or false? An IS-IS L1/L2 router is similar to an OSPF ABR.

Answer: True. L1/L2 routers maintain separate link-state databases for Level 1 and Level 2 routes. ABRs maintain separate link-state databases for each area they are connected too.

18.   You use _____ to connect a nondirectly connected OSPF area to the backbone.

Answer: Virtual links. You use virtual links to temporarily connect an OSPF area to the backbone.

19.   What is the benefit of designing for stub areas?

Answer: You do not need to flood external LSAs into the stub area, which reduces LSA traffic.

20.   What constraint does the OSPF network design have for traffic traveling between areas?

Answer: All traffic from one area must travel through Area 0 (the backbone) to get to another area.

21.   True or false? The OSPF and IS-IS default costs for Fast Ethernet interfaces are the same.

Answer: False. For Fast Ethernet, the OSPF cost is 1 and the IS-IS cost is 10.

22.   True or false? The OSPF and IS-IS default costs for Ethernet interface are the same.

Answer: True. For Ethernet, the OSPF cost is 10. The IS-IS cost for any interface is 10.

Use Figure 13-9 to answer the following questions.

Figure 13-9   *Path Selection*

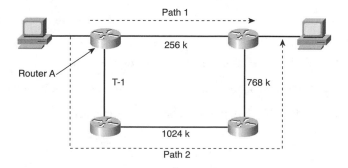

23. If IS-IS is enabled on all routers with the default metrics unchanged, what path is taken?

    a. Path 1

    b. Path 2

    c. Unequal load balance with Path 1 and Path 2

    d. Equal load balance with Path 1 and Path 2

    Answer: a. From Router A, Path 1 has an IS-IS cost of 10 + 10 = 20. Path 2 has an IS-IS cost of 10 + 10 + 10 + 10 = 40. Path 1 is selected.

24. If OSPF is enabled on all routers with the default metrics unchanged, what path is taken?

    a. Path 1

    b. Path 2

    c. Unequal load balance with Path 1 and Path 2

    d. Equal load balance with Path 1 and Path 2

    Answer: b. From Router A, the OSPF cost for Path 1 is $10^8/256$ kbps $=390$. The OSPF cost for Path 2 is $(10^8/1536$ kbps$) + (10^8/1024$ kbps$) + (10^8/768$ kbps$) = 65 + 97 + 130 = 292$. OSPF selects Path 2 because it has a lower cost.

Chapter 14

"Do I Know This Already?"

1. **b.** You use External Border Gateway Protocol (eBGP) to exchange routes between autonomous systems.

2. **c.** The current version of BGP is Version 4. BGPv4 includes support for CIDR.

3. **a.** Redistribution occurs automatically if EIGRP and IGRP are configured with the same autonomous system number.

4. **d.** PBR changes the route of packets based on configured policies.

5. **b.** You use IGMP between hosts and local routers to register with multicast groups.

6. **b.** The lower 23 bits of the IP multicast address are mapped to the last 23 bits of the Layer 2 MAC address.

7. **a.** The administrative distance of eBGP routes is 20. The administrative distance of Internal BGP (iBGP) routes is 200.

8. **d.** CIDR provides the capability of forwarding packets based on IP prefixes only, with no concern for IP address class boundaries.

Chapter 14   561

Q&A

1. True or false? You use iBGP to exchange routes between different autonomous systems.

    Answer: False. You use eBGP to exchange routes between different autonomous systems.

2. True or false? BGP Version 4 includes support for CIDR.

    Answer: True. BGPv4 added support for Classless Inter-Domain Routing (CIDR), which provides the capability of forwarding packets based on IP prefixes only, with no concern for the address class.

3. True or false? EIGRP and IGRP redistribute automatically on a router if the two protocols are configured with the same AS number.

    Answer: True.

4. Use _____ to modify the next hop of packets based on source IP address.

    Answer: PBR.

5. eBGP routes have an administrative distance of _____ and iBGP routes have an administrative distance of _____.

    Answer: 20, 200.

6. True or false? IGMP snooping and CGMP are methods to reduce the multicast traffic at Layer 2.

    Answer: True.

7. True of false. PIM has a 32 hop-count limit.

    Answer: False. PIM does not have a hop-count limit. DVMRP has a 32 hop-count limit.

8. True or false? PIM-SM routers use the multicast 224.0.0.13 address to request a multicast group to the RP.

    Answer: True.

9. True or false? AS path is the only attribute BGP uses to determine the best path to the destination.

    Answer: False. BGP uses several attributes in the BGP decision process.

10. List three IP routing protocols that use multicast addresses to communicate with their neighbors.

    Answer: RIPv2, OSPF, and EIGRP.

11. Match the IP multicast address with its description:

i. 224.0.0.1	**a.** All OSPF routers
ii. 224.0.0.2	**b.** All routers
iii. 224.0.0.5	**c.** EIGRP routers
iv. 224.0.0.10	**d.** All hosts

Answer: i = d, ii = b, iii = a, iv=c.

12. Match the BGP attribute with the description:

i. Local preference	**a.** An IP address
ii. MED	**b.** Indicates path used to exit the AS
iii. AS path	**c.** Tells external BGP peers the preferred path into the AS
iv. Next hop	**d.** List of AS numbers

Answer: i = b, ii = c, iii = d, iv = a.

13. Which Cisco feature can you use instead of local preference to influence the selected path to external BGP routers?

Answer: Weight. Weight is configured locally and not exchanged in BGP updates. On the other hand, the local-preference attribute is exchanged between iBGP peers and is configured at the gateway router.

14. What is the purpose of route reflectors?

Answer: Route reflectors reduce the number of iBGP logical mesh connections.

15. When using BGP confederations, which number do external peers see?

Answer: External peers see the confederation ID. The internal private AS numbers are used within the confederation.

16. With _____ all routers peer with each other within the private AS, and with _____ client routers only peer with the reflector.

Answer: BGP confederations, route reflectors.

17. Which of the following shows the correct order that BGP uses to select a best path?

a. Origin, lowest IP, AS path, weight, local preference

b. Weight, local preference, AS path, origin, MED, lowest IP

c. Lowest IP, AS path, origin, weight, MED, local preference

d. Weight, origin, local preference, AS path, MED, lowest IP

Answer: b. Only answer b has the correct order of BGP path selection, which is weight, local preference, AS path, origin, MED, and lowest IP.

18. What feature did BGPv4 implement to provide forwarding of packets based on IP prefixes?

Answer: CIDR was first implemented in BGPv4.

Refer to Figure 14-15 to answer the questions that follow.

Figure 14-15 *Network Scenario*

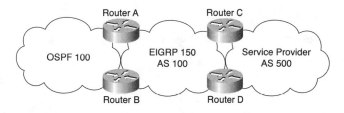

19. Where should you configure BGP?

   a. Routers A and B

   b. Routers C and D

   c. Answers a and b

   d. Routers A and C

Answer: b. BGP should be configured between AS 100 and AS 500.

20. On which router should you configure redistribution for OSPF and EIGRP?

   a. Router A only.

   b. Router B only.

   c. Routers A and B.

   d. Redistribution will occur automatically.

Answer: c. Both Routers A and B perform the redistribution with route filters to prevent route feedback.

21. To announce the networks from AS 100 to AS 500, which routing protocols should you redistribute into BGP?

   a. OSPF only

   b. EIGRP only

   c. OSPF and EIGRP

   d. iBGP

   Answer: b. The OSPF routes are redistributed into EIGRP. Then you can redistribute EIGRP routes into BGP.

22. Where should you use filters?

   a. Routers A and B

   b. Routers C and D

   c. Routers A and C

   d. Answers a and b

   Answer: d. You should use filters on all routers performing redistribution.

Chapter 15

"Do I Know This Already?"

1. **b.** Man-in-the-middle attacks sniff packets to obtain information, but if you encrypt the packet, the information that is sniffed becomes useless.

2. True. Encrypted packets can be compromised if the hacker is able to obtain the keys that were used to encrypt the packet.

3. **d.** Using Layer 3 filtering contains the hackers and prevents access to networks.

4. **c.** Brute force is a password attack that uses random guesses to try to access systems.

5. **a.** A large server presence on segments usually is associated with applications and should be assessed for vulnerability to application-layer attacks.

6. **a.** An IDS attempts to thwart attacks by sending an alert or by taking an action.

7. **d.** This scanning is a common aspect of a worm attack, which does not require human intervention to spread.

8. **c.** Cisco Security Policy Manager (CSPM) is the name of the tool you use to centralize the management of several policy-based tools such as firewalls and IDSs.

9.   **d.** Out-of-band management enables you to access devices via a serial connection to a modem or direct connection.

10.   **b.** SSH replaces Telnet access.

Q&A

1.   You can use private IP addresses to prevent which types of attacks?

    a. DoS

    b. Trojan horses

    c. IP spoofing

    d. Unauthorized access

Answer: c. RFC 2827 and 1918 prevent locally originated spoofed packets and limit remote spoof attempts.

2.   What is a backdoor?

    a. A type of attack

    b. Another name for a Trojan

    c. An automatic result of a hacker gaining access to the network

    d. A method left by the hacker to gain access at a later time

Answer: d. This method is often how hackers ensure that they can continually gain access to the network.

3.   What does HIDS refer to?

    a. Host-based intrusion-detection system

    b. Host intrusion-detection sources

    c. Hacker information-data system

    d. Hacker intrusion-detection system

Answer: a. HIDS is a host-based IDS that operates by inserting agents into the host to be protected.

4.   Port-redirection attacks are associated with which type of attack?

    a. Password attack

    b. Trust exploitation

    c. Application-layer attacks

    d. Unauthorized access

Answer: b. Port redirection is a trust-exploitation attack. For example, it uses a breached host to pass traffic through a firewall that would otherwise be dropped.

5. Packet sniffing is most common in which type of functional area?

   a. E-commerce module

   b. Enterprise Edge

   c. VPN and remote access

   d. ISP

   Answer: b. Packet sniffing is most common in the Enterprise Edge.

6. Which of the following mitigation tactics can you use to thwart a man-in-the-middle attack?

   a. Encrypt traffic

   b. Switched infrastructure

   c. IDS

   d. Firewall

   Answer: a. If you encrypt the traffic, the data cannot be "hijacked" and then read.

7. In which module should you place content filtering on applications such as e-mail?

   a. Corporate module

   b. Management module

   c. Server module

   d. Corporate Internet module

   Answer: d. You use the Corporate Internet module as a demilitarized zone (DMZ) to separate inbound Internet traffic. This spot is ideal for checking for viruses on a Simple Mail Transfer Protocol (SMTP) gateway prior to passing the packet onto the email server.

8. A TCP SYN flood is categorized as which type of attack?

   a. Password attack

   b. Man-in-the-middle

   c. DoS

   d. Network reconnaissance

   Answer: c. Attackers use a TCP SYN flood to cause failure in a system because of its inability to process SYN requests. DoS attacks are some of the easiest to launch and are difficult to completely block.

9. What is the most common method used to prevent IP spoofing?

    a. Encryption

    b. Operating-system upgrades

    c. IP address management

    d. Access control lists (ACLs)

    Answer: d. ACLs should be the first defense against IP spoofing.

10. True or false? Host-based IDSs are a viable solution in the server module of the Enterprise Campus functional area.

    Answer: True. You use HIDS to monitor servers.

11. What is a secure method for remotely accessing applications?

    Answer: SSH is an application and a protocol that replaces rsh, rlogin, and rcp. You also can use IPSec and SSL to secure a remote-access session to an application.

12. How would you achieve remote access to a device for remote management when the network is not available?

    Answer: You use out-of-band management by adding an alternate connection means to a device, such as a modem or direct connection via a console port.

13. What type of management does the Cisco Security Policy Manager application provide?

    Answer: CSPM is the name of the tool you use to centralize the management of several policy-based tools, such as firewalls and IDSs. You use CSPM in a large network with various security deployments to avoid misconfigured and inconsistent security devices such as firewalls and IDS.

14. What other advantage aside from historical information can logging provide?

    Answer: Logging can be useful to determine whether any malicious attacks were launched and to determine the source. In addition, logging is a helpful tool to reverse configuration changes or provide a backout plan.

15. What does the abbreviation NIDS stand for?

    Answer: NIDS is network-based intrusion-detection system.

16. Which application can serve as a secure alternative to Telnet access to devices?

Answer: SSH is an alternative to Telnet.

17. True or false? Packet encryption is a good mitigation strategy for man-in-the-middle attacks, which sniff packets to obtain information.

Answer: True. Packet encryption can be used as an efficient strategy for man-in-the-middle attacks.

18. Which are the most commonly affected modules in the SAFE blueprint that are targeted by reconnaissance attacks?

   a. Management module

   b. Edge distribution module

   c. WAN module

   d. Corporate Internet module

   Answer: a, b, d. The management, edge distribution, and corporate Internet modules are targeted by reconnaissance attacks.

19. Which are the most commonly affected modules in the SAFE blueprint that are targeted by man-in-the-middle attacks?

   a. Management module

   b. Edge distribution module

   c. Building access module

   d. Corporate Internet module

   Answer: a, c. Man-in-the-middle attacks target the management and building access modules.

20. Which are the most commonly affected modules in the SAFE blueprint that are targeted by DoS attacks?

   a. Management module

   b. E-commerce module

   c. WAN module

   d. Corporate Internet module

   Answer: b, c, d. DoS attacks target the e-commerce, WAN, and corporate Internet modules.

21. Which type of attack is common to core modules in the Enterprise Campus?

   a. Unauthorized access

   b. Packet sniffing

   c. IP spoofing

   d. Trust exploitation

   Answer: b. Packet sniffing is a type of attack common to core modules in the Enterprise Campus.

22. An attacker who connects to multiple devices because an authorized user has set all his access codes the same has used what type of attack?

   a. DoS

   b. Trojan

   c. Password attack

   d. Unauthorized access

   Answer: c. Password attacks are used to connect to multiple devices using an access code set by an authorized user.

23. An attack that tries to access your data phone numbers might use what type of device?

   a. IDS

   b. War dialer

   c. Terminal server

   d. Modem

   Answer: b. War dialers are used to access your data phone numbers.

Chapter 16

"Do I Know This Already?"

1. **d.** The corporate Internet is part of the Enterprise Edge because it is a service that lies between the Service Provider Edge and the Enterprise Campus.

2. **b.** The corporate security policy ensures the security solution meets the corporate security objectives that are established at the highest levels of management. Although the security audit and the customer needs are also important, the corporate security policy is the best answer.

3. **a.** Security Architecture for Enterprise is the blueprint developed by Cisco as a guideline for best-practice security design methodology.

4. **b.** A defense-in-depth approach means that there are layers of network-security solutions; if one is breached, the others would halt the attack.

5. **c.** SAFE divides the network into sections. The first major category of sections is functional areas.

6. **c.** VPNs are connections that are secured by encryption and authentication.

7. **c, e.** The Enterprise Edge and Enterprise Campus compose the Enterprise network, and the SP Edge is the third functional area.

8. **a.** Internal users such as disgruntled employees, visiting guests, and users making common mistakes cause the majority of attacks.

9. **c.** The Cisco ecosystem is a web of partners and vendors with services and solutions that you can use in conjunction with SAFE to provide a complete solution.

10. **b.** You determine security solutions for each module based on security threats and the mitigation strategies needed to thwart the attacks.

Q&A

1. Cisco defines five elements that are key to providing network security. Which of these choices are not one of the five elements?

   a. Secure connectivity

   b. Intrusion detection

   c. Security monitoring

   d. Identity

   e. Perimeter security

   Answer: b. Intrusion detection is not part of the five elements; policy management is the missing element.

2. Support for emerging network appliances is an objective of the SAFE blueprint. What is the result of achieving this objective?

   a. Resilience

   b. Performance

   c. Protection

   d. Management

   e. Scalability

   Answer: e. Meeting this objective ensures that the architecture is scalable and can use new technologies that become available.

3. Using vendor partners and consulting firms to create a best-of-breed solution is part of what strategy?

    a. SAFE

    b. Cisco network assurance

    c. Cisco Security ecosystem

    d. Cisco channel

    Answer: c. This step is part of the Cisco Security ecosystem strategy.

4. Which of the following modules is not a part of the SP Edge functional area?

    a. ISP

    b. Frame Relay

    c. Corporate Internet

    d. ATM

    Answer: c. The Corporate Internet is part of the Enterprise Edge functional area.

5. True or false? Layering network solutions in the SAFE blueprint provides resilience in a network.

    Answer: True. Layers enable SAFE to include multiple security measures so that if one fails, another will halt the attack.

6. True or false? Most attacks are launched by hackers.

    Answer: False. Most network attacks are launched by internal users.

7. Which of the following is a module part of the Enterprise Edge functional area?

    a. WAN

    b. ISP A

    c. Core

    d. PSTN

    Answer: a. WAN is part of the Enterprise Edge functional area.

8. Which of the following is not part of the five key areas that are used as a basis for the development of SAFE?

  a. Perimeter security

  b. Identity

  c. Secure management and reporting

  d. Policy management

  Answer: c. Secure management and reporting is an objective of SAFE.

9. Which of the following statements describes SAFE's focus on identity?

  a. Use encryption.

  b. Authorized users have access to specific systems.

  c. Use network-security scanners.

  d. Manage the state of a security policy.

  Answer: b. Allowing authenticated access to only certain systems is part of establishing identity within SAFE.

10. True or false? Corporate Internet is part of the functional area Enterprise Campus.

  Answer: False. Corporate Internet is part of the functional area Enterprise Edge.

11. A _____ is recommended by Cisco as the foundation of any deployed security solution.

  Answer: Cisco recommends that a corporate security policy be the foundation of any deployed security solution.

12. The Cisco security architecture called SAFE stands for what?

  Answer: The Cisco security architecture called SAFE stands for Security Architecture for Enterprise.

13. Which functional areas compose the Enterprise Edge?

  a. a. Enterprise ISP

  b. E-commerce

  c. Corporate Internet

  d. Enterprise access

  e. WAN

Answer: b, c, and e. The Enterprise Edge consists of e-commerce, corporate Internet, VPN and remote access, and WAN.

14. True or false? The Cisco ecosystem increases the effectiveness of security systems by using various partners as well as supporting products.

Answer: True. The Cisco ecosystem increases the effectiveness of security systems by using various partners as well as supporting products.

Chapter 17

"Do I Know This Already?"

1. **c.** H.323 is the ITU standard that provides a framework for the transport of voice, video, and data over packet-switched networks.

2. **d.** The default codec in Cisco VoIP dial peers is G.729, which has an 8 Kbps bit rate.

3. **c.** RTP operates in the transport layer of the OSI model.

4. **c.** The H.225 standard defines the procedures for call setup and signaling.

5. **b.** An erlang is a unit that describes the number of calls in an hour.

6. **b.** VAD reduces traffic by not transmitting packets when there is silence in voice conversations.

7. **c.** CRTP compresses the RTP, UDP, and IP headers.

8. **b.** LLQ is recommended in integrated VoIP networks.

9. **a.** The local loop is located between the traditional phone and the CO switch.

10. **c.** Jitter is the variable delay of packets at the receiving end of a connection, including an IP telephony voice call.

Q&A

1. True or false? LLQ is recommended for VoIP networks.

    Answer: True. Cisco recommends Low Latency Queuing for VoIP Networks.

2. True or false? H.323 is an IETF standard, and SIP is an ITU standard for multimedia protocols.

    Answer: False. H.323 is an ITU standard and SIP is an IETF standard for multimedia.

3. True or false? An Erlang is a unit that describes the number of calls in a hour.

    Answer: True. An Erlang is a unit of telecommunications traffic measurement representing the continuous use of one voice path for one hour.

4. Implement _____ to stop packets from being transmitted when there is silence in a voice conversation.

   Answer: VAD Voice Activity Detection (VAD) suppresses packets when there is silence.

5. The variable delay of received VoIP packets is corrected with _____ buffers.

   Answer: de-jitter. The de-jitter buffers are used at the receiving end to smooth out the variable delay of received packets.

6. True or false? Common-channel signaling uses a separate channel for signaling.

   Answer: True. With common channel signaling (CCS), a separate channel (from the bearer channels) is used for signaling.

7. True or false? FXO ports are used for phones, and FXS ports connect to the PSTN.

   Answer: False. Use FXS ports to connect to phones and FXO ports to connect to the PSTN.

8. True or false? SS7 provides mechanisms for exchanging control and routing messages in the PSTN.

   Answer: True. SS7 implements call setup, routing, and control, ensuring that intermediate and far-end switches are available when a call is placed.

9. An organization will use a _____ system to gather and provide information for the customer before transferring her to an agent.

   Answer: Interactive Voice Response (IVR) System. IVR systems connect incoming calls to an audio playback system that queues the calls, provides prerecorded announcements, prompts the caller for key options, provides the caller with information, and transfers the call to another switch extension or agent.

10. An organization will use a _____ system to route calls to agents based on the agent skill group or call statistics.

    Answer: Automatic Call Distribution (ACD) System. ACD is used by airline reservation systems, customer service departments, and other call centers.

11. In addition to codec selection, both _____ and _____ can be used to reduce the bandwidth of VoIP calls.

    Answer: CRTP and VAD. Both CRTP and VAD reduce the amount of bandwidth used by VoIP calls. G.729 calls can be reduced from 26.4 kbps to 11.2 with CRTP and to 7.3 with CRTP and VAD.

12. Label the delays as fixed or variable:

a. Processing

b. De-jitter buffer

c. Serialization

d. Queuing

e. Propagation

Answer: a, b, c, and **e** = fixed; **d** = variable. Fixed-delay components include processing, serialization, de-jitter, and propagation delays. Variable-delay components include only queuing delays.

13. How can you reduce serialization delay?

Answer: You reduce the frame size with fragmentation or increase the link bandwidth. The formula is serialization delay = frame size/link BW.

14. Which two queuing techniques use a strict priority queue for IP RTP traffic?

Answer: PQ-WFQ and LLQ. Both of these queuing techniques use a strict priority queue. LLQ also provides class-based differentiated services.

15. True or false? The maximum one-way delay in the G.114 recommendation for acceptable voice is 200 ms.

Answer: False. The G.114 recommendation specifies 150 ms one-way maximum delay.

16. True or false? FRF.12 is an LFI standard used in networks with VoFR and VoIP over Frame Relay.

Answer: True. FRF.12 specifies LFI for Frame Relay networks.

17. Match the protocol with the description:

i. DHCP	**a.**	Transports coded voice streams
ii. SSCP	**b.**	Controls Cisco IOS gateways
iii. RTP	**c.**	Provides call signaling between Cisco IP phones and CM
iv. H.323	**d.**	Provides IP address
v. TFTP	**e.**	Provides phone configuration

Answer: i = d, ii = c, iii = a, iv = b, v = e.

18. Match the CM deployment model with the description:

    i. Single-site deployment   **a.** Single CM cluster with SRST at remote sites

    ii. Distributed WAN   **b.** Single CM cluster implemented in large building

    iii. Centralized WAN   **c.** Multiple CM clusters

    Answer: i = b, ii = c, iii = a.

19. Match the component with the AVVID functional area:

    i. CM   **a.** Service applications

    ii. L3 switch   **b.** Call processing

    iii. Digital gateway   **c.** Clients

    iv. Unity   **d.** Infrastructure

    Answer: i = b, ii = d, iii = c, iv = a.

20. The _____ standard establishes specifications for call setup and packet formats for VoFR.

    Answer: FRF.11.

21. Based on the current network diagram, which deployment model should you recommend?

    Answer: The current network is a hub-and-spoke architecture with many small remote sites; the solution should follow the centralized WAN call-processing architecture.

22. What feature should you recommend to provide call processing in the event of a WAN failure?

    Answer: You can implement SRST to use the PSTN in the event of a WAN failure.

23. Which queuing technique should you recommend?

    Answer: Recommend LLQ. LLQ provides a strict priority queue for voice streams and class-based WFQ service for other data types. SNA could get preferential priority over FTP traffic.

24. For Site 1, the current data traffic is 512 kbps and video traffic is 0. What circuit speed should be provisioned if 4 concurrent VoIP G.729 calls will be permitted to the site?

    Answer: The VoIP traffic will be 24 kbps x 4 = 96 kbps. The total traffic will be 96 kbps + 512 kbps = 608 kbps. The provisioned bandwidth for the circuit should be 608 kbps/.75 = 608 (4/3) = 804 kbps or higher.

25. Should you implement a CM cluster?

    Answer: Yes. Implement a CM cluster in the main site data center with redundant switches.

26. What feature can you use to reduce bandwidth over the WAN links?

    Answer: CRTP. Configure IP RTP compression to reduce the bandwidth used by VoIP traffic.

27. Which LFI technique should you use to reduce the serialization delay?

    Answer: FRF.12. FRF.12 provides LFI on Frame Relay networks.

Chapter 18

"Do I Know This Already?"

1. **b, c.** SNMPv2 and SNMPv3 both have mechanisms to secure SNMP traffic.

2. **d.** SNMP stands for Simple Network Management Protocol.

3. False. RMON is a Management Information Base (MIB) definition that defines objects for managing remote network-monitoring devices.

4. **c, d.** RMON architecture consists of RMON management applications and RMON agents (probes and monitors) that transmit information and collect statistics.

5. **a.** Cisco Discovery Protocol collects information from neighboring Cisco devices.

6. **a.** Management Information Base (MIB) is the virtual information store used within SNMP.

7. **c.** ASN.1 is the standard language used to store device information in SNMP.

8. **b.** Community is not an operation.

9. **b.** The remote monitoring agent in RMON is called a probe.

10. **b.** Cisco Discovery Protocol (CDP) is based on a Hello protocol.

Q&A

1. How are the features available in an MIB branch determined?

    Answer: Vendors decide which features will be available in the MIB tree.

2. On which devices is CDP available?

    Answer: All Cisco infrastructure equipment is CDP compliant.

3. What is an MIB variable?

    Answer: An MIB variable is the individual configurable feature of an MIB.

4. Why is the SNMP protocol considered simple?

    Answer: SNMP is considered simple because it is designed to implement compact efficient agents with data transfer on demand or driven by events to reduce routine bandwidth consumption. This design is important because it minimizes the cost of network devices and the impact on network bandwidth.

5. What method does network-management software communicating to managed devices with SNMP use to periodically gather information from agents?

   Answer: Polling is the process of regularly checking devices to assess their state and to establish connectivity. This connection is used to periodically gather the SNMP information from a device.

6. What are some examples of information transferred by SNMP using SNMP PDUs?

   Answer: The SNMP PDU exchanges can perform configurations, collect statistics and performance information, manage security, and monitor devices.

7. What is the purpose of a trap?

   Answer: It notifies the NMS when a threshold has been exceeded.

8. How does the managed device communicate with the NMS station?

   Answer: Network-management agent software on the managed device communicates with the NMS and translates the information on the managed device to a SNMP-compatible form.

9. What are the SNMP basic commands?

   Answer: get monitors the device, **set** controls the device, and **trap** is sent when a threshold is exceeded.

10. What are the three SNMP management components?

    Answer: SNMP describes three network-management components: the managed device, the agent that resides in the managed device, and the management server that collects the information.

11. Why is CDP not limited in multiprotocol environments?

    Answer: CDP is independent of any network-layer protocol; two devices that do not have a common network-layer protocol can discover each other.

Chapter 19

"Do I Know This Already?"

1. **d.** The Performance management function of the FCAPS model can be used to assess network behavior.

2. **c.** The ITU-T is responsible for creating the FCAPS architecture.

3. The Fault management function of the FCAPS model is responsible for finding network problems that reduce availability.

4. **d.** FCAPS is the abbreviation for fault, configuration, accounting, performance, and security management, described in ITU-T Recommendation X.700.

5. **c.** Accounting management allows the network manager to track utilization of network resources for even distribution and to bill them according to use.

6. **a.** SLM is a component of the Service Manager Solution of CiscoWorks.

7. **b.** There are four defined SLA types in the Cisco SLM: latency, network services, VoIP, and SLA violation traps.

8. **c.** SLCs are agreements between a service customer and a service provider that contain information about monitored services. Each SLC contains one or more SLAs.

9. **b.** An SLA defines expected performance between devices.

10. **a.** Service providers often write an SLA to define the expected level of performance from a service. In addition, the SLA can be a distinguishing point for multitier services.

Q&A

1. Which FCAPS function would you use to "stress test" a pilot network to determine how well it functions under various conditions?

   a. Fault management

   b. Security management

   c. Network management

   d. Performance management

   Answer: d. The Performance management function of the FCAPS model can be used to "stress test" a pilot network.

2. What is a grouping of SLAs called that are created to define an end-to-end service?

   a. Total Service Management (TSM)

   b. CM

   c. SLM

   d. SLC

   Answer: d. SLCs are defined by one or more SLAs to represent a service.

3. Monitoring logs to assess whether a user has used proper authentication procedures is considered part of which FCAPS function?

   a. Fault management

   b. Accounting management

    c. Security management

    d. Performance management

Answer: c. Monitoring logs can be part of the Security management function of the FCAPS model.

4. Managing variables that need to be set for a device to function the way you expect it to is included in which FCAPS function?

    a. Security management

    b. Accounting management

    c. Performance management

    d. Configuration management

Answer: d. Managing variables can be part of the Configuration management function of the FCAPS model.

5. What is the SLM component that you use to collect and aggregate performance data from devices that need to be monitored based on SLA thresholds?

    a. CM

    b. SLC

    c. TSM

    d. SLA

Answer: a. You use the CM to gather performance information from compatible devices.

6. Inventory and Cisco IOS Software versions are managed as part of which FCAPS function?

    a. Security management

    b. Accounting management

    c. Performance management

    d. Configuration management

Answer: d. Configuration management allows you to perform those functions.

7. Which of the following functions can the Cisco NetFlow product perform to provide accounting management?

    a. Baseline a network

    b. Measure utilization

    c. Detect network faults

    d. Define network services

Answer: b. Cisco NetFlow can measure utilization to bill back end users for services used or to collect data for performance analysis.

8. What do you place in Cisco IOS Software to provide Layer 3 and Layer 4 service metrics?

    a. SLA

    b. SLM

    c. SAA

    d. SLC

Answer: c. Cisco SAA is embedded in Cisco IOS software to obtain Layer 3 and 4 service metric data through synthetic testing and monitoring service performance.

9. What does Cisco provide to monitor the delivery of services against the terms of an SLA?

    a. SLC

    b. SLM

    c. CM

    d. SAA

Answer: b. SLM is a tool developed by Cisco to provide this service.

10. Intrusion detection can be categorized as part of which FCAPS function?

    a. Fault management

    b. Accounting management

    c. Configuration management

    d. Security management

Answer: d. Security management.

11. True or false? You can use the performance-management function in FCAPS to assess a network and to determine how well it functions under various conditions.

Answer: True.

12. True or false? You can use the accounting-management function in FCAPS to monitor logs to assess whether a user has used proper authentication procedures.

Answer: False. The security-management function is where you monitor authentication.

The OSI Reference Model and Numeric Conversion

The Open Systems Interconnection (OSI) model is a mandatory topic in any internetworking book. The CCDA candidate needs to understand the OSI model and identify which OSI layers host the different networking protocols. This appendix provides an overview and general understanding of the OSI reference model.

Also covered in this appendix is the numeric conversion of binary, decimal, and hexadecimal numbers. Quickly converting these numbers will help you answer test questions.

OSI Model Overview

The International Organization for Standardization (ISO) developed the OSI model in 1984, and revisited it in 1994, to coordinate standards development for interconnected information-processing systems. The model describes seven layers that start with the physical connection and end with the application. As shown in Figure 2-1, the seven layers are physical, data link, network, transport, session, presentation, and application.

Figure B-1 *Seven-Layer OSI Model*

Layer Number	OSI Layer Name
7	Application
6	Presentation
5	Session
4	Transport
3	Network
2	Data Link
1	Physical

The OSI model divides the tasks involved in moving data into seven smaller, more manageable layers. Each layer provides services to the layer above, performs at least the functions specified by the model, and expects the defined services from the layer below. The model does not define the precise nature of the interface between layers or the protocol used between peers at the same layer in different instantiations of a protocol stack. The design of the model encourages each layer to be implemented independently. For example, you can run an application over IP (Layer 3), Ethernet (Layer 2), Frame Relay (Layer 2), or Gigabit Ethernet (Layer 2). As the packets route through the Internet, the Layer 2 media changes independently from the upper-layer protocols. The OSI model helps standardize discussion of the design and construction of networks for developers and hardware manufacturers. It also provides network engineers and analysts with a framework useful in understanding internetworking.

Layered implementations of internetworking technologies do not necessarily map directly to the OSI model. For example, the TCP/IP architecture model describes only four layers, with the upper layer mapping to the three upper layers of the OSI model (application, presentation, and session). The development of IP predates the OSI model. For a more thorough discussion of the TCP/IP model, see Chapter 9, "Internet Protocol Version 4 (IPv4)."

The following sections provide a description and sample protocols for each OSI layer.

Physical Layer (OSI Layer 1)

The physical layer describes the transportation of raw bits over physical media. It defines signaling specifications and media types and interfaces. It also describes voltage levels, physical data rates, and maximum transmission distances. In summary, it deals with the electrical, mechanical, functional, and procedural specifications for links between networked systems.

Examples of physical layer specifications are

- EIA/TIA-232 (Electronic Industries Association/ Telecommunications Industry Association)
- EIA/TIA-449
- V.35
- IEEE 802 LAN and metropolitan-area network (MAN) standards
- Physical layer (PHY) groups Synchronous Optical Network/Synchronous Digital Hierarchy (SONET/SDH)
- Maximum cable distances of the Ethernet family, Token Ring, and Fiber Distributed Data Interface (FDDI)

Data Link Layer (OSI Layer 2)

This layer is concerned with the reliable transport of data across a physical link. Data at this layer is formatted into frames. Data link specifications include frame sequencing, flow control, synchronization, error notification, physical network topology, and physical addressing. This layer converts frames into bits when sending information and converts bits into frames when receiving information from the physical media. Bridges and switches operate in the data link layer.

Because of the complexity of this OSI layer, the IEEE subdivides the data link layer into three sub-layers for LANs. Figure 2-2 shows how Layer 2 is subdivided. The upper layer is the logical link sublayer, which manages the communications between devices. The bridging layer, defined by IEEE 802.1, is the middle layer. The lowest layer is the MAC sublayer, which manages the protocol access to the physical layer and ultimately the actual media. Systems attached to a common data link layer have a unique address on that data link layer.

Figure B-2   *IEEE Data Link Sublayers*

OSI Model	IEEE 802 Specifications
Data Link Layer	802.2 Logical Link
	802.1 Bridging
	Medium Access

Examples of data link layer technologies are

- Frame Relay
- ATM
- Synchronous Data Link Control (SDLC)
- High-Level Data Link Control (HDLC)
- Point-to-Point Protocol (PPP)
- Ethernet implementations (IEEE 802.3)
- Token Ring (IEEE 802.5)
- Wireless LAN (IEEE 802.11)

Network Layer (OSI Layer 3)

The network layer is concerned with routing information and methods to determine paths to a destination. Information at this layer is called packets. Specifications include routing protocols, logical network addressing, and packet fragmentation. Routers operate in this layer.

Examples of network layer specifications are

- Routed protocols
  - IP
  - Internetwork Packet Exchange (IPX)

- Routing protocols
    - Routing Information Protocol (RIP)
    - Open Shortest Path First (OSPF)
    - Enhanced Interior Gateway Routing Protocol (EIGRP)
    - Intermediate System–to-Intermediate System (IS-IS)
    - Connectionless Network Protocol (CLNP)

Transport Layer (OSI Layer 4)

The transport layer provides reliable, transparent transport of data segments from upper layers. It provides end-to-end error checking and recovery, multiplexing, virtual circuit management, and flow control. Messages are assigned a sequence number at the transmission end. At the receiving end, the packets are reassembled, checked for errors, and acknowledged. Flow control manages the data transmission to ensure that the transmitting device does not send more data than the receiving device can process.

Examples of transport layer specifications are

- TCP
- Real-Time Transport Protocol (RTP)
- Sequenced Packet Exchange (SPX)
- AppleTalk's Transaction Protocol (ATP)
- User Datagram Protocol (UDP)

Session Layer (OSI Layer 5)

The session layer provides a control structure for communication between applications. It establishes, manages, and terminates communication connections called sessions. Communication sessions consist of service requests and responses that occur between applications on different devices.

Examples of specifications that operate at the session layer are

- AppleTalk's Zone Information Protocol (ZIP)
- DECnet's Session Control Protocol (SCP)
- H.245, H.225

Presentation Layer (OSI Layer 6)

The presentation layer provides application layer entities with services to ensure information is preserved during transfer. Knowledge of the syntax selected at the application layer allows selection of compatible transfer syntax if a change is required. This layer provides conversion of character-representation formats as might be required for reliable transfer. Voice coding schemes are specified at this layer.

An example of a specification that operates at the presentation layer is Abstract Syntax Notation 1 (ASN.1)

Application Layer (OSI Layer 7)

The application layer provides the user or operating system access to the network services. It interacts with software applications by identifying communication resources, determining network availability, and distributing information services. It also provides synchronization between the peer applications residing on separate systems.

Examples of application layer specifications are

- Telnet
- File Transfer Protocol (FTP)
- Simple Mail Transfer Protocol (SMTP)
- Simple Network Management Protocol (SNMP)
- Network File System (NFS)
- Association Control Service Element (ACSE)

Example of Layered Communication

Suppose that you use a Telnet application. Telnet maps into the top three layers of the OSI model. In Figure B-3, a user on Host 1 enables the Telnet application to access a remote host (Host 2). The Telnet application provides a user interface (application layer) to network services. As defined in RFC 854, ASCII is the default code format. There is no session layer defined for Telnet (not an OSI protocol). Per the RFC, Telnet uses TCP for connectivity (transport layer). The TCP segment is placed into an IP packet (network layer) with a destination IP address of Host 2. The IP packet is placed into an Ethernet frame (data link layer), which is converted into bits and sent onto the wire (physical layer).

Figure B-3 *Telnet Example*

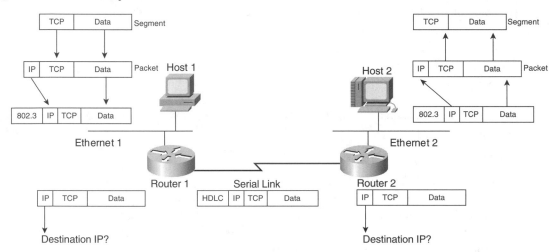

When the frame arrives at Router 1, it converts the bits into a frame; removes the frame headers (data link); checks the destination IP address (network); places a serial link header to the packet, making it a serial frame; and forwards the frame to the serial link (data link), which sends it as bits.

Router 2 receives the bits, converts to a frame; removes the serial encapsulation headers; checks the destination IP address (network); adds an Ethernet header to the packet, making it a frame; and places a frame on Ethernet 2 (data link). Host 2 receives bits (physical) from the Ethernet cable and converts the bits into a frame (data link). Then, the IP protocol is examined and the packet data is forwarded to TCP, which checks the segment number and for errors and then forwards the segment to TCP port 23 (Telnet), which is the application.

Numeric Conversion

This section focuses on the techniques for converting between decimal, binary, and hexadecimal numbers. Although the exam might not have a specific question about converting a binary number to decimal, you need to know how to convert these numbers to do problems on the test. A diagram might show a Token Ring with a decimal number, but the routing information field (RIF) might be shown as hexadecimal. An IP address could be shown as binary, as hexadecimal, or in traditional dotted-decimal format. Some **show** commands have output information in hexadecimal or binary formats.

Hexadecimal Numbers

The hexadecimal numeric system uses 16 digits, instead of 10 digits used by the decimal system. Table B-1 shows the hexadecimal digits and their decimal equivalent values.

Table B-1 *Hexadecimal Digits*

Hexadecimal Digits	Decimal Value
0	0
1	1
2	2
3	3
4	4
5	5
6	6
7	7
8	8
9	9
A	10
B	11
C	12
D	13
E	14
F	15
10	16

Hexadecimal Representation

It is common to represent a hexadecimal number with "0x" before the number so that it is not confused with a decimal number. The hexadecimal number of decimal 16 is written as 0x10, not 10. Another method is to put a subscript h to the right on the number, such as 10_h. It is also common to use the term hex when speaking of hexadecimal. Much of the text that follows uses hex.

Converting Decimal to Hexadecimal

First things first: memorize Table B-1. For larger numbers, there are two methods. The first method is to convert decimal to binary and then from binary to hex. The second method is to divide the decimal number by 16—the residual is the rightmost hexadecimal digit—and then keep dividing until the number is not divisible anymore. For the first method, use the schemes described in later sections. For the second method, follow the examples described here.

First, divide the decimal number by 16. The remainder of the division is the least significant (first) hexadecimal digit. Continue to divide the quotients (answer) of the divisions by 16 until the quotient is 0. The remainder value of each later division is converted to a hexadecimal digit and prepended to the previous value. The final remainder is the most significant digit of the hexadecimal equivalent. For large numbers, you might have to divide many times, This process will be clearer in the following examples.

Conversion Example B-1: *Convert 26 to Its Hex Equivalent*

Divide by 16:

$$16\,\overline{)\,26}$$

Answer: **1A$_h$**

Conversion Example B-2: *Convert 96 to Its Hex Equivalent*

Not divisible by 256; divide by 16:

$$16\,\overline{)\,96}$$

Answer: **60$_h$**

Conversion Example B-3:   *Convert 375 to Its Hex Equivalent*

Divide by 16 first:

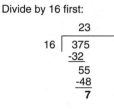

```
          23
      _____
16 |  375
      -32
       55
      -48
        7
```

Now divide 23 by 16:

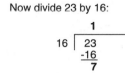

```
           1
       _____
16 |  23
     -16
       7
```

Now take the residual from the first division (7) and concatentate it with the residual from the second division (7), plus the result of the second division (1), and the answer is 177h.

Conversion Example B-4:   *Convert 218 to Its Hex Equivalent*

Divide by 16:

```
          13 = Dh
      _____
16 |  218
      -16
       58
      -48
       10 = Ah
```

Answer: **DAh**

Converting Hexadecimal to Decimal

To convert a hex number to decimal, take the rightmost digit and convert it to decimal (for example, 0xC = 12). Then, add this number to the second rightmost digit * 16 and third rightmost digit * 256. Don't expect to convert numbers larger than 255 on the CCDA exam because the upper limit of IP addresses in dotted-decimal format is 255 (although Token Ring numbers do reach 4096). Some examples follow.

Conversion Example B-5:   *Convert 177$_h$ to Decimal*

$$
\begin{array}{rcl}
1 \times 256 & = & 256 \\
7 \times \ 16 & = & 112 \\
7 \times \ \ 1 & = & \underline{\ \ \ 7} \\
& & \mathbf{375_d}
\end{array}
$$

Conversion Example B-6:   *Convert 60$_h$ to Decimal*

$$
\begin{array}{rcl}
6 \times 16 & = & 96 \\
0 \times \ 1 & = & \underline{\ \ 0} \\
& & \mathbf{96_d}
\end{array}
$$

Conversion Example B-7:   *Convert 100$_h$ to Decimal*

$$
\begin{array}{rcl}
1 \times 256 & = & 256 \\
0 \times \ 16 & = & \ \ 0 \\
0 \times \ \ 1 & = & \underline{\ \ 0} \\
& & \mathbf{256_d}
\end{array}
$$

Conversion Example B-8:   *Convert 1DA$_h$ to Decimal*

$$
\begin{array}{rcl}
1 \times 256 & = & 256 \\
13 \times \ 16 & = & 208 \\
10 \times \ \ 1 & = & \underline{\ 10} \\
& & \mathbf{474_d}
\end{array}
$$

Alternative Method to Convert from Hex to Decimal

Another way is to just convert from hex to binary and then binary to decimal. Conversion from binary to decimal follows.

Binary Numbers

The binary number system uses two digits: 1 and 0. Computer systems use binary numbers. IP addresses and MAC addresses are represented by binary numbers. The number of binary 1s or 0s is the number of *bits*, short for binary digits. For example, 01101010 is a binary number with 8 bits. An IP address has 32 bits, and a MAC address has 48 bits. As shown in Table B-2, IP addresses are usually represented in dotted-decimal format; therefore, it is helpful to know how to convert between binary and decimal numbers. MAC addresses are usually represented in hexadecimal numbers; therefore, it is helpful to know how to convert between binary and hexadecimal numbers.

Table B-2   *Binary Representation of IP and MAC Addresses*

IP Address in Binary	IP Address in Dotted Decimal
00101000 10001010 01010101 10101010	= 40.138.85.170
MAC Address in Binary	**MAC Address in Hexadecimal**
00001100 10100001 10010111 01010001 00000001 10010001	= 0C:A1:97:51:01:91

The CCDA candidate should memorize Table B-3, which shows numbers from 0 to 16 in decimal, binary, and hexadecimal formats.

Table B-3   *Decimal, Binary, and Hexadecimal Numbers*

Decimal Value	Hexadecimal	Binary
0	0	0000
1	1	0001
2	2	0010
3	3	0011
4	4	0100
5	5	0101
6	6	0110
7	7	0111
8	8	1000
9	9	1001
10	A	1010
11	B	1011
12	C	1100
13	D	1101
14	E	1110
15	F	1111
16	10	10000

Converting Binary to Hexadecimal

To convert binary numbers to hex, group the bits into groups of four, starting with the right-justified bits. Groups of four bits are often called *nibbles*. Each nibble can be represented by a single hexadecimal digit. A group of two nibbles is an octet, 8 bits. Examples follow.

Conversion Example B-9:   *Convert 0010011101 to Hex*

Group the bits:
00 1001 1101
Answer: **09D$_h$**

Conversion Example B-10:   *Convert 0010101001011001000010110001 to Hex*

Group the bits:
0010 1010 0101 1001 0000 1011 0001
Answer: **2A590B1$_h$**

Converting Hexadecimal to Binary

This procedure is also easy. Simply change the hex digits into their 4-bit equivalent. Examples follow.

Conversion Example B-11:   *Convert 0DEAD0 into Hex*

Hex: 0   D   E   A   D   0
Binary: 0000 1101 1110 1010 1101 0000
Answer: **000011011110101011010000**

Conversion Example B-12:   *Convert AA0101 into Hex*

Hex: A   A   0   1   0   1
Binary: 1010 1010 0000 0001 0000 0001
Answer: **101010100000000100000001**

Converting Binary to Decimal

To convert a binary number to decimal, multiply each instance of 0 or 1 by the power of 2 associated with the position of the bit in the binary number. The first bit, starting from the right, is associated with $2^0 = 1$. The value of the exponent increases by 1 as each bit is processed, working leftward. As shown in Table 2-4, each bit in the binary number 10101010 has a decimal equivalent from 0 to 128 based on the value of the bit multiplied by a power of 2 associated with the bit position. It is similar to decimal numbers where the numbers are based on powers of 10: 1s, 10s, 100s, and so on. In decimal, the number 111 is $(1*100) + (1*10) + (1*1)$. In binary, the number 11111111 is the sum of $(1*2^7) + (1*2^6) + (1*2^5) + (1*2^4) + (1*2^3) + (1*2^2) + (1*2^1) + (1*2^0) = 128 + 64 + 32 + 16 + 8 + 4 + 2 + 1 = 255$. For 10101010, the result is $128 + 0 + 32 + 0 + 8 + 0 + 2 + 0 = 170$. Examples follow.

Table B-4   *Decimal Values of Bits in a Binary Number*

Power of 2	$2^7 = 128$	$2^6 = 64$	$2^5 = 32$	$2^4 = 16$	$2^3 = 8$	$2^2 = 4$	$2^1 = 2$	$2^0 = 1$
Binary	1	1	1	1	1	1	1	1

NOTE   Just memorize 1, 2, 4, 8, 16, 32, 64, and 128. Use it as you read a binary number from right to left. This technique should be helpful in fast conversions.

Conversion Example B-13:   *Convert 10110111 to Decimal*

Sum: 128 + 0 + 32 + 16 + 0 + 4 + 2 + 1
Answer = **183**

Conversion Example B-14:   *Convert 11011 to Decimal*

Sum: 16 + 8 + 0 + 2 + 1
Answer = **27**

Conversion Example B-15:   *Convert 11111111 to Decimal*

Sum: 128 + 64 + 32 + 16 + 8 + 4 + 2 + 1
Answer = **255**

Converting Decimal to Binary Numbers

This procedure is similar to converting from hex to decimal (by dividing), but now you divide the decimal number by 2. You use each residual to build the binary number, by prepending each residual bit to the previous bit starting with the right. Repeat the procedure until you cannot divide anymore. The only problem is that for large numbers, you might have to divide many times. The number of divisions can be reduced by first converting the decimal value to a hexadecimal value and then converting the intermediate result to binary representation. After the following example, you will find an alternate method suitable for use with decimal values between 0 and 255 that can be represented in a single octet.

Conversion Example B-16:   *Convert 26 to Binary*

The first bit is 0; now divide 13 by 2. [0]

The second bit is 1; now divide 6 by 2. [10]

The third bit is 0; now divide 3 by 2. [010]

The fourth bit is 1; the leftmost bit is the division result at the top, which is one. [11010]

Answer: **11010**

Alternative Method

The dividing procedure described earlier works; it just takes a lot of time. Another way is to remember the bit position values within a byte—128, 64, 32, 16, 8, 4, 2, 1—and play with the bits until the sum adds up to the desired number. This method works when converting integer values between 0 and 255 inclusive. Table B-5 shows these binary numbers and their decimal value.

Table B-5 *Bit Values*

Binary Number	Decimal Value
10000000	128
01000000	64
00100000	32
00010000	16
00001000	8
00000100	4
00000010	2
00000001	1

For example, to convert 26, you know that it is a number smaller than 128, 64, and 32, so those three bits will be 0 (000?????). Now, you need to find a combination from 16, 8, 4, 2, and 1 that adds up to 26. This method involves using subtraction to compute the remaining number. Start with the largest number, and make the bit at 16 a 1 (0001????). The difference between 26 and 16 is 10 so what combination of 8, 4, 2, and 1 gives 10? (1010.) Therefore, the answer is 00011010. You might think this method involves too much guesswork, but it becomes second nature after some practice.

Conversion Example B-17:   *Convert 137 to Binary*

> The number is larger than 128; enable that bit. [1???????]
>
> How far is 137 from 128: 9; enable the remaining bits for a value of 9 [1???1001].
>
> The answer is 10001001.

Conversion Example B-18:   *Convert 211 to Binary*

> The number is larger than 128; enable that bit. [1???????]
>
> Because 211–128 is greater than 64, enable that bit. [11??????] (Remember that 11000000 = 192.)
>
> Because 211–192=19, enable bits 16, 2, and 1. [11?1??11]
>
> The answer is 11010011.

In addition to remembering the bit-position values (128, 64, 32, 16, 8, 4, 2, 1), it helps to remember network subnet masks values. Remembering them makes it easier to figure out whether you need to enable a bit. Table B-6 summarizes the binary subnet mask numbers and their decimal values.

Table B-6 *Binary Masks and their Decimal Values*

Binary Mask	Decimal
10000000	128
11000000	192
11100000	224
11110000	240
11111000	248
11111100	252
11111110	254

References and Recommended Readings

The references and recommended reading suggestions in this appendix are organized by chapter and are categorized in the following order:

- Books
- White papers
- Magazine and journal articles
- Websites
- Other

For those chapters that are not listed here, there were no particular references or recommended readings suggested.

Chapter 1: Design Principles

Cisco Systems, Inc. T. Thomas, and A. Khan. *Cisco CCIE Fundamentals: Network Design and Case Studies*. Indianapolis, Indiana: Cisco Press; 1998.

Retana, A., D. Slice, and R. White. *CCIE Professional Development: Advanced IP Network Design*. Indianapolis, Indiana: Cisco Press; 1999.

Quinn-Andry, T. and K. Haller. *Designing Campus Networks*. Indianapolis, Indiana: Cisco Press; 1998.

Convery, S. and B. Trudel. "SAFE: A Security Blueprint for Enterprise Networks." [white paper]; available from http://www.cisco.com.

Chapter 2: Network Design Methodology

Cisco Systems, Inc. *Internetworking Technologies Handbook*, Second edition. Indianapolis, Indiana: Cisco Press; 1998.

Chapter 3: Network Structure Models

Oppenheimer, P. *Top-Down Network Design*. Indianapolis, Indiana: Cisco Press; 1999.

"Removing Content Switching Performance Barriers: A Discussion of the Cisco CSM Pipelined Network Processor Architecture." [white paper]; available from http://www.cisco.com.

Chapter 4: LAN Design

"CSMA/CD Access Method," IEEE 802.3-2002. Piscataway, New Jersey: Institute of Electrical and Electronics Engineers; 2002.

"Token-Ring Access Method," IEEE 802.5-1998, Piscataway, New Jersey: Institute of Electrical and Electronics Engineers; 1998.

"Wireless LAN MAC and Physical Layer (PHY) Specifications," IEEE 802.11-1999, Piscataway, New Jersey: Institute of Electrical and Electronics Engineers; 1999.

10 Gigabit Ethernet Alliance. http://www.10gea.org.

Cisco Catalyst G-L3 Series Switches Server Load Balancing. http://www.cisco.com/en/US/products/hw/switches/ps672/products_configuration_guide_chapter09186a008007f253.html#35346.

Ethernet Technologies. http://www.cisco.com/univercd/cc/td/doc/cisintwk/ito_doc/ethernet.htm#xtocid3.

Remote Access VPN Solution, Design Guides. http://www.cisco.com/en/US/netsol/ns110/ns170/ns171/ns125/networking_solutions_design_guidances_list.html.Chapter 4: LAN Design

Chapter 5: Wide-Area Networking Technologies

Bruno, A. *CCIE Routing and Switching Exam Certification Guide*. Indianapolis, Indiana: Cisco Press; 2002.

Cisco Systems, Inc. *CCNA Self-Study: CCNA Basics (CCNAB)*. Indianapolis, Indiana: Cisco Press; 2002.

Cisco Systems, Inc. *Cisco IOS Wide Area Networking Solutions*. Indianapolis, Indiana: Cisco Press; 2001.

http://www.cisco.com/pcgi-bin/Support/browse/index.pl?i=Technologies&f=1587

WAN Introduction, Technology Family Matrix. http://www.cisco.com/en/US/tech/tk713/tech_topology_and_network_serv_and_protocol_suite_home.html.

Chapter 6: Designing Wide-Area Networking Solutions

Bruno, A. *CCIE Routing and Switching Exam Certification Guide*. Indianapolis, Indiana: Cisco Press; 2002.

Cisco Systems, Inc. *Cisco IOS Wide Area Networking Solutions*. Indianapolis, Indiana: Cisco Press; 2001.

Quality of Service Networking. http://www.cisco.com/univercd/cc/td/doc/cisintwk/ito_doc/ qos.htm.

Chapter 7: Backup Options and Sample WAN Designs

Bruno, A. *CCIE Routing and Switching Exam Certification Guide*. Indianapolis, Indiana: Cisco Press; 2002.

Cisco Systems, Inc. *Cisco IOS Wide Area Networking Solutions*. Indianapolis, Indiana: Cisco Press; 2001.

Chapter 8: VPN and DSL WAN Design

Pepelnjak, I. and J. Guichard. *MLPS and VPN Architectures*. Indianapolis, Indiana: Cisco Press; 2001.

Wenstrom, M. *Managing Cisco Network Security*. Indianapolis, Indiana: Cisco Press; 2001.

DSL and LRE, Protocol Groups. http://www.cisco.com/en/US/tech/tk175/ tech_protocol_families.html

E. Rescorla. "Diffie-Hellman Key Agreement Method," RFC 2631; available from http:// www.ietf.org/rfc.

Hamzeh, K., G. Pall, W. Verthein, J. Taarud, W. Little, and G. Zorn. "Point-to-Point Tunneling Protocol (PPTP)," RFC 2637; available from http://www.ietf.org/rfc.

Hanks, S., T. Li, D. Farinacci, and P. Traina. "Generic Routing Encapsulation (GRE)," RFC 1701; available from http://www.ietf.org/rfc.

Harkins, D. and D. Carrel. "The Internet Key Exchange (IKE)," RFC 2409; available from http:// www.ietf.org/rfc.

Kent, S. and R. Atkinson. "IP Authentication Header," RFC 2402; available from http:// www.ietf.org/rfc.

Kent, S. and R. Atkinson. "IP Encapsulating Security Payload (ESP)," RFC 2406; available from http://www.ietf.org/rfc.

Kent, S. and R. Atkinson. "Security Architecture for the Internet Protocol," RFC 2401; available from http://www.ietf.org/rfc.

Madson, C. and R. Glenn. "The Use of HMAC-MD5-96 within ESP and AH," RFC 2403; available from http://www.ietf.org/rfc.

Chapter 9: Internet Protocol Version 4 (IPv4)

Almquist, P. "Type of Service in the Internet Protocol Suite," RFC 1349; available from http://www.ietf.org/rfc.

Croft, B., Gilmore, J. "BOOTSTRAP PROTOCOL (BOOTP)," RFC 951; available from http://www.ietf.org/rfc.

Droms, R. "Dynamic Host Configuration Protocol," RFC 2131; available from http://www.ietf.org/rfc.

Egevang, K., Francis, P. "The IP Network Address Translator (NAT)," RFC 1631; available from http://www.ietf.org/rfc.

Information Sciences Institute. "Internet Protocol," RFC 791; available from http://www.ietf.org/rfc.

Mockapetris, P. "DOMAIN NAMES-CONCEPTS AND FACILITIES," RFC 1034; available from http://www.ietf.org/rfc.

Mockapetris, P. "DOMAIN NAMES-IMPLEMENTATION AND SPECIFICATION," RFC 1035; available from http://www.ietf.org/rfc.

Nichols, K., Blake, S., Baker, F., Black, D. "Definition of the Differentiated Services Field (DS Field) in the IPv4 and IPv6 Headers," RFC 2474; available from http://www.ietf.org/rfc.

Plummer, D. "An Ethernet Address Resolution Protocol -- or -- Converting Network Protocol Addresses to 48.bit Ethernet Address for Transmission on Ethernet Hardware," RFC 826; available from http://www.ietf.org/rfc.

Rekhter, Y., Moskowitz, B., Karrenberg, D., de Groot, G.J., Lear, E. "Address Allocation for Private Internets," RFC 1918; available from http://www.ietf.org/rfc.

Srisuresh, P., Egevang, K. "Traditional IP Network Address Translator (Traditional NAT)," RFC 3022; available from http://www.ietf.org/rfc.

Chapter 10: Internet Protocol Version 6 (IPv6)

Doyle, J. and J. DeHaven Carroll. *Routing TCP/IP*, Volume II. Indianapolis, Indiana: Cisco Press; 2001.

Coltun, R., Ferguson, D., Moy, J. "OSPF for IPv6," RFC 2740; available from http://www.ietf.org/rfc.

Conta, A., Deering, S. "Internet Control Message Protocol (ICMPv6) for the Internet Protocol Version 6 (IPv6) Specification," RFC 2463; available from http://www.ietf.org/rfc.

Deering, S., Hinden, R. "Internet Protocol, Version 6 ((IPv6) Specification," RFC 2460; available from http://www.ietf.org/rfc.

Fink, R. and R. Hinden. "6bone (IPv6 Testing Address Allocation) Phaseout" [draft]; available from http://www.potaroo.net/ietf/ids/draft-fink-6bone-phaseout-04.txt.

Hinden, R., Deering, S. "IP Version 6 Addressing Architecture," RFC 2373; available from http://www.ietf.org/rfc.

Hinden R., O'Dell, M., Deering, S. "An IPv6 Aggregatable Global Unicast Address Format," RFC 2374; available from http://www.ietf.org/rfc.

Hopps, C. "Routing IPv6 for IS-IS" [draft]; available from http://www.simpleweb.org/ietf/internetdrafts/complete/draft-ietf-isis-ipv6-03.txt.

http://www.cisco.com/application/pdf/en/us/guest/tech/tk373/c1482/ccmigration_09186a008019d70b.pdf

Kent, S. and R. Atkinson. "IP Authentication Header," RFC 2402; available from http://www.ietf.org/rfc.

Kent, S. and R. Atkinson. "IP Encapsulating Security Payload (ESP)," RFC 2406; available from http://www.ietf.org/rfc.

Kent, S. and R. Atkinson. "Security Architecture for the Internet Protocol," RFC 2401; available from http://www.ietf.org/rfc.

McCann, J., Deering, S., Mogul, J. "Path MTU Discovery for IP version 6," RFC 1981; available from http://www.ietf.org/rfc.

Narten, T., Nordmark, E., Simpson, W. "Neighbor Discovery for IP Version 6 (IPv6)," RFC 2461; available from http://www.ietf.org/rfc.

Malkin, G., Minnear, R. "RIPng for IPv6," RFC 2080; available from http://www.ietf.org/rfc.

Marques, P., Dupont, F. "Use of BGP-4 Multiprotocol Extensions for IPv6 Inter-Domain Routing," RFC 2545; available from http://www.ietf.org/rfc.

Thomson, S., Huitema, C. "DNS Extensions to support IP version 6," RFC 1886; available from http://www.ietf.org/rfc.

Tsirtsis, G., Srisuresh, P. "Network Address Translation – Protocol Translation (NAT-PT)," RFC 2766; available from http://www.ietf.org/rfc.

Chapter 11: Routing Protocol Selection Criteria

Bruno, A. *CCIE Routing and Switching Exam Certification Guide*. Indianapolis, Indiana: Cisco Press; 2002.

Hedrick, C. "Routing Information Protocol," RFC 1058; available from http://www.ietf.org/rfc.

Malkin, G. "RIP Version 2," RFC 2453; available from http://www.ietf.org/rfc.

Moy, J. "OSPF Version 2," RFC 2328; available from http://www.ietf.org/rfc.

Oran, D. "OSI IS-IS Intra-domain Routing Protocol," RFC 1142; available from http://www.ietf.org/rfc.

Chapter 12: RIP, IGRP, and EIGRP Characteristics and Design

Bruno, A. *CCIE Routing and Switching Exam Certification Guide*. Indianapolis, Indiana: Cisco Press, 2002.

Doyle, J. *Routing TCP/IP*, Volume I. Indianapolis, Indiana: Cisco Press; 1998.

Enhanced Interior Gateway Routing Protocol. http://www.cisco.com/en/US/tech/tk365/tk207/technologies_white_paper09186a0080094cb7.shtml

Enhanced IGRP. http://www.cisco.com/univercd/cc/td/doc/cisintwk/ito_doc/en_igrp.htm.

Hedrick, C. "Routing Information Protocol," RFC 1058; available from http://www.ietf.org/rfc.

Malkin, G. "RIP Version 2," RFC 2453; available from http://www.ietf.org/rfc.

Routing Information Protocol. http://www.cisco.com/univercd/cc/td/doc/cisintwk/ito_doc/rip.htm.

Tech Notes: How Does Unequal Cost Path Load Balancing (Variance) Work in IGRP and EIGRP? http://www.cisco.com/warp/public/103/19.html.

Chapter 13: OSPF and IS-IS

Bruno, A. *CCIE Routing and Switching Exam Certification Guide*. Indianapolis, Indiana: Cisco Press; 2002.

Doyle, J. *Routing TCP/IP*, Volume I. Indianapolis, Indiana: Cisco Press; 1998.

Martey, A. *IS-IS Network Design Solutions*. Indianapolis, Indiana: Cisco Press; 2002.

Coltun, R., Fuller, V. "The OSPF NSSA Option," RFC 1587; available from http://www.ietf.org/rfc.

D. Oran, Editor, "OSI IS-IS Intra-domain Routing Protocol, " RFC 1142 ; available from http://www.ietf.org/rfc.

Moy, J. "OSPF Version 2," RFC 2328; available from http://www.ietf.org/rfc.

Chapter 14: Border Gateway Protocol (BGP), Redistribution, and IP Multicast

Doyle, J. *Routing TCP/IP*, Volume I. Indianapolis, Indiana: Cisco Press; 1999.

Doyle, J. and J. Carroll. *Routing TCP/IP*, Volume II. Indianapolis, Indiana: Cisco Press; 2001.

Halabi, S. *Internet Routing Architectures*. Indianapolis, Indiana: Cisco Press; 2000.

Williamson, B. *Developing IP Multicast Networks*. Indianapolis, Indiana: Cisco Press; 1999.

"Internet Protocol (IP) Multicast Technology Overview" [white paper]; available from http://www.cisco.com/warp/public/cc/pd/iosw/tech/ipmu_ov.htm.

Chandra, R., P. Traina, and T. Li, "BGP Communities Attribute," RFC 1997; available from http://www.ietf.org/rfc.

Border Gateway Protocol. http://www.cisco.com/univercd/cc/td/doc/cisintwk/ito_doc/bgp.htm.

Deering, S. "Host Extensions for IP Multicasting," RFC 1112; available from http://www.ietf.org/rfc.

Estrin, D., D. Farinacci, A. Helmy, D. Thaler, S. Deering, M. Handley, V. Jacobson, C. Liu, P. Sharma, and L. Wei. "Protocol Independent Multicast-Sparse Mode (PIM-SM): Protocol Specification," RFC 2362 (Experimental); available from http://www.ietf.org/rfc.

Fenner, W. "Internet Group Management Protocol, Version 2," RFC 2236; available from http://www.ietf.org/rfc.

Fuller, V., T. Li, J. Yu, and K. Varadhan. "Classless Inter-Domain Routing (CIDR): an Address Assignment and Aggregation Strategy," RFC 1519; available from http://www.ietf.org/rfc.

Meyer, D. "Administratively Scoped IP Multicast," RFC 2365; available from http://www.ietf.org/rfc.

Rekhter, Y. and T. Li, "A Border Gateway Protocol 4 (BGP-4)," RFC 1771; available from http://www.ietf.org/rfc.

Waitzman, D., Partride, C., Deering, S. "Distance Vector Multicast Routing Protocol," RFC 1075; available from http://www.ietf.org/rfc.

Chapter 15: Common Security Flaws and Monitoring

SAFE Blueprint from Cisco. http://www.cisco.com/en/US/netsol/ns110/ns170/ns171/ns128/networking_solutions_package.html.

Chapter 17: Traditional Voice Architectures and Integrated Voice Design

Keagy, S. *Integrating Voice and Data Networks*. Indianapolis, Indiana: Cisco Press; 2000.

Lovell, D. *Cisco IP Telephony. Indianapolis*, Indiana: Cisco Press; 2002.

McQuerry, S., McGrew, K., Foy, S., *Cisco Voice over Frame Relay, ATM, and IP*, Indianapolis, Indiana: Cisco Press; 2001

Kotha, S. "Deploying H.323 Applications in Cisco Networks." [white paper]; available from http://www.cisco.com/warp/public/cc/pd/iosw/ioft/mmcm/tech/h323_wp.htm.

Arango, M., Dugan, A., Elliott, I., Huitema, C., Pickett, S., Pickett, S. "Media Gateway Control Protocol (MGCP) Version 1.0," RFC 2705; available from http://www.ietf.org/rfc.

Audio-Video Transport Working Group and H. Schulzrinne. "RTP Profile for Audio and Video Conferences with Minimal Control," RFC 1890; available from http://www.ietf.org/rfc.

Audio-Video Transport Working Group, H. Schulzrinne, S. Casner, R. Frederick, and V. Jacobson. "RTP: A Transport Protocol for Real-Time Applications," RFC 1889; available from http://www.ietf.org/rfc.

Handley, M., H. Schulzrinne, E. Schooler, and J. Rosenberg. "SIP: Session Initiation Protocol," RFC 2543; available from http://www.ietf.org/rfc.

Reference Guide, Packet Voice Networking. http://www.cisco.com/warp/public/cc/pd/rt/mc3810/prodlit/pvnet_in.htm.

Tech Notes: Voice Network Signaling and Control. http://www.cisco.com/warp/public/788/signalling/net_signal_control.html

Voice over IP: Per Call Bandwidth Consumption. http://www.cisco.com/warp/public/788/pkt-voice-general/bwidth_consume.htm.

GLOSSARY

µ-law   A North American companding standard used in conversion between analog and digital signals in pulse code modulation (PCM) systems. Similar to the European A-law.

1G mobile network   2.5G mobile network   second-generation-plus mobile network. A category of mobile wireless networks that supports higher data rates than 2G mobile networks. An example of a 2.5G mobile network standard is general packet radio service (GPRS).

10BASE2   The 10-Mbps baseband Ethernet specification using 50-ohm thin coaxial cable. 10BASE2, which is part of the IEEE 802.3 specification, has a distance limit of 606.8 feet (185 meters) per segment.

10BASE5   The 10-Mbps baseband Ethernet specification using standard (thick) 50-ohm baseband coaxial cable. 10BASE5, which is part of the IEEE 802.3 baseband physical layer specification, has a distance limit of 1640 feet (500 meters) per segment.

10BASE-T   The 10-Mbps baseband Ethernet specification using two pairs of twisted-pair cabling (Category 3, 4, or 5): one pair transmits data, and the other receives data. 10BASE-T, which is part of the IEEE 802.3 specification, has a distance limit of approximately 328 feet (100 meters) per segment.

100BASE-TX   The 100-Mbps baseband Fast Ethernet specification using two pairs of either unshielded twisted-pair (UTP) or shielded twisted-pair (STP) wiring. The first pair of wires receives data; the second transmits data. To guarantee the proper signal timing, a 100BASE-TX segment cannot exceed 328 feet (100 meters) in length. Based on the IEEE 802.3 standard.

100BASE-X   The 100-Mbps baseband Fast Ethernet specification that refers to the 100BASE-FX and 100BASE-TX standards for Fast Ethernet over fiber-optic cabling. Based on the IEEE 802.3 standard.

2B1Q   2 binary 1 quaternary. An encoding scheme that provides a 2-bits per baud, 80-kilobaud per second, 160-kbps transfer rate. The most common signaling method on Integrated Services Digital Network (ISDN) U interfaces. The 1988 ANSI specification T1.601 defines this protocol in detail.

2G mobile network   second-generation mobile network. A category of mobile wireless networks and services that implements digital technology. An example of a 2G mobile network standard is global system for mobile communication (GSM).

2.5G mobile network   second-generation-plus mobile network. A category of mobile wireless networks that supports higher data rates than 2G mobile networks. An example of a 2.5G mobile network standard is general packet radio service (GPRS).

3G mobile network   third-generation mobile network. A category of mobile networks with data, voice, and multimedia capabilities and always-on connections. Examples include Universal Mobile Telephone Service (UMTS) and IMT-2000.

4B/5B local fiber   4-byte/5-byte local fiber. A set of fiber-channel physical media used for Fiber Distributed Data Interface (FDDI) and ATM. 4B/5B local fiber supports speeds of up to 100 Mbps over multimode fiber.

4B3T   4 binary 3 ternary. A baseband line code (modulation and signaling structure) that maps a group of 4 binary bits into true three-state ternary code, achieving a baud-rate reduction of 25 percent. This line-code technique supports Integrated Services Digital Network (ISDN) Basic Rate Interface (BRI) in European countries. The corresponding line code used in the United States to support ISDN BRI is 2B1Q.

6BONE   The Internet's experimental IPv6 network.

802.x   A set of IEEE standards for the definition of LAN protocols.

8B/10B local fiber   8-byte/10-byte local fiber. A set of fiber-channel physical media that supports speeds of up to 149.76 Mbps over multimode fiber.

AAL   ATM Adaptation Layer. A service-dependent sublayer of the data link layer. The AAL accepts data from different applications and presents it to the ATM layer in the form of 48-byte ATM payload segments. AALs consist of two sublayers: CS and SAR. AALs differ on the basis of the source-destination timing used (CBR or VBR) and whether they are used for connection-oriented or connectionless mode data transfer. As of 2002, the four types of AAL recommended by the ITU-T are AAL1, AAL2, AAL3/4, and AAL5.

AAL1   ATM adaptation layer type 1. One of four AALs recommended by the ITU-T. AAL1 is used for connection-oriented, delay-sensitive services requiring constant bit rates, such as uncompressed video and other isochronous traffic.

AAL2   ATM adaptation layer type 2. One of four AALs recommended by the ITU-T. AAL2 is used for connection-oriented services that support a variable bit rate, such as some isochronous video and voice traffic.

AAL3/4   ATM adaptation layer type 3/4. One of four AALs, merged from two initially distinct adaptation layers, recommended by the ITU-T. AAL3/4 supports both connectionless and connection-oriented links but is used primarily to transmit SMDS packets over ATM networks.

AAL5   ATM adaptation layer type 5. One of four AALs recommended by the ITU-T. AAL5 supports connection-oriented VBR services and is used predominantly for the transfer of classical IP over ATM and LANE traffic. AAL5 uses SEAL and is the least complex of the current AAL recommendations. It offers low-bandwidth overhead and simpler processing requirements in exchange for reduced bandwidth capacity and error-recovery capability.

ABR   **1.** available bit rate. A quality of service (QoS) class defined by the ATM Forum for ATM networks. ABR is used for connections that do not require timing relationships between source and destination. ABR provides no guarantees in terms of cell loss or delay, providing only best-effort service. Traffic sources adjust their transmission rate in response to information they receive describing the network's status and its capability to successfully deliver data. **2.** Area Border Router. A router located on the border of one or more OSPF areas that connects those areas to the backbone network. ABRs are considered members of both the OSPF backbone and the attached areas. ABRs, therefore, maintain routing tables describing both the backbone topology and the topology of the other areas.

Abstract Syntax Notation 1   ASN.1. The OSI standard language to describe data types.

access layer   Provides workgroup and user access to the network.

access list   A list kept by routers and switches to control access to or from the router or switch for a number of services (for example, to prevent packets with a certain IP address from leaving a particular interface on the router or switch).

accounting management   Tracking the usage of network segments to determine usage-based billing of services.

ACD   **1.** automatic call distributor. A programmable device at a call center that routes incoming calls to targets within that call center. After the Cisco Intelligent Contact Management (ICM) software determines the call's target, the call is sent to the ACD associated with that target. The ACD must then complete the routing as determined by the Cisco ICM. **2.** automatic call distribution. A device or service that automatically reroutes calls to customers in geographically distributed locations served by the same central office (CO).

ACELP   Algebraic Code-Excited Linear Prediction. A compression method used in the G.723.1 codec that produces a 5.3 kbps bit rate.

ACR   Allowed Cell Rate. A parameter defined by the ATM Forum for ATM traffic management. ACR varies between the MCR and the PCR and is controlled dynamically using congestion-control mechanisms.

ACS   Access Control Server. Cisco Secure ACS provides authentication, authorization, and accounting (AAA) services to network devices that function as AAA clients, such as a network access server, PIX Firewall, or router.

active monitor   The device responsible for managing a Token Ring. A network node is selected to be the active monitor if it has the highest MAC address on the ring. The active monitor is responsible for management tasks such as ensuring that tokens are not lost or that frames do not circulate indefinitely.

adjacency   When two routers exchange hellos and establish two-way communication.

administrative distance   A rating of the trustworthiness of a routing information source.

ADSL   Asymmetric Digital Subscriber Line. Provides asymmetric DSL speeds up to 8 Mbps for the downlink.

AFI   Authority and Format Identifier. The part of an NSAP-format ATM address that identifies the type and format of the IDI portion of the address.

aggregatable-global addresses   IPv6 addresses that are globally unique and routable.

AH   Authentication Header. IPSec protocol for connection integrity and data origin. Does not provide data encryption.

A-law   An ITU-T companding standard used in the conversion between analog and digital signals in PCM systems. The A-law is used primarily in European telephone networks and is similar to the North American μ-law standard.

ANSI   American National Standards Institute. A voluntary organization composed of corporate, government, and other members that coordinates standards-related activities, approves U.S. standards, and develops positions for the United States in international standards organizations. ANSI helps develop international and U.S. standards relating to, among other things, communications and networking. ANSI is a member of the IEC and the ISO.

AP   access point. Provides communication between wireless clients and connects the WLAN with the wired LAN.

AppleTalk   A series of communications protocols designed by Apple Computer that consists of two phases. Phase 1, the earlier version, supports a single physical network that can have only one network number and be in one zone. Phase 2 supports multiple logical networks on a single physical network and allows networks to be in more than one zone.

Application layer   Layer 7 of the OSI reference model. This layer provides services to application processes (such as e-mail, file transfer, and terminal emulation) that are outside the OSI model. The application layer identifies and establishes the availability of intended communication partners (and the resources required to connect with them), synchronizes cooperating applications, and establishes an agreement on the procedures for error recovery and the control of data integrity.

area   A logical set of network segments (CLNS-, DECnet-, or OSPF-based) and their attached devices. Areas usually are connected to other areas via routers, making up a single autonomous system.

ARP   Address Resolution Protocol. An Internet protocol used to map an IP address to a MAC address. Defined in RFC 826.

ARPANET   Advanced Research Projects Agency Network. A landmark packet-switching network established in 1969. ARPANET was developed in the 1970s by BBN and was funded by ARPA (and later DARPA). It eventually evolved into the Internet. The term ARPANET was retired officially in 1990.

AS   autonomous system. A collection of networks under a common administration sharing a common routing strategy. An autonomous system must be assigned a unique 16-bit number.

ASBR   autonomous system boundary router. An OSPF router that injects external LSAs into the OSPF network.

ASN.1   Abstract Syntax Notation 1. An OSI language for describing data types independent of particular computer structures and representation techniques. Described by ISO International Standard 8824.

ATM   Asynchronous Transfer Mode. The international standard for cell relay in which multiple service types (such as voice, video, or data) are conveyed in fixed-length (53-byte) cells. Fixed-length cells allow cell processing to occur in hardware, thereby reducing transit delays. ATM is designed to take advantage of high-speed transmission media, such as E3, SONET, and T3.

ATM layer   The service-independent sublayer of the data link layer in an ATM network. The ATM layer receives the 48-byte payload segments from the AAL and attaches a 5-byte header to each, producing standard 53-byte ATM cells. These cells are passed to the physical layer for transmission across the physical medium.

AUI Attachment Unit Interface. An IEEE 802.3 interface between a media access unit (MAU) and a network interface card (NIC). The term AUI also can refer to the rear panel port to which an AUI cable might attach. Also called a transceiver cable.

authentication The process of identifying an individual, usually based on a username and password.

authorization The process of giving individuals access to system objects based on their identity.

AVVID Architecture for Voice, Video, and Integrated Data. Cisco AVVID provides an enterprise foundation that combines IP connectivity with security, high availability, and quality of service.

B channel bearer channel. A DS0 time slot that carries analog voice or digital data over ISDN. In ISDN, a full-duplex, 64-kbps channel used to send user data.

B8ZS Binary 8-zero Substitution. A line code type, used on T1 and E1 circuits, in which a special code is substituted whenever eight consecutive zeros are sent over the link. This code then is interpreted at the remote end of the connection. This technique guarantees ones density independent of the data stream. Sometimes called bipolar 8-zero substitution.

backbone router An OSPF router with at least one interface attached to Area 0.

Backdoor A method left by the hacker to gain access to a system at a later time.

bandwidth The difference between the highest and lowest frequencies available for network signals. Also, the rated throughput capacity of a given network medium or protocol. The frequency range necessary to convey a signal is measured in hertz (Hz); for example, voice signals typically require approximately 7 kHz of bandwidth, and data traffic typically requires approximately 50 kHz of bandwidth.

BDR Backup Designated Router. An OSPF BDR provides redundancy in the event of the failure of the DR in an OSPF multiple-access network.

Be excess burst. The negotiated tariff metric in Frame Relay internetworks. The number of bits that a Frame Relay internetwork attempts to send after Bc is accommodated. Be data, in general, is delivered with a lower probability than Bc data because the network can mark Be data as discard eligible (DE).

beacon A frame from a Token Ring or FDDI device indicating a serious problem with the ring, such as a broken cable. A beacon frame contains the address of the station assumed to be down.

BECN Backward Explicit Congestion Notification. A bit set by a Frame Relay network in frames traveling in the opposite direction of frames encountering a congested path. DTE receiving frames with the BECN bit set can request that higher-level protocols take flow control action as appropriate.

BER Bit Error Rate. The percentage of bits that have errors relative to the total number of bits received.

BGP Border Gateway Protocol. The interdomain routing protocol used in the Internet. BGP exchanges reachability information with other BGP systems. It is defined in RFC 1163.

BGP4 Border Gateway Protocol version 4. Version 4 of the predominant interdomain routing protocol used on the Internet. BGP-4 supports CIDR and uses route aggregation mechanisms to reduce the size of routing tables.

Bit-error rate A measure of link quality expressed as the ratio of errored bits to some total number of bits, often 1,000,000.

BOOTP Bootstrap Protocol. Allows a booting host to configure itself by dynamically obtaining its IP address parameters from a remote server.

BPDU Bridge Protocol Data Unit. A Spanning-Tree Protocol hello packet that is sent out at configurable intervals to exchange information among bridges in the network.

bps bits per second. A measure of bandwidth identifying the rate at which data is transmitted.

BRI Basic Rate Interface. An ISDN interface composed of two bearer (B) channels (each of which is 64 kbps) and one data (D) channel (16 kbps) for circuit-switched communication of voice, video, and data.

BSR Bootstrap Router. A BSR is configured in a PIMv2 network to automatically select the RP of the multicast network.

BSS Basic Service Set. A wireless LAN mode where all stations communicate with the AP.

BW Bandwidth. The rated throughput capacity of a given network medium or protocol.

byte A series of consecutive binary digits that are operated on as a unit (for example, an 8-bit byte).

Cable A new WAN technology that is a hybrid of coaxial cable and fiber-optic media over cable distribution systems.

CAS   Channel Associated Signaling. The transmission of signaling information within the voice channel. CAS often is called robbed-bit signaling because user bandwidth is "robbed" or used by the network for other purposes.

Category3 cabling   One of five grades of UTP cabling described in the EIA/TIA-586 standard. Category3 cabling is used in 10BASE-T networks and can transmit data at speeds up to 10 Mbps.

Category4 cabling   One of five grades of UTP cabling described in the EIA/TIA-586 standard. Category4 cabling is used in Token Ring networks and can transmit data at speeds up to 16 Mbps.

Category5 cabling   One of five grades of UTP cabling described in the EIA/TIA-586 standard. Category5 cabling can transmit data at speeds up to 100 Mbps.

CBR   constant bit rate. A quality of service (QoS) class defined by the ATM Forum for ATM networks. CBR is used for connections that depend on precise clocking to ensure undistorted delivery.

CBT   Core Based Tree. A sparse multicast routing protocol.

CBWFQ   Class-Based Weighted Fair Queuing. This form of queuing extends the standard Weighted Fair Queuing (WFQ) functionality to provide support for user-defined traffic classes.

CCDA   Cisco Certified Design Associate. The associate level network design certification from Cisco Systems.

CCDP   Cisco Certified Design Professional. The professional level network design certification from Cisco Systems.

CCIE   Cisco Certified Internetworking Expert. The expert-level networking certification from Cisco Systems.

CCK   Complimentary Code Keying. A keying method used with wireless LANs. CCK uses a set of 64 8-bit unique code words to transfer data.

CCS   Common Channel Signaling. A signaling system used in telephone networks that separates signaling information from user data. A specified channel is dedicated to carrying signaling information for all other channels in the system.

CCSS7   Common Channel Signaling System 7. A protocol used by the AT&T signaling network. The Cisco Intelligent Contact Management (ICM) software's NIC receives routing requests from the CCSS7 network and returns a routing label to the CCSS7 network.

CDP   Cisco Discovery Protocol. A Cisco proprietary protocol used for network discovery and management. Informs neighboring devices of their attributes.

CDR   call detail record. A record written to a database for use in post-processing activities. CDR files consist of several CDBs. These activities include many functions, but primarily billing and network analysis. The Cisco CallManager writes CDR records to the SQL database as calls are made in a manner consistent with the configuration of each individual Cisco CallManager.

Cell switching   WAN technologies where the network divides data into units of fixed-size units called cells.

Centrex   With Centrex services, the CO acts as the company's voice switch, giving the appearance that the company has its own PBX.

CER   cell error ratio. In ATM, the ratio of transmitted cells that have errors to the total cells sent in a transmission for a specific period of time.

CGMP   Cisco Group Management Protocol. A Cisco protocol to reduce multicasts on local-area segments and to control multicast traffic at Layer 2.

Channelized E1   An access link operating at 2.048 Mbps that is subdivided into 30 B channels and one D channel. Supports DDR, Frame Relay, and X.25.

Channelized T1   An access link operating at 1.544 Mbps that is subdivided into 24 channels (23 B channels and one D channel) of 64 kbps each. The individual channels or groups of channels connect to different destinations. Supports DDR, Frame Relay, and X.25. Also called fractional T1.

CIDR   Classless Interdomain Routing. A technique supported by BGP-4 and based on route aggregation. CIDR allows routers to group routes to reduce the quantity of routing information carried by the core routers. With CIDR, several IP networks appear to networks outside the group as a single, larger entity. With CIDR, IP addresses and their subnet masks are written as four octets, separated by periods and followed by a slash and a two-digit number that represents the subnet mask.

CIR   Committed Information Rate. The rate at which a Frame Relay network agrees to transfer information under normal conditions, averaged over a minimum increment of time. CIR, measured in bits per second, is one of the key negotiated tariff metrics.

Circuit switching   WAN technologies that establish a connection between two end points and then terminate the connection upon completion of the data transfer. Although the connection is not permanent, it is dedicated.

CO   Central Office. The local telephone company office to which all local loops in a given area connect and in which circuit switching of subscriber lines occurs.

CODEC   Coder Decoder. **1.** An integrated circuit device that typically uses pulse code modulation to transform analog signals into a digital bit stream and digital signals back into analog signals. **2.** coder-decoder. In voice over IP, voice over Frame Relay, and voice over ATM, a DSP software algorithm used to compress and decompress speech or audio signals.

coding   A series of electrical techniques used to convey binary signals.

collision domain   In Ethernet, the network area within which frames that have collided are propagated. Repeaters and hubs propagate collisions; LAN switches, bridges, and routers do not. A hub/repeater has a single collision domain and a single broadcast domain. A switch/bridge has multiple collision domains and a single broadcast domain.

configuration management   Modifying and tracking configuration changes.

Core layer   Provides fast transport between distribution sites.

CoS   class of service. A Layer 2 differentiation of network services.

counting to infinity   A problem that can occur in routing algorithms that are slow to converge, in which routers continuously increment the hop count to particular networks. Typically, a routing protocol imposes a hop-count limit to prevent this problem.

CPE   customer premises equipment. Terminating equipment, such as terminals, telephones, and modems, supplied by the telephone company, installed at customer sites, and connected to the telephone company network. This term can also refer to any telephone equipment residing on the customer site. In cable environments, CTE also refers to set-top boxes or modems.

CQ   Custom Queuing. A Cisco queuing mechanism that allows a user to define up to 16 queues plus the system queue. The queue is serviced in a round robin fashion.

CRC   Cyclic Redundancy Check. An error-checking technique in which the frame recipient calculates a remainder by dividing frame contents by a prime binary divisor and compares the calculated remainder to a value stored in the frame by the sending node.

CRTP   Compressed Real Time Transport Protocol. Used to compresses the RTP/UDP/IP header in VoIP networks.

CS-ACELP Conjugate Structure Algebraic Code Excited Linear Prediction. A CELP voice compression algorithm providing 8 kbps, or 8:1 compression, standardized in ITU-T Recommendation G.729.

CSMA/CA Carrier sense multiple access with collision avoidance. An access method used with wireless LANs.

CSMA/CD Carrier sense multiple access with collision detection. An access method used with Ethernet networks.

CSPM Cisco Secure Policy Manager. Manages security devices in the network.

CTI computer telephony integration. The merger of traditional telecommunications (PBX) equipment with computers and computer applications. The use of caller ID to retrieve customer information automatically from a database is an example of a CTI application.

DBPSK Differential Binary Shift Phase Keying Modulation technique used by IEEE 802.11-compliant wireless LANs for transmission at 1 Mbps.

DCE **1.** data communications equipment (EIA expansion). Provides clocking to the data terminal equipment (DTE). **2.** data circuit-terminating equipment (ITU-T expansion). Devices and connections of a communications network that compose the network end of the user-to-network interface. The DCE provides a physical connection to the network, forwards traffic, and provides a clocking signal used to synchronize data transmission between DCE and DTE devices. Modems and interface cards are examples of DCE.

delay The time from transmission of the first byte of a packet to receipt of that byte at the destination. Along a single traffic path, the causes of delay are characterized as fixed or variable.

DES **1.** Data Encryption Standard A standard cryptographic algorithm developed by the U.S. National Bureau of Standards. **2.** destination end station. An ATM termination point that is the destination for a connection's ATM messages and that is used as a reference point for ABR services

DHCP Dynamic Host Configuration Protocol. Allows a booting host to configure itself by dynamically leasing its IP address and obtaining IP address parameters from a remote server.

dial backup A WAN backup solution that features a dial-up asynchronous or ISDN link that acts as a backup in the event of a primary link failure.

dial peer An addressable call endpoint. Voice over IP has two kinds of dial peers: POTS and VoIP.

Dial-up   The use of the PSTN to carry data,

Diffie-Hellman key exchange   A public key cryptography protocol that allows two parties to establish a shared secret over insecure communications channels. Diffie-Hellman is used in Internet Key Exchange (IKE) to establish session keys. Diffie-Hellman is a component of Oakley key exchange. Cisco IOS Software supports 768-bit and 1024-bit Diffie-Hellman groups.

Dijkstra's algorithm   An algorithm that is sometimes used to calculate routes given a link- and nodal-state topology database. The Open Shortest Path First (OSPF) protocol relies on Dijkstra's algorithm for correct operation.

distance-vector routing algorithm   A routing algorithm that iterates the number of hops in a route to find a shortest-path spanning tree. Each router sends its entire routing table in each update to only its neighbors.

Distribution layer   Provides policy-based connectivity.

DLCI   Data-Link Connection Identifier. A value that specifies a PVC or SVC in a Frame Relay network. In the basic Frame Relay specification, DLCIs are locally significant—connected devices might use different values to specify the same connection. In the LMI extended specification, DLCIs are globally significant—DLCIs specify individual end devices.

DLSw+   data-link switching plus. The Cisco implementation of the data-link switching (DLSw) standard for SNA and NetBIOS traffic forwarding. DLSw+ goes beyond the standard to include the advanced features of the current Cisco RSRB implementation. It also provides additional functionality to increase the overall scalability of data-link switching.

DMZ   Demilitarized Zone. A DMZ network is used to provide services to the outside world. DMZ Servers are typically placed in a data center. The basic policy is to allow anyone on the Internet to connect to the WWW, FTP, and SMTP services on the DMZ network, and to make DNS queries to it.

DNS   Domain Name System. DNS servers return destination IP addresses given a FQDN.

DoS   Denial of Service. Prevents legitimate users access to services.

DQPSK   Differential Quadrature Phase Shift Keying. Modulation technique used by IEEE 802.11-compliant wireless LANs for transmission at 2 Mbps.

DR   designated router. A router selected in multiaccess networks to generate the OSPF network (Type 2) LSA.

DS0   Digital signal level 0. A framing specification used in transmitting digital signals over a single channel at 64 kbps.

DS1   Digital signal level 1. A framing specification used in transmitting digital signals at 1.544 Mbps on a T1 facility (in the United States) or at 2.108 Mbps on an E1 facility (in Europe).

DSCP   Differentiated Service Code Point. Replaces the Type of Service (ToS) of the IP header and uses 6-bits for service differentiation.

DSL   digital subscriber line. A modem technology that uses existing twisted-pair telephone lines to transport high-bandwidth data, such as multimedia and video, to service subscribers.

DSSS   Direct Sequence Spread Spectrum. A wireless LAN mode that divides data into separate sections, each section is sent over different frequencies at the same time.

DTE   data terminal equipment. A device at the user end of a user-network interface that serves as a data source, destination, or both. DTE connects to a data network through a DCE device (such as a modem) and typically uses clocking signals generated by the DCE. DTE includes devices such as computers, protocol translators, and multiplexers.

DTMF   Dual Tone Multi Frequency. Tones generated when a button is pressed on a telephone. Primarily used in the United States and Canada.

DUAL   EIGRP's Diffusing Update Algorithm. A convergence algorithm used in EIGRP that provides loop-free operation at every instant throughout a route computation. Allows routers involved in a topology change to synchronize at the same time while not involving routers that are unaffected by the change.

dynamic routing   Routing that adjusts automatically to network topology or traffic changes.

E&M   **1.** recEive and transMit (or ear and mouth). (Telephony) A trunking arrangement generally used for two-way switch-to-switch or switch-to-network connections. The Cisco analog E&M interface is an RJ-48 connector that allows connections to PBX trunk lines (tie-lines). E&M also is available on E1 and T1 digital interfaces. **2.** recEive and transMit (or ear and mouth). A type of signaling traditionally used in the telecommunications industry. Indicates the use of a handset that corresponds to a telephone's ear (receiving) and mouth (transmitting) component.

E1   A WAN digital transmission facility that carries data at a rate of 2.048 Mbps.

EAP   Extensible Authentication Protocol. A framework that supports multiple optional authentication mechanisms for PPP, including cleartext passwords, challenge-response, and arbitrary dialog sequences.

EGP   Exterior gateway protocol. An Internet protocol used to exchange routing information with other autonomous systems. BGP is the only exterior gateway protocol available.

EIGRP   Cisco hybrid routing protocol. Supports CIDR and VLSMs. Uses composite metric with bandwidth and delay parameters.

Enterprise Campus   Campus network with backbone, distribution, and access infrastructure; also includes server farm and network management.

Enterprise Composite Network model   A scalable, hierarchical network model that divides networks into the campus network, the Enterprise Edge, and the SP Edge.

Enterprise Edge   Includes modules for Internet, e-commerce, VPN/remote access, and WAN access.

erlang   A unit that measures the total voice traffic volume in one hour.

ESP   Encapsulating Security Payload. IPSec protocol that provides confidentiality by encrypting the payload.

Ethernet   A baseband LAN specification invented by Xerox Corporation and developed jointly by Xerox, Intel, and Digital Equipment Corporation. Ethernet networks use CSMA/CD and run over a variety of cable types at 10 Mbps. Ethernet is similar to the IEEE 802.3 series of standards.

fault management   Detecting, isolating, and correcting problems.

FCAPS model   Model representing network-management functions: Fault, Configuration, Accounting, Performance, Security.

FCC   Federal Communication Commission. Governs frequency allocation in the United States.

FDDI   Fiber Distributed Data Interface. Layer 2 media.

feasible distance   The lowest calculated metric of a path to reach the destination.

feasible successor   The second best path selected by DUAL.

FECN   Forward Explicit Congestion Notification. A bit set by a Frame Relay network to inform DTE receiving the frame that congestion was experienced in the path from source to destination. DTE receiving frames with the FECN bit set can request that higher-level protocols take flow-control action as appropriate.

FHSS   Frequency Hopping Spread Spectrum. Uses a frequency-hopping sequence to send data in bursts.

floating static route   A static route configured with an artificially high administrative distance; this route is viewed as less desirable than a dynamic routing protocol's route. The static route is called upon if there is a failure of the main link, and thus the dynamic route is removed from the routing table.

flush timer   Removes a route from the routing table.

FQDN   Fully Qualified Domain Name. A system's full name, rather than just its host name. For example, aldebaran is a host name, and aldebaran.interop.com is an FQDN.

Frame Relay   A packet-switching protocol for WAN access that uses virtual circuits over shared physical media.

FRF.11   Frame Relay Forum implementation agreement for Voice over Frame Relay (v1.0 May 1997). This specification defines multiplexed data, voice, fax, DTMF digit-relay, and CAS/Robbed-Bit Signaling frame formats but does not include call setup, routing, or administration facilities. See www.frforum.com.

FRF.9   Defines data compression over Frame Relay using the DCP.

FRTS   Frame Relay traffic shaping. A queuing method that uses queues on a Frame Relay network to limit surges that can cause congestion. Data is buffered and sent into the network in regulated amounts to ensure that the traffic can fit within the promised traffic envelope for the particular connection.

full-mesh topology   A topology in which each node (router) connects to every other node in the network design; this design features the greatest level of redundancy and performance in the design.

functional area   First layer of modules in SAFE blueprint.

FXO   Foreign Exchange Office. Used to connect to the PSTN.

FXS   Foreign Exchange Station. Used to connect to end devices.

G.711   Describes the 64-kbps PCM voice-coding technique. In G.711, encoded voice is already in the correct format for digital voice delivery in the PSTN or through PBXs. Described in the ITU-T standard in its G-series recommendations.

G.723.1   Describes a compression technique that can be used to compress speech or audio signal components at a very low bit rate as part of the H.324 family of standards. This CODEC has two bit rates associated with it: 5.3 and 6.3 kbps. The higher bit rate is based on ML-MLQ technology and provides a somewhat higher quality of sound. The lower bit rate is based on CELP and gives system designers additional flexibility. Described in the ITU-T standard in its G-series recommendations.

G.726   Describes ADPCM coding at 40, 32, 24, and 16 kbps. ADPCM-encoded voice can be interchanged between packet voice, PSTN, and PBX networks if the PBX networks are configured to support ADPCM. Described in the ITU-T standard in its G-series recommendations.

G.728   Describes a 16-kbps low-delay variation of CELP voice compression. CELP voice coding must be translated into a public telephony format for delivery to or through the PSTN. Described in the ITU-T standard in its G-series recommendations.

G.729   Describes CELP compression in which voice is coded into 8-kbps streams. Two variations of this standard (G.729 and G.729 Annex A) differ mainly in computational complexity; both provide speech quality similar to 32-kbps ADPCM. Described in the ITU-T standard in its G-series recommendations.

gatekeeper   **1.** The component of an H.323 conferencing system that performs call address resolution, admission control, and subnet bandwidth management. **2.** An H.323 entity on a LAN that provides address translation and control access to the LAN for H.323 terminals and gateways. The gatekeeper can provide other services to the H.323 terminals and gateways, such as managing bandwidth and locating gateways. A gatekeeper maintains a registry of devices in the multimedia network. The devices register with the gatekeeper at startup and request admission to a call from the gatekeeper.

gateway   In the IP community, an older term referring to a routing device. Today, the term router describes nodes that perform this function, and *gateway* refers to a special-purpose device that performs an application-layer conversion of information from one protocol stack to another.

Gbps   gigabits per second.

GMII   Gigabit Media Independent Interface. A standard for a high-speed Ethernet, approved by the IEEE 802.3z standards committee in 1996.

GoS   grade of service. The probability that a call will be blocked when making an attempt.

GRE   Generic Routing Encapsulation. Cisco tunneling protocol. Encapsulates network layer packets such as IP, IPX, and AppleTalk.

H.225.0   An ITU standard that governs H.225.0 session establishment and packetization. H.225.0 actually describes several different protocols: RAS, use of Q.931, and use of RTP.

H.245   An ITU standard that governs H.245 endpoint control.

H.320   A suite of ITU-T standard specifications for videoconferencing over circuit-switched media, such as ISDN, fractional T1, and switched-56 lines. This is an extension of ITU-T standard H.320 that enables videoconferencing over LANs and other packet-switched networks, as well as video over the Internet.

H.323   ITU framework for multimedia protocols. Used to control Cisco IOS gateways.

HDLC   High-Level Data Link Control. A bit-oriented synchronous data link layer protocol developed by the International Organization for Standardization (ISO).

hierarchical routing   Routing based on a hierarchical addressing system.

HMAC-MD5   Hash-based Message Authentication Codes with MD5. A keyed version of MD5 that lets two parties validate transmitted information using a shared secret. Documented in RFC 2104.

holddown timer   Sets an allowed time for which routing information regarding different paths is suppressed.

HSRP   Hot Standby Router Protocol. A proprietary Cisco protocol that provides high network availability and transparent network-topology changes.

IANA   Internet Assigned Number Authority.

ICMP   Internet Control Message Protocol. A network-layer Internet protocol that reports errors and provides other information relevant to IP packet processing. Documented in RFC 792.

ICMPv6   Internet Control Message Protocol Version 6. Provides diagnostics, errors, and reachability information.

IDS   Intrusion detection system. Detects network intrusions.

IEEE 802.1   An IEEE specification that describes an algorithm that prevents bridging loops by creating a spanning tree. The algorithm was invented by the former Digital Equipment Corporation. The Digital algorithm and the IEEE 802.1 algorithm are not exactly the same, nor are they compatible.

IEEE 802.11   A wireless LAN standard that divides the unlicensed 2.45-GHz band into three switched segments, each with up to 11 Mbps of shared bandwidth.

IEEE 802.3   An IEEE LAN protocol that specifies an implementation of the physical layer and the MAC sublayer of the data link layer. IEEE 802.3 uses CSMA/CD access at a variety of speeds over a variety of physical media. Extensions to the IEEE 802.3 standard specify implementations for Fast Ethernet. Physical variations of the original IEEE 802.3 specification include 10BASE2, 10BASE5, 10BASE-F, 10BASE-T, and 10Broad36. Physical variations of Fast Ethernet include 100BASE-T, 100BASE-T4, and 100BASE-X.

IEEE 802.5   An IEEE LAN protocol that specifies an implementation of the physical layer and media access control (MAC) sublayer of the data link layer. IEEE 802.5 uses token passing access at 4 or 16 Mbps over STP cabling and is similar to IBM Token Ring.

IEEE   Institute of Electrical and Electronics Engineers. Defines standards for Layer 2 technologies.

IETF   Internet Engineering Task Force. A task force consisting of more than 80 working groups responsible for developing Internet standards. The IETF operates under the auspices of ISOC.

IGMP   Internet Group Management Protocol. Used in multicast networks for clients to register to multicast groups.

IGP   Interior gateway protocol. An Internet protocol used to exchange routing information within an autonomous system. Examples include RIPv1, RIPv2, IGRP, EIGRP, OSPF, IS-IS.

IGRP   Cisco routing protocol that broadcasts its routing table every 90 seconds. Does not support CIDR and VLSMs. Uses composite metric with bandwidth and delay parameter.

in-band management   Network management setup using the network for communication with the security devices.

Integrated IS-IS   A routing protocol based on the IS-IS OSI routing protocol but with support for IP and other protocols. Integrated IS-IS implementations send only one set of routing updates, making it more efficient than two separate implementations. Formerly called *Dual IS-IS*.

internal router   A router whose interfaces all belong to the same OSPF area.

invalid timer   Marks a route as invalid when updates are not received.

Inverse ARP Inverse Address Resolution Protocol. A method of building dynamic routes in a network. Allows an access server to discover the network address of a device associated with a virtual circuit.

IP Internet Protocol. The network layer protocol in the TCP/IP stack that offers a connectionless internetwork service. IP provides features for addressing, type of service (ToS) specification, fragmentation and reassembly, and security. Defined in RFC 791.

IP fragmentation The division or fragmentation of IP packets into smaller units to pass through small MTU links.

IP multicast A routing technique that allows IP traffic to be propagated from one source to a number of destinations or from many sources to many destinations. Rather than sending one packet to each destination, one packet is sent to a multicast group identified by a single IP destination group address.

IP Spoofing An IP spoofing attack occurs when an attacker outside your network pretends to be a trusted user. He does this either by using an IP address that is within the range of IP addresses for your network or by using an authorized external IP address that you trust and to which you want to provide access to specified resources on your network. Should an attacker get access to your IPSec security parameters, he can masquerade as the remote user authorized to connect to the corporate network.

IP telephony The transmission of voice and fax phone calls over data networks that uses the Internet Protocol (IP). IP telephony is the result of the transformation of the circuit-switched telephone network to a packet-based network that deploys voice-compression algorithms and flexible and sophisticated transmission techniques. This network delivers richer services using only a fraction of traditional digital telephony's usual bandwidth. IP telephony relies on an IP network to transmit voice. Voice is treated as the payload in an IP packet.

IPSec IP Security. A framework of IETF-proposed standards that provides data confidentiality, data integrity, and data authentication between participating peers.

IPv4 Internet Protocol version 4. The defacto IP version used in the Internet today that uses 32-bit logical addresses.

IPv6 Internet Protocol version 6. A replacement for the current version of IP (version 4). IPv6 includes support for flow ID in the packet header, which can be used to identify flows. Formerly called *IPng* (IP: The Next Generation).

IPv6 anycast address Identifies a set of routers within an area.

IPv6 autoconfiguration   Stateless method of IPv6 address assignment.

IPv6 multicast address   Identifies a set of hosts. The "all-nodes" multicast represents a broadcast.

IPv6 ND   Neighbor discovery. Discovers all other nodes in the same link, checks for duplicate addresses, and finds the routers in the link.

IPv6 unicast address   Logical identifier of a single interface.

IPX   Internetwork Packet Exchange. A Novell NetWare network layer (Layer 3) protocol used to transfer data from servers to workstations. IPX is similar to IP and XNS.

ISDN   Integrated Services Digital Network. An international communications standard for sending digital voice, digitized video, and data over digital telephone lines or normal telephone wires.

IS-IS   Intermediate System–to-Intermediate System. An OSI link-state hierarchical routing protocol whereby ISs (routers) exchange routing information based on a single metric to determine the network topology.

ISL   Inter-Switch Link. Cisco VLAN tunneling protocol.

ISM   Industrial, Scientific, and Medical. Wireless LANs use ISM frequency bands.

ISP   Internet service provider. A company that provides Internet access to other companies and individuals.

ITU   International Telecommunication Union. An organization established by the United Nations to set international telecommunications standards and to allocate frequencies for specific uses.

IVR   Interactive Voice Response. IVR systems provide recorded announcements, prompt the caller for key options, and provide information.

jitter   The variability of delay between traffic source and destination.

kbps   kilobits per second. A bit rate expressed in thousands of bits per second.

LAN   local-area network. A high-speed, low-error data network covering a relatively small geographic area (up to a few thousand square meters). LANs connect workstations, peripherals, terminals, and other devices in a single building or in another geographically limited area. LAN standards specify cabling and signaling at the OSI reference model's physical and data link layers.

LAT   Local Area Transport. A network virtual terminal protocol developed by Digital Equipment Corporation.

LEAP   Lightweight Extensible Authentication Protocol. Used for centralized user-based authentication.

Leased lines   Reliable and expensive WAN technologies that are completely reserved for transmissions and are always available.

LFI   Link Fragmentation & Interleaving. QoS mechanism that reduces serialization delay by fragmenting large packets and interleaving them with smaller (usually voice) packets.

link-local addresses   IPv6 addresses that are significant only to the nodes on a single link.

link-state routing algorithm   A routing algorithm in which each router broadcasts or multicasts information regarding the cost of reaching each of its neighbors to all nodes in the internetwork.

LLC   Logical Link Control. The higher of the two data link layer sublayers defined by the IEEE. The LLC sublayer handles error control, flow control, framing, and MAC-sublayer addressing. The most prevalent LLC protocol is IEEE 802.2, which includes both connectionless and connection-oriented variants.

LLQ   Low Latency Queuing (also known as PQ-CBWFQ). LLQ provides a single priority queue for voice traffic, all other traffic can be configured with guaranteed bandwidth for different classes of traffic.

LOS   **1.** loss of signal. Occurs when *n* consecutive zeros are detected on an incoming signal. **2.** line of sight. A clear, unobstructed path between the transmitters and receivers in a wireless network. A clear LOS is essential for LMDS products. It enhances general performance in every RF deployment as opposed to partial or completely obstructed data paths. The opposite of LOS is NLOS, or non-line-of-sight.

LRE   Long-Reach Ethernet, or Ethernet in the First Mile (EFM). a broadband networking technology that uses Ethernet to deliver 5-15 Mbps performance over existing telephone-grade (Category 1/2/3) wiring.

LSA   Link-state advertisement. A broadcast packet used by OSPF that contains information about neighbors and interface status.

LZS   Lempel-Ziv Stack. An implementation of a compression algorithm frequently used for WAN traffic.

MAC   Media Access Control. Layer 2 physical address.

MAN   metropolitan-area network. A network that serves a metropolitan area. Generally, a MAN spans a larger geographic area than a local-area network (LAN) but a smaller geographic area than a wide-area network (WAN).

MBONE   Multicast Backbone. A virtual multicast network composed of multicast LANs and the point-to-point tunnels that interconnect them. MBONE is the Internet's multicast backbone.

MGCP   Media gateway Control Protocol. Used to control Cisco IOS gateways.

MIB   Management Information Base. A database of objects that can be monitored by a network management system. Both SNMP and RMON use standardized MIB formats that allows any SNMP and RMON tools to monitor any device defined by a MIB.

MLPPP   Multi Link Point to Point Protocol. An extension of the PPP that allows the B-channels of ISDN lines to be used in combination as a single transmission line, doubling throughput to 128 Kbps.

module   A functional block of the network.

MOS   Mean Opinion Score. A measure used to describe the quality of speech in which '5' being the best toll-quality sound.

MOSPF   Multicast OSPF. An intradomain multicast routing protocol used in Open Shortest Path First (OSPF) networks. Extensions are applied to the base OSPF unicast protocol to support IP multicast routing.

MPLS   Multiprotocol Label Switching. A high-speed method for moving data through networks by encapsulating packets with a label and then making forwarding, QoS, or traffic engineering decisions based upon the Layer 2 label.

MPPC   Microsoft Point-to-Point Compression. A scheme used to compress PPP packets between Cisco and Microsoft client devices.

MTU   Maximum transmission unit.

multicast address   Sends packets to all hosts that are registered to a group.

NAT   network address translation. Translates private addresses to public addresses.

NBMA   Non-Broadcast Multiple Access. A term describing a multiaccess network that does not support broadcasting (such as X.25) or in which broadcasting is not feasible.

neighbor loss detection   Process used by routers and routing protocols to confirm the failure of a WAN link.

NET   network entity title. A network address, defined by the ISO network architecture, used in IS-IS networks.

NetBEUI   NetBIOS Extended User Interface. An enhanced version of the NetBIOS protocol used by network operating systems, such as LAN Manager, LAN Server, Windows for Workgroups, and Windows NT. NetBEUI formalizes the transport frame and adds other functions. NetBEUI implements the OSI LLC2 protocol.

NetBIOS   Network Basic Input/Output System. An application programming interface (API) used by applications on an IBM LAN to request services from lower-level network processes. These services might include establishing and terminating sessions and transferring information.

network analyzing   A set of tools and techniques used to collect and analyze data.

network auditing   A set of tools and techniques used to generate reports on the existing network infrastructure.

network constraints   A number of limitations a network designer must work around to comply with the network blueprint.

network documentation   A way of representing the network design in paper format.

network requirements   Minimum network functionality available after completion of the network-design process.

network simulation   A set of tools and techniques used to imitate network traffic.

network threat   Vulnerabilities exposed by attackers to your network.

NLSP   Netware Link Services Protocol. **1.** A link-state routing protocol based on Intermediate System-to-Intermediate System (IS-IS). **2.** Network Layer Security Protocol. An OSI protocol (ISO 11577) for end-to-end encryption services at the top of OSI Layer 3. NLSP is derived from an SDNS protocol, SP3, but is much more complex.

NRZ   Non Return to Zero. An encoding method where a logical 'zero' is represented by a particular line state, and a logical 'one' by another with no return to zero voltage level.

NSAP   Network Service Access Point. A point at which OSI network service is made available to a transport layer (Layer 4) entity.

NSSA   Not So Stubby Area. An OSPF area with on type 5 external LSAs where an ASBR injects type 7 LSAs.

OC-3   Optical Carrier 3. A physical layer protocol defined for SONET optical signal transmission with a rate of 155 Mbps.

on-demand routing   Cisco mechanism used to provide routing with reduced overhead without having to configure dynamic routing protocols or static routes at a remote stub router.

OSI   Open Systems Interconnection. An international standardization program created by ISO and ITU-T to develop data networking standards that facilitate multivendor equipment interoperability.

OSPF   Open Shortest Path First. A link-state, hierarchical routing protocol where routers exchange routing information and use Dijkstra's SPF algorithm to determine the network topology.

OSPF Area 0   The backbone of an OSPF network.

OSPFv3   Version 3 of the Open Shortest Path First routing protocol for use in IPv6 networks.

out-of-band management   Network management setup using a backup network for communication with the security devices.

overlapping   Maps registered internal IP addresses to outside registered IP addresses.

overloading   Maps multiple unregistered IP addresses to a single registered IP address by using different ports.

PABX   private automatic branch exchange. A telephone switch used within an organization or company to connect private and public telephone networks. PABX is the preferred term in Europe, whereas PBX is used in the United States.

Packet switching   WAN technologies that have network equipment create "virtual circuits" through the shared WAN provider's network.

partial-mesh topology   A point-to-point network design topology that features circuits that connect many but not all of the routers in the topology.

PAT   Port Address Translation. IPv4 many to one translation that uses separate port numbers to identify each translation.

PBR   policy-based routing. Used when traffic engineering of paths is required.

PBX   private branch exchange. A telephone switch used within an organization or company to connect private and public telephone networks. PBX is the preferred term in the United States, whereas PABX is used in Europe.

PCM   pulse code modulation. A technique of encoding analog voice into a 64-kbps data stream by sampling with 8-bit resolution at a rate of 8000 times per second.

PDIOO   Plan, Design, Implement, Operate, Optimize. The technology lifecycle of internetworks.

PDU   Protocol Data Unit. An OSI term for *packet*.

performance management   Measuring network behavior and its effectiveness in data delivery.

PIM   Protocol Independent Multicast. A multicast routing architecture that allows the addition of IP multicast routing to existing IP networks.

Policing   WAN performance option that typically drops excess traffic or at least modifies it in some way (for example, manipulating IP precedence).

Policy Management   SAFE element that specifies, manages, and audits the state of a security policy.

PPP   Point-to-Point Protocol. A successor to Serial Line Internet Protocol (SLIP) that provides router-to-router and host-to-network connections over synchronous and asynchronous circuits. PPP was designed to work with several network layer protocols, such as IP, IPX, and AppleTalk Remote Access (ARA).

PQ   Priority queuing. A queuing method that establishes four interface output queues and allows the designer to assign each queue a priority.

PQ/CBWFQ   Priority Queuing/Class-Based Weighted Fair Queuing. A feature that brings strict priority queuing to CBWFQ. Strict priority queuing allows delay-sensitive data, such as voice, to be dequeued and sent first (before packets in other queues are dequeued), giving delay-sensitive data preferential treatment over other traffic.

PQ-WFQ   Priority Queuing – Weighted Fair Queuing. A queuing mechanism that adds a single priority queue to WFQ. The priority queue is used for VoIP packets. All other traffic is queued based on the WFQ algorithm.

Predictor A public-domain compression algorithm that tries to predict the next sequence of characters in a data stream by using an index to look up a sequence in the compression dictionary.

PRI Primary Rate Interface. An Integrated Services Digital Network (ISDN) interface to primary rate access. Primary rate access consists of a single 64-kbps D channel plus 23 (T1) or 30 (E1) B channels for voice or data.

private addresses Range of addresses defined in RFC 1918 for use in private networks; they are 10/8, 172.16/12, and 192.168/16.

protocol-dependent modules Used by EIGRP to independently support IP, IPX, and AppleTalk.

PSTN Public Switched Telephone Network. A general term referring to the variety of telephone networks and services in place worldwide.

PTT Post, Telephone, and Telegraph. A government agency that provides telephone service. PTTs exist in most areas outside North America and provide both local and long-distance telephone service.

PVC Permanent virtual circuit created through a WAN.

Q.931 An ITU-T specification for signaling to establish, maintain, and clear

QoS quality of service. A measure of performance for a transmission system that reflects its transmission quality and service availability.

QPSK quadrature phase shift keying. A digital frequency modulation technique used to send data over coaxial cable networks. Because it is both easy to implement and fairly resistant to noise, QPSK is used primarily to send data from the cable subscriber upstream to the Internet.

RADIUS Remote Authentication Dial-In User Service. A database for authenticating modem and Integrated Services Digital Network (ISDN) connections and for tracking connection time.

Reliability A measure of how often an application is available when network users attempt to access it.

resources Assets available to network designers.

Response time The time between the entry of a command or data at a source system and the target system's execution of the command or the target's response.

RFC   Request For Comments. A series of documents used as the primary means of communicating information about the Internet. Some RFCs are designated by the Internet Architecture Board (IAB) as Internet standards. Most RFCs document protocol specifications, such as Telnet and File Transfer Protocol (FTP), but some are humorous or historical. RFCs are available online from numerous sources.

RIP   Routing Information Protocol. An Interior Gateway Protocol (IGP) considered the most common IGP in the Internet that uses hop count as a routing metric.

RIPng   Routing Information Protocol next generation. Version of RIP for use in IPv6 networks.

RIPv1   Distance-vector routing protocol that broadcasts its routing table every 30 seconds. Does not support CIDR and VLSMs. Has a 15-hop limit.

RIPv2   Distance-vector routing protocol that multicasts its routing table every 30 seconds. Supports CIDR and VLSMs. Has a 15-hop limit.

RMON   Remote Monitoring remotely monitors network devices.

RSVP   Resource Reservation Protocol. A protocol that supports the reservation of resources across an IP network. Applications running on IP end systems can use RSVP to indicate to other nodes the nature (bandwidth, jitter, maximum burst, and so on) of the packet streams they want to receive. Also known as *Resource Reservation Setup Protocol*.

RTCP   Real Time Transport Control Protocol. A protocol that monitors the quality of service (QoS) of a Real-Time Transport Protocol (RTP) connection and conveys information about the ongoing session.

RTP   Real-Time Transport Protocol. Carries coded (digitized) voice; runs over UDP. Used by EIGRP to ensure reliable delivery of route updates.

SAFE   Cisco Security Architecture for Enterprise.

SDH   Synchronous Digital Hierarchy. A European standard that defines a set of rate and format standards that are transmitted using optical signals over fiber. SDH is similar to SONET, with a basic SDH rate of 155.52 Mbps, designated as STM-1.

SDSL   Symmetrical DSL. Provides equal bandwidth for both the uplink and downlink lines up to 2.3 Mbps.

Secure Connectivity   SAFE element that protects confidential information by implementing virtual private network.

security ecosystem   Linkage of various partners and supporting products.

security management   Authentication, access control, data confidentiality, data integrity, and nonrepudiation.

Security Monitoring   SAFE element that proactively identifies areas of weakness with network vulnerability scanners, and monitors and responds to security events as they occur with intrusion-detection systems.

security policy   Foundation for SAFE implementation.

SHA-1   Secure Hash Algorithm. An algorithm that takes a message of less than 264 bits in length and produces a 160-bit message digest. The large message digest provides security against brute-force collision and inversion attacks. SHA-1 [NIS94c] is a revision to SHA that was published in 1994.

shadow PVC   A secondary permanent virtual circuit provisioned as a backup for the main WAN connection.

SIP   Session Initiation Protocol. IETF framework for multimedia protocols.

site-local addresses   IPv6 addresses that are analogous to IPv4 private addresses. These addresses are not globally unique.

SLA   service level agreement.

SLB   Server Load Balancing. Cisco IOS feature that provides IP-based server balancing.

SLC   service level contract.

SLM   service level manager.

SMDS   Switched Multimegabit Data Service. A high-speed, packet-switched, datagram-based WAN networking technology for communication over PDNs.

SNMP   Simple Network Management Protocol is used as communication vehicle between the Network Management Station and the Agent.

SNMP agent   Collects local management data.

SNMP manager   A central store that collects all agent data.

SOHO   small office, home office. A set of networking solutions and access technologies for offices that are not directly connected to large corporate networks.

SONET   Synchronous Optical Network. A standard format for transporting a wide range of digital telecommunications services over optical fiber. SONET is characterized by standard line rates, optical interfaces, and signal formats. SONET is a high-speed (up to 2.5 Gbps) synchronous network specification developed by Bellcore and designed to run on optical fiber. STS-1 is SONET's basic building block. Approved as an international standard in 1988.

SP Edge   Provides Internet, PSTN, and WAN services.

SPF   shortest path first algorithm. (Routing) A routing algorithm that iterates on length of path to determine a shortest-path spanning tree. Commonly used in link-state routing algorithms. Sometimes called Dijkstra's algorithm after its creator.

split horizon   A routing technique in which information about routes is prevented from exiting the router interface through which that information was received.

split horizon with poison reverse   A routing technique in which information about routes are sent with an infinite (unreachable) metric out the router interface through which that information was received.

SS7   Signaling System 7. Allows voice and network calls to be routed and controlled by central call controllers; permits modern consumer telephone services. Protocol used in the PSTN.

SSID   Service Set Identifier. Identifies the "network name" of the wireless LAN.

SSL   Secure Sockets Layer. A protocol developed by Netscape for transmitting private documents via the Internet. SSL works by using a public key to encrypt data that's transferred over the SSL connection.

star topology   A point-to-point network design topology that features a core router that serves as the hub for the WAN connections to remote locations.

static routing   Routes that are explicitly configured and entered into the routing table.

STM-1   Synchronous Transport Module level. One of a number of Synchronous Digital Hierarchy (SDH) formats that specifies the frame structure for the 155.52-Mbps lines used to carry ATM cells.

STP   Spanning Tree Protocol. Used by bridges and switches to determine a loop-free topology.

STS-1 synchronous transport signal. Level 1. A basic building block signal of Synchronous Optical Network (SONET), operating at 51.84 Mbps. Faster SONET rates are defined as STS-*n*, where *n* is a multiple of 51.84 Mbps.

STS-3c synchronous transport signal Level 3, concatenated. A Synchronous Optical Network (SONET) format that specifies the frame structure for the 155.52-Mbps lines used to carry ATM cells.

successor The best path selected by DUAL.

SVC Switched (nonpermanent) virtual circuit through a WAN.

T1 A digital WAN carrier facility. T1 carries DS1–formatted data at 1.544 Mbps through the telephone-switching network, using AMI or B8ZS coding.

TACACS+ Terminal Access Controller Access Control System Plus. A proprietary Cisco enhancement to Terminal Access Controller Access Control System (TACACS) that provides additional support for authentication, authorization, and accounting.

TCP/IP Transmission Control Protocol/Internet Protocol. A common name for the suite of protocols developed by the U.S. Department of Defense in the 1970s to support the construction of worldwide internetworks. TCP and IP are the two best-known protocols in the suite.

TDMA time-division multiplex access. A type of multiplexing in which two or more channels of information are transmitted over the same link by the allocation of a different time interval (*slot* or *slice*) for the transmission of each channel; that is, the channels take turns using the link. Some kind of periodic synchronizing signal or distinguishing identifier is usually required so that the receiver can identify the channels.

throughput The amount of data transferred in a portion of the network during a specific time interval.

TIA Telecommunications Industry Association. An organization that develops standards relating to telecommunications technologies. Together, the TIA and the Electronic Industries Alliance (EIA) have formalized standards, such as EIA/TIA-232, for the electrical characteristics of data transmission.

Token Ring A token-passing LAN developed and supported by IBM. Token Ring runs at 4 or 16 Mbps over a ring topology.

ToS type of service. An 8-bit field carried in the header of an Internet Protocol Version 4 (IPv4) header that can be used to identify packets designated to receive preferential treatment on a class of service (CoS) basis. Based on their configuration, switches and routers determine whether to implement ToS.

ToS   Type-of-service field. Indicates QoS parameters.

traffic policing   A process used to measure the actual traffic flow across a given connection and compare it to the connection's total admissible traffic flow. Traffic outside the agreed-upon flow can be tagged (where the cell loss priority [CLP] bit is set to 1) and can be discarded en route if congestion develops. Traffic policing is used in ATM, Frame Relay, and other types of networks. Traffic policing is also called *admission control*, *permit processing*, *rate enforcement*, and *usage parameter control (UPC)*.

traffic shaping   WAN performance option that delays excess packets by holding them in buffers and then releasing them at preconfigured rates.

UBR   unspecified bit rate. A quality of service (QoS) class defined by the ATM Forum for ATM networks. UBR allows an amount of data up to a specified maximum to be sent across the network, but with its use, there are no guarantees in terms of cell loss rate and delay.

UDP   User Datagram Protocol. A connectionless transport layer protocol in the TCP/IP protocol stack. UDP is a simple protocol that exchanges datagrams without acknowledgments or guaranteed delivery, requiring that error processing and retransmission be handled by other protocols. UDP is defined in RFC 768.

U-law   A companding technique commonly used in North America. U-law is standardized as a 64-kbps codec in ITU-T G.711.

unicast addresses   Sent to a single interface.

UNII   Unlicensed National Information Infrastructure. Frequencies used in IEEE 802.11a wireless devices.

update timer   Specifies the frequency of the periodic routing-table broadcasts.

VAD   Voice Activity Detection. When this is enabled, packets are not transmitted when there is silence.

Van Jacobson header compression   TCP/IP header compression that reduces the size of the TCP/IP headers to as few as three bytes.

VBR   variable bit rate. A quality of service (QoS) class defined by the ATM Forum for ATM networks. VBR is subdivided into a real-time (RT) class and a nonreal time (NRT) class. VBR RT is used for connections that have a fixed timing relationship between samples. VBR NRT is used for connections that have no fixed timing relationship between samples but that still need a guaranteed QoS.

VLAN   Virtual LAN. Group of devices in different physical segments that communicate with each other as if they are all in the same segment.

VLSMs   Variable-length subnet masks. Used to subdivide a network into subnets of various sizes to prevent wasting IP addresses.

VOD   video on demand. A system using video compression to supply video programs to viewers when requested via ISDN or cable.

VoFR   voice over Frame Relay. VoFR lets a router carry voice traffic (for example, telephone calls and faxes) over a Frame Relay network. When voice traffic is sent over Frame Relay, it is segmented and encapsulated for transit across the Frame Relay network using FRF.12 encapsulation.

VoIP   voice over IP. The capability to carry normal telephony-style voice over an IP-based Internet with POTS-like functionality, reliability, and voice quality. VoIP lets a router carry voice traffic (for example, telephone calls and faxes) over an IP network. In VoIP, the DSP segments the voice signal into frames, which then are coupled in groups of two and stored in voice packets. These voice packets are transported using IP in compliance with ITU-T specification H.323.

VPI   virtual path identifier. An 8-bit field in the header of an ATM cell. The VPI, together with the VCI, identifies a cell's next destination as it passes through a series of ATM switches on the way to its destination. ATM switches use the VPI/VCI fields to identify the next VCL through which a cell needs to transit on the way to its final destination. The VPI's function is similar to that of the DLCI in Frame Relay

VPN   virtual private network. Allows IP traffic to travel securely over a public TCP/IP network by encrypting all traffic from one network to another. A VPN uses *tunneling* to encrypt all information at the IP level.

WAN   wide-area network. A data communications network that serves users across a broad geographic area and often uses transmission devices provided by common carriers.

WECA   Wireless Ethernet Compatibility Alliance. WECA defined the Wi-Fi standard.

WEP   Wired Equivalent Privacy. WEP provides encryption in wireless LANS. There two types of WEP keys used in WLANs: 64-bit and 128-bit.

WFQ   Weighted fair queuing. A queuing methodology that prohibits high-volume senders from "crowding out" low-volume senders.

Wi-Fi   Wireless Fidelity. An interoperability certification for IEEE 802.11b devices.

Window size   The amount of data a device sends on the network before requiring the receipt of an acknowledgment.

WINS   Windows Internet Naming Service. A naming services used in Microsoft networks that provides the IP address given the NetBIOS name.

Wireless   An exciting area of telecommunications in which data travels by electromagnetic waves instead of wire or glass fibers.

WLAN   Wireless LANs. These are LANs that use radio frequencies as media.

WRED   Weighted Random Early Detection. A congestion-avoidance mechanism that ensures that high-precedence traffic has lower loss rates than other traffic during times of congestion.

X.25   An ITU-T WAN protocol.

Index

D

U-V

X